VAMPS & TRAMPS

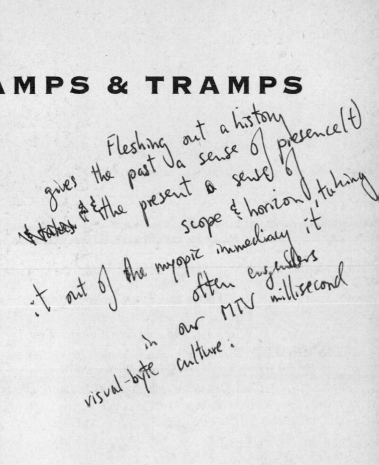

Fleshing out a history
gives the past a sense of presence(t)
~~makes~~ & the present a sense of
scope & horizon, taking
it out of the myopic immediacy it
often engenders
in our MTV millisecond
visual-byte culture.

Books *by* **CAMILLE PAGLIA**

Vamps and Tramps: New Essays

Sex, Art, and American Culture: Essays

Sexual Personae:
Art and Decadence from Nefertiti to Emily Dickinson

VAMPS
&
TRAMPS

NEW ESSAYS

CAMILLE PAGLIA

VINTAGE BOOKS

A Division of Random House, Inc.

New York

A VINTAGE ORIGINAL, NOVEMBER 1994
FIRST EDITION

Copyright © 1994 by Camille Paglia

All rights reserved under International and Pan-American Copyright
Conventions. Published in the United States by Vintage Books,
a division of Random House, Inc., New York, and simultaneously
in Canada by Random House of Canada Limited, Toronto.

Paglia, Camille
Vamps and tramps : new essays / Camille Paglia.—1st ed.
p.   cm.
Includes bibliographical references (p.   ) and index.
"A Vintage original."
ISBN 0-679-75120-3
1. Popular culture—United States—History—20th century.
2. Arts, American.   3. Arts, Modern—20th century—United
States.   4. American literature—20th century—History and
criticism.   I. Title.
E169.12.P334   1994
306.4′0973—dc20   94-12191
CIP

Pages 531–32 constitute an extension of this copyright page.

Manufactured in the United States of America
10 9 8 7 6 5 4 3 2 1

CONTENTS

POP THEATER

MASTERS AND MISTRESSES

MEMOIRS AND ADVENTURES

ON LITERATURE AND ART

BOOK REVIEWS

SATIRES AND SHORT TAKES

APPENDICES

INDEX

INTRODUCTION

Vamps & tramps

The title of this book evokes the missing sexual personae of contemporary feminism. Vamps are queens of the night, the primeval realm excluded and repressed by today's sedate middle-class professionals in their orderly, blazing bright offices. The prostitute, seductress, and high-glamour movie star wield woman's ancient vampiric power over men. That power is neither rational nor measurable. The Apollonian rules we pass to govern the workplace will never fully control the demonic impulses of Dionysian night. Sexual equality before the law—the first great goal of modern feminism—cannot so easily be transferred to our emotional lives, where woman rules. Art and pornography, not politics, show us the real truth about sex.

I want a revamped feminism. Putting the vamp back means the lady must be a tramp. My generation of Sixties rebels wanted to smash the bourgeois codes that had become authoritarian totems of the Fifties. The "nice" girl, with her soft, sanitized speech and decorous manners, had to go. Thirty years later, we're still stuck with her—in the official spokesmen and anointed heiresses of the feminist establishment. White middle-class personae have barely changed. Getting women out of the kitchen and into the office, we have simply put them into another bourgeois prison. The panoramic Sixties

vision, inspired by Buddhism and Hinduism, called the entire Western career system into question. But that insight has been lost.

   The beatniks, the generation of dissenters before mine, went "on
the road"—not just physically, like Jack Kerouac, but spiritually.
Allen Ginsberg, the New York Walt Whitman, made wayfaring
songs of an exile in his own land. Fusing Hindu and Hebrew chant
with African-American jazz rhythms, Ginsberg reenergized the pur-
ist folk style of Bob Dylan, my generation's hobo troubadour, who
went on to make rock"n' roll an art form. In "Like a Rolling Stone,"
Dylan forces his faithless heroine to confront the blank-eyed "mystery tramp," who is both the artist and personified death, the reality
of extinction that defines life itself. "Think for yourself," said the
Beatles, and let your mind roam "where it will go." The tramp is
a rover, exploring the wilderness outside the status quo.

   Until the end of the Fifties, a sexually free woman was called a
"tramp," that is, a vagrant or streetwalker, a whore. Joan Rivers's
gleefully insatiable Heidi Abromowitz, dashing to the dock to greet
the fleet, was the dark alter ego of the chaste middle-class girl. We
must reclaim the Whore of Babylon, the nature goddess of that
complex city of arrogant male towers and hanging female gardens.
Vamps and tramps are Babylonian personae, pagan outcasts. They
live again in our bold drag queens and gay hustlers, midnight cow-
boys of the urban canyons. An episode of the *Perry Mason* television
series, starring Raymond Burr, was called *The Case of the Vagabond
Vixen*. Female sexuality, freed from Judeo-Christian sequestration,
returns to animal nature. The woman "on the stroll" (streetwalking)
is a prowler and predator, self-directed and no one's victim.

   Equal opportunity feminism, which I espouse, demands the removal of all barriers to woman's advance in the political and
professional world—but not at the price of special protections for
women, which are infantilizing and anti-democratic. As a Sixties
libertarian, I also oppose overregulation of sexuality, which has risen
to a totalitarian extreme over the past decade in America. The
culture is at risk when civil liberties are sacrificed on the altar of
career success. Professional functioning in the Apollonian capitalist
machine—which I laud as the vehicle of woman's modern liberation—must not be confused with full human identity. Nor can office

"Arrogant male towers" & "hanging female gardens"

Sexuality is a force of nature outside the social realm

politics dictate our understanding of sexuality, which begins as a force of nature outside the social realm.

White middle-class style, despite the Sixties rebellion, still tyrannizes us, because corporate business, with the streamlined efficiency of the profit-based work ethic, was born in Protestant Northern Europe, before and after the industrial revolution. It has been puritanical and desensualized from the start. Bland on the surface and seething with Darwinian hostility below, office manners grind down and homogenize all ethnic and racial differences. The world is going WASP. We must scrutinize and monitor business operations when corporations corner monopolies or mushroom into faceless global mega-entities rivaling nation-states, but business style, fetishizing the white Protestant persona, may be beyond reform, because it is simply too effective.

We need to recast the daily dramas of our public theater. Meditating on vamps and tramps makes us see the decorous borders of professional life. In calling for a "room of one's own," Virginia Woolf created a central metaphor of twentieth-century feminism. Emily Dickinson, by a turn of the key, had achieved that secure mental space, but she was the daughter and sister of successful lawyers. A perquisite of privilege and prosperity, the "room of one's own" was already too bourgeois for my subversive generation, whose brash rock spirit counsels: Get out of the house, and keep on running. A car of one's own, the great equalizer, is more the mode of American Amazonism. On the open highway, battling stormy nature and dodging mammoth eighteen-wheelers (today's piratical tramp freighters), woman has never been more mobile, more capable of the archetypal journey of the heroic quest, a traditionally masculine myth.

The new tramp is not a displaced person, except insofar as he or she is a refugee from the prison of the nuclear family. Life is a condition of searching for meaning—an active and affirmative process, unlike the bunkered defeatism of modernism and postmodernism. The multicultural twenty-first century will also require research, as we drift further and further from our ethnic origins. By the principle of what I call creative duality, we must recover and celebrate our ethnic roots, while at the same time identifying ourselves with the spiritual homelessness of the tramp. The task is to balance phil-

Toughen us up

osophical detachment, the isolated consciousness, with a sense of community and engagement with social issues.

Overprotected in the paternalistic past, women have a special obligation to liberate their personae. Male adventurism has always been a costly, painful privilege. When the office—by which I mean the whole complex of word-based, smoothly cooperative white-collar work, in business or academe—becomes the primary paradigm of new female achievement, women have cut themselves off from the risk-taking, rough-and-tumble experiences that have always toughened men. Women will never succeed at the level or in the numbers they deserve until they get over their genteel reluctance to take abuse in the attack and counterattack of territorial warfare. The recent trend in feminism, notably in sexual harassment policy, has been to overrely on regulation and legislation rather than to promote personal responsibility. Women must not become wards and suppliants of authority figures. Freedom means rejecting dependency.

Creative duality also applies to female self-definition. Hyperdevelopment of the Apollonian office persona during the day—crucial if women are to advance to leadership—necessitates contrary measures for psychic health. Vamp and tramp, as vivid mental states, must be given nocturnal Dionysian license. My brand of streetwise feminism demands aggressive guerrilla tactics of speed, subterfuge, and surprise. The street walk and street talk, big and brassy, are polar opposites of the reserved, compressed body language and modest, subdued voices required by the professional world in its contained spaces. The street is nature, the open savanna with its long sightlines and the raw, exuberant energies of hunt and pursuit. Communication is African call-and-response, loud because it must cover great distances. I am acutely aware of the difficult transition from working class to middle class, since I have identified, to my career detriment, with the assertive, theatrical style of my grandparents' generation (my maternal grandfather worked in a shoe factory) rather than with the discreet good manners of my parents' generation, who sought social assimilation in America.

Vamps and tramps are the seasoned symbols of tough-cookie feminism, my answer to the smug self-satisfaction and crass materialism of yuppie feminism. I admire the hard-bitten, wisecracking realism of Ida Lupino and the *film noir* heroines. I'm sick of simpering

antiphony

white girls with their princess fantasies. The twenty-first hexagram of the *I Ching* is Shih Ho, "Biting Through," which represents the forcible overcoming of obstacles. No more sweets. No more placebos or false assurances. The eating disorders that plague bourgeois feminism are the regressive rituals of docile daughters who, on some level, refuse to fend for themselves. As an Italian-American child, I was fed wild black mushrooms, tart dandelion greens, spiny artichokes, and tangy olives flecked with red pepper flakes. These were life lessons in the sour and prickly, the bitter herbs eaten in the tramp's clothes of leavetaking. Auntie Mame, my campy guru, liked to say, "Life is a banquet, and most poor suckers are starving to death." The theme of *Vamps and Tramps* is wanderlust, the erotic, appetitive mind in free movement.

The word "vamp," in the sense of a sexual seductress, is Slavic in origin and descends from the Serbo-Croatian vampire legends of the bloody Balkans. Our language has a second, less glamourous "vamp," this one with French roots, by way of Middle English. Derived from shoemaking (the ancestral trade of my mother's region in Italy), it describes the leather instep of a boot, the thing that is "in the front," *"avant,"* as in the military and later artistic term, "avant-garde" or vanguard. Eventually, to "vamp" meant saving or repairing something old by patching it with a new piece—that is, using ingenuity, cleverness, and commonplace practicality to achieve your aims. From there it entered vaudeville and jazz: in musical accompaniment, "vamping" means improvising, ornamenting, pumping up the excitement.

I take vamping in this second sense to describe my interpretative style, in classroom teaching, public lectures, and cultural criticism. Improvisation in the modern performing arts is ultimately a product of Romanticism's stress on energy, originality, spontaneity, and emotional truth, as opposed to the gleaming technical perfection, architectural symmetry, and cerebral didacticism of neoclassicism. I don't want to throw out the old songs; I want to update, customize, and supercharge them. I want to put the bomp back into the bomp-de-domp. Improv, analogous to Freudian free association, takes you by startling leaps and pulses to the heart of the matter. It is Dionysian logic, sensory and surreal. Vision comes in psychedelic flashes. "Hot tramp!" David Bowie says to a pagan rogue in "Rebel, Rebel." The

Go on while paying homage.

guardians of culture must return to homage and ecstasy. Riffing and jamming on the classics, we can both corrupt and redeem them.

Vamps and Tramps began a year ago as a proposal by my editor for a second collection of essays. My first, *Sex, Art, and American Culture* (1992), documented the period following the release of my 700-page scholarly study, *Sexual Personae* (1990), when I was drawn into national controversies over date rape, sexual harassment, censorship, political correctness, poststructuralism, the literary canon, women's studies, gay studies, multiculturalism, the role of television, and, last but not least, Madonna. The second volume of *Sexual Personae*, on modern popular culture, was completed in 1981 but is currently being revised to incorporate the thousands of note cards that have accumulated over the intervening decade and a half. That volume, like the first, will be released in hardcover by Yale University Press.

she uses note cards

I was asked to write an essay, to serve as the centerpiece of *Vamps and Tramps*, about the newly contentious debate over homosexuality and biology, on which I had begun to speak out. I felt I should produce instead a more general statement of my sexual philosophy, in which homosexuality would have its place. Hence the main essay here, "No Law in the Arena: A Pagan Theory of Sexuality," which systematically presents my libertarian views of rape, abortion, battering, sexual harassment, prostitution, stripping, pornography, homosexuality, pedophilia, and transvestism. My guiding principle is a strict separation between the public and private spheres. The sanctity of the latter must be preserved and defended. The state should have no power to oversee or regulate solitary or consensual activities, such as suicide or sodomy. Hence I strongly support the legalization of drugs and prostitution, and I am an extreme advocate of the most lurid forms of pornography.

In the four years since I arrived on the scene (after an ill-starred career that included job problems, poverty, and the rejection of *Sexual Personae* by seven major publishers), there has been a dramatic shift in thought in America. The fascist rigidity of political correctness, in academe and the media, has begun to melt. Heretical ideas that, when I expressed them in essays and lectures in 1991 and 1992, got me pilloried and picketed, in a torrent of abuse and defamation, have now become common coin. My terminology and frame of analysis have passed into general usage. These are matters for the historical record, always clearer from a distance than in the chaotic present. My strategy has been to change the climate of ideas *around* the academic and feminist establishment, in order to shrink its power base. I have used aggressive "strikes," based on war and (my favorite sport) football, to damage and punish false leaders. My favorite weapon has been satire, which I studied in Horace, Juvenal, Rabelais, Pope, Swift, Oscar Wilde, Bob Dylan, and *Mad* magazine.

My meteoric rise—actually, this was the axiomatic "overnight success that took twenty years"—was partly due to a restlessness in America, a fatigue with dated ideology and an impatience with establishment insularity and impotence. These forces contributed to the 1992 presidential election of Bill Clinton, a relatively unknown governor of a provincial agricultural state (whom I continue to support, despite my public criticism of his managerial errors). As an ornery outsider of prickly eccentricity and raw populist humor, I was a parallel phenomenon to businessman-turned-politician Ross Perot and radio personalities Rush Limbaugh and Howard Stern, with their gigantic nationwide following. We have widely different political views, but all four of us, with our raging egomania and volatile comic personae tending toward the loopy, helped restore free speech to America.

Since the publication of *Sex, Art, and American Culture*, I have been particularly encouraged by three books. One was published by Cambridge University Press in 1989: Colin Falck's intricately interdisciplinary *Myth, Truth, and Literature: Towards a True Postmodernism*. When it came my way in early 1993, I immediately ordered twenty copies and sent them to leading scholars around the country: this, I prophesied, was the future of literary criticism—after the long overdue death of that ugly octopus, poststructuralism. The first words I saw on flipping open Falck's book were "Susanne Langer." I whooped with joy. Langer is the distinguished philosopher whose work on aesthetics was widely read and admired in the Sixties. When, in the process of writing my academic exposé, "Junk Bonds and Corporate Raiders," I spent six months reviewing the past two decades of jargon-ridden literary theory, I was appalled at the total absence of Langer's name—more proof of the ineptitude of the current humanities professoriat.

The two other works deal with feminism. Last year appeared 27-year-old Katie Roiphe's *The Morning After: Sex, Fear, and Feminism on Campus*, an eloquent, thoughtful, finely argued book that was savaged from coast to coast by shallow, dishonest feminist book reviewers (a welcome exception being Wendy Kaminer). Just released in 1994 is Christina Hoff Sommers's landmark study *Who Stole Feminism?*, which uses ingenious detective work to unmask the shocking fraud and propaganda of establishment feminism and the servility of American media and academe to Machiavellian feminist manipulation. This bracingly precise, fact-based book should be required reading for every journalist. Sommers is a courageous academic philosopher who was one of the very first to systematically critique current feminist ideology and who took tremendous abuse for it. Her activism predated by several years the publication of my long-delayed first book. Sommers has done a great service for women and for feminism, whose fundamental principles she has clarified and strengthened.

The themes of *Vamps and Tramps* continue those of *Sex, Art, and American Culture*. The progressive principles of the Sixties must be rescued from the brackish bog of political correctness into which they have sunk. My highest ideals are free thought and free speech. I condemn all speech codes and espouse offensiveness for its own sake, as a tool of attack against received opinion and unexamined assumptions. My heroes are the libertines of the Enlightenment and the aesthetes of the nineteenth-century Decadence. Science and art—intellect and imagination—must be reintegrated for a complete vision of the universe.

As a militant reformer of feminism and academe, I have followed the Sixties design of protest and opposition. The corrupt palace elites, arrogant with power, must be exposed and brought to justice everywhere, whether they are in the literature departments at Harvard and Princeton or in the headquarters of the National Organization for Women, which at the moment is merely an outpost of the Gloria Steinem coterie. Those who have poisoned the cultural atmosphere in America or gained high position by unethical means must be held accountable. It's Nuremberg time.

Sex, Art, and American Culture was secretly aimed toward students and seems to have succeeded in its mission. It is a handbook for the Resistance. I am arming the rebels. For example, "Junk Bonds and Corporate Raiders," paragraph by paragraph, is a set of can openers by which dissenters can pry open the solipsistically sealed discourse of poststructuralism. I seek no followers. I am an irascible Aries warrior rather than a politician or diplomat. My kind takes the beachhead and pushes the Nazis back; others make the treaties. Neither was I a "follower" *per se* of Allen Ginsberg, Marshall McLuhan, Norman O. Brown, or Leslie Fiedler. But those radical thinkers broke through the conventions of tradition and allowed us of the Sixties to *find our own voices*. That is what I would like to do for the students of the Nineties.

We need a general theory of culture. Without it, multiculturalism is nonsense. My synoptic work, taking in the full spectrum from high art to popular culture, was inspired by German philology, which I encountered via my childhood passion for archaeology. The great Schools of Oriental Studies—now routinely defamed as racist and imperialist by puerile New Historicists and others—were posited on the philological model. The latter represents a multilayered view of society, where everything, from trivia to treasure, counts. Religion, politics, law, language, literature, art, architecture, agriculture, husbandry, medicine, commerce, courtship, food preparation, domestic management: the analyst of culture must be able to range freely among all the elements of ordinary and extraordinary life. The story is in the details, scattered fragments into which the scholar breathes life.

My program of educational reform begins on the primary-school level, which has been irresponsibly ignored by our academic pseudo-leftists, whose idea of political action is nattering about Foucault to each other at conferences. Urban public schools have been allowed to decline disastrously since my mother emigrated from Italy in the Thirties and since I was rigorously educated in the Fifties and early Sixties. I favor a simple, back-to-basics curriculum centered on world history, science, and the arts, and I call for a return to the strict

If you don't really want to learn, I suggest you find another class

immigrant-era policy of expulsion of disorderly students, to protect the classroom for economically disadvantaged children who want to learn. Education is the foundation stone of true social justice.

National standards, like those of the New York State Regents exams that ruled my youth, are necessary, but administrative bureaucracies must be reduced and teachers given more power. I view bilingual instruction as shortsighted and counterproductive, and I oppose all social-welfare meddling in public education: condom distribution belongs in public health clinics, not schools, and forcing gay issues into the curriculum is an outrageous act of cultural imperialism by white middle-class ideologues against the working class for whom they claim to speak. Deep social change takes time and cannot be achieved by fiat. Sex must be kept out of the totalitarian grip of philanthropists and preachers of every stripe.

On the college level, reform has been stymied by two forces. First, a sterile liberal versus conservative debate has polarized the campuses and prevented authentic self-critique. These political positions are simplistic and outmoded. We must take the best from the left and the best from the right to devise new strategies for the global twenty-first century. The reluctance of liberal professors to speak out against rampant abuses committed on their side (e.g., suppression of free speech, the excesses of women's studies and French theory) has simply increased the power of the right.

Progressive values are damaged when the left has lost touch with reality and when the plain voice of common sense is heard mainly on the right. Conservative Christian organizations have made enormous gains in America because most of their issues are legitimate ones that have been misunderstood, misrepresented, or treated with sophomoric disrespect by what Dan Quayle correctly called the "cultural elite." The only way to slow or stop the national drift to the right is for intellectuals to reclaim these issues and methodically recast them, one by one, in a new progressive language comprehensible to middle America but divested of narrow Christian moralism. The people can and must be pulled back toward the center. Civil liberties, as the Sixties understood them, are at stake.

The process of curricular reform has been complicated by the insularity of humanities faculty, most of whom seem naively oblivious to the political complexities and inner turbulence of contem-

Totalitarian grip of philanthropists + preachers

porary America. The second force frustrating reform is the academic career system, which has gotten tangled up with politics, since ambitious, apolitical literature teachers discovered in the Seventies and Eighties that easily learned leftist posturing brought professional prestige and advancement. The politics of these vinyl carpetbaggers consist mainly of empty rhetoric—and of currying favor with other academics.

Economic analysis is the first principle of Marxism. Professors who were genuine leftists would have challenged the entire economics-driven machinery of American academe—the wasteful multidepartmental structure, the divisive pedantry of overspecialization, the cronyism and sycophancy in recruitment and promotion, the boondoggling ostentation of pointless conferences, the exploitation of graduate students and part-time teachers, the subservience of faculty to overpaid administrators, the mediocrity and folly of the ruling cliques of the Modern Language Association.

The failure of academe to reform itself from within was compounded by the negligence and inertness of what used to be called the "alternative press," which in the political correctness debate astonishingly aligned itself with the tenured professors of the elite schools. For example, *The Village Voice*, which I read devoutly in the Sixties and early Seventies, had so collapsed into confusion and irrelevance that its derisive 1991 cover story denying the existence of political correctness (and picturing me as a "counterfeit feminist" bandit "Wanted for Intellectual Fraud") was quickly accepted for republication by the *Yale Journal of Criticism*. Something is wrong in the culture when there is such collusion between the establishment and the old forces of critique. For twenty years, the alternative press, nationwide, has been irresponsibly mute about the venal careerism of academe, which drove my generation into the wilderness.

Most professors know that American higher education in the humanities is in a deplorable state. Yet many remain silent, perhaps through prudent self-preservation, which is starting to look a lot like moral cowardice. They have put loyalty to their colleagues before loyalty to their students, ostensibly the *raison d'être* for educational institutions. How many more young minds must be distorted or destroyed before the faculty decides to defend the Western intellectual values of free inquiry and orderly acquisition of knowledge?

Great western skill!

XX

INTRODUCTION

Only the West produced the scientific techniques and speculative analysis of geology, paleontology, and archaeology, which have revealed and preserved the world past.

I end my public lectures with a mantra for the students: "Hate dogma. Love learning. Love art." What sorry pass have we come to when such sentiments are judged dangerously radical? Learning, not facile theory, must be the primary criterion (with teaching ability second) for the hiring and promotion of faculty. The new interdisciplinary era, which I support, requires an even deeper commitment to learning than before, but standards have actually weakened. The venerable emeritus professors still at Yale when I entered graduate school may have been reserved, puritanical WASPs, but they were men of honor who had given their lives to scholarship. Today in the elite schools, honor and ethics are gone.

My aim is to build a coalition for educational reform consisting of concerned persons across the political spectrum. The supreme principles of free thought and free speech transcend all party affiliations. I think I am alone in proposing a plan for *world* education. International understanding must have some basis in common terminology, which can best be articulated through traditional means, the solid scholarship of a revamped old historicism. We need a plan that is simultaneously a great expansion and a great simplification—that is, a moving outward to take in the vastness of global multiculturalism and a reordering, by severe process of elimination, of the organizing themes for that huge body of material.

My program offers comparative religion as a core curriculum for the world. I do not believe in God, but I believe God is man's greatest idea. Those incapable of religious feeling or those (like hardcore gay activists) who profane sacred ground do not have the imagination to educate the young. Flicking the radio dial in America, one hears bursts of beautiful, spellbinding poetry. But it is neither academics nor contemporary writers who are filling the air with dazzling imagery and profound spiritual truths. Alas for progressive politics, these are the voices of white and black Christian ministers, reading from the Bible. Why have intellectuals abandoned the people? This is the shame of modernism. High Romanticism at least gave poetry as the prize of rebellion and, turning from God, put nature in his place.

Everyone in the world should know all the great religions of the world: Hinduism; Buddhism; Greco-Roman and Near Eastern paganism; Judeo-Christianity; Islam; African, North American, and Oceanic tribal cults; pre-Columbian imperial myth. Art, history, and philosophy are intertwined with the evolution of religion. This is the true multiculturalism. The secularism of the Enlightenment was meant to free the mind, not kill the soul. In the spirit of the eighteenth-century encyclopedists and revolutionaries, we must keep church and state separate, even while we preserve the eternal insights and metaphors of religion. Authority belongs to the classroom, not the pulpit.

Until the left comes to its senses about the cultural power of religion, the right will continue to broaden its appeal. The Sixties wanted to break the oppressive moral codes of organized religion, to attain vision by a daring individualism. But we left the generations who came after us in a spiritual vacuum. The young are struggling for identity in a world defined by material uncertainties and inequities, surreally juxtaposed pockets of feast and famine. Hence their vulnerability to political correctness, the only religion they know. They crave spiritual food, and the elite schools have given them the bitter ashes of nihilism. Everything inspiring or ennobling has been befouled for them by their crabbed, callous professors, who do not deserve the name "teacher." My efforts to restore the unfashionable concept of "greatness" to critical discourse are part of my evangelical mission in the service of the Hellenic religion of art, whose homoerotic prophets have risen again and again since the Renaissance.

My plan is a fusion of archaism and futurism. Much of the acrimony of academic debate has come from a misapplication of the Sixties' demand for "relevance." Universities should not be brokers of the contemporary. The purpose of education is to open the remote past to the students, so that they can learn from the voluminous human record of mistakes and triumphs. Professors have no business telling students about the present. The students *are* the present, and month by month, they are creating the future. Stop oppressing them with exhausted paradigms of the recent past. Each time a professor sets foot in the classroom, he or she is already history.

The "vamping" style that I endorse weaves references to the present throughout all interpretation of the past. Every teacher must become a bard, a living archive and singer of sagas. "Only connect," said E.M. Forster. Education must center on primary texts, the major artworks so complex and elusive that they have haunted generation after generation. None of us understands them fully. We must present them to the students, then get out of the way. Great art radiates—an uncanny aura beyond good or evil. We literally "expose" ourselves to it, never knowing its deepest effects until years or decades later.

On the Moebius strip of the human psyche, the future meets the past. I recognize the austere elegance and gravity of ancient Egyptian ritualism in *Star Trek: The Next Generation*, a television series (1987–94) that speaks to the universalist longings of the post-Sixties era. Technology has become like a second skin. The heroic spirit of maligned Columbus still pushes into space, *Star Trek*'s "final frontier." Its plot lines wavering between cooperation and militance, the program recapitulates the *Oresteia*'s contest between law and lawlessness, civilization and barbarism. And *Star Trek* accepts, without paternalistic sentimentality, the grotesque *differentness* of peoples, even their mutual physical repulsiveness.

The current multicultural metaphor of the "rainbow" is completely wrong. Cultures will never coexist in placid, symmetrical bands. There is no way, for example, that the opulent African aesthetic of luxurious textures and brilliant colors, produced by the tropical sun, can ever fully comprehend or be comprehended by the sensuality-suppressing corporate WASP aesthetic of clean-lined "understated" designs and "tasteful" muted tones—beige, bone, charcoal, navy. One cancels out the other. Conflict is unavoidable.

My master metaphor for culture is *the river*, with its nourishing tributaries and churning cataracts. It conveys the real majesty of the world's historical traditions. Art comes cascading down to us from shadowy origins, like the allegorical Nile whose head is mysteriously wrapped in Bernini's Piazza Navona fountain. Not critics but artists make the canon, which is simply the long stream of influences that create and sustain a civilization.

We must construct a curriculum that balances the arts and sciences in a simple, rational way. I have written and spoken extensively about the need to demolish women's studies, a corrupt

No TALKING!!! Just watch, do!!!

autocracy that was flung together without regard for scholarly standards or objective criteria of professional credentialing. Gay studies is even worse—a cul-de-sac microfield that guarantees bias and self-interest. My proposed substitute, sex studies, would put men and women, as well as gay and straight, into the same program, and it would make basic study of biology, endocrinology, psychology, and anthropology requirements for anyone claiming expertise in gender issues or seeking employment in that area as a college instructor.

Good

Teaching of the arts also needs reform, to remove every trace of desiccated academicism—bibliographic, semiotic, or poststructuralist. The visual and performing arts must be liberated from the tyranny of words, the stock-in-trade of a snooty literary establishment whose superannuated worldview predates that of our colorful, image-dominated age of television. History of the international languages of music and dance should be built into the liberal arts core curriculum. It is disgraceful, for example, that jazz is more honored abroad than in its birthplace. Black music, in its half-dozen major phases, belongs at the heart of education for all young Americans.

The media so shapes our world that a survey course in its long development is indispensable, from the first mass-market newspapers in the 1830s through the birth of advertising and the invention of movies, radio, and television. Art films are a superb educational tool to introduce students to foreign languages as well as to dramatize the fleeting ambiguities and hypnotic compulsions of sexuality. Cinema is far more accurate about sex than is feminist theory. Public funds should be used not to support individual artists—no genuinely avant-garde artist would take money from the government—but to underwrite dance companies, musical groups, and a national film consortium, designated to produce and protect mint-condition prints of great films for constant circulation among primary and secondary schools. If we fail to take action to sophisticate our students, the intellectual and artistic creativity of America will suffer.

All the pieces in *Vamps and Tramps* were written in the two years since the release of *Sex, Art, and American Culture*. Many have been previously published in England and America, but the following were specially written for this volume: the main essay,

"No Law in the Arena," "The Saint," "Tournament of Modern Personae" (on D.H. Lawrence), "Sontag, Bloody Sontag," and "My Brothers in Crime," a memoir of four gay men who have heavily influenced me.

This is a multimedia book, in the Sixties style of Marshall McLuhan. Included are transcripts of several of the television and film projects I have recently participated in. I feel most fortunate to have an ongoing professional relationship with the brilliant producer-director Peter Stuart, whose staff and crew at Rapido TV in London have created four specials that I hosted on Channel 4, thanks to arts editor Waldemar Januszczak, over the past year and a half. Two of them, *The Penis Unsheathed* and *Lolita Unclothed*, are in this book. Censorship is such in America, on both the left and right wings, that neither program could have been made for mainstream television here. Transcripts of the two remaining shows, *Diana Unclothed* (which caused a press flap) and *Lesbians Unclothed*, were not included for reasons of space.

Other transcripts, in order of their film production: "Dr. Paglia," from *Female Misbehavior*, directed by Monika Treut and featuring Bruce Benderson; *Sex War*, directed by Luca Babini and starring Lauren Hutton; and *Glennda and Camille Do Downtown*, a video collaboration with New York drag queen and public-access television personality and producer Glennda Orgasm (Glenn Belverio). The Hutton film has not yet been publicly shown, but *Female Misbehavior* has appeared at film festivals and in commercial release around the world and is distributed in video by First Run Features. *Glennda and Camille*, despite being shown at the prestigious Sundance Festival in January 1994, was banned for reasons of political incorrectness this past spring by both the New York and San Francisco Lesbian and Gay Film Festivals. [Note: As this book went to press, *Glennda and Camille* won first prize for the best short documentary at the 1994 Chicago Underground Film Festival.]

Other pieces in the book deal with censorship, academic reform, and the Stalinism of the feminist and gay-activist establishment. There are articles on Diana and Jacqueline Kennedy Onassis, as well as on the Clintons (including a 1993 London cover story on Hillary). Popular culture figures profiled include Judy Garland, Woody Allen, Amy Fisher, Sandra Bernhard, Madonna, and Barbra

Streisand (another 1993 London cover story). Literary and artistic subjects, aside from D.H. Lawrence and Susan Sontag, include Lewis Carroll, Bizet's *Carmen*, Kenneth Clark's *The Nude*, an article on love poetry from the *Princeton Encyclopedia of Poetry and Poetics*, and a manifesto of Neo-Sexism, the pro-art project I cofounded with artist and curator Alison Maddex. Among books reviewed are those by Germaine Greer, Edward Said, and Warren Farrell. Previously published pieces have usually been retitled, and all material dropped for space at deadline editing has been restored.

"Satires and Short Takes" includes heterogeneous extracts and snippets, as well as the advice columns I wrote for *Spy*, which came to an end when commissioning editor Jamie Malanowski left the magazine. Scores of cartoons about me have appeared since my last book; some are reproduced here. They illustrate the degree to which I have become a sexual persona, apart from my ideas, at a moment when both feminism and academe are in flux. I seem to have passed into Pop Art, one of the formative influences of my college years. Last is a condensed media chronicle of my major appearances, as both subject and vamping commentator, in international newspapers and magazines.

I would like to thank my patient and supportive editor, LuAnn Walther, and my ace publicist and loyal advisor, Katharine Barrett, at Vintage Books. Luca Babini, artist and athlete, has been extraordinarily generous in taking portrait photographs of me for this book. Five people were directly involved, in different ways, with the production of the manuscript: Kent Christensen, Nina Lucas, Stephen Wolf, Bruce Benderson, and my partner, Alison Maddex. During the writing of the book, I benefited from conversations with the following people, in alphabetical order: Glenn Belverio, Robert Caserio, John DeWitt, Herbert Golder, Lauren Hutton, Ann Jamison, Stephen Jarratt, Elizabeth Kaspar Aldrich, Kristen Lippincott, M.G. Lord, Kenneth Manning, Harvey Mansfield, Rosemary Mayer, Lynn Nesbit, Lenora Paglia, Marilyn Roberts, Gillian Rose, Camelia Sanes, Heidi Jon Schmidt, Christina Hoff Sommers, Francesca Stanfill, Sarah Such, David Talbot, Monika Treut, Helen and Gregory Vermeychuk, Lydia Wills, and Ben and Rachel Wizner.

Camille Paglia
Philadelphia, June 1994

THE YEAR
OF THE PENIS

THE PENIS UNSHEATHED

After hours at a museum gallery of Greek and Roman sculpture. Next to a stately entryway of Doric pillars, we see a marble copy of Polycleitus' Dia-doumenos, a nude athlete tying on his headband. The camera pans down his body, from face to penis. To the brassy beat of Yma Sumac's "Goomba Boomba," a charwoman with mop and pail sashays through the gallery and flicks the statue's genitals with three flourishes of her orange dust rag. Cut to stage set adorned with racks of church candles and a red carpet leading to an altar-like platform, above which hangs a neon-bright Pop Art painting of the abdomen and thighs of Michelangelo's David. The background of the image is iridescent orange, the skin cobalt blue, the pubic hair green, and the penis hot-pink. CAMILLE PAGLIA, *in black jacket and pants, strolls out from the shadow of a church window, steps up on the platform, and addresses the camera.*

CAMILLE PAGLIA *(imitating Nancy Kulp as schoolmarmish Miss Jane on The Beverly Hillbillies):* The penis. Should we keep it? Or should we cut it off and *throw it away?* In the thirty years since the sexual revolution, we have thought obsessively about sex but come to no answers to any important sexual question. The

[A Rapido TV production for *World Without Walls*, Channel 4, London. Produced by Peter Stuart. Directed by Peter Murphy. Aired March 1, 1994.]

penis is shaping up to be the central metaphor of the gender crisis of the Nineties. *(Cut to black-and-white art photograph of a nude man holding a photo of the genitals of Michelangelo's* David *over his own.)* In too much feminist thought of the last several decades, the penis has been defined as an instrument of intimidation, aggression, violation, and destruction. I think we've gotten to the point where this kind of reductive definition of male anatomy is proving unsatisfactory to women of the Nineties. It would be useful for us to go backwards in time and to review the way the penis has been symbolized through history.

(Cut to prehistoric and classical depictions of men, penises, and dildos, including Greek vases and the monumental penis-on-a-pillar in the sacred precinct at Delos. Cut to art historian PETER WEBB, *seated against a black background with a spotlit statue of a nude Greek boy behind him.)*

PETER WEBB: The phallus has had a very positive image, a very positive power in history and in prehistory, as far back as we go. And this has not in any way been demonstrably anti-women. But it has been *pro*. It's been pro-fertility. It's been a sort of talismanic image, an image to bring fertility, an image to assure good luck, an image to ward off the evil eye. And in this way, it's had a strong role to play in all sorts of cultures that we can examine in history. Really, from prehistoric times right through. But I suppose the most interesting to evaluate is the world of Greece and Rome, where it's quite clear that the phallus played a vital role in worship.

(Cut to a reconstruction of a priapic dance, circa 300 A.D., from Derek Jarman's Sebastiane. *Ecstatically leaping acolytes with large phallic prostheses circle a writhing bald man in white body paint and red G-string, who obscenely laps his reddened tongue. Back to Paglia on the set.)*

PAGLIA: The Greeks had a rather comical little god named Priapus, who stood for phallic erection. There was a priapic element to the behavior of Aristophanes' comic actors on stage, some of whom had enormous leather penises attached to their bodies, with which they would hit each other *(she demonstrates)* and buffet each other about. It's very similar to the "slapstick" of commedia dell'arte and, later, vaudeville.

(Cut to more Greek vases and then the wild dance again. Cut to art critic Jack Fritscher, sitting in a park near a monumental fountain.)

JACK FRITSCHER: In art history, it's very difficult to find a favorite penis without going back to ancient times, where there are very frankly portrayed beautiful penises. We get into this period of Western culture where there's a terrible fear of penises. They're not allowed to be, I think, big, above a larger size than small. They just don't become the man, and as a result, they don't have a lot of appeal.

(The camera zooms in on the tiny penises of statues of a discus-thrower and a warrior with his shield. Return of the Latin beat.)

PAGLIA *(on set)*: The Greeks gave their statues the genitals of small boys. We have only recently found out what the reasons for this might be. It is that the classical Athenians regarded the large penis as a symbol of animality, of one's bestial instinct having primacy over the mind. Therefore, it was an exact reversal of modern days, where a large penis is prized.

(Cut to covers and advertisements from pornography magazines with headlines like Massive Meat *and* Big Men on Campus. *Fade-in to a muscular Archaic Greek kouros figure. Back to Peter Webb.)*

WEBB: I don't personally think they were deliberately made tiny. I think that we tend to think that because phalluses are large in the religious sphere, they look much smaller on human beings. I don't think there was a specific desire to make them tiny. Some people say that Michelangelo deliberately made the penises tiny in the Sistine Chapel. Personally, I don't think that that was deliberate, though, on his part. *(Cut to penis-to-face pan of Michelangelo's Adam, accompanied by Gregorian chant of the Kyrie Eleison.)* I think that he just saw that the human body was a perfect whole and he wanted to make it beautiful without drawing attention in particular to the sexual aspect.

(Cut to Michelangelo's Sistine fresco of the serpent's temptation of Eve and the banishment of Adam and Eve from the Garden of Eden. Cut to shots of various Sistine ignudi.)

PAGLIA *(on set)*: Perhaps the best example in Michelangelo of the disparity between the little boy's private parts and the bulky brawniness of the adult body would be the *ignudi* of the Sistine Chapel ceiling, the nude youths, where you have such a contrast between the beefiness of the torso and these *tiny* little genitals that have always reminded me of my grandmother's *gnocchi,* tiny little pasta pieces made out of potatoes. *(Mandolin music. Cut to bowl of fat, white* gnocchi, *which dissolve into an* ignudo*'s penis.)*

There is a tradition in Renaissance art of depicting the genitals either of the baby Jesus exposed, in ritual display, or of those of the dead Christ, bulging through the fabric of his loincloth, that seems very shocking to us in modern times. *(Cut to paintings of the passion and entombment of Christ.)* There is a symbolism here that Christ was *incarnated.* He was the Son of God, but he was put into mortal flesh and experienced, presumably, all of the impulses and temptations that we too are subject to.

(Cut to MARGARET WALTERS, *author of* The Nude Male. *She is seated in an artist's studio, filled with drawings of the male nude.)*

MARGARET WALTERS: The baby Christ often has a very obvious penis. Sometimes he is touching it; sometimes Mary is pointing to it. *(Cut to painting of Madonna and child. Mary seems to be gazing down at her son's penis.)* It's always visible. In some sense, a center, a proof of Christ's humanity as well as his godliness. But also in dead Christs—I mean, Mantegna's dead Christ, with its extraordinary foreshortening of the body—the loincloth actually emphasizes the bulge of his penis, and it's done very reverently. *(Cut to the Mantegna painting.)* This is an important point about humanity and godhead.

(Cut to an art class, where male and female students are sketching a nude male model with his arms over a pole resting, lancelike, across his upper back. The camera pans over several charcoal renderings of the penis.) The male nude has always been central to artistic training, because it was such a central image in figurative art. It kept that centrality until we moved into the mid-nineteenth century and the twentieth century, when figurative art was no longer so crucial. It's also interesting that the male nude was not available for women artists to study. They were absolutely excluded. It

was an absurd situation. And the great American painter Thomas Eakins lost his job teaching in Philadelphia when he removed the loincloth from a male model—this is in the late nineteenth century!—interestingly, probably because some of his women students complained. They were at that stage genuinely shocked by this. It seemed to be sexual rather than artistic.

(Cut to SARAH KENT, *art critic and author of* Women's Images of Men. *She is standing in front of a display of Robert Mapplethorpe's photographs.)*

SARAH KENT: Women have only very recently begun to make images of the male nude, and they're doing a lot of things that men find problematic. For instance, making fun of them or else showing them as vulnerable, soft and passive, in a way that appeals to *them* but in a way that men find very problematic.

(Cut to excerpts from a film, Dick: Women's Views on the Penis. *A question appears on screen: "What do they look like?" A series of American and British female voices is heard over a montage of black-and-white close-up photos of real-life penises. The women's tones vary, from affectionate to bitterly sarcastic.)*

It's kind of like a vacuum-cleaner hose or something *(laughs)*.

It's such a *(baby talk) cute little thing!*

I think it looks sort of bald.

Kind of heart-shaped.

Almost like a duck-billed platypus, I suppose.

A cluster of bananas.

It looked like a tea kettle.

A butt.

I always thought it looked like a belly button.

A little bit like a skinned chicken neck.

They're like young asparaguses!

PAGLIA: Throughout history, respectable women were expected to keep a modest gaze. That is, not stare, to keep their eyes cast downward. A woman with a very hard or what was called "free" gaze was always considered a prostitute. So here we are at the end of the twentieth century now, and respectable, middle-class women are—through the tutelage of modern commercial photography—being taught how to take pleasure in *looking*. Now, I think that this is a true revolution, and it is the end of that feminist idea of the "male gaze," which says that men stare aggressively and turn women into sex objects, because now we're in a period when it is permissible for women to make *men* into sex objects.

(Cut to the "Women Photograph Men Workshop," a photography course designed for women to study the male nude, offered by Exposures Gallery in London. Three young women giggle and sheepishly exchange glances as, cameras held aloft, they kneel in front of or lie below the nude model's penis and buttocks. The gung-ho female instructor, like a summer-camp counselor, cheerfully exhorts them onward.)

INSTRUCTOR *(motioning with her arms)*: Move in closer!

SARAH KENT: A lot of supposedly erotic male nudes are very funny because there's such *hysteria* in the image, you know, there's this terrible sense of, "Oh, my God! We've got to try to build up the mythology of this creature!" And it doesn't work because it's ludicrously inflated, in every sense of the word. It's incredibly difficult to look at an image of the penis for lots and lots of different reasons for men *and* for women. The man will probably have to identify *with* that subject and feel very uncomfortable, feel very vulnerable because he's been stripped of his accoutrements. He's been stripped of his covering.

(Cut to male and female visitors' bemused faces at "True Phallacy: The Myth of Male Power," America's first group art show since the Sixties devoted to imagery of the penis. On view from December 10, 1993, to January 19, 1994, at Clark & Company gallery, Georgetown, Washington, D.C. Among the works visible are Jeffrey Barron's Race Relations *(black and white plastic dildos encased, mummylike, in velvet boxes), Groover Cleveland's* Ce n'est pas un penis, *Reuven Kupperman's nude, cross-legged* Self-portrait, *a paint-*

ing from Joe Kaminski's Dick Series *(a gigantic swollen penis with a cock ring), and Nuki's* Untitled *(a penis head peeking out of a matador costume). Cut to artist* JOSÉ VILLARRUBIA, *standing in front of his* Minotaur, *a ritualistically frontal photograph of a nude black man who is wearing a silver bull mask and whose large penis has been painted silver.)*

JOSÉ VILLARRUBIA: The penis is a tremendous, tremendous taboo. People think that they're going to burn in hell if they see one. You never see it on television or in the media. And it's restricted only to pornography—and *(laughs)* fine art.

(Cut to ALISON MADDEX, *curator of* True Phallacy. *She is serenely seated behind a table covered with 60 shiny, gun-metal-gray erect penises pointing at different angles toward the ceiling. It is Jim Fotile's* Die Tannenwald: Self-portrait. *The artist plaster-casted his own penis and coated the images with metallic paint.)*

ALISON MADDEX: Artists can deal with it. In a situation like this penis "forest" here, where these take on figurative kind of characters. Even more so than trees, I would say they're *people* somehow—kind of *(laughs and gestures like a hiker plowing through underbrush)* making our way through the dicks of the world!

(Cut to a chic blonde woman at True Phallacy, *viewing the penis "forest." As the crowd looks on, she dramatically points out her favorite.)*

WOMAN VISITOR: I'll take *that* one! *(laughs uproariously with her female friend)*

(Cut back to England.)

SARAH KENT: If we come to the *female* viewer, what's *she* doing when she looks at the penis? Well, she's probably embarrassed, to start with. She looks at this little piece of flesh, and she thinks, "That's no use to *me*. What can I do with *that*? Nothing!" So this man is of no use to her in any metaphoric or literal way. Of course, the main problem is that it's illegal to show an erection. An erect penis is a very handsome object, *I* maintain, a very beautiful object, as people like Robert Mapplethorpe have *proved.* You know, he has shown some *wonderful* male nudes with semi-erect penises. And in pornography magazines the men usu-

*But everyone knows that, has potential! ☺
even a deflated penis*

ally have *slightly* massaged members, so that they appear to be
a bit erect, which helps a lot, because then you're getting nearer
to something that could actually be meaningful and useful and
could embody power.

(Cut to HELEN WILLIAMS, *editor of* For Women *magazine, who peers
through a magnifying glass at a proof sheet of color photos of a long-haired,
nude, heavily tanned and oiled hunk impishly kneeling with a metal baseball
bat. Montage of* For Women *covers. Headlines on a Patrick Swayze cover:
"I imagine my cock is encased in an icicle"; "Is it love or lust? and how to
tell the difference"; "Group Sex"; "Miss Whiplash and the cabinet minister."
Headlines on a Matt Dillon cover: "Is your clitoris ¼" long?"; "Women who
sleep with strangers night after night.")*

HELEN WILLIAMS: Women definitely *do* want to see an erection. We
get a lot of letters from women saying, you know, "*Love* the
magazine, but how come there aren't any erections?" Because
it doesn't make any sense to have kind of sexy shots of men
without an erection. Because the guidelines are so woolly about
what actually constitutes an erection. I mean, there is no angle
or degree that we're given. The law is very vague on this. You
know, we've tried kind of seeing how far we can go and what
the censors consider an erection. And basically, we've finally
decided that a penis that is kind of self-supporting, or freestanding in any way, if it's not leaning on something or
just . . . hanging, then we get into problems. And especially it
mustn't be pointing at you!

*Ha!
Of course!
Why shouldn't
they?*

(Flash of the baseball boy's cock. Then back to PAGLIA *on set, her head next
to* David's *hot-pink penis.)*

PAGLIA: For me, the erect penis is the ultimate symbol of human
sexual desire, because only *men* can show sexual excitation *externally*. We *never* know whether women are truly sexually aroused
or not. Their reproductive apparatus remains internal. Therefore, I think it is of crucial importance to feminism to put the
penis *back* to *stage center!*

*Not
wholly
true*

(Cut to bronze figurine of dancing Greek satyr with a huge, curved erection.)

JACK FRITSCHER: It seems ironic that here we're doing a show about the penis and we cannot show the erect penis. We *can*, however, show the penis that pees but not the penis that gives babies or grace. Ha!

(Cut to tourists crowded around the Mannekin-Pis, the seventeenth-century "pissing boy" fountain in Brussels. They leap back, laughing, as the spray hits them.)

PAGLIA: The motif of the pissing boy that is so common on fountains in Europe seems very remarkable, because one can't *imagine* a female equivalent. A young girl pissing would not in any way be humorous or touching. Young boys are literally *handling their tools* from early on. *(She demonstrates.)* They have to learn how to, for example, *aim*. I have often said that this is one of the moments when young boys learn linearity, concentration, focus, projection. *(Cut to rococo painting of a pastoral scene of nymphs and cherubs, two of whom are urinating into a brook.)* Right from the start, man has the idea of *building*, of something which is building and falling, okay? The idea of something that goes both hard and soft, that he is not totally in control of. So I think that the phallic paradigm underlies a lot of male cultural achievement in ways that women *too easily* ridicule. Interesting!

(Cut to a panorama of Manhattan's skyline. The camera pulls back to reveal a pensive, nude young man leaning languidly against a wall on a roof, with the Empire State and Chrysler buildings in the distance. In the next photo, the same man, clad only in sneakers and athletic socks, lounges on a Hudson River pier, as he contemplates the World Trade Center towers.)

SARAH KENT: You could argue that we live in a phallic environment. I mean, if you go to Manhattan, it's just one prick after another! The entire *place* is a kind of temple to the phallus. And of course, the *power* of the phallus, in terms of commerce and money. We see monuments everywhere that are basically large pricks: Cleopatra's Needle, Nelson's Column. So we don't have actual pricks on display, but we have phallic objects on display. I can't imagine a woman building a building that was tower-blocked in shape. It's inconceivable.

PAGLIA *(on set)*: One of Freud's most controversial theories is that of penis envy. That is, that woman feels a mutilated being, feels that she is an incomplete man. This has always been disputed by feminists. And indeed, it's probably the number-one reason Freud was thrown out of the feminist movement twenty years ago. It still remains controversial.

(Cut again to Dick: Women's Views on the Penis. *The question "Would you want one?" appears on screen. More black-and-white photos of penises flash by, while we hear women's responses, some of them heavily ironic.)*

Where would I keep it?

Maybe. Maybe if I had it in a little box—I mean, that I could take out and play with. But never connected to my body!

It looks like you'd get a backache. I mean, God! No thanks!

Besides, I've kicked enough guys in the dick, and seen the reaction that it gets, to *not want* that kind of pain.

But I've always wished that I could sort of lease one and have it around whenever I need it.

Like "Queen for a Day." I'd like to have a penis for a day.

If I had a dick, I think I'd probably piss on everything and, uh, I'd wank a lot.

I'd play with it by myself a lot. And I'd go around and stick it in as many women as I could, and I would just totally enjoy it all the time.

PAGLIA *(as lofty Dame Edna Everage)*: I myself, though I would find a penis useful when courting women, would think of it on a day-to-day basis as being *highly* inconvenient, *getting* in the way, *always* being *rubbed* and therefore a *constant problem!*

[handwritten: You don't quite get it.]

[handwritten: Wrong!]

OFFSCREEN VOICE *(director* PETER MURPHY*)*: But supposing you could have a penis just for a day, Camille. What would you do with it?

PAGLIA: *(Taken by surprise, goes blank for a moment. Then laughs, blushes, and shrugs.)* You don't want me to answer that question! I would—*(imitates Groucho Marx)* go find Catherine Deneuve in a hurry!

(Cut to film of annual Shinto fertility procession at Tagata Shrine in Japan. A boisterous team of men in traditional garb carry a giant blonde-wood phallus, the size of a tree trunk, on their shoulders through the village to the temple. Rows of women follow, cradling replicas like babies. A monk sprinkles coarse salt in the street. A young woman rings a penis-shaped bell. Businessmen rub the tip of a black stone phallus, for good luck. A woman bows and prays to an altar of phallic images.)

JACK FRITSCHER: I'm not saying that you just worship the penis. It's just that we're talking about *penis,* and penis as being something that *hasn't* been worshipped. Everybody's falling on their knees and worshipping vaginas in a sense, worshipping femininity. I mean, people just driven into *groups* because they want to get in touch with their feminine side. Well, hey! Get in touch with your *masculine* side. You need to get a grip on your *dick!* Hold *on* to it. Because if you don't, it will be turned into a Bobbitt!

(Cut to cover of People *magazine: "The War of the Bobbitts: The Cut Felt Round the World." Horror-movie music. Close-ups of Lorena and John Wayne Bobbitt in court and then the kitchen knife itself, placed in evidence.)*

PAGLIA *(on set)*: I think that the subliminal castration anxiety that men have *always* had has suddenly erupted into the open with the case in 1993 of Lorena Bobbitt, who cut off her husband's penis in the middle of the night. I think this is an event of major proportions in modern sexual history. I don't feel that most women want to support such an act of barbarism. But in some sense, Lorena Bobbitt has committed the ultimate revolutionary act of contemporary feminism.

(Cut to footage of Lorena Bobbitt walking from her car into the courthouse. Cut to Court TV cable coverage.)

ANCHORWOMAN: We turn now today to the trial of Lorena Bobbitt, accused, as most of the country now knows, of cutting off her husband's penis. After the opening statements in this case, which were quite brief by most standards, John Wayne Bobbitt himself was called to the stand as witness number one for the state. Here he describes what it was like when his wife attacked him.

(Cut to courtroom footage.)

JOHN WAYNE BOBBITT: And she just pulled up on my, you know, groin area. I mean . . . *(His voice trails off.)*

STATE'S ATTORNEY: She did what?

JOHN: She pulled on my groin area twice, I think. I felt a couple jerks and then I, I, I—After that she just, like, cut it off.

(Cut to Lorena Bobbitt on the stand.)

DEFENSE ATTORNEY: And the next thing you remember is when you were driving to your friend Janice's house—

LORENA BOBBITT *(distraught)*: Yes. Yes.

ATTORNEY: You were getting close to a stop sign—

LORENA: Yes.

ATTORNEY: And you realized that there was something in your left hand—

LORENA: Yes.

ATTORNEY: And you realized it was your husband's penis—

LORENA *(whimpering)*: Yes.

ATTORNEY: And you were just *horrified*. Isn't that right?

LORENA: Yes.

ATTORNEY: And you just wanted to get rid of it. Isn't that right?

LORENA *(sobbing but mysteriously dry-eyed)*: Yes, yes, yes.

ATTORNEY: And you went and got rid of it. Just like *that*. Isn't that right?

LORENA: Yes, I throw it out! Yes!

ATTORNEY: Just like that.

LORENA: No, I don't remember how I threw it just like that. I know I just—I just want to get *rid* of it!

(Lorena gropes for a handkerchief, buries her face in it, and works herself up into wracking sobs.)

JACK FRITSCHER: I think what we have is a society that's been so frightened by the penis, made frightened by a *version* of the woman's movement, not by feminism itself, but by an hysterical woman's movement that has so frightened people about the penis, that you have Lorena Bobbitt being applauded for chopping off the aptly named John Wayne Bobbitt's penis in his bedroom. *(Cut to Lorena leaving the courthouse after her acquittal. She is clutching a huge white teddy bear. A turbaned African-American woman, balancing a box of long-stemmed red roses, leads her forcefully by the arm. There are deafening cheers and chants from the crowd: "Lorena! Lorena! Lorena!")* If people think of the penis as an instrument of rape, then what message are they giving to their sons? What they're going to do is create a whole generation of men who are so afraid of their penis, they're not going to be able to *use* it for the procreation of the race. Because the self-esteem that people like to talk about is being taken away. No, that's wrong.

SARAH KENT: Virility has taken some hard knocks recently. And men feel very frightened of their own sexuality, because their sexual urges seem to be politically incorrect, if you like. Women have begun to think of men as aggressors and predators rather than as companions. *(Cut to photo of a nude youth in heroic profile, gazing up at the sun.)* And I think we're now moving on to a new phase in which both men and women are beginning to say, well, you know, "We *want* sexually active men. We *want* sexual partners. But let's rethink what virility is. Let's rethink what it means for the woman."

(Cut to photo of a nude young man cuddling a nude male infant. Then photos of penises juxtaposed with flowers, leaves, a mask, and donut-like baby's toys. Back to the opening pan of the Greek Diadoumenos, *from head to penis.)*

PAGLIA: I have intensely disliked the tendency of many feminists to want men to be remade in a kind of shy, sensitive form—to become, in essence, new kinds of women, contemporary eunuchs with a soft penis, which is less inconvenient to women. I think that this is *not* in the interests of the human race. We want a *hard penis*. We want *masculine vigor*. And I'm afraid that in order to get men macho again, we may have to endure a certain amount of instability in sexual relations. That is, there may have to be a kind of *honorable truce* between enemy camps.

So what would be my advice to the sexes at the end of the century? *(arms akimbo in fierce, campy drag queen mode)* I would say to men: *get it up!* And to women I would say: *deal with it!*

(Camera pulls in tight on David's hot-pink penis. Back to Diadoumenos standing guard amid the white pillars at the museum. As Yma Sumac's Latin beat returns, the credits roll.)

NO LAW IN THE

ARENA

So no one
could
learn to talk
about it! ↘

NO LAW IN THE ARENA:

A PAGAN THEORY

OF SEXUALITY

Because the media won't let it go

1. INTRODUCTION: THE HORSES OF PASSION

At the end of the Christian millennium and the century of Freud, sex is still shrouded in mystery. A question mark hangs over every important sexual issue. Despite bitter public controversy and heated private debate, we have no answers. Indeed, we have barely begun to formulate the questions accurately.

Sex, I have argued in my prior books, is animality and artifice, a dynamic interplay of nature and culture. To study it, one must weigh the testimony of art and draw on all the scholarly resources of the social and natural sciences. In my opinion, the many schools of modern psychology, whose roots were in the late nineteenth century, reached their height in the eclectic 1960s, which fused widely diverse theories and practices, from Freudian verbal analysis to Reichian body manipulation. In that decade in America, Western science and Asian Hinduism momentarily came together, but the brilliant insights gained from this encounter were experienced by isolated individuals and dissipated into the general culture. The psychedelic Sixties left their imprint in images and music more than in books.

For the last twenty-five years, sex theory has been in a state of chaos. Single-issue activism turned into fanaticism, on both the left and right. Understanding of eroticism has actually regressed, as ideology has become paramount. The major conceptual breakthrough of the Sixties was its Romantic movement back toward nature, the awesome, star-studded panorama dwarfing social conventions and forms. The Sixties flower-power view of nature had too much Rousseauist benevolence, but it was more right than wrong. Organicism is the true deconstruction. With the failure or reluctance of Sixties visionaries to enter the professions or mainstream politics, the Seventies suffered from an intellectual vacuum, which was filled by a narrow, blinkered social constructionism—the simplistic behaviorist belief that nature does not exist, that everything we are comes from social conditioning.

Social constructionism was a crude distortion of the vast Sixties cosmic vision. It was promulgated for sectarian political purposes by three groups. First, the new Seventies breed of Stalinist feminist tried, in the abortion crusade, to wipe out all reference to nature or religion—a misconceived strategy that backfired and simply strengthened the pro-life opposition. Second, ambitious literature academics, ignorant of science, used esoteric, language-based, social constructionist French theory to advance their careers after the collapse of the academic job market in the Seventies recession. Third, gay activists, after the identification of AIDS in the early Eighties, used fascist tactics to stop public discussion of it in anything but political terms—as if disease occurred in people's prejudices rather than in the suffering body.

But what AIDS shows us is nature itself, risen up with terrible force to mock our delusions of knowledge and control. AIDS, above all, forces nature back onto the agenda of sex theory. Unfortunately for the shallow ideology of current feminism and gay liberation, whose ultimate aims I support, this means that procreation must be dealt with much more fully and honestly than has yet been done. The avoidance of that issue by the left has simply ceded it to and helped the rise of the right, which frames the argument in moral or rather Judeo-Christian terms.

For me, the ultimate power in the universe is nature, not God, whose existence I can understand only as depersonalized vital energy. But as I have repeatedly said, merely because nature is supreme does not mean we must yield to it. I take the Late Romantic view that everything great in human history has been achieved in defiance of nature. Law, art, and technology are defense mechanisms, Apollonian lines drawn against the Dionysian turbulence of nature. Melville's Captain Ahab, crippled and scarred, shaking his fist at the stormy heavens, symbolizes the rebellion of imagination against fate.

There is a sex problem in the West because of Judeo-Christianity's ambivalence toward nature, the fallen realm of matter brought into being by a perfect transcendent deity. From its first book on, the Bible links sex to reproduction and condemns as perverted all male sexual activities, such as sodomy or onanism, that are wasteful of semen. Recent claims by gay activists that there is no explicit prohibition of homosexuality in the Old Testament, or that it is simply one of many defunct ritual formulas, or that "God is love" (which applies primarily to the New Testament and only to *agape* and *caritas,* not *eros*), beg the question in a foolish and reckless manner. Procreation, not fear or bias, underlies the Christian opposition to homosexuality.

Fundamentalist reading of the Bible is far from passé. On the contrary, religious faith, in particular evangelical Protestantism and Roman Catholicism, is spreading around the world. The goals and reputation of progressive politics have been harmed by the juvenile arrogance of the liberal establishment toward institutional religion, which may oppress by rules but which is also a repository of spiritual experience, as well as folk wisdom about life, far more truthful than anything in French poststructuralism. What I propose is an argument based on another Western tradition, the Greco-Roman or pagan, which was equal to the Judeo-Christian in the formation of our culture.

Feminists and gay activists must stop their self-destructive habit of jeering at the church and trying to twist it to their own purposes. We must concentrate instead on winning recognition of the pagan line as a countertradition whose major contributions have been science and art and whose philosophy of sexuality is both broader and subtler than the Judeo-Christian. It is to Athens and Rome that we also trace our political systems. The framers of American democracy were not conventional Christians but Enlightenment Deists who invoked a crosscultural "Creator." It is no coincidence that the principal monumental architecture of our national capital is pagan.

Even in classical antiquity, homosexuality was controversial, and despite the exaggerated claims of today's partisans, there was no period or place where it flourished in complete freedom from moral opprobrium. However, the urban centers of the ancient Mediterranean were magnets for prostitution, as well as male homosexuality. Indeed, in my view, development of a sexual underworld may be intrinsic to urbanization as a worldwide phenomenon, a process that can be checked only by ruthless repression by church or state. There are remarkably similar patterns in erotic behavior, as identity overlaps identity in the intensified space and pace of cities.

Whether rampant open homosexuality is or is not a symptom of social decadence remains one of the issues that must be fairly discussed, without hysterical charges of "homophobia," in the new age of sex theory. I am ready to defend both homosexuality and decadence, since I look at history from the perspective of art, not morality. For me, civilization *is* art, and art is the highest record of humanity. One day, when we represent ourselves to inhabitants of distant galaxies, it will be by our art that we will want to be known. Therefore, anything that contributes to art must be nurtured and preserved. What seems irrefutable from my studies is that male homosexuality is intricately intertwined with art, for reasons we have yet to determine.

The Greeks invented not only the major genres of literature and the disciplines of philosophy but organized athletics, in their mathematics-based track and field form. Dramatic competition is built into the agonistic plot structure of Greek tragedy as well as the oratorical Western mode of legal argumentation. I want to transfer that rhythmic choreography of opposition into sex theory. Late-twentieth-century America has more in common with imperial Rome than with classical Athens, and so it is to the Hellenized Roman world that I would look for pagan models. We need new living myths.

The current discourse about sex is too genteel. Freud's severe, conflict-based system has lost popularity to a casual, sentimental style of user-friendly psychological counseling that I find typically Protestant, in the glad-handing Chamber of Commerce way. The operatic perversions of Krafft-Ebing and the unsettling daemonism of Ferenczi are completely gone. Yet sex war remains, and is likely to be our permanent condition. Competition and conflict are operating at every level of even our cooperative ventures, at work or at home. Our dream life itself, as Freud has shown, is both power play and passion play.

In war there can also be honor, the code of aristocratic chivalry, applied by medieval knights (*chevaliers*, "horsemen") to battlefield, court, and bedchamber. If women want freedom and equality, they must learn the rules of the game. The title of this essay comes from *Ben-Hur* (1959), the Hollywood epic that depicts the explosive tension in Judaea under Roman occupation. An Arab sheik persuades the vengeful prince Judah Ben-Hur (Charlton Heston) to race his exquisite white horses at Jerusalem by promising a head-to-head showdown with the evil Roman tribune, Messala (Stephen Boyd). The sheik says, "There is no law in the arena."

Sex today occurs in the dust and clamor of the imperial circus. Private grievances are dragged into the glare of day and become meat for the masses. Plato's lofty metaphor of the charioteer, the soul subduing by cool rationality the horses of bestial passion, was brutally revised by Rome, with its grandiose gladiatorial spectacles. The chaste elegance of the contemplative Delphic Charioteer was inconceivable in the hurly-burly hippodromes of the Hellenistic Mediterranean. Under the empire, as we see from the sober writings of Marcus Aurelius, the philosophic ideal of Stoic detachment became a way to survive cultural instability. Then as now, there is no going back. Conservative paradigms deserve our respect but also our recognition that they are nostalgic longings for a simpler and irretrievable past.

Sex in our age has become gladiatorial, with male and female, gay and straight whipping and goading each other for position. This is our lot. We must accept it and devise a simple new rule book and training regime that puts the combatants on equal footing. Neither women nor gays should plead for special protections or preferential treatment. The arena is the social realm, marked off from nature but ritually formalizing nature's aggressions. My libertarian position is that, in the absence of physical violence, sexual conduct cannot and must not be legislated from above, that all intrusion by authority figures into sex is totalitarian.

The ultimate law of the sexual arena is personal responsibility and self-defense. We must be prepared to go it alone, without the infantilizing assurances of external supports like trauma counselors, grievance committees, and law courts. I say to women: get down in the dirt, in the realm of the senses. Fight for your territory, hour by hour. Take your blows like men. I exalt the pagan personae of athlete and warrior, who belong to shame rather than guilt culture and whose ethic is candor, discipline, vigilance, and valor.

2. SEX CRIME: RAPE

The area where contemporary feminism has suffered the most self-inflicted damage is rape. What began as a useful sensitization of police officers, prosecutors, and judges to the claims of authentic rape victims turned into a hallucinatory overextension of the definition of rape to cover every unpleasant or embarrassing sexual encounter. Rape became the crime of crimes, overshadowing all the wars, massacres, and disasters of world history. The feminist obsession with rape as a symbol of male-female relations is irrational and delusional. From the perspective of the future, this period in America will look like a reign of mass psychosis, like that of the Salem witch trials. Quite perhaps

Rape cannot be understood in isolation from general criminology, which most feminists have not bothered to study. Psychopathology was an early interest of mine, partly because of my own aggressive and deviant impulses as a tomboy in the Fifties. Two comprehensive, analytic, and nonjudgmental books I acquired as a teenager gave me the intellectual framework for my later approaches to abnormal behavior: Richard von Krafft-Ebing's *Psychopathia Sexualis* (1886) and Émile Durkheim's *Suicide* (1897). In college and graduate school, I gathered the material on rape, homosexuality, and other controversial themes that appears in *Sexual Personae*. By the time Susan Brownmiller's *Against Our Will* appeared in 1975, I knew enough to find its interpretative framework seriously inadequate. That book is one of many well-meaning feminist examples of the limitation of white middle-class assumptions in understanding extreme emotional states or acts.

The philistinism of feminist discourse on rape in the Eighties and Nineties has been astonishing. My generation was well-educated

; Limitations of white middle-class assumptions

in the Sixties in major literary texts that have since been marginalized by blundering women's studies: our sense of criminality and the mystery of motivation came principally from Dostoyevsky's *Crime and Punishment*, Camus's *The Stranger*, and Genet's *The Maids*. There was also Poe's "The Tell-Tale Heart" and "The Cask of Amontillado," as well as eerie films like Fritz Lang's *M*, Alfred Hitchcock's *Psycho*, and Richard Fleischer's *Compulsion* (on the Leopold and Loeb case). The shrill feminist melodrama of male oppressor/ female victim came straight out of nickelodeon strips of mustache-twirling villains and squealing maidens tied to train tracks. Those who revere and live with great art recognize Clytemnestra, Medea, Lady Macbeth, and Hedda Gabler—conspirators and death-dealers of implacable will—as equally the forebears of modern woman.

Rape should more economically be defined as either stranger rape or the forcible intrusion of sex into a nonsexual context, such as a professional situation. However, even the latter is excusable if a sexual overture is welcomed, as can be the case in both gay and straight life. There *is* such a thing as seduction, and it needs encouragement rather than discouragement in our puritanical Anglo-American world. The fantastic fetishism of rape by mainstream and anti-porn feminists has in the end trivialized rape, impugned women's credibility, and reduced the sympathy we should feel for legitimate victims of violent sexual assault.

What I call Betty Crocker feminism—a naively optimistic Pollyannaish or Panglossian view of reality—is behind much of this. Even the most morbid of the rape ranters have a childlike faith in the perfectibility of the universe, which they see as blighted solely by nasty men. They simplistically project outward onto a mythical "patriarchy" their own inner conflicts and moral ambiguities. In *Sexual Personae*, I critiqued the sunny Rousseauism running through the last two hundred years of liberal thinking and offered the dark tradition of Sade, Darwin, Nietzsche, and Freud as more truthful about human perversity. It is more accurate to see primitive egotism and animality ever-simmering behind social controls—cruel energies contained and redirected for the greater good—than to predicate purity and innocence ravaged by corrupt society. Nor does the Foucault view of numb, shapeless sensoriums tyrannically impinged on by faceless systems of language-based power make any more sense, in view of daily news reports of concretely applied and concretely suffered random beatings, mutilations, murders, arson, massacres, and ethnic exterminations around the world.

Rape will not be understood until we revive the old concept of the barbaric, the uncivilized. The grotesque cliché "patriarchy" must go, or rather be returned to its proper original application to periods like Republican Rome or Victorian England. What feminists call patriarchy is simply *civilization,* an abstract system designed by men but augmented and now co-owned by women. Like a great temple, civilization is a gender-neutral structure that all should respect. Feminists who prate of patriarchy are self-exiled in grass huts.

Ideas of civilization and barbarism have become unfashionable because of their political misuse in the nineteenth century. The West has neither a monopoly on civilization nor the right or obligation to impose its culture on others. Nor, as *Sexual Personae* argues, are any of us as individuals ever completely civilized. However, it is equally wrong to dismiss all progressive theories of history, which is not just scattered bits of data upon which we impose wishful narratives. Societies do in fact evolve in economic and political complexity.

Even though we no longer wish to call one society "higher" or "more advanced" than another, it is unwise to equate tribal experience, with its regimentation by tradition and its suppression of the individual by the group, with life under industrial capitalism, which has produced liberalism and feminism. Law and order, which protect women, children, and the ill and elderly, are a function of hierarchy, another of the big bad words of feminism. Law and order were achieved only a century ago in the American West, which still lives in our national mythology. Disintegration into banditry is always near at hand, as was shown in 1989 in the notorious case of the Central Park woman jogger—a savage attack significantly called "wilding" by its schoolboy perpetrators. Sex crime means back to nature.

When feminism rejected Freud twenty-five years ago, it edited out of its mental life the barbarities of the homicidal Oedipal psychodrama, which the annals of crime show is more than a metaphor. The irony is that Freud's master paradigm of "family romance," which structures our adult relationships in love and at work, has a special appropriateness to the current feminist debate. Too much of the date-rape and sexual harassment crisis claimed by white middle-class women is caused partly by their own mixed signals, which I have observed with increasing distress as a teacher for over two decades.

The predominant fact of modern sexual history is not patriarchy but the collapse of the old extended family into the nuclear family, an isolated unit that, in its present form, is claustrophobic and psychologically unstable. The nuclear family can work only in a pioneer situation, where the punishing physicality of farmwork keeps everyone occupied and spent from dawn to dusk. The middle-class nuclear family, where the parents are white-collar professionals who do brainwork, is seething with frustrations and tensions. Words are charged, and real authority lies elsewhere, in bosses on the job. Marooned in the suburbs or in barricaded urban apartments, upwardly mobile families are frantically overscheduled and geographically transient, with few ties to neighbors and little sustained contact with relatives.

Two parents alone cannot transmit all the wisdom of life to a child. Clan elders—grandparents, great-grandparents, aunts, uncles, cousins—performed this function once. Today, poor inner-city or rural children are more likely to benefit from the old extended family or from the surrogate family of long-trusted neighbors, since working-class people are less likely to make repeated moves for job promotions. The urban child sees the harshness of the street; the rural child witnesses the frightening operations of nature. Both have contact with an eternal reality denied the suburban middle-class child, who is cushioned from risk and fear and who is expected to conform to a code of genteel good manners and repressed body language that has changed startlingly little since the Victorian era.

The sex education of white middle-class girls is clearly deficient, since it produces young women unable to foresee trouble or to survive sexual misadventure or even raunchy language without crying to authority figures for help. A sense of privilege and entitlement, as well as ignorance of the dangers of life, has been institutionalized by American academe, with its summer-resort, give-the-paying-customers-what-they-want mentality. Europe has thus far been relatively impervious to the date-rape hysteria, since its tortured political history makes sugary social fantasies of the American kind less possible. Fun-and-fabulous teenage dating is not high on the list of priorities for nations which, in the lifetime of half their population, had firsthand knowledge of war, devastation, and economic collapse. The media-fueled disproportion and distortion of the date-rape debate are partially attributable to American arrogance and parochialism.

White middle-class girls at the elite colleges and universities seem to want the world handed to them on a platter. They have been sheltered, coddled, and flattered. Having taught at a wide variety of institutions over my ill-starred career, I have observed that working-class or lower-middle-class girls, who are from financially struggling families and who must take a patchwork of menial off-campus jobs to stay in school, are usually the least hospitable to feminist rhetoric. They see life as it is and have fewer illusions about sex. It is affluent, upper-middle-class students who most spout the party line—as if the grisly hyperemotionalism of feminist jargon satisfies their hunger for meaningful experience outside their eventless upbringing. In the absence of war, invent one.

The real turmoil is going on inside the nuclear family, which, with its caged quarters and cheerful ethic of "togetherness," must generate invisible barriers to the threat of incest. Here is the real source of the epidemic eating disorders, blamed by incompetent feminist analysts on the media. Anorexia, for example, remains primarily a white middle-class phenomenon. The daughter stops her disturbing sexual maturation by stripping off her female contours, the hormone-triggered fleshiness of breasts, hips, and buttocks. She wants to remain a child, when her innocent erotic stratagems had no consequence. Again and again, among students as well as the date-rape heroines canonized on television talk shows, I have seen the flagrant hair-tossing and eye-batting mannerisms of Daddy's little girl, who since childhood has used flirtation and seductiveness to win attention within the family.

Provocation and denial are built into the circuitry of the white middle-class girl, with her depressing flatness of sexual imagination, her strange combination of "low self-esteem" with hectoring moral superiority in groups, inflamed by feminist rhetoric. The eating disorders are symptomatic not of external forces or media conspiracies but of a major breakdown in the female sex role. In the Anglo-

American world, the successful woman is now defined in exclusively professional terms. The role of mother, still central in Latin and Asian cultures, has been devalued. Feminism should be about options. I myself have no talent for motherhood and have sought only a career. But I recognize that no role may be more important than bearing and raising children and that most men, whatever their contributions to the child's later development, are not and will never be proficient at infant care. *This may be mostly true. Why men leave, think it's OK.*

Over the past forty years, there has been an increasingly long postponement of marriage and childbirth by middle-class women. For example, my parents married at twenty-one in 1946, a year before I was born. Today, it would be unheard-of for a girl at an elite school to marry at that age. Maternity is considered an accident, a misfortune, the vulgar prerogative of misguided working-class teenagers. If a Yale sophomore were to drop out of school to marry, she would be treated as a traitor to her class, "throwing away" her expensive education, "wasting" her life. In the Sixties, by contrast, it was considered a radical gesture for a girl to disappoint her parents' expectations by leaving college and running off with her ragged hippie boyfriend to bake bread and have babies in a commune.

Modern society is now structured so as to put a crippling impediment between women's physical development and their career ambitions. Feminist ideology began by claiming to give women freedom, enlightenment, and self-determination, but it has ended by alienating professional women from their own bodies. Every signal from the body—like the sudden quiet inwardness and psychological reorientation of girls at puberty, when they mysteriously recede in classroom assertiveness—is automatically interpreted in terms of social oppression. Teachers are supposedly "discouraging" the girls; adjusting your behavior to attract a mate is dismissed as a voluntary or legitimate choice. Girls are taught the mechanics of reproduction and sexual intercourse as clinically as if they were learning to operate a car or computer. The repressed, sanitized style of the WASP managerial class now governs public discussion of sex. Anything dark or ambiguous is blamed on "ignorance," "superstition," or "lack of education." *Avoid the dark!*

It was after my tumultuous lecture at Brown University in March 1992 that I saw this process of cultural repression most clearly. Taking questions at the reception, I sat with an African-American security guard as several hundred students seethed around me. Those who doubt the existence of political correctness have never seen the ruthless Red Guards in action, as I have done on campus after campus. For twenty years, meaningful debate of controversial issues of sex or race was silenced by overt or covert intimidation.

As I watched a half-dozen pampered, white middle-class girls, their smooth, plump cheeks contorted with rage, shriek at me about rape, I had two thoughts. First, America is failing its young women; these are infantile personalities, emotionally and intellectually undeveloped. Second, it's not rape they're screaming about. Rape is simply a symbol of the horrors and mysteries of the body, which their education never deals with or even acknowledges. It was a Blakean epiphany: I suddenly saw the fear and despair of the lost, stripped of old beliefs but with nothing solid to replace them. Feminism had constructed a spectral sexual hell that these girls inhabited; it was their entire cultural world, a godless new religion of fury and fanaticism. Two months later, as I sat in London, discoursing at length with poised, literate, witty Cambridge University women of the same age as those at Brown, I became even more indignant at the travesty of Ivy League education.

Women are not in control of their bodies; nature is. Ancient mythology, with its sinister archetypes of vampire and Gorgon, is more accurate than feminism about the power and terror of female sexuality. Science is far from untangling women's intricate hormonal system, which is dauntingly intertwined with the emotions. Women live with unpredictability. Reproduction remains a monumental challenge to our understanding. The Eleusinian Mysteries, with their secret, torch-lit night rituals, represented woman's grandeur on the scale that she deserves. We must return to pagan truths.

The elite schools, defining women students only as "future leaders," masters of the social realm, limit and stunt them. The mission of feminism is to seek the full political and legal equality of women with men. There should be no impediments to women's social advance. But it is the first lesson of Buddhism, Hinduism, and Judeo-Christianity that we are much greater than our social selves. I envision two spheres: one is social, the other sexual and emotional. Perhaps one-third of each sphere overlaps the other; this is the area where feminism has correctly said, "The personal is political." But there is vastly more to the human story. Man has traditionally ruled the social sphere; feminism tells him to move over and share his power. But woman rules the sexual and emotional sphere, and there she has no rival. Victim ideology, a caricature of social history, blocks women from recognition of their dominance in the deepest, most important realm.

Ambitious young women today are taught to ignore or suppress every natural instinct, if it conflicts with the feminist agenda imposed on them. All literary and artistic works, no matter how great, that document the ambivalence of female sexuality they are trained to dismiss as "misogynous." In other words, their minds are being programmed to secede from their bodies—exactly the opposite of what the Sixties sexual and cultural revolution was all about. There is a huge gap between feminist rhetoric and women's actual sex lives, where feminism is of little help except with a certain stratum of deferential, malleable, white middle-class men. In contrast, Hollywood actresses, used to expressing emotional truths, are always reappearing after pregnancy to proclaim, "I'm not important. My child is important." The most recent was Kelly McGillis, who said, "Motherhood has changed me. I'm not as ambitious as I used to be." It is nature, not patriarchal society, that puts motherhood and career on a collision course.

My first inkling of the psychological maelstrom suffered by this generation of female students came in 1980, when I returned to New Haven after eight years away (at my first job at Bennington, which ended with a bang). Yale College had admitted its first women in 1969, while I was a graduate student. Returning to the Cross Campus Library, brand-new when I left, I was horrified to find the stalls of the women's toilets covered with bizarre, ranting graffiti. There was little humor or bawdiness; the principal imagery was of nausea, disgust, and self-loathing. "Something is going wrong with feminism," I said to friends at the time. The Yale graffiti seemed demented, psychotic, like those one would expect to find at New York's Port Authority Bus Terminal. When Brown girls created a national furor in 1990 by posting names of alleged rapists in the toilets, the media completely missed the real story: why were squalid toilets now the forum for self-expression by supposed future leaders? These

sewer spaces, converted to pagan vomitoria, offer women students
their sole campus rendezvous with their own physiology.

The strident rape discourse is a hysterical eruption from the
deepest levels of American bourgeois life. Early in this phase of
feminism, it was still possible to say, "Taste your menstrual
blood"—that is, reclaim your physicality. Today, with the callow
new brand of yuppie feminist with her simpering, prom-queen manner, we have regressed to the Fifties era of cashmere sweaters and
pearls. The blood and guts of women's reproductive cycle are light-
years beyond the reach of these dollhouse moppets. White middle-
class feminists of every age have shown themselves spectacularly
unable to confront the grossness of their own physiological processes.
The passages in *Sexual Personae* vividly depicting that humid, labyrinthine reality have made them flee like Victorian spinsters shriek-
ing at a mouse.

Until the bloody barbarousness of procreation is fully absorbed,
without the abstract jargon and genteel euphemisms that now dominate gender studies, rape will not be understood. By defining rape
in exclusively social terms—as an attack by the powerful against
the powerless—feminism has missed the point. It is woman, as
mistress of birth, who has the real power. As my colleague Jack
DeWitt likes to say, "Any woman is more powerful than any man."

Rape is an act of desperation, a confession of envy and exclusion.
All men—even, I have written, Jesus himself—began as flecks of
tissue inside a woman's womb. Every boy must stagger out of the
shadow of a mother goddess, whom he never fully escapes. Because
of my history of wavering gender and sexual orientation, I feel I
have a special insight into these matters: I see with the eyes of the
rapist. Hence I realize how dangerously misleading the feminist rape
discourse is. Rape is a breaking and entering; but so is the bloody
act of defloration. Sex is inherently problematic.

Women have it. Men want it. What is *it?* The secret of life,
symbolized in heroic sagas by the golden fleece sought by Jason, or
by the Gorgon's head brandished as a sexual trophy by Cellini's
Perseus. The rapist is sickened by the conflict between his humiliating neediness and his masculine rage for autonomy. He feels suf-
focated by woman and yet entranced and allured by her. He is
betrayed into dependency by his own impulses, the leaping urges of

the body. Stalking women like prey returns him to prehistoric freedom, when the wiliest, swiftest, and strongest survived. Rape-murder is a primitive theft of energy, a cannibalistic drinking of life force.

When toddlers or schoolgirls are kidnapped, brutally assaulted, and killed, the world is rightly horrified and sickened. But why are we surprised? Heinous acts of profanation and degradation fill the annals of history and great literature—Neoptolemus' slaughter of Priam at the altar, Herod's massacre of the innocents, the immurement and bestial death of Dante's Ugolino. Until recently, most societies had a clear idea of what constitutes "uncivilized" or "ungodly" behavior and punished it accordingly. Today, in contrast, there is a tendency to redefine the victimizer as himself a victim— of a broken home or abusive parents—and then, ironically, to broaden criminality to areas of consensual activities where women are equally responsible for their behavior. When feminist discourse is unable to discriminate the drunken fraternity brother from the homicidal maniac, women are in trouble.

Rape-murder comes from the brutish region of pure animal appetite. Feminist confidence that the whole human race can be "reeducated" to totally eliminate the possibility of rape is pure folly. Even if, very optimistically, 80 percent of all men could be reprogrammed, 20 percent would remain, toward whom women would still have to remain vigilant. Even if 99 percent were neutralized— absurdly unlikely—that would leave 1 percent, against whom women's level of self-defense would need to be just as high as against 90 percent. Wave after wave of boys hit puberty every year. Do feminists, with their multicultural pretensions, really envision a massive export of white bourgeois good manners all around the world? Speak of imperialism! When Balthasar, one of the Magi, advises Ben-Hur to leave vengeance to God, the sheik murmurs, "Balthasar is a good man. But until all men are like him, we must keep our swords bright."

The dishonesty and speciousness of the feminist rape analysis are demonstrated by its failure to explore, or even mention, man-on-man sex crimes. If rape were really just a process of political intimidation of women by men, why do men rape and kill other males? The deceptively demure persona of the soft-spoken, homosexual serial-murderer Jeffrey Dahmer, like that of handsome, charming Ted Bundy, should warn everyone that we still live in a sexual jungle. Nothing in feminist ideology addresses the grim truth that beauty itself may be an incitement to destroy, that there is a frenzy of primitive pleasure in torturing captives or smashing things. I learned from art about the willful violation of innocence. When babies, nuns, or grandmothers are raped, it can be understood only in terms of what pagan antiquity called "pollution," a sullying of the sacred. Feminist overstress on power differentials gets us nowhere; it cannot explain spasmodic bursts of slashing criminal lust.

The problem with America's current preoccupation with child abuse is that cultural taboos automatically eroticize what is forbidden. Marking off zones of purity increases their desirability and ensures their profanation. Children are not that innocent, and we must put an end to Anglo-American hypocrisy on this question. Children, sanctified by Victorian Romanticism, are quite capable of perverse and horrific fantasy, without adult suggestion. A century after Freud proposed his theory of infantile sexuality, most parents (outside of Malibu or Tribeca) still cannot intellectually accept it— partly because doing so would activate the incest taboo. The enormous publicity about child-abuse has certainly increased safety awareness, but I doubt it has lowered the crime rate. Snatching a perfect child from under the noses of society's guardians has become the ultimate subversive act of the outlaw. Such criminality, I maintained in *Sexual Personae,* is the product not of a bad environment but of the opposite, a failure of social conditioning. Serial rapemurderers, cool, logical, and precise, are not "insane" and deserve to be executed, not as deterrence but as justice for the survivors.

Far from being inhuman or "monstrous," sex crime is a ritual enactment of natural aggressions latent in all sexuality, which is primarily mating behavior and has only recently been redefined in recreational terms. The best survey I have yet seen of the clashing psychodynamics of eroticism is Edmund Spenser's *The Faerie Queene* (1590), which remains amazingly applicable today, four hundred years after it was written. Spenser sees the fine gradations of sexual behavior, from chivalrous courtship to duplicitous seduction and loutish brigandage. Studying the poem in depth in the Seventies, I identified what I called its "rape cycle." Like a specter stalking a college mixer, Spenser acutely describes the tantalizing sexual vulnerability of passive femininity and the militant warriorship of mature, self-reliant womanhood. Naiveté evokes its own destruction. This is not "blaming the victim"; it is saying victimhood cannot become a vocation.

Until feminism permits the return of the ancient identification of woman and nature in its full disturbing power, rape will remain an enigma. Rape is an invasion of territory, a despoilment of virgin ground. The radically different sexual geography of men's and women's bodies has led to feminist inability to understand male psychology. "She made me do it": this strange assertion by rapists expresses man's sense of subservience to woman's sexual allure. The rapist feels enslaved, insignificant: women seem enclosed, impervious. From the outside, female sexuality glows like the full moon. The stormy complexity of the rapist's inner life has been obscured by the therapeutic jargon he is soon speaking in prison, once he has been brainwashed by the social-welfare workers. Until women grasp the blood-sport aspect of rape, they will be unable to protect themselves.

Films of the mating behavior of most other species—a staple of public television in America—demonstrate that the female *chooses*. Males pursue, show off, brawl, scuffle, and make general fools of themselves for love. A major failing of most feminist ideology is its dumb, ungenerous stereotyping of men as tyrants and abusers, when in fact—as I know full well, from my own mortifying lesbian experience—men are tormented by women's flirtatiousness and hemming and hawing, their manipulations and changeableness, their humiliating rejections. Cock teasing is a universal reality. It is part of women's merciless testing and cold-eyed comparison shopping for potential mates. Men will do anything to win the favor of women. Women literally *size up* men—"What can you show me?"—in bed and out. If middle-class feminists think they conduct their love lives perfectly rationally, without any instinctual influences from biology, they are imbeciles.

Following the sexual revolution of the Sixties, dating has become a form of Russian roulette. Some girls have traditional religious values and mean to remain virgin until marriage. Others are leery of AIDS, unsure of what they want, but can be convinced. For others, anything goes: they'll jump into bed on the first date. What's a guy to do? Surely, for the good of the human species, we want to keep men virile and vigorous. They should feel free to seek sex and to persuade reluctant women. As a libertarian, I believe that we have absolute right to our own body and that no one may lay a hand on us without our consent. But consent may be nonverbal, expressed by language or behavior—such as going to a stranger's apartment on the first date, which I think should correctly be interpreted as consent to sex. "Verbal coercion" is a ridiculous concept: I agree with Ovid that every trick of rhetoric should be used in the slippery art of love.

Sexual personae are the key to this new age of uncertainty. I follow the gay male model in defining every date as a potential sexual encounter. Given that the rules are in flux, the issue of sexual availability must be negotiated, implicitly or explicitly, from the first moment on. Women must take responsibility for their share in this exchange, which means they must scrupulously critique their own mannerisms and clothing choices and not allow themselves to drift willy-nilly into compromising situations. As a teacher, I have seen time and again a certain kind of American middle-class girl who projects winsome malleability, a soft, unfocused, help-me-please persona that, in adult life, is a recipe for disaster. These are the ones who end up with the string of abusive boyfriends or in sticky situations with overfamiliar male authority figures who call them "honey."

Deconstruction of the bourgeois code of "niceness" is a priority here. My generation tried it but seems mostly to have failed. Second, white girls need a crash course in common sense. You get back what you put out. Or as I say about girls wearing Madonna's harlot outfits, if you advertise, you'd better be ready to sell! Suburban girls don't realize that they were raised in an artificially pacified zone and that the world at large, including the college campus, is a far riskier place. I call my feminism "streetwise" or "street-smart" feminism. Women from working-class families usually agree with my view of the foolhardiness of feminist rhetoric, which encourages girls to throbbingly proclaim, "We can dress just as we want and go anywhere we want at any time!" This is true only to the point that women are willing to remain in a state of wary alertness and to fight their own fights. Men are in danger too. In America, one sees over-protected white girls bopping obliviously down the city street, lost in their headphones, or jogging conspicuously and bouncingly bra-less, a sight guaranteed to invite unwanted attention.

It is tremendously difficult to convince feminist professional women of the existence of unconscious or subliminal erotic com-munication. As my friend Bruce Benderson says, their middle-class world has "no subtext." Women of the Sixties had far bolder and more salacious imaginations. The career system into which women have definitively won entry over the past twenty-five years seems to have rigidified their thinking. Stalinist literalism has become the norm. Shocked disbelief greets suggestions that many women may take pleasure in rape fantasies, established long ago by Nancy Friday in her pioneering 1973 study, *My Secret Garden*, and dramatized today in the staggering mass-market popularity of Harlequin Romances, where heroines are overwhelmed by passionate, impetuous men. My warning description of the buffoonish "fun element" and "mad in-fectious delirium" of gang rape particularly infuriated many middle-class feminists, even though the point is easily proved by movies like *Two Women, The Virgin Spring, A Clockwork Orange, Deliverance, Death Wish,* or *North Dallas Forty.* That men can satisfy their desires on an inert or unconscious object seems intolerable to such women, though it is a fact of life, palatable or not. Male sexual functioning does not depend on female response. And the illicit is always highly charged.

All crimes of sex or mutilation contain pagan paradigms, hidden ritual symbolism we must learn to read. Pious rubrics like "Violence Against Women"—the stentorian title of a 1993 Congressional bill—are too simplistic. Surges of instinctual power are going on beneath the surface of every human exchange. Having sex with a woman is an earned action and honorific for young men, who lack an internal rite of passage like menstruation and who must therefore create an adult sexual identity for themselves in ways that women do not. Sex crime is revenge against women as an abstract class for wounds already suffered by men as a class—the wound of birth and its consequent galling dependencies. Until we widen the lens to take in nature, women will not know what is happening or how to control it. Victimization is a dead end. Better to meditate instead on the great pagan archetypes of the mother, with her terrible duality of creation and destruction. Women must accept their own ambivalence in order to wield their birthright of dominion over men.

3. SEX WAR:
ABORTION, BATTERING, SEXUAL HARASSMENT

The principal controversies of recent feminism have usually in some way involved a failure to deal with the issue of aggression. In the hundred-year-old nature versus nurture debate, contemporary feminists have taken the Rousseauist position that we are born good and society makes us bad. The naturists among them are ultimately twin to the nurturists, or social constructionists, since the former see nature as uniformly benign, despite constant catastrophic evidence to the contrary. Sentimental overidealization of women runs throughout anti-male feminist thought, from the prim, solemn Carol Gilligan to the acridly cynical Marilyn French, with their flagrant misreadings of social history.

The campaign for abortion rights, which has polarized America, was systematically mismanaged by feminist leaders, partly because of their refusal to acknowledge the violence inherent in any termination of life. The same people who opposed capital punishment ironically fought for abortion on demand, showing a peculiar discrimination about whom to execute. Squeamishly sensitive about their humanitarian self-image, feminists have used convoluted casuistry to define the aborted fetus in purely material terms as inert tissue, efficiently flushed.

My views are more consistent: I support the death penalty for outrageous crimes, such as political assassination or serial rape-murder, and I am fervently pro-abortion—the term "pro-choice" is a cowardly euphemism. Women's modern liberation is inextricably linked to their ability to control reproduction, which has enslaved them from the origin of the species. It is nature, again, that is our real oppressor. Men's contribution to conception and gestation is minimal, compared to the burden borne by pregnant and nursing women. Patriarchy, routinely blamed for everything, produced the birth control pill, which did more to free contemporary women than feminism itself.

The vicious stereotyping of abortion opponents as "anti-woman" or "far right fanatics" has been one of the most deplorable habits of the feminist establishment. For years, mass mailings of the National Organization for Women were filled with hysterical rhetoric that repelled and alienated even abortion supporters like me. With their propagandistic frame of mind, feminist leaders never admitted that their opponents could be equally motivated by ethics. In fact, the ethical weight may be on the other side in this debate. We career women are arguing from expedience: it is personally and professionally inconvenient or onerous to bear an unwanted child. The pro-life movement, in contrast, is arguing that every conception is sacred and that society has a responsibility to protect the defenseless.

Among the most memorable moments in my career as a public speaker occurred in September 1992, when I pressed this issue during my lectures at the University of Washington in Seattle and at the Herbst Theater in San Francisco. It was risky: feminist orthodoxy had jelled around abortion rights, and challenge was not brooked. But as I, from the position of abortion advocacy, dramatized the injustice of feminist contempt for the pro-life position, an eerie silence fell over the crowd. It was as if we all felt the uneasy conscience of feminism.

The inflexible sectarianism of feminist leaders was on embarrassing public view during the 1990 Senate Judiciary Committee hearings for the nomination of David Souter to the Supreme Court. Present and past presidents of NOW (including Eleanor Smeal) and their partisans sat with querulous expressions of childish petulance and whined and sneered at the all-male panel before them. Abortion, just one of many pressing issues facing the nation, had become a low gate through which any nominee to the court had to stoop. The women's performance was loathsome. It is by such self-defeating exercises in solipsism that feminism has repeatedly injured itself.

That another, more intelligent and sophisticated approach is possible was proved by the next witness, Faye Wattleton, president of Planned Parenthood, who was accompanied by the ever-reasonable Kate Michaelman, head of the National Abortion Rights League. Dignified and articulate, Wattleton presented the pro-abortion case with crisp, cool professionalism. Unlike the others, she showed respect for the occasion and the historical setting. Beautiful, elegant, and grand, she demonstrated that it is African-American women, not white middle-class feminists, who have already created the ideal female persona of the twenty-first century.

The problem with the abortion rights crusade is that it is locked in a secular mind-set of me-first entitlement. Religious objections to abortion are based on devout study of the Bible, understood by believers as the word of God. "Be fruitful, and multiply" (Gen. 1:28): it is not enough to respond that this admonition to a small, struggling ancient people may no longer be applicable to an overpopulated world of dwindling resources. Theologians are not grocery managers taking inventory. For the faithful, God's plan is beyond human understanding, and one cannot pick and choose among his commands.

To rescue feminism, we must give religion its due but require it to stay in its place. Again, Judeo-Christianity is only half our tradition. Paganism has other paradigms to offer. The militant virgin goddesses, Athena and Artemis, with their cold autonomy, are heroines of mine. Plato speaks of two Aphrodites, a common one of physical childbirth and the other, the Uranian, patron of spiritual and intellectual influence, specially associated with homoerotic relations. Evasion of nature's biological imperative is distinctly human. I take the extreme view of that Enlightenment neopagan, the Marquis de Sade, who lauds abortion and sodomy for their bold frustration of mother nature's relentless fertility. My code of modern Amazonism says that nature's fascist scheme of menstruation and procreation *should* be defied, as a gross infringement of woman's free will.

Unlike the feminist establishment, I recognize that abortion is killing. But slaughter and harvest—symbolized by the sickle crescent of the moon goddess (which appears as a castrating blade in Picasso's *Les Demoiselles d'Avignon*)—are the record of human sustenance and survival for ten thousand years. A pagan vision, like that of Tennessee Williams's *Suddenly, Last Summer,* will see the terrifying mass destruction in nature's procreative plan. Nature scatters a billion seeds to the wind. We must philosophically strengthen feminist theory so that it can admit that abortion is an aggressive act, that it is a form of extermination. Modern woman has become an agent of Darwinian triage. It is or should be ethically troubling: abortion pits the stronger against the weaker, and only one survives. The feminist coat-hanger symbol, prophesying the return of back-alley butchery if abortion is regulated or banned, is dishonest. A small number of women may die in botched procedures, but in successful abortions, the fetus death rate is 100 percent.

As a libertarian, I support unrestricted access to abortion because I have reasoned that my absolute right to my body takes precedence over the brute claims of mother nature, who wants to reduce women to their animal function as breeders. Women who want to achieve are at war with nature, as is shown by the hormonally disordering effects of career stress or extreme athletic training. In the Seventies, women runners, developing amenorrhea and calcium-related shin splints, were the first to realize that nature is hovering over us, ready to shut down our systems if our fetus-feeding fat reserve drops below a certain percentage of body weight. In other words, in nature's eyes we are nothing but milk sacs and fat deposits. Women inspired by the Uranian Aphrodite to produce spiritual progeny should view abortion as a sword of self-defense put into their hands by Ares, the war god. Government, guaranteeing freedom of religion, has no right to interfere in our quarrel with our Creator, in this case pagan nature. Under the carnal constitution that precedes social citizenship, women have the right to bear arms. The battlefield is internal, and it belongs to us.

Aggression must be returned to the center of feminist thinking. The rape discourse derailed itself early on by its nonsensical formulation, "Rape is a crime of violence but not of sex," a mantra that, along with "No always means no," blanketed the American media until I arrived on the scene. Feminists had an astoundingly naive view of the mutual exclusiveness of sex and aggression, which, Freud demonstrates, are fused in the amoral unconscious, as revealed to us through dreams. That rape is simply what used to be called "unbridled lust," like gluttony a sin of insufficient self-restraint, seems to be beyond feminist ken. Rape is piggish, cave-man, hand-to-mouth gorging, the rudimentary, subsistence-level stage of moral development of tots at "the terrible twos," when they must be taught not to bash other children over the head to steal their sweets. Evolution *does* exist in history, and it is recapitulated in effective child-rearing.

The absence of a feminist theory of aggression is blatant in the so-called "battered woman syndrome," yet another major article of current dogma. We are instructed by the earnest social-welfare prelates, their faces permanently creased in ostentatious Christlike compassion, that women who have been beaten for years by lovers or husbands become lethargic prisoners of war, brainwashed hostages without free will who must be excused from any atrocious act they commit, in lieu of something so simple as actually packing up and leaving. Even cutting off a man's penis while he is sleeping is legitimized as "temporary insanity," as shown by the questionable acquittal in 1994 of Lorena Bobbitt, a Latin firecracker who knew exactly what she was doing not only when she wielded the knife but when she turned on the waterworks for the jury. The Bobbitt case, which brought to life the ancient mythic archetype of woman as castrator, demonstrated that women are as aggressive as men and that sex is a dark, dangerous force of nature. But of course the feminist establishment, stuck in its battered-woman blinders, learned nothing as usual from this lurid refutation of its normal views. Classic art works like Bizet's *Carmen* tell us more about the irrationality of love, jealousy, and revenge than do the pat formulas of the counseling industry.

Feminism as a world movement must continue to address the grave problem in economically underdeveloped countries of women being treated as chattel or even killed by husbands or families for being a financial burden. Feminists are to be commended when they provide legal advice and material resources for escape from such intractable conditions. However, that battered women in the industrialized democracies do not leave home because they are financially dependent on their mates is fast ceasing to be a credible excuse. A 1991 study of admissions of battered middle-class women to a San Francisco hospital emergency room found that 70 percent were not in fact financially dependent on their assailants—a rare example of a survey eluding control by the statistics-churning feminist propaganda machines, those "independent" think tanks with suspiciously close ties to government commissions.

Marxism rears its ugly head

For twenty years, armies of battered women and their counselor-spokesmen have trooped through television talk shows. From the start, I was troubled by a frequent discrepancy between the victims' demeanor and testimony and the simplistic, male-blaming rhetoric imposed on their experience by their smug professional escorts. The rigid political paradigm of oppressor/victim was the only one permitted. There was rarely much psychological inquiry into the sticky complexities of sexual attraction and conflict that implicate *both* partners in any long-running private drama. *Simplistic answers.*

As a feminist, I detest the rhetorical diminution of woman into passive punching bag, which is the basic premise of the "battered woman syndrome." Men strike women for quite another reason: because physical superiority is their only weapon against a being far more powerful than they. The blow does not subordinate; it equalizes. Aggression expresses itself in more than one way in the cycle of domestic violence (which includes underreported husband-battering). The polemical tactic of exhibiting garish mugshot photos of women's bruised faces evades the real issue. What led up to that moment in the emergency room? A video camera recording the episode before and after the assault would upset the received black-and-white view of male ogres and female martyrs. This is not to excuse men for their scurrilous behavior; it is to awaken women to their equal responsibility in dispute and confrontation.

Any woman who stays with her abuser beyond the first incident is complicitous with him. I conjecture the basic scenario of many cases as follows. The batterer, like the serial adulterer, is an infantile personality who is fixated on the mother archetype in his wife. He demands her undivided attention, the narcotic of her quiet consolation. But he compulsively enjoys shattering her composure and destroying the family equilibrium she tries so hard to maintain. It's a terrorist way of keeping her alert, focused on him. The more he misbehaves, the more she feels he needs her. She finds his adolescent rambunctiousness both daunting and endearing—and, it has to be said, sexually exciting.

She goads in her own way, little needling assertions of her territory and her rule over him. She implies he is inept, incapable of caring for himself without her. When he postures and demands, she is vague, vacillating; he can't reach her. He finds her serene self-containment intolerable because it ultimately represents women's priority to man, her unchallengeable control over procreation. No verbal argument can shake that. _TRUE!_

What leads up to the first blow is always the same: provoked or not, she has pushed his buttons of dependency. Once again, he faces his insignificance in women's eyes. He has dwindled back to boyhood, where women ruled him. To recover his adult masculinity, he lashes out at her with his fists. He savors her pain and fear, but her refusal to defend herself takes the fight out of him. He is sickened, desperate, apologetic.

Here is the crux of the relationship, which has to be defined as sadomasochistic on *both* sides. His pleading reactivates the maternal in her. She forgives him. Never is he more open, vulnerable, and intimate than when he begs for a second chance—"I'll never do it again." His tenderness and affection enamor her. *She is addicted to the apology.* She is overwhelmed by sensory ecstasy, by the heightened passions of rage and frenzy yielding to the melting reunion of boy and mother, who nestles her son against her bosom. As in the self-flagellation of medieval Catholicism, physical pain may produce spiritual exaltation. The battered woman stays because she thinks she sees the truth and because, secretly, she knows she is victorious.

Until it is recognized that women in these relationships are exerting their own form of aggression, battering will remain an enigma. Covert manipulation is just as powerful and far less easy to combat. The current etiology—that abuser and abused come from "dysfunctional" homes—makes little sense when one is also told that 90 percent of all families are dysfunctional. (The best critique of this mushy strain in recent American culture is Wendy Kaminer's *I'm Dysfunctional, You're Dysfunctional.*) Physical violence may be a form of simple catharsis, a ritualistic way of venting pent-up anxieties and hostilities originating outside the relationship. Bloody penitential techniques have pagan as well as Christian roots, notably among the Aztecs and Anatolians. Our culture lacks formal outlets for these universal urges, except in our notoriously violent movies.

The mutual war game concealed by the judgmental term "battered woman syndrome" may contain obscure cravings for deeper knowledge of life, for it is not patriarchy but matriarchy that is older and more fundamental. A Zen analysis of such a struggling pair would not find the man winning. In pondering why a battered woman does not leave, we must remember that gay men with a taste for violent "rough trade" have always paid for this kind of sex. Are women so perfect and angelic that we cannot imagine them having sadomasochistic impulses? When they are genuinely victimized, women deserve our pity. But victimization alone cannot explain everything in the tragicomedy of love.

Sexual harassment, the newest of the feminist issues, has degrees of severity, the worst being the terroristic stalking of women by ex-boyfriends or estranged husbands. By the time these painfully drawn out situations come to public notice, the woman may actually have been murdered.* Sometimes it is the woman who does the stalking, as in the 1989 Betty Broderick case, when an hysterical San Diego woman shot to death her lawyer ex-husband and his pretty new bride in their bed. These crime dramas are detailed on hour-long talk shows, where relatives, friends, neighbors, police, and the perpetrators themselves (often televised from prison) narrate the history of the conflict and its explosive finale. Then on come the therapists and crisis counselors to reduce these ambiguous sagas to bromides.

What are the roots of obsession? To interpret the crazed idolatry that turns into hostility and destruction, you need to immerse yourself in the psychological world of great plays and novels—Iago's mysterious motivation, Othello's paroxysmic rage. Men who kill the women they love have reverted to pagan cult. She whom a man cannot live without has become a goddess, an avatar of his half-divinized, half-demonized mother, a magic fountain of cosmic creativity. Without her, he cannot exist; he is obliterated. That anyone else should have her love, or even her gaze or presence, he cannot endure. It is an injustice, and so she becomes unjust: she must be punished. He interprets her refusal to see him as an act of war, so he lays siege to her citadel. To invade it and force himself into her attention restores his identity and importance. To harass, upset, and even kill her is to perpetuate his relationship with her. He would rather be hated than ignored. Like Richard III, he glories in his

*In June 1994, five months after this essay was completed, football star O.J. Simpson was charged with the brutal murder of his ex-wife and a male friend.

monstrosity, his ostracism by humanity. He goes willingly to prison and even to the gas chamber: this is "for her" and their love.

Until they understand the unstable dynamic of sexual attraction, women of heartbreakingly good intentions will continue to be drawn into these endless, agonizing struggles that may end in violence. It is not enough to say that men must change. Intimidation and assault are of course unacceptable in civilized society. Those who break the law must suffer the consequences. But emotion is a maelstrom. Polite, charitable people of unblemished records sometimes go completely haywire when tormented by love. Apollo and Dionysus are always at odds. Passion disorders.

What I am calling for is a massive restoration of psychology to feminist thought. For reasons still unclear, we have completely lost the hip Freudianism and shrewd self-satirizing insights that were common coin in my generation's all-night college bull sessions, which resembled Nichols and May comedy sketches. Whining and shrewishness are today's favored campus style. A purely political analysis cannot help the very pretty, too "nice" girl being pursued and shoved around by an oafish fellow she has dropped—a scene I witnessed as a student in a Harpur College parking lot. Several of us had to intervene, as the boy began breaking icy snow-chunks over her head. Even then, I was struck by the girl's maternal patience and melancholy affection, as she made no effort to fend off the blows but simply huddled, weeping, against the hood of a car. She saw, and we did too, that the violence came not from his sense of power but from its opposite, his wounded desperation and helplessness.

It may be a principle of womanliness to forgive men for their childish excesses. I certainly am deficient in this area, for, as part of my general sexual alienation, I forgive nothing. On the contrary, I have made it my business, as the record shows, to personally punish every male trespass on female rights. But much violence against women originates in emotional territory that they already command. By midlife and early old age, as the hormones of both genders change, women are in total, despotic control of their marriages. [Is this always true?]

First of all, wearisome as it may seem, women must realize that, in making a commitment to a man, they have merged in his unconscious life with his mother and have therefore inherited the ambivalence of that relation. Second, stalking by strangers is caused by projection, in which a woman (or boy) becomes an involuntary player in a shadowy fantasy that may recapitulate the stalker's childhood or that may, less predictably, be a psychotic crime-as-art drama. Defending against the wraithlike intangibility of the latter will always require wariness, wisdom, and personal responsibility on women's part.

The unpleasant truth is that we can never fully legislate the human psyche. Strange aberrations will continue to manifest themselves at every level of society. Since murder victims cannot be resurrected, we need to give women a shrewder view of the world, so that they can better manage problems or avoid them altogether. Too many girls want to be liked, and not always because, in the current line, they are socialized to seek approval. I suspect most women are genetically more empathic, not as a moral value (in the tedious Gilligan manner) but as an intuitive faculty of infant care. Women's well-documented superiority in reading facial expressions, as well as their hormonally produced, hypersensitive thinner skin, supports this. What I see is not a world of male oppression and female victimization but an international conspiracy by women to keep from men the knowledge of men's own frailty. A strange maternal protectiveness is at work.

In negotiating with rejected lovers or husbands, women must stop thinking they can make everyone happy. In many cases of harassment and stalking, it is clear that the women never learned how to *terminate the fantasy*—which requires resolution and decisiveness on their part. Wavering, dithering, or passive hysterical fear will only intensify or prolong pursuit. In war, one must counterattack and then cut clean and stand on one's own. Calm, contemptuous indifference, rather than panic, is more likely to succeed. Imprisoned serial rapists have constantly said that the pleading of victims actually inflamed their lust. Intimidation usually stops when it ceases to be effective, which is why I think the tactic of escalating restraining orders, endorsed by many crisis counselors, can be dangerous and counterproductive. In most cases, the police alone cannot stop a determined stalker. As best they can, women must fight their own fights and oversee their own defense.

In the less life-threatening area of the office, sexual harassment has become a key theme of contemporary professional life. I support moderate sexual harassment guidelines: after evaluating sample academic codes in my "Women and Sex Roles" class in 1986, I lobbied for their adoption at my university. Schools of the performing arts may be particularly vulnerable to this problem, since vocational teachers, unlike standard lecturers, must sometimes touch students as part of the instruction process. In dance class, a teacher may need to realign the arms, legs, or feet, or in cello class, to encircle a student with his or her arms to remedy weaknesses in bowing. Arts schools are also more likely to have a bigger roster of older, distinguished part-time faculty whose lives center elsewhere and whose commitment to the institution is minimal.

White middle-class freshmen girls seemed especially to need help in self-definition and self-expression, and sexual harassment guidelines were a promising way to embolden them to decide how they wanted to be treated. On the other hand, I was concerned about the possibility of false charges by grandstanding neurotics, with whom I'd had quite enough contact at Bennington. Every sexual harassment code should incorporate stiff penalties for false accusation, presently rarely mentioned. This is also a glaring omission from the national rape debate. It was clear, from my own observations as well as student testimony, that some girls know instinctively how to halt unwanted familiarities and others do not but even make things worse by blushing and brightly smiling in ways that mime flirtation and pleasure. Social conventions are partly to blame, but I think we must hold even teenaged girls responsible for the persona they choose, since for most of their lives it has brought them the rewards of attention and popularity.

I categorically reject current feminist cant that insists that the power differential of boss/worker or teacher/student makes the lesser party helpless to resist the hand on the knee, the bear hug, the sloppy kiss, or the off-color joke. Servility to authority to win favor is an old story; it was probably business-as-usual in Babylon. Objective research would likely show that the incidence of sycophancy by subordinates far exceeds that of coercion by bosses. That a woman, whether or not she has dependent children, has no choice but to submit without protest to a degrading situation is absurd. Women, as much as men, have the obligation to maintain their human dignity, without recourse to a posteriori tribunals (much less those a decade later, as with wily Anita Hill). It is an hour-by-hour, month-by-month, year-by-year process. Literally from the first moment of arrival at a job or in any social situation, a person is being tested and must set the tone by his or her responses. My entire Italian-immigrant extended family, in its transition over fifty years from blue-collar to white-collar work, has followed that policy of forth-rightness and self-respect. Lack of money does not excuse groveling.

The *quid pro quo* ruse—where a sex act is demanded for a promotion or job security—is the most grievous of sexual harassment offenses and should be suitably punished, but one wonders just how common so clumsily blatant a proposition is these days. I suspect some men just try for what they can get, and a few unprepared, overly trusting women fall for it. We cannot expect government to make up for ancient lapses in child rearing. The "hostile workplace" clause, on the other hand, which has become an integral part of sexual harassment policy and has even, to my regret, passed review by the Supreme Court, seems to me reactionary and totalitarian. Mere offensiveness, which is open to subjective interpretation, is not harassment. The problem with the "hostile workplace" concept is that it is culturally parochial: it imposes a genteel white lady's standard of decorum on everyone, and when blindly applied by management, it imperialistically exports white middle-class manners, appropriate to an office, into the vigorously physical and more realistic working-class realm. The mincing minuets and sexual etiquette of the scribal class of paperpushers make no sense outside their carpeted cubicles of fluorescent light.

The folly of this nomenclature is that *every* workplace is hostile, as any man who has worked his way up the cutthroat corporate ladder will testify. Teamwork requires cooperation, but companies without internal and external competition remain stagnant. Innovation and leadership require strategies of opposition and outstripping, however one wants to disguise it. The "transformative feminism" of thinkers like Suzanne Gordon (whose progressive politics I respect), which imagines a pleasant, stress-free work environment where the lion lies down with the lamb, is unreachably utopian. Once again, aggression is not being confronted here. For every winner, there are a hundred losers. The workplace is the pagan arena, where head-on crashes are the rule.

It is outrageous that the "hostile workplace" clause is now routinely applied to coarse or ribald language, as when in 1993 a *Boston Globe* writer jokingly called another male staffer "pussywhipped" and was reported by a female employee and fined by his editor. Nude images are also affected by this clause, as when laborers are puritanically forbidden to post risqué calendars or tape *Playboy* pictures to their lockers or even, as in Los Angeles firehouses, to read *Playboy* at work. A graduate student at the University of Nebraska was forced to remove a photo of his bikini-clad wife from his desk, when two female fellow students complained to the chairman that they felt sexually harassed by it. This used to be called "paranoia." ✷ Why are snippy neurotics running our lives?

In a highly publicized incident, a dowdy English instructor pressured Penn State administrators to take down a print of Goya's *Naked Maja* from her classroom in an arts building, where it had hung unmolested for decades. She complained that the students were looking at it instead of her (I can't imagine why). The situation has gotten so out of hand that, in 1993, in one of the first British cases, a plumber was fired for continuing to use the traditional term "ballcock" for the toilet flotation unit, instead of the new politically correct term, sanitized of sexual suggestiveness. This is insane. We are back to the Victorian era, when table legs had to be draped lest they put the thought of ladies' legs into someone's dirty mind.

My libertarian position is that, in a democracy, words must not be policed. Whatever good some people feel may be gained by restrictions on speech, it is enormously outweighed by the damage done to any society where expression is restricted. History shows that all attempts to limit words end by stifling thought. I am a Sixties free speech militant. As part of our rebellion, we middle-class girls flung around the raunchiest four-letter words we could find: we were trying to shatter the code of gentility, delicacy, and prudery that had imprisoned respectable women since the rise of the bourgeoisie after the industrial revolution. Pictures too are protected expression: I define images as pagan speech.

There are very few instances where speech properly falls under government scrutiny, and those involve either fraudulent representations in business contracts or disturbances of the peace, such as shouting "fire" in a crowded theater or disrupting residential neighborhoods or campuses by noisy late-night reveling. In the latter, if offensive epithets are used, it is not the content of the words that is punishable but the fact that anything at all is shouted at that hour. Epithets and stereotypes are not fraudulent in a commercial sense; they are crudely distorted or parodistic versions of a substratum of historical truth or perception, which no one, however well-meaning, has a right to erase.

I question the concept of "fighting words," except when an arresting officer or judge weighing sentencing considers whether a brawl that led to injury was provoked by an insult—which could be aspersions on one's beauty, taste, character, or virility as easily as on one's race or ethnicity. Attitudes are not changed by forbidding their expression; on the contrary, forcing social resentments underground simply increases the power of conservative ideologues or fascist extremists to speak for the silenced. Campus speech codes, that folly of the navel-gazing left, have increased the appeal of the right. Ideas must confront ideas. When hurt feelings and bruised egos are more important than the unfettered life of the mind, the universities have committed suicide.

Sexual harassment guidelines, if overdone, will end by harming women more than helping them. In the rough play of the arena, women must make their own way. If someone offends you by speech, you must learn to defend yourself by speech. The answer cannot be to beg for outside help to curtail your opponent's free movement. The message conveyed by such attitudes is that women are too weak to win by men's rules and must be awarded a procedural advantage before they even climb into the ring. Teasing and taunting have always been intrinsic to the hazing rituals of male bonding. The elaborate shouting matches and satirical putdowns of African tribal life can still be heard in American pop music ("You been whupped with the ugly stick!"—uproarious laughter) and among drag queens, where it's called "throwing shade." Middle-class white women have got to get over their superiority complex and learn to talk trash with the rest of the human race.

A sex-free workplace is neither possible nor desirable. Many people meet their spouses at work, just as students may marry their professors. After the mannish John Molloy dress-for-success look of the Seventies, when women first moved massively into fast-track

careers, the more glamourous Eighties professional style allowed
women to recover their femininity while still being taken seriously
on the job. But we must face the fact that women's formal dress is
inherently more erotic than men's. There is a subliminally arous-
ing sensuality to perfume, lipstick, nail lacquer, vivid colors, silky
fabrics, delicate jewelry, and high-heeled pumps. Exposed legs,
which early Neanderthal feminists saw as a symbol of subordination
(more exposed flesh = less power), are in the Nineties beginning to
be understood as a visible incarnation of women's sexual power.

For all the feminist jabber about women being victimized by
fashion, it is men who most suffer from conventions of dress. Every
day, a woman can choose from an army of personae, femme to butch,
and can cut or curl her hair or adorn herself with a staggering variety
of artistic aids. But despite the Sixties experiments in peacock dress,
no man can rise in the corporate world today, outside the entertainment industry, with long hair or makeup or purple velvet suits.
Men's aesthetic impulses have been stifled since the industrial revolution. Beautiful, fragile clothing is historically an aristocratic prerogative, signifying freedom from manual labor. The contemporary
clothing debate echoes the seventeenth-century standoff between
Cavaliers and Puritans, those earnest workaholics whose sober black
dress as our "Pilgrim Fathers" is foisted on us yearly in Thanksgiving
iconography.

In the modern workplace, men are drones, and women are queen
bees. Men's corporate costume, with its fore-and-aft jacket flaps,
conceals their sexuality. Woman's eroticized dress inescapably
makes her the center of visual interest, whether people are conscious
of it or not. Most women, as well as most men, straight or gay,
instantly appraise whether a woman has "good legs" or a big bosom,
not because these attributes diminish her or reduce her to "meat"
(another feminist canard) but because they unjustifiably add to her
power in ways that may destabilize the workplace. Woman's sexuality *is* disruptive of the dully mechanical workaday world, in which
efficiency means uniformity. The problems of woman's entrance into
the career system spring from more than male chauvinism. She
brings nature into the social realm, which may be too small to contain it.

One reason I favor reasonable sexual harassment guidelines is that they alert women to the erotic energies they inspire. But the matter is not asymmetrical, with virtuous women dutifully going about their tasks when—horrors!—jets of inky male lust spurt in their direction. (Cf. Hitchcock's Marnie madly bolting for the ladies room when red ink spots her sleeve.) I protest the recent creation, as if by dragon's teeth, of a master class of sexual harassment commissars, the cadres of specialists and consultants with their vested economic interest in this field. Like the campus kangaroo courts (the date-rape and speech-code grievance committees, with their haphazard roosters), the sexual harassment inquisitors are poorly trained for what they are doing. The dreary worldview of professional bureaucrats is untouched by Rabelais, Swift, Fielding, Wilde, or Shaw. How has the society that invented rock and roll ended up in the grip of these schoolmarmish monitors of sexual mores?

Class values have been seriously neglected in feminism, which takes a simplistic designer-Marxist view of the proletarian-as-victim. When they do not docilely act like victims, laborers are treated like heathen. For example, construction workers are demonized for their lunchtime diversion of staring, leering, whistling, and catcalling at passing female office workers, some of whom—lawyers and executives—regard themselves as very mighty indeed and far too lofty for such treatment. One side of me finds these spectacles annoying and sometimes enraging; the other cheers the workers on, for they are among the last remaining masculine men of action in a world where even soldiering has become computerized. We should applaud anything that challenges and explodes bourgeois decorum in our over-regimented nine-to-five world. There is likewise a class issue in the prohibiting of nude centerfolds on lockers, since the pictorials of men's magazines correspond, in my view, to museum prints of nude paintings and sculpture that middle-class men can generally collect and display without interference.

When pressed to excess, sexual harassment rules will inevitably frustrate women's aspirations in another area: breaking through the so-called "glass ceiling," the invisible barrier that allegedly stalls women at middle management positions and keeps them out of corporate boardrooms and top executive suites. Feminists blame the "glass ceiling" on gender discrimination and the "old boy" network. But many people, male and female, have difficulty forging a persona of leadership, which may require talents different from the people-oriented and clerical skills of middle managers.

When they are encouraged to overrely on the threat of sexual harassment claims, women are being institutionally deprived of development of precisely the hard-nosed, thick-skinned tactics they need to reach the upper echelons. It is not just a particular job but treacherous office politics that ambitious future executives must master. Hostility and harassment of all kinds lie before you. Men set traps for each other, as well as for women. A mirage of cordial fog covers the snakepits. Breaking into a group requires staking out one's territory, which among humans and other animals means fierce skirmishes and border disputes. Women must find their own place in the pecking order, for which open aggression is sometimes necessary. You must bare your own fangs and not someone else's, if you want to be leader of the pack. True.

Paradoxically, conservative women like Margaret Thatcher have found it easier to reach the highest post in their countries. Liberal women achieved political prominence in America under the early Clinton presidency because the status of domestic social issues rises in periods of peace. If we are ever to have a woman president, she must, like Thatcher, demonstrate her readiness and ability to command the military. Congresswoman Patricia Schroeder, for example, one of the beaming Betty Crockers who drive crabby Sixties feminists like me crazy, has not shown, despite her long experience on the Armed Services Committee, any of the qualities of reserved authority necessary to win the confidence and respect of the troops, whom, in an emergency, the president must lead. This constitutional obligation was self-destructively neglected by Bill Clinton himself, whose strong mother made him sensitive to women's concerns but whose lack of a positive father figure made him indifferent to military matters until it was too late (the mishandling of the controversy over gays in the military being one result).

Empathy alone will never propel a woman into the White House. Women will continue to become senators and governors, but the presidency will be won only by the female candidate who finds the correct sexual persona. Leadership is warm on the surface but cold at its heart. At the top, one must have the long view, a disciplined detachment. Every decision requires betraying something or some-

one else. In war, individuals may have to be cruelly sacrificed for the survival of the whole. Movies about the great age of sailing ships show what I mean: under fire, the captain is a still, stable point of steely consciousness. As events swirl around him, he transmits his orders in a low voice to the first mate, who shouts them to the crew and ensures their enforcement. In contemporary terms, the chief executive officer is not necessarily a "people person": he carries his solitude with him.

In America, the best model yet for the first woman president can be found among the Texas feminists, notably Governor Ann Richards. East Coast feminists, like Gloria Steinem, who created the smug, superior feminist smirk (done to an unctuous turn by NOW president Patricia Ireland), have failed to produce a credible persona for national leadership, partly because of their juvenile, jeering attitude toward men and masculinity. The irony is that the legal and media world inhabited by Steinem and her coterie is filled with bookish white-collar men who are the only ones in the world who actually listen to feminist rhetoric and can be guilt-tripped into trying to obey it. The younger feminists have not done much better. Though in their thirties, Susan Faludi and Naomi Wolf seem determined to cling to perpetual girlhood. Faludi is the Mary Tyler Moore of feminism ("Geeee, Mr. Grant!"), nice but easily flustered and cowed in public. These are bobbysoxer Fifties personae, a docile, good-daughter style also detectable in those spoiled, bland yuppies, the failed Clinton nominees, Zoë Baird and Kimba Wood.

In Texas, unlike the urban Northeast, men are men. Women politicians in that state have the toughness and grit to handle men at their most macho. Southern women, particularly those of the plantation-belt "iron magnolia" school, are able to get what they want and still retain their gracious femininity. Underneath the public persona of Ann Richards, like that of Attorney General Janet Reno, who has the mannish bearing of an admiral and whose Floridian mother wrestled alligators, one can still feel the American pioneer spirit. At moments, Richards and Reno seem like robust farm women (cf. brusque, hearty Marjorie Main in *The Women*). In that state of longhorn cattle, pit barbecue, and universal football, the Texas feminists have a vigorous physicality completely missing from the tame, sheltered, word-centered world of the Steinem politburo.

Ancient Roman matrons, with their fidelity to clan and state, had more *gravitas* than today's women politicians and professionals. We need to rethink and reappropriate the old personae of grande dame and dragon lady for new use today. Hanging on the walls of the Seven Sisters, the elite women's colleges of the Northeast, are stunning portraits of the early presidents and faculty, whose air of distinction recalls a period in feminism when women accepted, and were determined to match, the highest levels of male achievement. I call them the "battle-ax maiden ladies," and they remain my inspiration.

Another of my role models is St. Teresa of Avila (*not* that tender teen, St. Therese of Lisieux, cradling her dainty roses). Obscure until her flaming forties, Teresa fought with the bishops and singlehandedly reformed the Spanish convents. She was an irascible, hands-on mystic. My American patron saint is Annie Oakley, the real-life sharpshooter known around the world from her tours with Buffalo Bill's Wild West Show. This great home-grown persona demonstrates that the best argument for women in combat is combative women.

My prescription for women entering the war zone of the professions: study football. It is a classic textbook of the strategies and controlled aggression of the ever-hostile workplace. A chapter in the second volume of *Sexual Personae* analyzes the pagan motifs of football, which is not only my favorite sport but my only real religion. Indeed, I credit my success in attacking the academic and feminist establishment to a lifetime mania for football, which provides intricate patterns of offense and defense, as well as impetus for hard hits and my trademark open-field tackling. Women who want to remake the future should look for guidance not to substitute parent figures but to the brash assertions of pagan sport.

4. SEX POWER: PROSTITUTION, STRIPPING, PORNOGRAPHY

The bourgeois limitations in feminist theory are clearly demonstrated by its difficulty in dealing with prostitution, which is interpreted solely in outworn terms of victimization. That is, feminists profess solidarity with the "sex workers" themselves but denounce

prostitution as a system of male exploitation and enslavement. I protest this trivializing of the world's oldest profession. I respect and honor the prostitute, ruler of the sexual realm, which men must pay to enter. In reducing prostitutes to pitiable charity cases in need of their help, middle-class feminists are guilty of arrogance, conceit, and prudery.

An early admirer of *Sexual Personae* who came to Philadelphia to interview me was Tracy Quan, a working prostitute and activist with P.O.N.Y. (Prostitutes of New York), who supported the stand I had taken and described her violent fights with the doctrinaire feminists overrunning the world prostitute movement. I maintained, and Quan agreed, that the popular portrait of the hapless single mother forced into prostitution by poverty or a vicious pimp was a sentimental exaggeration. Psychologists were ushering ex-prostitutes onto television programs to make tearful recantations of their former careers and to testify that prostitutes hated their work and were merely misguided victims of child abuse. Listening to the radio at home, I heard Dr. Joyce Brothers confidently proclaim, "There are no happy prostitutes"—to which I angrily blurted aloud, "Dr. Brothers, there are no happy therapists!"

Moralism and ignorance are responsible for the constant stereotyping of prostitutes by their lowest common denominator—the sick, strung-out addicts, crouched on city stoops, who turn tricks for drug money. Every profession (including the academic) has its bums, cheats, and ne'er-do-wells. The most successful prostitutes in history have been *invisible*. That invisibility was produced by their high intelligence, which gives them the power to perceive, and move freely but undetected within, the social frame. The prostitute is a superb analyst, not only in evading the law but in intuiting the unique constellation of convention and fantasy that produces a stranger's orgasm. She lives by her wits as much as her body. She is psychologist, actor, and dancer, a performance artist of hyperdeveloped sexual imagination. And she is shrewd entrepreneur and businesswoman: the madams of brothels, along with medieval abbesses, were the first female managers.

The power of ancient harlots, ancestors of Renaissance courtesans and chic modern call-girls, is suggested in *The Egyptian* (1954), the film of Mika Waltari's novel about the reign of Akhnaten and

Nefertiti. For assignations with a hypnotically beautiful Babylonian
temptress, the brilliant young Egyptian doctor surrenders his wealth,
his house, his precious medical instruments, and finally, most shockingly, the embalming of his parents' bodies for the afterlife. When
he has nothing left, her servants slam the door in his face. *The
Egyptian* shows the prostitute as a sexual adept of magical skill and
accurately documents men's excruciating obsession with and subordination to women.

Temple prostitution seems to have occurred in the ancient Near
East, in association with goddess cults. In the Christian era, typified
by St. Augustine's condemnation of Cybele and her mutilating sac-
rificial rites, the prostitute remains our point of contact with repressed pagan nature. We completely lack the fusion of sexual and
sacred found in Hinduism, notably the Tantric school, where ini-
tiation in erotic arts by a sexually experienced woman is considered
a form of spiritual instruction. Christianity splits woman into divided
halves: Mary, the Holy Mother, and Mary Magdalene, the whore.
Maternity and sexuality don't mix well in our tradition, with its
transcendent, earth-shunning deity. In the Madonna-whore complex, which particularly affects Latin Catholics (e.g., Frank Sinatra),
a man loses sexual interest in his wife when she becomes pregnant,
activating memories of his sainted mother. The home becomes a
shrine, and the man seeks sexual satisfaction elsewhere with whores,
"bimbos," defensively minimized to evade woman's hegemony.

When they posit prostitutes as lost souls to be saved from satanic
male clutches, feminists are collaborating in the systematic deni-
gration of a class of women who, under dangerous conditions,
perform a necessary social service. Governments that try to ban
prostitution never succeed for long. Prostitution is always reinvented
and flourishes, underground or in light of day. During the Sixties
sexual revolution, I believed that, in a reformed future, prostitution
would be unnecessary, since emancipated female desire would expand to meet men's needs. However, over time, I realized that
sexuality can never be fully contained within social forms and that
the old double standard was no misogynous fiction: promiscuity is
risky to the health of procreative woman and her fetus. Hence the
prostitute has come to symbolize for me the ultimate liberated

woman, who lives on the edge and whose sexuality belongs to no
one.

Often over the past decade, as I arrive at 8 A.M. at my classroom
building on South Broad Street in Center City, I have been stunned
to encounter a working whore sashaying cheerfully along in full
brazen regalia—red-leather bolero jacket and bulging halter, white-
leather or lavender-suede thigh-high boots, black-spangle or gold-
lamé micro-miniskirt with no underwear and bare buttocks. White,
black, or Latina, she dominates the street for two blocks in every
direction. You can see the stir, as people hurrying to work break
step, turn, or furtively stare. Working-class men brashly hail her in
humorous admiration; middle-class men are startled, embarrassed,
but fascinated; middle-class women, uneasily clutching their attaché
cases, are frozen, blank, hostile.

Of the great sexual personae I have seen in my lifetime, Philadelphia prostitutes rank very high. They are fearless and aggressive,
waving down businessmen in sedans or bringing traffic to a halt as
they jaw with taxi drivers. They rule the street. "Pagan goddess!"
I want to call out, as I sidle reverently by. Not only are these women
not victims, they are among the strongest and most formidable
women on the planet. They exist in the harshest reality, but they
laugh and bring beauty out of it. For me, they are heroines of outlaw
individualism.

Prostitution should be decriminalized. My libertarian position
is that government may not under any circumstances intervene in
consensual private behavior. Thus, despite their damage to my generation, I support the legalization of drugs, consistent with current
regulation of alcohol. And I would argue for the absolute right to
homosexual sodomy. It is reasonable, however, to ask that sex acts
remain private and that they not *visibly* occur in shared public spaces
like streets and parks—the latter a favorite haunt of gay men, to
the despair of neighbors. Neither Judeo-Christian nor pagan may
dominate common ground.

Solicitation for sex should be tolerated and treated exactly like
the vending of any commercial product: that is, pedestrians have
the right not to be crowded, touched, or fondled by salesmen, ped-
dlers, or whores. Police may keep building entrances unobstructed,

guarantee a clear zone around schools and churches, and control noisy late-night auto traffic cruising in residential neighborhoods. But harassment of whores and their clients must cease. Government should concern itself only with public health matters: hence free testing and treatment of venereal disease, without censoriousness, should be required of prostitutes working in licensed brothels.

Mainstream feminist propaganda claims that prostitutes must "do whatever men want." This is true only of the amateurish and weak-willed. Most professional prostitutes are in complete charge of the erotic encounter and do nothing they don't want. Things can certainly go wrong, with painful or fatal results—as is also the experience of gay men, whose sexual adventurousness over the centuries has often cost them their lives. Stranger sex will never be risk-free; it is just as challenging an exploration of hazardous nature as cliff-climbing, sailing, car racing, big-game hunting, bungee-jumping, hang-gliding, or parachuting. The thrill is partly due to the nearness of disaster or death.

The prostitutes on window display in Amsterdam's famous red-light district, with their opulent fleshiness, earthy practicality, and bawdy sang-froid, impressed me enormously when I first saw them in 1969, as a graduate student still optimistic about bringing sophisticated European sexual values to puritan America. By 1993, when I visited Amsterdam again, the scene had changed: it is now less homey and, influenced by the dance revolution in stripping, more theatrical. The whores are dazzlingly multicultural. A conventional feminist analysis would see these women writhing and beckoning in glass cubicles as degradingly accessible cream pastries in a male automat. But I see, as always, pure female power. The men shopping in the street cluster together to bolster their confidence; most are awkward, uncertain, abashed. The young, lithe Thai whores boldly flaunt their breasts and buttocks in skinny white bikinis, blazing under violet Day-glo light. They are a pagan epiphany, apparitions of supreme sexual beauty. Jerusalem has never vanquished Babylon.

A luminous moment of this kind occurred in Naples in 1984, when I was walking with family friends near the bay late at night. A tall, striking, raven-haired whore in a tight white dress, who may or may not have been a transvestite, was bantering with a truck

driver, her long leg perched raffishly on the running board. Spotting
the flowing red hair of a mature married woman in our party, she
grinned wickedly and yelled out, in a rich, gravelly, flirtatious voice,
"Ciao, rossa!" ("Hey, redhead!") Everyone stared stonily ahead and
kept moving. The group as a whole, with its middle-class American
propriety, was not as powerful as this one extraordinary being, whose
perverse, worldly consciousness seemed to take in and dominate the
entire waterfront. This was her territory; we were the intruders.
Lagging behind, I smiled conspiratorially and nodded back in homage. She was my confederate. Her humor and vitality were like those
of Caravaggio's lewd urchins. I had an eerie sense of the Neapolitan
side of my heritage (my father's people were from the inland towns
of Benevento, Avellino, and Caserta), the stream of sensuality and
decadence going back to Pompeii and ancient Capri, where the
emperor Tiberius had his villa.

Strippers are not prostitutes, as they firmly point out. I first
became aware of their free-lance lifestyle while I was teaching at
Bennington in the Seventies, when several of my women students
earned tuition money by dancing in topless bars in metropolitan
New York and New Jersey. I questioned them closely and read their
research projects compiling interviews with their fellow workers. The
other dancers were often enterprising single mothers whose experiences depended on the quality of the clubs, the best of which
protected women employees by escorting them to their cars and
squelching overeager customers. At worst, the dancers had to fight
off the managers themselves, but this was usually considered an
occupational hazard that plucky women could handle.

Why do so many men want to see women undress? I have written
about the pagan origins of striptease, the ritual unveiling of a body
that will always remain mysterious because of the inner darkness of
the womb, from which we all came. Sexual exhibitionism plays a
part in most nature cults, such as Hinduism. My interest in this
subject dates from a New York State Fair in Syracuse in the late
Fifties, when I was around ten. A midway barker introduced a belly
dancer, who undulated from a tent and struck a pose at one end of
the platform. A trance came over me. I bolted from my startled
family and darted through the dense male crowd to stare up at her
in stupefied wonder. My parents told the story for years, since the

dancer, used to women giving her a wide berth, eyed me back with alarmed perplexity. I'm sure I looked like a moron, with mouth agape and eyes like saucers.

Sexual dancing, which handsome boys also do for gay men, is a great art form with ancient roots. I reject feminist cant about the "male gaze," which supposedly renders passive and inert everything it touches. As I maintained in my first book, sexual objectification is characteristically human and indistinguishable from the art impulse. There is nothing degrading in the display of any part of the human body. Those embarrassed or offended by erotic dancing are the ones with the problem: their natural responses have been curtailed by ideology, religious or feminist. The early Christian church forbade dancing because of its pagan associations and its very real incitement to lust.

In modern times, dance has become progressively more sexually explicit, as the performers of classical ballet, once aristocrats of the *ancien régime,* shed clothing from the nineteenth century on. The calf-length ballerina's skirt, for example, became the tutu, just a fringe of chiffon at the hips. The molded Renaissance tights of male dancers accent bulging genitals and buttocks. Half the appeal of today's classical ballet productions, I would argue, is their ravishing semi-nudity. It's striptease in the name of high art. Modern dance, from the Greek-inspired free movement and bare feet of Isadora Duncan to the tribal pelvic thrusts and spasmodic contractions of Martha Graham, has always been sexually revolutionary. Jazz dancing is also boldly erotic, thanks to Bob Fosse's appropriation of burlesque moves, which he witnessed as a child in the demimondaine.

Since the Twenties, popular dance has been sexualized by wave after wave of African and Latin (really Afro-Caribbean) influences. As Eldridge Cleaver said in *Soul on Ice,* the 1960 twist craze activated the dead white pelvis, in an early skirmish of the sexual revolution. Grinding, provocative wiggles and shimmies are now the everyday recreational language of the white middle class. The line between striptease and respectable social dancing has blurred. Hence the recent evolution toward total nudity in topless clubs. Today, straight or gay men, tucking tribute bills into a woman's garter belt or a guy's motorcycle boot, can inspect the sexual terrain at microscopic

proximity. Unescorted female customers are still disappointingly rare, as I can report from my own midnight forays.

In virtually all venues, the nude dancer is in total control of the stage and audience. The feminist scenario of a meat rack of ribs and haunches priced and fingered by reeking buffoons is another hysterical projection. Hard as it may be to believe, men in strip clubs *admire* what they see and are even awed by it. They gather round the women to warm themselves, as if the stage were a bonfire on a medieval winter's night. The dancers exert a magnetic force. The men don't know exactly why they must come there, but they sense that their ordinary lives and official religion don't fulfill their longings or answer all their questions. To reduce these ritual visitations to a matter of mechanical masturbation is unintelligent and unimaginative. The nude dancer can never be captured or completely known. She teases and eludes, like the female principle itself.

Extreme forms of sexual expression can only be understood through a sympathetic study of pornography, one of the most controversial issues in feminism. For more than fifteen years, the syllabi and reserve reading shelves of women's studies courses have been dominated by two sex-killing styles, the anti-art puritanism of the Catharine MacKinnon school and the word-obsessed, labyrinthine abstraction of Lacanian analysis. The pro-sex wing of feminism was virtually invisible until very recently, for two reasons. First, its adherents outside academe wrote fiction or journalism and never produced major theoretical statements anywhere near MacKinnon's level of argument. Second, its adherents inside academe shut themselves off in jargon-spouting conferences, which had no cultural impact or purpose beyond personal careerism. Free-speech feminists mobilized to defeat MacKinnon-inspired anti-porn statutes in Minneapolis and Indianapolis but then fell back into torpor, abandoning academe to the virulent ideologues, who seized administrative power in campus-life issues.

The pro-sex feminists were never able to stop MacKinnon, whose reputation rose steadily until she was canonized in a disgracefully uncritical cover story of *The New York Times Magazine* in October 1991. During the Clarence Thomas hearings that year, she was everywhere in the media. Even public radio and television were

hopelessly biased, trotting out dozens of radical and establishment feminists pushing one party line. The sexual harassment crisis was the Waterloo of the pro-sex feminists, who lost all perspective and collapsed into rampant MacKinnonism. Not one leading feminist voice but mine challenged the sentimental Anita Hill groupthink or the creeping fascism of the date-rape and sexual harassment hysteria. Nor did any critique of MacKinnon gain ground until I called her a "totalitarian" and exposed the drastically limited assumptions in her cultural worldview. In late 1993, the free-speech feminists finally—and far too late—launched a searing personal attack on MacKinnon (over her gross exploitation of the Bosnian rapes) in central feminist territory, *Ms.* magazine.

My skepticism about the courage and sincerity of the pro-sex feminists was confirmed by my own experience with them. The refusal or inability of the academic feminists to engage my work has eloquently demonstrated their insularity and hypocrisy. Of the best-known names outside academe, only film director Monika Treut and performance artist Annie Sprinkle took an interest in or publicly supported me and my views. Treut's avant-garde thinking was shaped by the greater cosmopolitanism of Europe, while Sprinkle's iconoclastic comedy draws on her intimate knowledge of the worlds of prostitution and stripping, which I celebrate. The parochialism and conventionalism in even the most ostensibly radical feminist views of sexuality were shown by Pat Califia's long silence about and then open attack on me, as well as by Susie Bright's catty impugning of my positions and right to speak. The latter's cliquish removal from the general culture was evident in her public dismissal of Dr. Ruth Westheimer, whose contributions to sex education of the American mass audience have been enormous.

A major problem with pro-sex feminism has been its failure to embrace the men's magazines, without which no theory of sexuality will ever be complete. I have gone out of my way to publish in and endorse *Playboy* and *Penthouse*, which have been vilified by both mainstream and anti-porn feminists, as well as by mainstream members of NOW. I love the irony of bringing contemporary feminism full circle, back to where Gloria Steinem made her name by infiltrating a Playboy Club. In the Eighties, feminists and religious conservatives pressured convenience stores and drugstore chains to ban the men's

magazines. This has led to a massive cultural ignorance on the part of feminists, inside and outside academe, about what is actually *in* those magazines.

Idiotic statements like "Pornography degrades women" or "Pornography is the subordination of women" are only credible if you never look at pornography. Preachers, senators, and feminist zealots carry on about materials they have no direct contact with. They usually rely on a few selectively culled inflammatory examples that bear little resemblance to the porn market as a whole. Most pornography shows women in as many dominant as subordinate postures, with the latter usually steamily consensual. Specialty mail services can provide nonconsensual sadomasochistic scenarios, but they are difficult to find, except in the vast underground of cartoon art, so subversively individualistic that it has thus far escaped the feminist thought police. Cartoons in R. Crumb's fabled Sixties style show the comic, raging id uncensored. Despite hundreds of studies, the cause-and-effect relationship between pornography and violence has never been satisfactorily proved. Pornography is a self-enclosed world of pure imagination. Feminist claims that porn actresses are coerced and abused are wildly exaggerated and usually based on one or two atypical tales.

Feminist anti-porn discourse virtually always ignores the gigantic gay male porn industry, since any mention of the latter would bring crashing to the ground the absurd argument that pornography is by definition the subordination of women. I have learned an enormous amount from gay porn, which a few lesbians have commendably tried to imitate but not with sterling success. The greatest erotic images of women remain those created by male artists and photographers, from Botticelli, Titian, Ingres, and Courbet to Richard Avedon and Helmut Newton. The advertising pages of gay newspapers are adorned with stunning icons of gorgeous male nudes, for which I have yet to see an impressive lesbian equivalent. Men, gay or straight, can get beauty and lewdness into one image. Women are forever softening, censoring, politicizing.

Unlike the art-illiterate anti-porn fanatics, gay men glory in every angle on the sexual body, no matter how contorted. A sleek, pretty boy in cowboy boots spreading his buttocks for an up-close glimpse of his pink anus is an alluring staple of gay magazines. In that world, everyone knows this splendid creature is victor, not slave. Sexual power defies or *reverses* rigid political categories. Feminists who see the bare-all, pubic "beaver shot" as a paradigm of women's historical oppression are cursed with the burden of their own pedestrian prejudices. Until we solve the mystery of sexuality, contemplation of our kaleidoscopic genitalia—from glossy and nubile to lank and withered—will remain an interesting and important exercise in human self-discovery.

Since paganism must give its due to Judeo-Christianity, we should respect the desire of the religious not to be assaulted with nude images in public spaces. Thus sex magazines should be freely available at newsstands but not necessarily displayed on them. Sealed plastic or paper sleeves don't seem unreasonable to me, though I would like opponents and proponents of pornography to be able to leaf through magazines to stay informed. Since television is also a public space, it is fair to ask, but not require, that stations schedule adult programming during late-night hours, when parents can best supervise their children. Unlike Frank Zappa, I feel that a ratings system is merely informational and infringes on no one's right to free speech. On the contrary, an "X" designation positively helps the lascivious to locate juicy material in every medium. The music industry must not confuse free speech rights with lucrative placement of product in suburban malls.

Far from poisoning the mind, pornography shows the deepest truth about sexuality, stripped of romantic veneer. No one can claim to be an expert in gender studies who is uncomfortable with pornography, which focuses on our primal identity, our rude and crude animality. Porn dreams of eternal fires of desire, without fatigue, incapacity, aging, or death. What feminists denounce as woman's humiliating total accessibility in porn is actually her elevation to high priestess of a pagan paradise garden, where the body has become a bountiful fruit tree and where growth and harvest are simultaneous. "Dirt" is contamination to the Christian but fertile loam to the pagan. The most squalid images in porn are shock devices to break down bourgeois norms of decorum, reserve, and tidiness. The Dionysian body fluids, fully released to coat every gleaming surface, return us to the full-body sensuality of the infant condition. In crowded orgy tableaux, like those on Hindu temples, matter and energy melt. In the cave spaces of porn, camera lights are torches of the Eleusinian Mysteries, giving us flashes of nature's secrets.

Gay men appreciate pornography as I do because they accept the Hellenic principle that some people are born more beautiful than others. Generic granola feminists are likely to call this "lookism"— an offense against equality. I take the Wildean view that equality is a moral imperative in politics but that the arts will always be governed by the elitism of talent and the tyranny of appearance. Pornography's total exposure of ripe flesh, its dynamic of vigor and vitality, is animated by the cruel pre-Christian idolatry of beauty and strength.

Pornography *is* art, sometimes harmonious, sometimes dissonant. Its glut and glitter are a Babylonian excess. Modern middle-class women cannot bear the thought that their hard-won professional achievements can be outweighed in an instant by a young hussy flashing a little tits and ass. But the gods have given her power, and we must welcome it. Pornography forces a radical reassessment of sexual value, nature's bequest and our tarnished treasure.

5. REBEL LOVE: HOMOSEXUALITY

Homosexuality may be the key to understanding the whole of human sexuality. No subject cuts in so many directions into psychology, sociology, history, and morality. The incidence, as well as visibility, of homosexuality has certainly increased in the Western world in the past twenty-five years. But discussion of it rapidly became overpoliticized after the Stonewall rebellion of 1969, which began the gay liberation movement. Viewpoints polarized: people were labeled pro-gay or anti-gay, with little room in between. For the past decade, the situation has been out of control: responsible scholarship is impossible when rational discourse is being policed by storm troopers, in this case gay activists, who have the absolutism of all fanatics in claiming sole access to the truth.

Stonewall was an act of resistance to police authority by multiracial drag queens mourning the death of Judy Garland, long divinized by gays. Therefore Stonewall had a cultural meaning beyond the political: it was a pagan insurrection by the reborn transvestite priests of Cybele. But the Seventies gay scene immediately turned away from the drag spirit that gave birth to it: a macho clone look took over the men's bars, and queens were scorned as an embarrassing reminder of a time when gayness meant effeminacy. Paradoxically, drag was more acceptable in heterosexual rock music, then in its decadent sci-fi phase, typified by Alice Cooper, Kiss, and David Bowie, whose roots, via the New York Dolls, were in Andy Warhol's charismatic Superstars, whom I worshiped.

From Stonewall to the first AIDS alert was only twelve short years. In the Eighties and early Nineties, displaced anxiety over the horror of AIDS turned gay activists into rampaging nihilists and monomaniacs, who dishonestly blamed the disease on the government and trampled on the rights of the gay majority, and whose errors of judgment materially aided the rise and consolidation of the far right. AIDS did not appear out of nowhere. It was a direct result of the sexual revolution, which my generation unleashed with the best intentions, but whose worst effects were to be suffered primarily by gay men. In the West, despite much propaganda to the contrary, AIDS *is* a gay disease and will remain one for the foreseeable future.

That is, of all those stricken with AIDS throughout the world—whether through drug use, blood transfusion, or prenatal or heterosexual transmission—no other group has experienced it so uniquely as a collective spiritual crisis or as a traumatic assault upon personal identity. The newness of the disease, the long delay of symptoms after infection, the rapid speed of degeneration (syphilis could take a lifetime) were shocking. Medicine and science had become so advanced that gay men, heady after Stonewall, were caught up in the arrogant Western confidence in free will and self-determination. And without the fear of pregnancy that hovers over heterosexual liaisons, homosexuality had no inherent biological controls; its use of the body seemed unlimited. Came the apocalypse: AIDS is a systems breakdown of a body that has lost its defenses against nature. The ugliness and premature aging of this wasting disease were especially painful and grotesque in view of gay men's historic idealization of youth and beauty.

The gargantuan promiscuity of the Seventies gay male world was a pagan phenomenon, unequaled in scale since the Roman empire. Its joyful, perilous excess was a response to the long suppression of homosexual behavior and expression following the trial and conviction of Oscar Wilde in 1895. Wilde, a Hellenophile, was to relapse into Christian morality in prison, but his uncompromising aestheticism lingered on in the underground sensibility of gay men, right up to Stonewall. The masculine cultism of the Seventies bar scene was laudable in view of feminism's bitter assault on the very notion of masculinity, building at that moment. However, ancient Greek idealizations of the athletic male form were always grounded in a larger context of both aesthetics and religion. And, it must be remembered, Athenian boy-lovers always married and never stopped honoring female divinities.

The twentieth century has seen two holocausts—one by politics and one by nature. The massacre of gay men has had and will continue to have devastating consequences in the worlds of art and fashion, where gays have exercised enormous, often invisible influence as tastemakers. But the destruction began from within. I believe that the shocking toll of AIDS on gay men in the West was partly due to their Seventies delusionalism that a world without women was possible. All-male energies, unbalanced and ravenous, literally tore the body apart.

When he refused to sacrifice to Aphrodite, Hippolytus was destroyed—dragged to death by his own horses (i.e., sexual impulses), spooked by a chthonian monster from the sea. No eroticism can be complete that denies the power of the female principle, which is nature itself, what Hinduism calls the cycle of birth and death. Pre-Stonewall gay culture *was* complete. Not only did lesbians and gay men, due to the paucity of gay bars, socialize more regularly, but gay men were bound together by a grandiose international aesthetic that spectacularly glamourized women—chiefly Hollywood stars and opera divas (recently documented by Wayne Koestenbaum). Female impersonation, as campy nightclub entertainment, flourished. For centuries, gay aesthetes—the brilliant makeup artists, hair stylists, and couturiers—have shaped and enhanced women's sexual image. They accurately saw and hugely increased women's power over men—even as they refused to yield to it in their personal erotic lives.

The post-Stonewall decade, rejecting drag queens and closing the doors of the orgiastic men's bars to women, created a paradise

of pleasure that collapsed into the hell of AIDS. Is obsessive mono-
sexuality really a solution to the libidinal limitations of socially enforced heterosexuality? A gay versus straight opposition simply
perpetuates a false dualism and guarantees the oppression of gay
men, who will always lose that conflict and, because of their vulnerability when cruising, will pay with their blood in the streets.
Surely the real revolution is to establish the fluid continuum of
human sexuality and to win acceptance from heterosexuals of the
presence of pleasure-promising homosexual impulses in themselves.

The gay activist establishment has been stupid and narrow in
the way it has conducted its civil rights campaign. An authentically
Sixties libertarian vision would argue for the protection of *all* nonconformist behavior, to which homosexual love is just a subset. There
is no gay leader remotely near the stature of Martin Luther King,
because black activism has drawn on the profound spiritual traditions of the church, to which gay political rhetoric is childishly
hostile. Activists have disrupted church services in New York and
Philadelphia (flinging the Communion host on the floor; throwing
condoms at and striking the archbishop conducting a Mass for the
AIDS dead). Shrilly self-interested and doctrinaire, gay activism is
completely lacking in philosophical perspective. Its sorrow became
the only sorrow, its disease the only disease.

The parallel claimed by gay leaders between blacks and gays
as oppressed minorities has always been questionable, and some
African-Americans have angrily rejected it. Since the argument that
gays are a distinct class, deserving special protection against discrimination, is based on this premise, the controversy over issues
like Colorado's Amendment 2 (passed in 1992) is confused and
simplistic, with knee-jerk responses of outrage expected of all loyal
gays. But discrimination against skin color is not wholly comparable
to the complicated resistance of virtually all societies in history to
open homosexuality, which involves thorny questions of morality
and psychology. Most gays can "pass" whenever they want—an
option available to few blacks.

Homosexuality is not "normal." On the contrary, it is a challenge to the norm; therein rests its eternally revolutionary character.
Note I do not call it a challenge to the *idea* of a norm. Queer theorists—that wizened crew of flimflamming free-loaders—have tried

to take the poststructuralist tack of claiming that there is no norm, since everything is relative and contingent. This is the kind of silly bind that word-obsessed people get into when they are deaf, dumb, and blind to the outside world. Nature exists, whether academics like it or not. And in nature, procreation is the single, relentless rule. That is the norm. Our sexual bodies were designed for reproduction. Penis fits vagina: no fancy linguistic game-playing can change that biologic fact.

However, my libertarian view, here as in regard to abortion, is that we have not only the right but the obligation to defy nature's tyranny. The highest human identity consists precisely in such assertions of freedom against material limitation. Gays are heroes and martyrs who have given their lives in the greatest war of them all. Fate, not God, has given us this flesh. We have absolute claim to our bodies and may do with them as we see fit. To develop and expand our sensory responses is a pagan strategy, reverent in its own way toward nature. Homosexual potential is in everyone, and evidence suggests that under the right circumstances it will out. But the instinctual imperative to mate is also in all of us.

Given the intense hormonal surge of puberty, the total absence of adult heterosexual desire is neither normal nor natural, and it requires explanation. Gay activists are guilty of Stalinist disinformation when they assert that homosexuality is no different than and equivalent to heterosexuality, and that anus and vagina are interchangeable, except for our political conditioning to the contrary. Toleration of dissenting behavior, which I am calling for, does not necessarily mean approval by society. Pagan and Judeo-Christian will never, and should never, agree. Disapproval is not "ignorance" or "bigotry"—gay activists' tiresome crutch terms—when it is motivated by principle. Similarly, there are legitimate medical questions about the safety and sanitation of tissue-rupturing anal sex, even though the latter belongs, in my view, to the private realm outside government control.

Since Romanticism, sexuality has been asked to bear too much of the burden of identity, formerly supplied by affiliation to religion, nation, or clan. Recreational sex has expanded in importance, so that it is now a substitute for other forms of communication. Between intimates, who may not be capable or desirous of procreation, sex "revelatory descent to primal levels of nonverbal experience."

permits revelatory descent to primal levels of nonverbal experience. It emotionally reawakens and heals the "family romance" of our personal biography. Between strangers, sex can have a ritual character. It is an act of pagan homage to some archetypal reality, outside the social frame. The reveler in pure beauty is pillager but also devotee.

If can have a ritual character between strangers, too.

It's not always battlefield combat.

Here is where gay men have distinguished themselves. The idealism of the Seventies gay bacchanalia lay in its glorification of the masculine, which throughout history has striven to be free of female dominance and, in the process, made the great breakthroughs in art and technology. But as politics began to take over gay as well as feminist discourse, psychology dropped away. When questions ceased to be asked about the origins of homosexuality, woman was eliminated from the picture, with disastrous consequences for men unaccustomed to custodianship of their bodies. Homosexual experimentation will naturally occur whenever social or moral barriers are removed. Homosexual acts have been an institutionalized part of rites of passage in some tribal cultures, but significantly only when the warrior code of violent masculine action is present as a corrective. *Exclusive* homosexual relations among *adults* have never been sanctioned before modern times. Their recent appearance seems to me directly connected to the crisis in sex roles after the industrial revolution. Probably

Why?

but far from the only ones.

Gay men are mythmakers, poetically re-creating a masculinity that has been culturally lost, but they are also fleeing a female power that has become frustrated and all-consuming. Again we must reconsider that pivotal transition from the extended to the nuclear family, which has isolated incomplete parents with their incomplete children. There may indeed be a genetic component predisposing some people toward homosexuality, but social factors in childhood play an enormous role in determining whether that tendency manifests itself or not. Parents are not specifically to blame, insofar as they themselves are affected by historical forces of disintegration. But the family matrix is central to the sexual story.

They can't handle it.

No one is "born gay." The idea is ridiculous, but it is symptomatic of our overpoliticized climate that such assertions are given instant credence by gay activists and their media partisans. I think what gay men are remembering is that they were born *different*. Here is where my personal observation may dovetail with Simon LeVay's hypothesis, based on admittedly fragmentary evidence, about the enlarged hypothalamus in the brains of a small group of gay men who died of AIDS. LeVay observed that in size the gland resembled that of women rather than heterosexual men, but whether this characteristic was congenital or the effect of disease or homosexual practice itself was inconclusive.

Media reports, manipulated by gay activists, trumpeted that LeVay, despite his careful qualifiers, had incontrovertibly established that gay people were born that way and that moral opposition to gayness would hence cease, since homosexuality is not a matter of choice. Censored out was the common-sense point that this marked an astonishing return to the old idea, discarded after Stonewall, that gay men are like women. Lesbians and gay men are very different, and so is the etiology of their homosexuality. Genetic factors, if they exist, are probably more likely to appear in men, because of the complex process of hormonal masculinization of the fetus (always initially female in form), where variations or disturbances might occur. But we must be cautious about a theory that defines gays as *a priori* incomplete men. Excessive masculinization of the female *in utero* is a possible explanation for some but certainly not most lesbianism, which seems to be primarily produced by social pressures.

My tentative conclusions are based on a lifetime of observation and experience in the modern sex wars. As a tomboy in the Fifties, I questioned my own gender and had early infatuations with women and later purely physical attractions to men, whom I dated intermittently. One reason I so dislike recent gay activism is that my self-identification as a lesbian preceded Stonewall: I was the only openly gay person at the Yale Graduate School (1968–72), a candor that was professionally costly. That anyone with my aggressive and scandalous history could be called "homophobic," as has repeatedly been done, shows just how insanely Stalinist gay activism has become.

As a teacher of twenty-three years, most of which were spent in art schools, I have been struck by the rarity, not the frequency, of homosexuality. From the start of my media career, I attacked the much-touted activist claim that 10 percent of the population is gay—

which was always a distortion of Kinsey's finding that 10 percent had had some homosexual experience over their lifetime. Tracking my students, acquaintances, and the world in general, I guessed the number hovered at 3 percent, and recent surveys (ranging from 1 or 2 to 4 percent) have borne this out.

The 10 percent figure, servilely repeated by the media, was pure propaganda, and it made me, as a scholar, despise gay activists for their unscrupulous disregard for the truth. Their fibs and fabrications continue, now about the still-fragmentary evidence for a genetic link to homosexuality and for homosexual behavior among animals. The incidence of the latter is enormously exaggerated, in proportion to conventional procreative pairings throughout nature, and acknowledgment is rarely made of the exceptional conditions of environmental stress or population pressure under which it occurs. I am also unpersuaded, thus far, by multigenerational and twin studies that claim to have found evidence for a genetic basis for homosexuality, since the samplings have been weakly constructed and since homosexuality was treated as an isolated factor, without broader consideration of family dynamics, ethnic history, or personality typology.

Because of my admiration of and deep friendship with gay men (four of whom I have written about elsewhere in this book), I used to feel that the old psychoanalytic model was inadequate in describing the origins of homosexuality as, essentially, arrested development. But it was true that all my gay male friends had powerful, dominating mothers in the prototypical style. In college, I was already complaining about my difficulties in meeting or communicating with lesbians. My mental and imaginative life was absorbed more and more with gay men, with whom I felt totally free. To this day, the dichotomy remains. I have found few lesbians with whom I can discourse for more than five minutes without hitting some tiresome barrier of resentment or ideology. My romantic life has been spent primarily with bisexual or heterosexual women. I fail to see why lesbians must pursue other lesbians; it's illogical. Straight women, with their radiant sexual aura, began it all.

Again and again over the decades, as I did my time, in frustrated boredom, in lesbian bars, trying with spectacular lack of success to make friends or just converse, I would end up gabbing for hours

opinion - taste - energy - wit

with some stray gay man. He might have dropped out of school at fourteen, but he had opinions, tastes, energy, wit. Is there something innately different about the gay male brain? And do family factors and gay culture reinforce that difference? Answers will not soon be coming. But what I do know is that gay male consciousness, as I have experienced it, is stunningly expansive and exquisitely precise. Gay men have collectively achieved a fusion of intellect, emotion, and artistic sensibility that resembles Goethe's or Byron's integration of classicism and Romanticism. The intellectual of the twenty-first century, trained by an academic system I am trying to reshape, will think like a gay man.

After my career in art schools, I know that artistic talent cannot be created, only developed. It is inborn. Similarly, I conclude that men are not born gay; they are born with an artistic gene, which may or may not lead to an artistic career. More often, they are connoisseurs, aesthetes, or simply arch, imperious commentators with stringent judgments about everything. (At a Yale party, a gay fellow whom I hardly knew muttered waspishly to me about a woman across the room, "That dress does *nothing* for her!") There are gay men without such talent, but they are a minority. The effeminacy of gay men—which emerges as soon as the macho masks drop—is really their artistic sensitivity and rich, vulnerable emotionalism.

In *Sexual Personae*, I studied the psychic duality of the artist, who combines male and female in the act of creation. It is possible that gay men are caught midway between the male and female brains and therefore share the best of both. Talent in the visual arts may be related to a sensory or perceptual openness, detectable (as responsiveness to light and color) in early childhood and perhaps related to autism, where the flux of sensations is cognitively uncontrolled. The gay male brain seems to me permanently switched "on."

Here is my speculative scenario, constructed after teaching and advising so many apprentice artists. A sensitive boy is born into a family of jocks. He is shy and dreamy from the start. His father is uncomfortable with him, and his brothers are harsh and impatient. But he is his mother's special favorite, almost from the moment he is born. He and she are more alike. Repelled by male roughhousing, he is drawn to his mother's and sisters' quietness and delicacy. He becomes his mother's confidant against her prosaic husband, a half-eroticized relationship that may last a lifetime and block the son from adult contacts with women.

He is fascinated by his mother's rituals of the boudoir, her hypnotic focus on the mirror as she applies magic unguents from vials of vivid color, like paints and palette. He loves her closet, not because he covets her clothes but because they are made of gorgeous, sensuous fabrics, patterns, and hues denied men in this post-aristocratic age. Later, he feels like an outsider in the schoolyard. There is no male bonding; he tries to join in but never fully merges with the group. Masculinity is something beautiful but "out there"; it is not *in* him, and he knows he is feigning it. He longs for approval from the other boys, and his nascent sexual energies begin to flow in that direction, pursuing what he cannot have. He will always be hungry for and awed by the masculine, even if and when, through bodybuilding or the leather scene, he adopts its accoutrements.

Thus homosexuality, in my view, is an *adaptation*, not an inborn trait. When they claim they were gay "as far back as I can remember," gay men are remembering their isolation and alienation, their differentness, which is a function of their special gifts. Such protestations are of little value in any case, since it is unlikely that much can be recalled before age three, when sexual orientation may already be fixed. Heaven help the American boy born with a talent for ballet. In this culture, he is mocked and hounded and never wins the respect of masculine men. Yet this desperation deepens his artistic insight and expressiveness. Thus gay men create civilization by fulfilling the pattern of Coleridge's prophesying, ostracized poet, dancing alone with "flashing eyes" and "floating hair."

Other patterns of homosexual etiology certainly exist, including one of hatred toward and revulsion from women. But that ambivalence may already be built into the story I have sketched, since the mother who turns away from her dull spouse to make a subliminally incestuous marriage with her sensitive son may be suffocating the boy and stunting his development. Indeed, the developmental theory of homosexuality, which I rejected in college, returned to haunt me because of the misbehavior of ACT UP, a chain of small protest groups that I probably would have joined in my youth, since its style of Sixties guerrilla theater is my own. ACT UP won substantial practical victories in its mobilizations against the political and medical establishment, but its most crazed extremists also did enormous damage to the public image of gay men that will take a generation to undo.

Flashed across the nation's television screens were contorted male faces, raging, ranting, bawling like infants—"Me, me, me!" What we were seeing in ACT UP's worst tantrums was the disintegration, under pressure of implacable reality, of the gay male persona. Horrifyingly exposed were the unevolved emotions just beneath the surface. Male authority figures—the disapproving, rejecting father—were blamed for everything. Total attention and an instant cure were demanded, even though science had failed to find a cure for any virus, even the common cold. It is no coincidence that ACT UP never could expand its membership beyond the white middle class, with its footstamping sense of entitlement. Civil rights demonstrators, anti-war protesters, and those facing death from any disease had rarely behaved with such juvenile lack of dignity.

Meanwhile, more women were dying yearly from breast cancer than had succumbed to AIDS in America over a decade. In April 1991, a monsoon hit Bangladesh and killed 125,000 people over one weekend—exactly the number of American AIDS casualties to that point. I angrily asked a friend, "Where is the quilt for those who died in Bangladesh? Who will go to Bangladesh and find those names? What privileges the deaths of so many white middle-class gay men?" ACT UP was selfishly selective in what it got angry about.

The government's policy of neglect toward AIDS (not so different from its slow response to service-related chronic diseases and terminal cancers among veterans) may have been preferable to the alternative—identification and quarantine of the infected, which some observers were demanding. Civil liberties won over the public health, an ethically problematic choice that I, as a libertarian, supported. ACT UP's hysteria made me reconsider those vilified therapists and ministers who think change of homosexual orientation is possible and whose meetings are constantly disrupted by gay agitators. Is gay identity so fragile that it cannot bear the thought that some people may not wish to be gay? The difficulties in changing sexual orientation do not spring from its genetic innateness. Sexuality is highly fluid, and reversals are theoretically possible. However, habit is refractory, once the sensory pathways have been blazed and deepened by repetition—a phenomenon obvious in the struggle with obesity, smoking, alcoholism, or drug addiction.

The injustice and impracticality are in trying to "convert" totally from homosexuality to heterosexuality, an opposition I think false. However, helping gays learn how to function heterosexually, if they so wish, is a perfectly worthy aim. We should be honest enough to consider whether homosexuality may not indeed be a pausing at the prepubescent stage when children anxiously band together by gender. Indeed, the instantly recognizable house voice of many gay men—thin, reedy, and pinched—dates from that pre-adult period. But artistic creativity is also a prolonged childhood, as the Romantics first observed. Hence the eternal youthfulness of gay men, their inquisitiveness and *joie de vivre*, so different from the plodding earnestness of lesbians, laboring in yokes of political correctness. When I meet gay men anywhere in the world, there is a spontaneity and a spirit of fun and mischief that lesbians seem incapable of.

A pagan design for living would be a sexual mosaic, a high-contrast Greek-key meander pattern. Gay men should confront the elements of haphazard choice in their erotic history, which began in the confusion, shame, and inarticulateness of childhood. Judeo-Christian morality, following the Bible, would call for a renunciation of all homosexual behavior. I don't agree. Why shouldn't all avenues of pleasure remain open? But it is worthwhile for gays to retrace their developmental steps and, if possible, to investigate and resolve the burden of love-hate they still carry for the opposite-sex parent. Behavior may not change, but self-knowledge—Socrates' motto—is a philosophic value in its own right.

If a gay man wants to marry and sire children, why should he be harassed by gay activists accusing him of "self-hatred"? He is more mature than they are, for he knows woman's power cannot be ignored. And if a married man wants to pursue beautiful young men from time to time, why shouldn't he have the same freedom of sexual self-determination as husbands who patronize whores? Why must he be charged with vacillation or evasion, when his eroticism is the most fully developed? If counseling can allow a gay man to respond sexually to women, it should be encouraged and applauded, not strafed by gay artillery fire of reverse moralism. Heterosexual love, as Hindu symbolism dramatizes, is in sync with cosmic forces. Not everyone has the stomach for daily war with nature.

It is much easier for women to live bisexually, since their erotic performance is not measured by the unforgiving yardstick of erection and ejaculation. Men who shrink from penetration of the female body are paralyzed by justifiable apprehension, since they are returning to our uncanny site of origin. Lingering on the unconscious level in every act of heterosexual intercourse are two male terrors: that when the penis goes in, it won't come out again; and second that as he approaches the womb, a man will, as in a nightmare, be sucked back to boyhood and infancy and be reabsorbed into the maternal body.

These fantasies, detectable in the vampire legends of world mythology, have led me to argue that "misogyny" is one of feminism's more useless ideas. It is not male hatred of women but male *fear* of woman that is the great universal. Gay activists who spout feminist rhetoric are actually the most misogynous, for they love the idea of woman as victim, small, passive, and in need of their help. Such men, of course, are usually helplessly dominated by imposing mothers.

The sexual segregation of gay bars following Stonewall was bad for everyone. The men slid into orgiastic narcissism, and the women entombed themselves in a gigantic burrow, the clogged honeypot of lesbian feminism. I got along well with pre-Stonewall butches, the diesel dykes who had a working-class realism about life. They never whined about the awful patriarchy; most of them liked men, and men liked them—man to man. They were plainspoken, spunky, and self-reliant, with simple military honor. In a crisis, they'd break a beer bottle at the neck and vault over the table to grab a guy by the throat. Today, vapid bourgeois niceties permeate the sorority-house world of white lesbians, even when they doll themselves up in black leather. (As a female ex-lover said disgustedly to me about the San Francisco scene, "I could be more s&m in a *dress!*")

Now that twenty-five years have passed, it's time to admit that lesbian feminism has produced only the ghettoization and miniaturization of women. No great works of art or intellect have emerged from it. On the contrary, it has asphyxiated young women with propaganda and stunted their talent by limiting their vision and constricting their emotions. Women never grow from the moment they enter the lesbian world. Hence one is deafened in bars by the juvenile whooping and hollering of packs of lesbians greeting each other like screeching teens arriving at a slumber party. Gay men as a whole are far more sophisticated in demeanor. In America, gay men brunch—where interesting conversation is a *sine qua non*. Gay women are off planning the next softball match. Music in the men's bars is pumping, pelvic, and sweatily sexual; there is an edge of menace, a darkness or artistic ambiguity. Music in too many women's bars is bland, defanged disco, with a monotonous tick-tock beat ideal for bad dancers. A complex Latin polyrhythm clears the floor. Classic dance tunes, numbingly overplayed, have a chirpy, cheerleading, middlebrow tone.

It is woman's destiny to rule men. Not to serve them, flatter them, or hang on them for guidance. Nor to insult them, demean them, or stereotype them as oppressors. Gay men and artists create a realm marked off from woman's power, but most men require women to center them and connect them to the underworld of emotional truth. When women withdraw from men, as has been done on a massive scale in lesbian feminism, we have a cultural disaster on our hands. In such a situation, men are divided from themselves, and women simply fail to mature. Lesbian feminists, for all their ideals of sisterhood and solidarity, can treat each other with a fickleness, parasitic exploitativeness, and vicious spite that have to be seen to be believed.

One of the most startling discoveries of my career was when I realized that the strongest women in the world are not lesbians but heterosexual women, who know how to handle men. It began with my disillusion with Martina Navratilova, the darling of the lesbian world, who used to symbolize for me the athletic new militance of my generation of feminists. Her rival, Chris Evert, was the nice Catholic girl, the goody-two-shoes whom I loathed, since she was everything we who were reared in the Fifties were expected to be. However, I came to see that Chris is the stronger of the two—that Martina has a childish streak and that that childishness is inextricable from her lesbianism.

At key moments in important matches, Martina would glance up toward the stands and shrug or grin shamefacedly at Judy Nelson, her mature blonde lover, who was nodding and clapping like a hovering kindergarten teacher. It drove me crazy. Why did the premier Amazon of our time need a substitute mother figure? When things went wrong, Martina couldn't conceal her self-pity; the mask of strength would crumble, and she'd storm around the court in a snit. Meanwhile, Chris Evert never threw a tantrum, groused at opponents, or blamed officials. A bad call produced a steely stare, at most. Chris behaved like an adult, taking full responsibility for her performance and deportment.

Classy Chris Evert is a better role model for young women than Martina, whose hyperdeveloped masculine musculature is overcompensation for her creampuff interior. The real butches are straight. Lauren Hutton and rock star Chrissie Hynde, for example, are far tougher chicks than k. d. lang, with her lugubrious singing style and her passé persona of a baby-faced desexed boy (early Wayne Newton). Dealing with and controlling men make you stronger.

Lesbians are mournful sentimentalists, dragging around ancient family baggage. The very worst are the sour political activists, who look like stumpy trolls. Virginia Woolf described the type well in clunky Doris Kilman in *Mrs. Dalloway*. A once-lesbian friend, now married, declared to me that lesbians suffer from "buried rage, with a desperate need for consolation." I see a persistent pattern among white middle-class lesbians: they often have a decorous, passive-aggressive mother, who uses her daughter as a proxy to act out her secret ambivalence toward men, in the person of the never directly confronted husband. Caretakers on the surface, lesbians are seething with unacknowledged hostility that erupts when someone (like me) challenges them. Freud saw hidden anger as the root of depression— the cause, in my view, of so many lesbians' notorious humorlessness. Imagination and creative energy are killed at their source.

Gay men inhabit the bar scene as free radicals, competitive individualists scanning each other, preening, and scuffling for territory. Strangers can walk off the street in any country and enter the fray. Aggressive wit is an instrument of flirtation and seduction. Solitary cruising and pickups do occur among lesbians, but they are not the rule. Lesbian bars are organized in huge kinship groupings, which I identify as family regressions (the usual grass huts). Trying to break into these shifting cliques could drive you mad—unless you join one of their sports leagues. Musical beds is the name of the game. But each person sets up the next affair before she breaks off the last, so there is intricate overlapping, producing endless amounts of what Alison Maddex calls, with exasperation, "lesbian drama from hell." Lushly eroticized push-pull emotion, rather than genital sexuality, is the real heart of lesbianism. It's All About Mom.

Today, when a freshman has an affair with another girl, all the campus social-welfare machinery pushes her toward declaring herself gay and accepting and "celebrating" it. This is a serious mistake. I encourage bisexual experimentation, and I want a world in which people, throughout their lives, freely cross the gender lines in love. But it is absurd to say that one, two, or more homosexual liaisons make you "gay"—as if lavender ink ran in your veins. Young women are often attracted to each other during a transitional period when they are breaking away from their parents, expanding their world-views, and developing their personalities.

To identify these fruitful Sapphic idylls with a permanent condition of homosexuality is madness, and the campus counselors who encourage such premature conclusions should be condemned and banished. They are preying, for their own ideological purposes, on young people at their most vulnerable. I want to cry out to these girls: Stop! Think! Continue to love women, but resolve your problems with men. If you expect to achieve, learn how to live in the real world. Men must be confronted, fairly and honestly. And for heaven's sake, don't fall down the rabbit hole of the lesbian scene. You will never escape, and your talent will wither on the vine. Your energy will be wasted and absorbed in repetition without progression. Women alone are Spenser's Bower of Bliss, enclosed, comfortable, and dangerous.

The hypocrisy of lesbian feminist politics is clear in the increasing use among lesbians, over the past decade, of sex toys and esoteric sex practices. Thanks to advances in industrial plastics, dildos, a staple of ancient pornographic art, now flood what used to be called the "marital aids" market. In the early feminist Seventies, lesbian lovemaking was constrained by taboos: anything echoing heterosexual penetration had to be avoided or disguised. By the Eighties, the

phobic MacKinnon–Dworkin school, which identifies penetration
with violence and exploitation, was ascendant, but there were un-
dercurrents of change. Susie Bright's comic dildo rap in Monika
Treut's hit film, *Virgin Machine* (1988), exposed the liberal new San
Francisco attitude toward sex toys to a national feminist audience.

Here, as in Tantric yoga, we should welcome any ingenious
techniques of pleasure. But what bothers me is that the lesbian dildo
craze stubbornly avoids acknowledging its anatomy-as-destiny implications. Why stop at dildos? If penetration excites, and if receptive
female genitalia are so suited to friction by penis-shaped objects,
why not go on to real penises? Dildos, used for thousands of years
around the world, have always been understood as temporary stop-
gap measures, in the absence of men. Lesbian adoption of dildos
should have been a first step toward a new bisexual awareness in
feminism. Instead, the lines were drawn more firmly. Susie Bright
used her prominence not to reconcile the sexes but to preach
"fisting," a lesbian vaginal version of the notorious (and risky) gay–
male anal practice. Without reconsideration of men as potential sex
partners, such evasive maneuvers are grotesque.

Because women have no external gauge of arousal, the erect
penis is, and will remain, the ultimate symbol of human sexual
desire. Its massive use in Hindu iconography descends from ancient
fertility cults. Any woman, gay or straight, who cannot respond to
penises or who finds them hideous or laughable (a puerile theme in
the stage acts of lesbian comedians like Robin Tyler and Lea Delaria)
has been traumatized by some early experience. She is neither complete as a woman nor healthy as a person. We can no longer allow,
without protest, obsessives and neurotics to preach a mutilated
brand of feminism to trusting young women. Here is where pornography plays a crucial cultural role, for at its raunchiest it shows
the penis in all its fascinating erotic modalities.

Lesbians who use dildos but shun penises must start admitting
that they operate sexually not just *for* women but *against* men. Probably because of the maternal embraces of nursing and childcare, a
greater, caressing physicality is permitted among women in virtually
every culture. Thus lesbianism, with its diffuse tactility, is always
less threatening than male homosexuality, which involves legitimate
issues of manhood and masculinity. Women are biologically and

psychologically more flexible than men, whom nature coldly confines to a narrow instrumentality.

Sexual attraction may begin visually, but it is essentially an animal interaction of pheromones, the hormonal sex chemicals exuded in sweat and urine which act on us subliminally. Those exclusively homosexual as adults are signaling an aversion to the smell of the opposite-sex parent. For lesbians, women's sweet smell and cushiony contours are a euphoric return to a lost maternal union. The same smell and sensations strike gay men as cloying and claustrophobic. Men's sharper, testosterone-based body odor seems aggressively unsettling to lesbians, who associate it with invasion of maternal turf by a rival who is known by words rather than touch and who represents harsh external judgment. (We did not need Lacan to tell us about the father as "law"; it's everywhere in Western literature from Aeschylus' *Oresteia* to Virginia Woolf's *To the Lighthouse*.)

Hence the roots of male homosexuality go back further than those of lesbianism, whose unarticulated resentment toward social order may explain its later vulnerability to philanthropic ideology. Lesbians, said a lesbian friend wearily to me, are "program heads": "They need the structure. They have all the answers." Hence lesbians' omnipresence in the social-welfare industry. Rejecting the father's competitive system, they substitute another that they imagine is based on female "caring" and "compassion" but is, in dismal effect, repressive, totalitarian, and hostile to art and dissent. The same friend memorably said to me long ago that lesbianism is caused by either "too much tit or not enough."

The case of lesbianism demonstrates that sexual desire, which has moved to the foreground of modern life and dominates our pagan popular culture, now incorporates many longings that are beyond the physical. Visiting the elite schools on my lecture jaunts, I am struck by how the most militantly gay, Foucault-addled male students look like orphans, with 12-year-old Huck Finn clothing styles and haunted, starved eyes. They are spiritually unfathered. My friends Robert Caserio and Kristoffer Jacobson call them "lesboyans"—scrubbed, arrogant clones with bright, shallow smiles who mouth political clichés but whose sexual imaginations are completely undeveloped. Caserio says, "Queer theory insulates them from reality." This is one reason why gay studies, in its current separatist form, must be opposed. Cultivated, cosmopolitan, pre-Stonewall gay men like Gore Vidal were the real revolutionaries. They lived in the world and accepted and advanced cultural history, the heritage of gay and straight alike.

The unhappy truth is that male homosexuality will never be fully accepted by the heterosexual majority, who are obeying the dictates not of "bigoted" society or religion but of procreative nature. All of us emerge from the body of a mystical female giant. Boys are swamped in the female realm. Note how mothers take male children into the women's toilets: the boys are officially neuter and still part of the mother's body. To progress into manhood, boys must leave the women's world behind. In tribal cultures, men may kidnap a boy, slash his body with knives, throw him into a pit, or abandon him in the woods, cruel rites of passage still evident in the brutal, sometimes homicidal hazing of modern fraternities, which flourishes despite every effort to ban it. How many women students fall to their death while walking, drunk, on a balcony railing during Florida spring fling, or drown, stunned by a rock, when they dive off a cliff into a quarry at midnight?—an actual incident at Bennington, which killed one of my most attractive male students. Testing is integral to masculine development. The old epithets "mama's boy" and "sissy" (i.e., "sister") still harbor psychological truth.

At the transition to manhood, most boys pass through a homophobic stage, where "gay" is a term of contempt (applied indiscriminately today to anything uncool) and where recreational gaybashing may be a criminal means of group self-affirmation. Because boys lack a biological marker like menstruation, to be a man is to be *not female*. Contemporary feminism called this "misogyny," but it was wrong. Masculine identity is embattled and fragile. In the absence of opportunity for heroic physical action, as in the modern office world, women's goodwill is crucial for preserving the male ego, which requires, alas, daily maintenance. It is in the best interests of the human race, and of women themselves, for men to be strong. Inspired by my Italian heritage, with its blazingly assertive personae, I call for strong men and strong women, not strong women and castrated men. Hot sex and healthy children cannot be produced by eunuchs. Women, the stronger sex from birth to death, better get their priorities straight. Male swagger is erotic.

Unfortunately for the gay cause, hostility toward, or discomfort with, male homosexuality is built into this dynamic. Paradoxically, gay men themselves understand the arrogant imperviousness of heterosexual masculinity, since its steely forms dominate their erotic iconography. Male homosexuality may therefore be inherently tragic, for it posits as glamourous perfection precisely what most loathes it and cancels it out. From this agonizing and irresolvable contradiction came some of our greatest art, such as that of Donatello, Botticelli, and Michelangelo. When feminism tries to eliminate or severely revise historical standards of masculinity without honoring what they have stood for, both men and women drift farther from secure identity. That the masculine, which exists only in moments of assertion, is condemned to transience does not diminish its beauty or glory as an ideal.

Gay activism has been naive in its belligerent confidence that "homophobia" will eventually disappear, with proper "education" of the benighted. Reeducation of fractious young boys on the scale required would mean fascist obliteration of all individual freedoms. Furthermore, no truly masculine father will ever welcome a feminine or artistic son *at the start,* since the son's lack of virility not only threatens but liquidates that father's identity, dissolving husband into wife. Later there may be public rituals of acceptance, but the damage will already have been done. Gay men are aliens, cursed and gifted, the shamans of our time.

Gays must demand not to be physically harassed, but they have no more claim to legal protection than any other group of citizens, large or small. I oppose the concept of "hate crimes": as a libertarian, I am suspicious of government inquiries into psychological motivation, except when fixing length of sentence after criminal conviction. Democracies should not be burdened with excess legislation, and Big Brother should stay out of our souls. "Hate crimes," currently applied on sometimes shaky evidence to racial, ethnic, or sexual incidents, would also describe the feuding of Hatfields and McCoys, the shootouts of urban street gangs, rioting among British soccer fans, or any violent dispute among family members or neighbors. Why wasn't it a hate crime when two brothers shotgunned their affluent parents while watching TV, or when a woman severed her sleeping husband's penis, or when a skater tried to cripple her rival? The term has simply become a stalking horse for sentimental liberalism and should be dropped.

The worst misjudgments of gay activism were on view during its botched campaign to end the ban on gays in the military. Before and after the inauguration of Bill Clinton, a pontificating parade of self-appointed gay leaders marshaled a series of men and women whose military service had been terminated because of homosexuality. My position is that no institution may control what one does in one's free time and that gays therefore have every right to join and be promoted in the military. But gay activists, in pushing their agenda, told lie after lie. The television camera was not kind to the gay leaders or their martyred male servicemen. The former seemed shifty and weasely, and the latter strangely childish and undeveloped. Pictures of plaintiff gay soldiers with big, frightened, rabbity eyes gave new life to the idea that gay men are not as masculine as others. We were being lectured about sameness, but what we saw was difference. The gay establishment, cocooned in conceit, never caught or corrected this costly public relations error.

The biggest activist lie was the claim that openly gay soldiers would not disrupt military cohesion. Of course they would, and it should have been admitted. But commanding officers must restore unit discipline, at home or abroad. Again, I question special protections of gays; if they choose to reveal their sexual preference, they are not entitled to greater consideration than anyone else. Until America gets a more sophisticated sense of sexuality, in the decadent European style, young heterosexual men will never serve comfortably with gay men in close quarters. Hostility and rejection are inevitable and may have to be tolerated, as long as professionalism of the mission is maintained. Given the probable permanence of the homophobic stage in male development, open homosexuality in the military, even if officially permitted, will remain risky.

It is ridiculous to assert that gay men are interested only in other gay men and would never ogle straight men in barracks showers. When I heard this on TV, I burst out laughing. Anyone who belongs to a health club knows better. Sexual tension and appraisal are constants, above all among gay men, who never stop cruising everything in sight. Seduction of straight studs is a highly erotic motif in gay porn. The problem with the gay–activist position is that, for philosophic consistency, it should have argued for integration of male and female military quarters, like college dormitories. Continued segregation by gender makes no sense, if the cohabitation of gays with straights is really so benign. Everyone should be free to ogle everyone else, as long as looks don't cross over to touch. Similarly, everyone should be free to insult everyone else, as long as words don't escalate into violence.

While they force themselves into public schools, demanding curricular representation and free condom distribution (both of which I oppose as a deformation of education), most gay activists have shown very little courage in dealing with pedophilia, which they dismiss as a hoary libel by religious fundamentalists. Man-boy love is perfectly obvious in the pagan homoerotic art tradition, from Greek sculpture to Donatello and Caravaggio and late nineteenth-century poetry. NAMBLA (the North American Man-Boy Love Association) is consistently banned from gay marches and events. The narrow political focus of gay activism prevented it from addressing larger questions about sexuality. Pedophilia, for example, is yet another indicator of sexual difference, since it applies only to gay men, never lesbians. By keeping NAMBLA at arm's length, activists apparently think they can broaden their acceptability and sell their agenda, which includes a preposterous demand for openly gay Boy Scout leaders. (What would feminists say about grown men dying to take pubescent Girl Scouts on hikes, sleep-overs and camp-outs?)

Public hysteria has made objective discussion of this subject very difficult. I was nearly lynched by a furious audience on a television talk show in 1992, when the host asked me about my defense of man-boy love in *Sexual Personae*. I have no erotic interest in children, but I protest the thought-blocking and context-blind value judgments inherent in automatically referring to every adult-juvenile physical encounter as "abuse," "molestation," or "assault." There are certainly atrocious incidents of genuine rape, which we must condemn. But in some cases the contact is actually initiated by the youth; in others, the relationship may be a positive one, but of course one never hears about it, since the affair doesn't end up in court. Loaded terminology is self-defeating, since it coarsens distinctions and prevents us from recognizing authentic abuse when it occurs.

In *Sex and Destiny* (1984), Germaine Greer documents the far freer sensuous physicality of adults with children in non-Western cultures but unfortunately stops short of my conclusions. The moment was right for a searching critique of our priggish sexual assumptions in this area, which have been institutionalized by a banal social-welfare bureaucracy. I have been thanked for my views by many men, by letter and in person after lectures, because of their own adolescent liaisons with supportive adults. At Bennington, I became aware (when Polaroid photos of a kneeling boy's golden genitals fell out of a book) of a private connection between a genial aging male poet and a good-looking local youth in his early teens. It was against the law, but I saw nothing wrong with it.

The problem is in trying to define the cutoff point, where coercion is incontrovertible. Sex with an infant certainly falls into this category. But our present age of consent is far too high and treats adolescents as an enslaved class owned by their parents. Who is to say whether or not a juvenile is capable of informed choice? When does protection of children become oppression? Does anyone really believe that Jocy Buttafuoco, convicted of statutory rape of a minor (the Long Island shark goddess, Amy Fisher), took advantage of a helpless child? Because of the incest taboo, most people cannot admit how the pagan conventions of Baroque putti and Valentine's Day Cupids represent an eroticization of fleshy infant bodies. My position on child pornography is that no images, if drawn, painted, or sculpted, may be banned. As for the use of actual children in erotic photographs and videos, some restriction may seem reasonable, given our modern repugnance to child labor, but there is no easy answer, since government is notoriously unable to discriminate among kinds of art.

The damage from many pedophiliac encounters probably comes, as some psychologists suggest, less from the contact itself than from the culturally enforced stress and secrecy surrounding it. In a recent scandal in New Jersey, a seventy-seven-year-old man was arrested after years of visitations by droves of teenaged boys, who permitted mild physical liberties in exchange for money, liquor, and drugs. Neighbors reported boys scaling the wall of the senior-citizens apartment building at all hours of the night. Aside from the public disturbance, why shouldn't both parties in this case be free to make such a voluntary commercial transaction? Why shouldn't a juvenile have the right to dispose of his body as he wishes? At this time, I favor lowering the age of consent to fourteen.

Our hypocrisy about pedophilia has simply forced the problem into the Third World, to which Westerners go for sun-and-sex vacations with underage boys. That economic exploitation will not end until our strict Judeo-Christian position is challenged by a more liberal pagan one. In the Anglo-American world, there is an endless postponement of adulthood, which the Catholic Church once dated from age seven. In pre-industrial rural life, where children went to work young, sexual maturity was defined by internal natural processes. We need to reexamine the way bourgeois values of professional job readiness, which have so distorted male-female relations, have also curtailed the sexual freedom and self-determination of the young.

Homosexuality is *necessary* now to heal the fissures in the Western psyche, in this period following the industrial revolution. But is homosexuality a permanent solution to the problems of the nuclear family? Do we want the sexes forever divorced, in a state of perpetual alienation? Middle-class men, neutered by office life and daunted by feminist rhetoric, are shrinking. Lesbianism is increasing, since anxious, unmasculine men have little to offer. Women are simply more interesting. Male homosexuality is increasing, because masculinity is in crisis and because maternal consciousness, severed from the support network of the extended family, has become a psychotic system, forcing the young to struggle for life against clinging parental fantasy.

Current gay cant insists that homosexuality is "not a choice," that no one would choose to be gay in a homophobic society. But there *is* an element of choice in all behavior, sexual or otherwise. It takes an effort to deal with the opposite sex; it's safer with your own kind. The issue is one of challenge versus comfort. In the modern world, homosexuality has become a self-perpetuating lifestyle. The more its practitioners have become preoccupied with self-definition, the less meaningful that definition is, since it is predicated on provincialism and tautology.

Homosexuality as erotic expression has to be liberated from gay activism, which systematically oversimplifies issues or evades their implications. Instead of arguing for legal recognition of gay marriages, for example, it should have attacked the favored economic status given to marriage at all, a position more consistent with antibourgeois Sixties radicalism. Ceremonies of commitment do fill a psychological need and bind the larger community together; domestic-partner legislation benefits heterosexuals as well. But if gay marriages are permitted (a prerogative of the most decadent Roman emperors), why not polygamy?—a pagan and early Hebrew practice later banned by Judeo-Christianity. We should also beware of the potentially pernicious intermingling of gay activism with science, which produces more propaganda than truth. Gay scientists must be scientists first, gays second.

Midway through the AIDS epidemic, the media, having ignored homosexuality or treated it in a lurid manner, did a quick flip-flop under activist pressure and now continues its policy of unthinking cant by parroting the gay-establishment party line on every occasion. Like Elizabethan Papists or seventeenth-century French Jesuits, gay activists have earned a reputation as conspirators and casuists, because of their amoral tactics of deceit, defamation, intimidation, and extortion. By politicizing homosexuality and isolating it from the continuum of human life, they have managed to make it pathological again.

Policed by gay censors, the cultural debate over homosexuality has been stifled, to the spiritual detriment of gays themselves. For example, the Christian Fundamentalist charge that AIDS is "God's punishment" was summarily rejected twenty years ago and never adequately dealt with, so that it remains, unanswered and alive as ever. There *was* a cause and effect connection between promiscuity and the epidemic, as well as an "Après moi, le déluge" attitude on the part of many gays. Self-questioning is crucial.

The conservative moral argument, positing a guilt that had to be expiated, was closer to the truth than the left's callow shunting off of blame onto negligent social authorities. The gay activist obsession with condom distribution (as if condoms were 100 percent effective) is a displacement of anxiety from the real horror of AIDS: that men are carrying poisoned semen in their scrotums. As in the Theban plague of *Oedipus Rex,* there is a blight on the seed: the heart of nature has been contaminated. If we reject the extreme Christian reading of the epidemic, as I do, then we must offer new metaphors, a mythopoetic pagan alternative. Our inner turbulence must be acknowledged and addressed. In the collective unconscious, gay and straight suffer together.

6. CONCLUSION: CITIZENS OF THE EMPIRE

As America's pagan popular culture expands around the world, and as multicultural influences flow back and are absorbed by us in turn, we have re-created the polyglot complexity of the Roman empire at its height. We should accept the imperial model of moral dichotomy, the state of perpetual tension between the sober virtues of the republican past and the luxury and decadence of the present. Opposition, rather than approval, produces the sculptural carving out of selfhood.

Creative duality is my master principle. We must belong simultaneously to the mainstream culture and to our ever-receding ethnic origins. Imperialism may begin as a system of unilateral domination, but it ends as artistic and intellectual cosmopolitanism, revolutionary in its own right. In today's global existence, the alternative to imperialism is not unconditional freedom but tribalism, fractious and fragmented.

In sexual and racial matters, the parochial tribal entity is now "identity politics," a barricaded secessionism that is a spiritual dead end. Hostile respect, rather than pluralism, may be the best we can hope for. The new extended family, no longer linked by blood, will be both patriotic and internationalist, preserving history without being trapped by it.

Imperial sexuality, typified by the syncretism of the Mediterranean goddess cults, was grounded in both civilization and nature. In practice, this means that while homosexuality is a brave and necessary drive for male autonomy, gay men must render unto Cybele the things that are Cybele's. And women, in rightly seizing social power, must not neglect what they owe to, and need from, the ancient rites of phallicism.

I see the dynamic of history as an oscillation between Apollonian and Dionysian principles, order and energy, which become, at their extremes, fascism or chaos. In sexual terms, this promises eternal conflict between repression and debauchery. We must learn how to make tiny corrections to avoid the uncontrolled swing of the pendulum that, over a generation, swept us from Fifties conformism to Sixties rebellion to Seventies excess and the cataclysm of AIDS. We now live with the smell of funeral pyres.

Dual vision allows us to hail the epochal liberation of the senses in post-Stonewall gay culture and at the same time to acknowledge its massive destructiveness. There has been a contemptible failure by gay leaders to admit the slightest moral responsibility for the enormous part the gay community played, helped by jet travel, in the rapid spread of AIDS throughout the world. That the harm was not intentional makes the gay role all the more tragic, in the original Greek sense. The Stonewall victory was in many ways Pyrrhic.

The fatalism of imperial philosophy gives death a simple, secular dignity. Life is dust to dust, without the trick ending of salvation. Hit plays and films of the moment use mawkish Victorian sentimentality to present AIDS sufferers as noble victims whose only problem is lack of acceptance and love from society. But gay men challenged nature and lost. What is "safe sex" but a return to the normative?—as dictated by tyrant nature. Promiscuity is a pagan choice, but then be prepared to pay the price. Of short, intense Romantic lives, represented in our time by gay men and rock stars, it can be said (revising a famous motto of the American Revolution), "Live free and die!"

My model of dualism is the drag queen, who negotiates between sexual personae, day by day. I sometimes call my system "drag queen feminism." Queens are "fierce," in every sense. Masters of aggressive, bawdy speech, they know the street and its dangers and fight it out without running to authority figures, who would hardly be sympathetic. Queens, unlike feminists, know that woman is dominatrix of the universe. They take on supernatural energy when ritualistically donning their opulent costume, the historical regalia of woman's power. Prostitute and drag queen are sexual warriors who offer a pagan challenge to bourgeois gentility, now stultifying modern life from corporate boardrooms to academia to suburban shopping malls.

Bisexuality is our best hope of escape from the animosities and false polarities of the current sex wars. Whether or not we can put it into practice, bisexuality is a great pagan ideal. Perhaps bisexual *responsiveness* is all we can hope for. Indeed, that is the lesson of art history, which exposes us to the many ravishing forms of human beauty. The homosexual Botticelli produced, in *The Birth of Venus*, one of the most sublime images of the power of woman. And Michelangelo, adorning the Sistine Chapel with twenty homoerotic *ignudi* (nude Greek youths), made the most radical statement yet of the enduring duality of pagan and Christian in our culture.

A pagan education would sharpen the mind, steel the will, and seduce the senses. Our philosophy should be both contemplative and pugilistic, admitting aggression (as Christianity does not) as central to our mythology. The beasts of passion must be confronted, and the laws of nature understood. Conflict cannot be avoided, but perhaps it can be confined to a mental theater. In the imperial arena, there is no law but imagination.

THE CULTURE

WARS

THE NURSERY-SCHOOL CAMPUS:
THE CORRUPTING OF THE
HUMANITIES IN THE U.S.

Is there intellectual life in America? At present, the answer is no. Since the decline of the great era of literary journalism, when Edmund Wilson, the Algonquin wits, and the politically engaged *Partisan Review* writers were active, America has lacked a general literate culture hospitable to ideas. Mary McCarthy went off to Paris, and Susan Sontag, after half-a-dozen promising years, withdrew into French preciosity and irrelevance. When she was attacked for her laudable interest in pop culture, Sontag dropped it like a hot potato and has never since regained the status she enjoyed in the 1960s.

During that decade, a vital artistic and intellectual consciousness was taking shape. Passionate, prophetic voices, heirs to the visionary tradition of Emerson, Whitman, and Hart Crane, spoke in the central works of Allen Ginsberg, Norman O. Brown, and Leslie Fiedler, but they had few successors. The actual achievements of 1960s thinkers were few and limited, and the line of continuity was broken.

America's current intellectual crisis originates in the tragic loss of the boldest and most innovative members of the 1960s generation. Drugs may have expanded the mind, but they arrested its long-term

[*Times Literary Supplement,* London, May 22, 1992]

productivity, whose promise was glimpsed in the so-called "psychedelic" phase of rock music.

The students most affected by the Sixties did not as a rule enter the professions, whose stultifying rules for advancement have remained unchanged for fifty years. Instead, they surrendered their places to less talented contemporaries, careerists in the dull, timid Fifties style.

Nowhere was this truer than in academia. The effect upon American universities of the student rebellions was fleeting. Genuine radicals did not go on to graduate school. If they did, they soon dropped out, or were later defeated by the faculty recruitment and promotion process, which rewards conformism and sycophancy. The universities were abandoned to the time-servers and mercenaries who now hold many of the senior positions there. Ideas had been relegated to the universities, but the universities belonged to the drudges.

There is a widespread notion that these people are dangerous leftists, "tenured radicals" in Roger Kimball's phrase, who have invaded the American establishment with subversive ideas. In fact, they are not radicals at all. Authentic leftism is nowhere to be seen in our major universities. The "multiculturalists" and the "politically correct" on the subjects of race, class, and gender actually represent a continuation of the genteel tradition of respectability and conformity. They have institutionalized American *niceness*, which seeks, above all, not to offend and must therefore pretend not to notice any differences or distinctions among people or cultures.

The politically correct professors, with their hostility to the "canon" of great European writers and artists, have done serious damage to the quality of undergraduate education at the best American colleges and universities. Yet they are people without deep beliefs. Real radicals stand for something and risk something; these academics are very pampered fat cats who have never stood on principle at any point in their careers. Nothing has happened to them in their lives. They never went to war; they were never out of work or broke. They have no experience or knowledge of anything outside the university, least of all working-class life. Their politics are a trendy tissue of sentimental fantasy and unsupported verbal categories. Guilt over their own privilege has frozen their political discourse into a simplistic world melodrama of privilege versus deprivation.

Intellectual debate in the humanities has also suffered because of the narrowness of training of those who emerged from the over-departmentalized and overspecialized universities of the postwar period. The New Criticism, casting off the old historicism of German philology, produced a generation of academics trained to think of literature as largely detached from historical context. This was ideal breeding ground for French theory, a Saussurean paradigm dating from the 1940s and '50s that was already long *passé* when American academics got hold of it in the early 1970s. French theory, far from being a symbol of the 1960s, was on the contrary a useful defensive strategy for well-positioned, pedantic professors actively resisting the ethnic and cultural revolution of that subversive decade. Foucault, a glib game-player who took very little research a very long way, was especially attractive to literary academics in search of a short cut to understanding world history, anthropology and political economy.

The 1960s failed, I believe, partly because of unclear thinking about institutions, which it portrayed in dark, conspiratorial, Kafkacsque terms. The positive role of institutions in economically complex societies was neglected. The vast capitalist distribution network is so efficient in America that it is invisible to our affluent, middle-class humanists. Capitalism's contribution to the emergence of modern individualism, and therefore feminism, has been blindly suppressed. This snide ahistoricism is the norm these days in women's studies programs and chi-chi, Foucault-afflicted literature departments. Leftists have damaged their own cause, with whose basic principles I as a 1960s libertarian generally agree, by their indifference to fact, their carelessness and sloth, their unforgivable lack of professionalism as scholars. The Sixties world-view, which integrated both nature and culture, has degenerated into clamorous, competitive special-interest groups.

The universities led the way by creating a ghetto of black studies, which begat women's studies, which in turn begat gay studies. Not one of these makeshift, would-be disciplines has shown itself capable of re-creating the broad humane picture of Sixties thought. Each has simply made up its own rules and fostered its own selfish clientele, who have created a closed system in which scholarship is inseparable from politics. It is, indeed, questionable whether or not the best interests of blacks, women, and gays have been served by these political fiefdoms. The evidence about women's studies suggests the opposite: that these programs have hatched the new thought police of political correctness. No conservative presently in or out of government has the power of intimidation wielded by these ruthless forces. The silencing of minority opinion has been systematic in faculty recruitment and promotion. The winners of that rat-race seem genuinely baffled by such charges, since, of course, their conventional, fashionable opinions have never been stifled.

While lecturing at major American universities this year, I have come into direct conflict with the politically correct establishment. At Harvard and elsewhere I was boycotted by the feminist faculty, and at several colleges leaflets were distributed, inaccurately denouncing me as a voice of the far right. Following my lecture at Brown, I was screamed at by soft, inexperienced, but seethingly neurotic middle-class white girls, whose feminist party-line views on rape I have rejected in my writings. Rational discourse is not possible in an atmosphere of such mob derangement.

Sociologically, the roots of the campus crisis can be found in the rapid expansion of the college-going population in America in the decades following the Second World War. After the "baby-boomers," the post-war demographic bulge, passed through, colleges were forced to retrench, and they turned to aggressive marketing strategies to maintain enrollment. As costs continued to rise, they were locked into a strictly commercial relationship with parents. Intellectual matters soon took a back seat to the main issue: providing a "nice time" for students with paying parents.

By the early 1970s, American universities had become top-heavy with full-time administrators who took to speaking of the campus as a "community," which, faculty soon discovered, was governed by invisible codes of acceptable speech, opinions, and behavior. In the past fifteen years, some of these administrators, especially Student Life deans and the freshmen orientation staff, have forged a disquieting alliance with women's studies programs, and are indoctrinating their charges with the latest politically correct attitudes on dating, sexual preference, and so on. Many of the students, neglected by their prosperous, professional parents, are pathetically grateful for these attentions. Such coddling has led, in my view, to the outrageous speech codes which are designed to shield students from the realities of life. The campus is now not an arena of ideas but a nursery school where adulthood can be indefinitely postponed. Faculty who are committed to the great principle of free speech are therefore at war with paternalistic administrators in league with misguided parents.

In the summer-camp mentality of American universities, the ferocity of genuine intellectual debate would just seem like spoiling everyone's fun. Ambitious humanities professors go about their business behind a brick wall of "theory," which they imagine is the *dernier cri,* but which has long been out of fashion, even in Paris. Drab, uncultivated philistines, without broad knowledge of the arts, have seized the top jobs in the Ivy League, simply because they have the right opinions and know the right people. In the past twenty years, conferences became the infernal engine driving the academic profession. The conference crowd, an international party circuit of literary luminaries ever on the move, was put together by the new humanities centers. These programs had the initially laudable aim of fostering interdisciplinary exchanges outside the repressive framework of the conservative, static and over-tenured university departments. But the epidemic of French theory was abroad in the world. The humanities centers quickly became careerist stockyards, where greedy speculation and insider trading were as much the rules of the game as on Wall Street.

Quieter, more traditional academics were outmaneuvered by the conference crowd, and scholarship was the victim. The humanities centers are now controlled by small, amoral cadres that are intricately intertwined with each other nationally by cronyism, favoritism, patronage and collusion It is essential for American intellectual life that they be brought under scrutiny. And, indeed, that is beginning to happen: in April, a prominent woman scholar filed a lawsuit against the Massachusetts Institute of Technology for tolerating an internal *putsch* by a cabal of politically correct faculty members with close ties to the cultural studies center at Harvard University.

The solution to the present dilemma is for academic liberals to speak out against the rampant corruption of their profession. The reform of education is too often being left to the neoconservatives these days. My own proposals for reform include the abolition of all literary conferences and the replacement of women's studies with sex studies, based on the rigorous study of world history, anthropology, psychology, and science. Today, in politically correct America, questions of quality, learning, and intellectual distinction are out of style.

GAY STALINISM

HAS THE GAY PRESS BEEN UNFAIR

TO CAMILLE PAGLIA?

Not all the gay press has been hostile. My X-rated book received
warm attention in gay publications from San Francisco to London.
But the scourge of political correctness is clearest in my own city:
neither of the Philadelphia gay newspapers has mentioned my name
in the two years since *Sexual Personae* was published.

Strident, repressive gay activists persistently distort my views.
For example, an article in *The Advocate* ["The Newsroom Becomes
a Battleground," Issue 603] claimed that I had called lesbians "pathological"—a flat-out lie. I am compared to Nazis and denounced
as a "neoconservative"—a ridiculous label for someone who publicly
defends pornography, prostitution, homosexuality, transvestism,
and sadomasochism. I am constantly called "homophobic," despite
the fact that I spent most of my adult life as an open lesbian and
paid my dues for it. My militancy and general obnoxiousness preceded both the present women's movement and Stonewall. I will
match my credentials as an Amazon and feminist pioneer against
those of my boring, lockstep critics any day.

I hate dogma in any form. I hated it in the Catholic Church
and Girl Scout troops of the 1950s, and I hate it in gay activism

[*The Advocate*, September 22, 1992]

and established feminism today. We must no longer tolerate narrow, rigid thinking, pious clichés, and humorless party-line rhetoric. What attracted me to gay men in college in the 1960s was their fierce independence of mind, their whiplash tongues, and their scorn for bourgeois decorum, saccharine sentimentality, and empty ideology. They came from ordinary middle-class homes in the suburbs or the Midwest, yet they had taste, distinction, and style—a sense of beauty that I believe is innate and surely connected with the artistic gene.

Gay men saw movies, television, art, opera, and fashion in a new way—learned, enthusiastic, and brilliantly imaginative. And they integrated sex with culture: they were bawdy, lewd, and adventurous—at home on the dangerous midnight streets.

This bold, cultivated cosmopolitan sensibility is still alive in many gay men, but you would never know it from the gay press, whose political commentary too often smacks of wheel-spinning Stalinist hackwork. How did it get this bad? One can't keep blaming AIDS, since feminism had already sunk chin-deep into mindless propaganda before the epidemic started. I think the Stonewall rebellion, a central event in cultural history, had one unfortunate effect: Gay liberation also led to sexual segregation, which has been disastrous for both men and women.

In the pre-Stonewall period, the few discreet, shabby gay bars outside major cities usually mixed the sexes. After Stonewall, the men's bars exploded in number and luxury. I vividly remember when the doors of the men's bars closed in my face. It was 1974, the dawn of the orgy-room and bathhouse era. Strange parasitic diseases soon began appearing, and by 1981 a "gay cancer" was identified as AIDS. The price of the Sixties sexual revolution, which I supported, was paid by gay men. We must honestly admit that gay men's attempt to create a world without women failed catastrophically. Pre-Stonewall gays revered goddesslike female stars, while the post-Stonewall scene went macho clone. The female principle was lost.

Lesbian feminism of the last twenty years also suffered, with its mushy do-gooder anti-art egalitarianism and its adolescent antimale petulance. I tend to get along with pre-Stonewall lesbians, who are

refreshingly free of political sloganeering. It is no coincidence that
the only intelligent feminist review of *Sexual Personae* was by Lillian
Faderman or that when I recently met comedian Robin Tyler in
London, we instantly seemed to speak the same language of brass-
balls individualism. There is an insurgent protest movement of lesbians fed up with the dreariness and sex phobia of the old guard,
but it's still marginal. Susie Bright and Pat Califia, with all their
many virtues, have not produced work of intellectual weight equal
to that of the puritanical Catharine MacKinnon.

My first proposal for the gay world: Get rid of dead abstract
"theory" and rabid social constructionism, the limp legacy of academic know-nothings. The Sixties were about nature, in the Romantic way. You cannot understand sex or AIDS until you
reacquaint yourself with nature and its dark mysteries. Our guide
should be not the frigid, head-tripping nerd Michel Foucault but
prophetic Allen Ginsberg, who fused Hinduism with Walt Whitman to give us a radical vision of energy, passion, and sensuality—of homosexual desire grounded in the amoral rhythms of
nature.

Next, get rid of victimology and oppression politics. The real
revolution will come when we are free of the false dichotomy of gay/
straight and when bisexual responsiveness is accepted as the universal norm. Finally, reposition AIDS in the philosophical context
of world history. Fanatical ranting rage, the favorite face of ACT
UP, is infantile. Martin Luther King learned from Gandhi how to
make the sufferings of your people the sufferings of all humanity.
You do not invade or insult churches; you do not silence dissent or
smear as "bigots" people who oppose your practices on religious
grounds. Gay activism has got to get off its knee-jerk oppositional
mode and into an affirmative articulation of first principles, which
in my view have to be based on pagan pansexuality, a complex,
reasoned alternative to Judeo-Christian ethics.

[*Afterword:* Just before this article went to the printer, the headline
was sabotaged in the *Advocate* offices to read: "Camille Paglia Defends
Her Rotten Record." The editors launched an investigation and
apologized. In an indignant letter to the editor (Oct. 6), Paglia

stated: "Incidents like this prove my point: smug, juvenile political correctness is strangling free speech in too much of the gay and feminist world. I invite others to join my campaign against the Stalinists among us." The reference to Robin Tyler also caused controversy: see the index.]

THE RETURN OF CARRY NATION:
CATHARINE MACKINNON AND
ANDREA DWORKIN

I am a pornographer. From earliest childhood, I saw sex suffusing the world. I felt the rhythms of nature and the aggressive energies of animal life. Art objects, in both museum and church, seemed to blaze with sensual beauty. The authority figures of church, school, and family denied or suppressed what I saw, but like Madonna, I kept to my pagan vision. I belong to the Sixties generation that tried and failed to shatter all sexual norms and taboos. In my book, *Sexual Personae*, I injected lewdness, voyeurism, homoeroticism and sadomasochism into the entire Western high-art tradition.

Because I am a pornographer, I am at war with Catharine MacKinnon and Andrea Dworkin. These obsessed, moralistic women, feminism's oddest odd couple, are Carry Nation reborn. They were co-authors of the Minneapolis and Indianapolis ordinances against pornography that were declared unconstitutional. They have produced, individually and in collaboration, an enormous amount of material ranging from tortured autobiographical confessions to legal case histories and academic Marxist critiques.

MacKinnon was among the first to argue for the establishment

[*Playboy*, October 1992]

of sexual harassment as a legal category. But her positive contributions to women's issues must be weighed against the responsibility she bears for fomenting the crazed sexual hysteria that now grips American feminism. Date rape has swelled into a catastrophic cosmic event, like an asteroid threatening the earth in a Fifties science-fiction film. Anita Hill, a competent but priggish, self-interested yuppie, has been canonized as a virgin martyr ruined by the depraved emperor—who never laid a hand on her.

MacKinnon is a totalitarian. She wants a risk-free, state-controlled world. She believes rules and regulations will solve every human ill and straighten out all those irksome problems between the sexes that have been going on for five thousand years. As a lawyer, MacKinnon is deft and pragmatic. But as a political thinker, cultural historian, or commentator on sex, she is incompetent. For a woman of her obvious intelligence, her frame of reference is shockingly small. She has the dull instincts and tastes of a bureaucrat. It's all work and no play in MacKinnon Land. Literature, art, music, film, television—nothing intrudes on MacKinnon's consciousness unless it has been filtered through feminism, which has taught her, she likes to say, "everything I know." There's the rub. She is someone who, because of her own private emotional turmoil, locked on to Seventies-era feminism and never let go.

MacKinnon has a cold, inflexible, and fundamentally unscholarly mind. She is a propagandist and casuist, good at constructing ad hoc arguments from expedience for specific political aims. But her knowledge of intellectual or world history is limited, and as a researcher she has remarkably poor judgment in evaluating sources. She wildly overpraises weak feminist writers and has no feeling whatever for psychology, a defect that makes her conclusions about sex ridiculous. She is a Stalinist who believes that art must serve a political agenda and that all opposing voices are enemies of humanity who must be silenced. MacKinnon and Dworkin are fanatics, zealots, fundamentalists of the new feminist religion. Their alliance with the reactionary, antiporn far right is no coincidence.

MacKinnon is a classic WASP who painstakingly builds huge, rigid structures of words in complete obliviousness to the organic, sensual, and visual. She is a twentieth-century puritan whose upbringing—a stern Minnesota judge as father, Episcopalian and conservative Republican—seems straight out of Hawthorne. MacKinnon's pinched, cramped, body-denying Protestant culture made her peculiarly susceptible to Andrea Dworkin, whose let-it-all-hang-out ethnicity was initially liberating. MacKinnon's stolid lack of psychology drew her to Dworkin's boiling emotionalism and self-analytic, self-lacerating Jewishness. In return, MacKinnon, the third-generation Smith College WASP insider, satisfied Dworkin's longings for establishment acceptance, a nagging theme in her writing.

Dworkin, like Kate Millett, has turned a garish history of mental instability into feminist grand opera. Dworkin publicly boasts of her bizarre multiple rapes, assaults, beatings, breakdowns and tacky traumas, as if her inability to cope with life were the patriarchy's fault rather than her own. She pretends to be a daring truth-teller but never mentions her most obvious problem: food. Hence she is a hypocrite. Dworkin's shrill, *kvetching*, solipsistic prose has a sloppy, squalling infantilism. This attracted MacKinnon, with her dour background of Protestant high seriousness, which treats children like miniature adults. MacKinnon's impersonal prose is dry, bleached, parched. Her hereditary north-country, anal-retentive style, stingy and nitpicking, was counterbalanced by Dworkin's raging undifferentiated orality, her buckets of chicken soup spiked with spite.

Dworkin, wallowing in misery, is a "type" that I recognize after twenty-two years of teaching. I call her The Girl with the Eternal Cold. This was the pudgy, clumsy, whiny child at summer camp who was always spilling her milk, dropping her lollipop in the dirt, getting a cramp on the hike, a stone in her shoe, a bee in her hair. In college, this type—pasty, bilious, and frumpy—is constantly sick from fall to spring. She coughs and sneezes on everyone, is never prepared with tissue and sits sniffling in class with a roll of toilet paper on her lap. She is the ultimate teacher's pest, the morose, unlovable child who never got her mama's approval and therefore demands attention at any price. Dworkin seized on feminism as a mask to conceal her bitterness at this tedious, banal family drama.

MacKinnon and Dworkin have become a pop duo, like Mutt and Jeff, Steve and Eydie, Ron and Nancy. MacKinnon, starved

and weather-beaten, is a fierce gargoyle of American Gothic. With
her witchy tumbleweed hair, she resembles the batty, gritty pioneer
woman played by Agnes Moorehead on *The Twilight Zone.* Or she's
Nurse Diesel, the preachy secret sadist in Mel Brooks's *High Anxiety.*

Dworkin is Pee-wee Herman's Large Marge, the demon trucker
who keeps returning to the scene of her fatal accident. I see
MacKinnon and Dworkin making a female buddy picture like *Thelma
& Louise.* Their characters: Penny Wise and Pound Foolish, the
puritan Gibson Girl and her fuming dybbuk, the glutton for punishment. Or they'd be perfect for the starring roles in a TV docu-
drama about prissy, repressed J. Edgar Hoover and his longtime
companion, Clyde Tolson, bugging hotel rooms and sticking their
noses into everyone's business.

MacKinnon and Dworkin detest pornography because it symbolizes everything they don't understand and can't contol about their
own bodies. Current feminism, with its antiscience and social constructionist bias, never thinks about nature. Hence it cannot deal
with sex, which begins in the body and is energized by instinctual
drives. MacKinnon and Dworkin's basic error is in identifying pornography with society, which they then simplistically define as patriarchal and oppressive. In fact, pornography, which erupts into
the open in periods of personal freedom, shows the dark truth about
nature, concealed by the artifices of civilization. Pornography is
about lust, our animal reality that will never be fully tamed by love.
Lust is elemental, aggressive, asocial. Pornography allows us to explore our deepest, most forbidden selves.

The MacKinnon–Dworkin party line on pornography is preposterous. "Pornography is sex discrimination," they declared in
their Minneapolis ordinance. In a manifesto, they call pornography
"hate literature." "Most women hate pornography; all pornography
hates women." MacKinnon and Dworkin display an astounding
ignorance of the ancient, sacred pornographic tradition of non-
Western societies, as well as that of our own gay male culture.
Dworkin's blanket condemnation of fellatio as disgusting and violent
should make every man furious.

MacKinnon and Dworkin are victim-mongers, ambulance chas-
ers, atrocity addicts. MacKinnon begins every argument from big,

flawed premises such as "male supremacy" or "misogyny," while Dworkin spouts glib Auschwitz metaphors at the drop of a bra. Here's one of their typical maxims: "The pornographers rank with Nazis and Klansmen in promoting hatred and violence." Anyone who could write such a sentence knows nothing about pornography *or* Nazism. Pornography does not cause rape or violence, which predate pornography by thousands of years. Rape and violence occur not because of patriarchal conditioning but because of the opposite, a breakdown of social controls. MacKinnon and Dworkin, like most feminists today, lack a general knowledge of criminology or psychopathology and hence have no perspective on or insight into the bloody, lurid human record, with its disasters and triumphs.

In this mechanized technological world of steel and glass, the fires of sex have to be stoked. This is why pornography must continue to play a central role in our cultural life. Pornography is a pagan arena of beauty, vitality, and brutality, of the archaic vigor of nature. It should break every rule, offend all morality. Pornography represents absolute freedom of imagination, as envisioned by the Romantic poets. In arguing that a hypothetical physical safety on the streets should take precedence over the democratic principle of free speech, MacKinnon aligns herself with the authoritarian Soviet commissars. She would lobotomize the village in order to save it.

An enlightened feminism of the twenty-first century will embrace all sexuality and will turn away from the delusionalism, sanctimony, prudery, and male-bashing of the MacKinnon–Dworkin brigade. Women will never know who they are until they let men be men. Let's get rid of Infirmary Feminism, with its bedlam of bellyachers, anorexics, bulimics, depressives, rape victims, and incest survivors. Feminism has become a catch-all vegetable drawer where bunches of clingy sob sisters can store their moldy neuroses.

Pornography lets the body live in pagan glory, the lush, disorderly fullness of the flesh. When it defines man as the enemy, feminism is alienating women from their own bodies. MacKinnon never deals with woman as mother, lover, or whore. Snuff films are her puritan hallucinations of hellfire. She traffics in tales of terror, hysterical fantasies of death and dismemberment, which shows that she does not understand the great god Dionysus, with his terrible duality. The demons are within us. MacKinnon and Dworkin, peddling their diseased rhetoric, are in denial, and what they are blocking is life itself, in all its grandeur and messiness. Let's send a message to the Mad Hatter and her dumpy dormouse to stop trying to run other people's tea parties.

THE NEW SEXISM:

LIBERATING ART AND BEAUTY

Washington had a sizzling hit show with "Walk the Goddess Walk: Power Inside Out," recently on view at the District of Columbia Arts Center and curated by artist Alison Maddex. The September 10 opening, featuring performance and video artists such as Manhattan drag queen Glennda Orgasm, drew a crowd of over a thousand.

Above all, "Walk the Goddess Walk" demonstrated that, in the current unadventurous Washington art scene, there is a great craving for excitement and the challenge of something new. I suspect that we were also seeing a rejection of the political correctness that is stunting the cultural development of a whole generation of young women emerging from elite American colleges and universities.

Like Maddex, with whom I collaborated in the show, I have despaired about the tendentiousness, ignorance, and mediocrity of feminist attitudes toward art and beauty. Issues of quality and standards have been foolishly abandoned by liberals, who now interpret aesthetics as nothing but a mask for ideology. As a result, the far

[*The Washington Post*, September 26, 1993]

right has gained enormously. What madness is abroad in the land when only neoconservatives will defend the grandeur of art?

Ironically, today's fashion magazines and supermodels, embodying the cult of beauty for a mass audience, are in the main line of art history. Cultural authenticity has shifted to them and away from the establishment ideologues like those running the Whitney Museum in New York, who are obsessed with a passé political agenda.

When Maddex and I toured the Whitney's rape exhibit this summer, we were appalled and incredulous. Visitors were wandering around with tears in their eyes, as rape victims recited their sorrows on a video monitor. When the offerings of a major museum are indistinguishable from the victimization soap opera of television talk shows, art has ceased to exist. The intelligent, courageous artist and curator would defy the rape hysteria, not surrender to it.

Danger signs are everywhere that we are sliding into a new era of the Red Guards. As I know from my visits to campuses across the country, abuse and intimidation await anyone who dares to reject the party line on sexual and political issues. There is a trend among followers of the ideas of Catharine MacKinnon which has resulted in vandalism of art works that fail to conform to feminist orthodoxy. The pro-sex wing of feminism sat around smugly for years, content that it had signed a list or two defending pornography and never realizing that its total silence on the date rape and sexual harrassment issues facilitated MacKinnon's rise.

One of the many lies of women's studies is that European art history was written by white males and that feminism has conclusively rewritten that history by discovering and restoring major female artists excluded from the pantheon by patriarchal conspiracy. But European art history was not just written but created by white males. We may lament the limitations placed on women's training and professional access in the past, but what is done cannot be undone.

The last twenty years of scholarship have brought many forgotten women artists to attention, but too often their presentation has been marred by anachronistic feminist rhetoric. Nancy G. Heller's lucid, evenhanded *Women Artists* is a noteworthy exception to this depressing trend. Germaine Greer's *The Obstacle Race* regrettably veers again and again into agitprop, worst of all on the last page, where Greer declares that the reason there have been no great female artists is that you cannot get great art from "mutilated egos." I would argue that great art comes *only* from mutilated egos.

Feminism, for all its boasts, has not found a single major female painter or sculptor to add to the canon. It did revive the reputations of many minor women, like Frida Kahlo or Romaine Brooks. Mary Cassatt, Georgia O'Keeffe, and Helen Frankenthaler were known and did not need rediscovery. Artemisia Gentileschi was simply a polished, competent painter in a Baroque style created by men.

Women's studies has not shifted the massive structure of art history one jot. It is scandalous that our most talented women undergraduates are being tutored in attitudes of juvenile resentment toward major male artists of the rank of Degas, Picasso, and Marcel Duchamp, who have become virtual untouchables. We will never get great art from women if their education exposes them only to the second-rate and if the idea of greatness itself is denied. Greatness is not a white male trick. Every important world civilization has defined its artistic tradition in elitist terms of distinction and excellence.

Now is the time for all pro-sex, pro-art, pro-beauty feminists to come out of the closet. Maddex and I have created what we call Neo-Sexism, or the New Sexism. It is a progressive feminism that embraces and celebrates all historical depictions of women, including the most luridly pornographic. It wants mythology without sentimentality and every archetype, from mother to witch and whore, without censorship. It accepts and welcomes the testimony of men.

The New Sexism puts sensuality at the center of our responsiveness to life and art. Rejecting the bourgeois feminist obsession with anorexia and bulimia, it sets food and sex into the same continuum of the pleasure principle. It calls for a new, vivid language of art criticism that reveres the art work instead of talking down to it. No more dead jargon and empty theory; no more ideology substituting for appreciation; no more moralism masquerading as politics.

All art belongs to its social context, but great art by definition

transcends that context and speaks universally. Sex is one of the
supreme subjects of art and literature of the last two hundred years.
It deserves to be treated in a way that respects its mystery and
complexity. That is what "Walk the Goddess Walk" tried to do. It
was designed to overthrow the tyranny of false politics and to open
the mind toward art—the spiritual and carnal record of mankind.

AN OPEN LETTER TO THE
STUDENTS OF HARVARD

Anyone concerned with the future of literature and art in America should be repelled by that witches' brew of hypocrisy and sanctimony called "political correctness," which has poisoned the professional life of the elite colleges and universities. If there is to be a spiritual and intellectual revival, it is today's students who must do it. The academic establishment, paralyzed by cronyism, greed, and moral cowardice, is incapable of reforming itself.

For twenty-five years, I have watched from a distance as Harvard's distinguished tradition of literary scholarship has self-destructed. In 1968, when I left college (I attended the State University of New York at Binghamton), the graduate English programs of Harvard and Yale were nationally rated as equivalent in stature. Accepted at both, I chose Yale rather than Harvard, since Harvard required graduate students to teach—a questionable practice that allowed senior faculty to minimize direct contact with undergraduates.

My Sixties generation, with its irreverence and confrontational style, was determined to make profound changes in America's political and cultural life. Education in the humanities had become

[*Harvard Crimson,* February 17, 1994]

narrow and desiccated, imprisoned by an overspecialized, over-departmentalized curricular structure. Those of us who were most influenced by popular culture, psychedelia, and the sexual revolution felt that the universities had lost touch with reality. We wanted to end authoritarian overcontrol of our private lives. And we were militant about free speech, which had launched the first student demonstrations at Berkeley.

What is most disgusting about current political correctness on campus is that its proponents have managed to convince their students and the media that they are authentic Sixties radicals. The idea is preposterous. Political correctness, with its fascist speech codes and puritanical sexual regulations, is a travesty of Sixties progressive values. And except for the sociologist Todd Gitlin, not a single Sixties political activist holds a tenured professorship at any of the elite schools, coast to coast.

On the contrary, the boldest and most original Sixties people either did not go on to graduate school or refused to play the sycophantic career game required for advance in academe. The tenured Ivy League literature faculty who are in their forties are chronologically my generation, but they made their way up the ladder not because they were of the Sixties but because there was nothing Sixties about them. I know, because I was in graduate school with these characters. They never challenged or threatened the status quo—which is exactly why they were handpicked to succeed the conservative old guard.

In literary studies, text-centered New Criticism had reached a dead end and needed to be widened and deepened, through the study of history and sexuality, respectively. Important North American writers who helped Sixties students to rechart the mental landscape in an interdisciplinary way were Allen Ginsberg, Norman O. Brown, Marshall McLuhan, and Leslie Fiedler. But my fellow graduate students, far from absorbing these radical thinkers, were soon off chasing dull, pedantic European poststructuralists, who were trapped in cynical, verbose mind games that my generation had gotten rid of when we substituted Elvis Presley for Samuel Beckett (Foucault's idol). Despite their inflated reputations, none of the French theorists, including Foucault, is competent at speculation about either history or sexuality. Those who claim otherwise simply don't know what they're talking about.

Let me give just one example of how the Ivy League awards its highest honors. A leading Harvard woman professor rose to prominence by her discipleship of Paul de Man and Derrida. Then it was revealed that de Man was a Nazi sympathizer. As deconstruction sank, she switched into feminism and African-American studies, neither of which her books had shown prior interest in. This was capped off by her dramatic avowal, at an October 1991 Harvard Yard rally, of her lesbianism, which is now chic.

Excuse me for my contempt. As the only openly gay person at the Yale graduate school (1968–72), I paid the career price for my pre-Stonewall candor. Where were all these lesbians when it mattered? They stayed in the closet until tenure—and other people's sacrifices—made it safe to come out and claim the spoils. The then-bizarre themes of my dissertation—homosexuality, transvestism, transsexualism, sadomasochism—also ensured that no research university would hire me. I am just one of incalculable numbers of people of my generation whose fidelity to Sixties principles led to their exclusion from the establishment. That is tolerable, since we disdain money and status. What is intolerable is that frauds and poseurs, who rejected American culture to make shiny new gods out of French theorists, should now claim to be the heirs of Sixties thought.

The bottom fell out of the Harvard literature departments in the Seventies. They had failed to find new blood to continue Harvard's reputation into the next generation, while Yale, after a bitter battle with undertones of anti-Semitism, secured Harold Bloom and Geoffrey Hartman, followed by established names from Johns Hopkins. Harvard waited too long to respond to contemporary changes; no younger faculty came remotely near the great scholarly level of Harry Levin and Walter Jackson Bate. The English department nearly went into receivership. Ten years after I entered grad school, Harvard's reputation in literature hit rock bottom.

Desperate, the Harvard administration went on a fast shopping expedition and filled the faculty with the current hot property, theorists, many of them women, as an affirmative action sop. Now you're stuck with them. Theory is moribund everywhere, but Harvard, which sacrificed scholarly standards for expedience, has condemned itself to at least two generations of mediocrity in the humanities, since these people are certain to hire only those who will prop up their decaying reputations. Harvard students are sadly mistaken if they think the literature faculty in their thirties and forties are the best America has to offer. It was the cliquish conference circuit, a crassly commercial phenomenon only twenty years old, that put those opportunistic trend-chasers in your classrooms. Under its hip varnish, their work is shoddy and shallow.

When will Ivy League students wake up to the corruption that is all around them? The leftist press in America has been grossly negligent in not identifying and attacking the slick career system that has made deception, pretension, and manipulation business-as-usual in the humanities since the Seventies. Economic analysis should be the first principle of authentic leftism. Phony, obfuscatory, elitist French theory became the ticket to ride for an amoral coterie that is intricately interconnected from Berkeley to Duke to Princeton and Harvard. These days, they pretend to be doing "cultural studies," an amateurish mishmash of this and that, without scholarly command of any area. Student newspapers, which used to question authority and attack the establishment, have been lazily oblivious to a national scandal equal to that of the Wall Street junk-bond crash.

The solution is in your hands. You can bring learning back to the center of the university. You can end the era of gimmicky theory. You can demand that quality of scholarship, rather than slick wordplay, be the standard for employment at Harvard. How? First make the library your teacher. Rediscover the now neglected works of the great scholars of the last 150 years, who worked blessedly free of the mental pollutants of poststructuralism. Immerse yourself in the reference collection, and master chronology and etymology. Refuse to cooperate with the coercive ersatz humanitarianism that insultingly defines women and African-Americans as victims. Insist on free thought and free speech. Offensiveness is a democratic right. The university should be organized around vigorous intellectual inquiry, not therapy or creature comforts. Harvard has become a nursing home for kids.

I have elsewhere detailed my proposals for massive reform of the university: an end to departmentalization of literature by nationalities; sex studies, rather than the overideological and unscientific women's studies and gay studies; and a world plan for a truly scholarly and depoliticized multiculturalism, based on comparative religion, archaeology, art history, and anthropology. The liberal versus conservative argument is pointless and passé. Its rhetoric has simply concealed the venality and sycophancy of the academic marketplace, which has in actuality driven the conflicts of the past fifteen years. In the twenty-first century, we will want something new. Today's students can create it.

ON CENSORSHIP

OBSERVER. Are you for or against censorship?

CAMILLE PAGLIA. I am opposed to censorship because of my over-arching theory that what we define—what tradition defines—as morally reprehensible and worthy of suppression is, in fact, the pagan element in Western culture that was never defeated. The elements of sex and violence that most disturb people, all the untidy and amoral forces of nature the pagan tradition was more honest about, are what the Judeo-Christian tradition has always struggled with.

OBSERVER. Is there any case for censorship?

CAMILLE PAGLIA. There should be no censorship of any kind. On the other hand, I think one can raise questions of appropriateness. If you're teaching children, I think it is reasonable to believe that teachers should not impose their sophisticated sexual visions on them. I wouldn't call it censorship if a school said, "That's inappropriate for young children."

[*The Observer*, London, April 10, 1994]

OBSERVER. What is your position on the censorship of pornography?

CAMILLE PAGLIA. My point in *Sexual Personae* is that one cannot make any kind of firm line between high art and pornography. In fact, porn permeates the high art tradition. Even Michelangelo's *Pietà*, the supreme artifact of the Vatican, is a work of pornography—when you look at it up close.

OBSERVER. Does that mean all pornography should be freely available to adults?

CAMILLE PAGLIA. I am on record as saying that one can reasonably restrict public displays of pornography. The public spaces, the free spaces, and so on belong to both traditions—the Judeo-Christian and the pagan—and, therefore, a person should not have to have naked ladies overwhelming the eye from a newsstand. On the other hand, those magazines should be available at the newsstand.

I hate the way feminists in America have managed to pressure the drugstore chains so that you can no longer buy *Playboy* or *Penthouse*. The major men's magazines are all but censored, because no one is able to find them outside the urban centers. This has occurred without a ripple over here.

OBSERVER. Why?

CAMILLE PAGLIA. There has been this incredible alliance between the feminists, the Catholic schools, and the far right. As a result, something very bad has happened.

In the Sixties, part of what my generation did was the sexual revolution. Women of my period were bawdy in our speech. We were trying to break down the old middle-class conventions, and part of this was the fabulous sex magazines of the time   men and women looked at them. They were artistic, they were funky, they were radical in their politics.

Also, you had middle-class women going with their boyfriends and husbands to porn theaters to see *Deep Throat*. That was a breakthrough. We'd never even heard about oral sex, much less seen it demonstrated.

But now, in the puritanical revisionism of things, it's like *Deep*

Throat is the ultimate symbol of a woman being raped—being forced to perform oral sex. It's loathsome. There has been a horrible retreat into puritanism since the Sixties.

OBSERVER. Is that a failing of imagination?

CAMILLE PAGLIA. My explanation is usually that the most interesting and innovative and bawdy members of my generation did not go on into the standard professions. They took drugs. They sort of cancelled themselves out.

OBSERVER. What is your position on child pornography?

CAMILLE PAGLIA. I maintain that Donatello's *David*, one of the most important, revolutionary works in the whole history of art, is, in fact, a work of child pornography.

Then there's the Valentine thing, the Valentine's Day Cupid with its plush infant body. That's an eroticization of the child's body that we're used to seeing. It goes back to ancient Rome, where you find babies presented as sensuous.

Germaine Greer says in her book *Sex and Destiny* that non-Western cultures are very open about the kind of physicality they permit between adults and children. Pleasures are taken with children's bodies that would be defined, in our culture, as abuse or rape.

OBSERVER. So it's a cultural issue, not a legal one?

CAMILLE PAGLIA. I believe that the abolition of child labor was one of the great reform movements of the last 200 years. If you have children posing for pornographic pictures and videos, that is an infringement—not of something sexual—but of what we now feel is civilized, that children should not be forced to labor.

OBSERVER. Isn't that a dangerous opinion?

CAMILLE PAGLIA. As far as any visual, imaginary representations that are sketched or painted of children in pornographic acts—again, I'm considered pretty radical here, on the lunatic fringe with this one—I feel: so what? Anything that can be imagined should be depicted.

OBSERVER. Are you sure?

CAMILLE PAGLIA. I feel that that's the only way we can keep ourselves from sliding into dogmatism. To most people, these kinds of things are abhorrent. They can't look at them without being disturbed. So I feel that intellectuals and artists are obliged to force themselves to depict them, to write about them.

That's why I'm a great fan of the Marquis de Sade. He was trying, in prison, to reach the limits of the human sexual imagination, and to put it down on paper.

OBSERVER. You yourself were recently the subject of censorship over a film in which you confronted anti-porn campaigners on the streets of New York. Can you explain this?

CAMILLE PAGLIA. For years, these women have harassed people on the sidewalks in Greenwich Village. They hold out these pictures of women bound with ropes, from *Hustler* or wherever, and force them in people's faces and scream and yell.

My sister, who lives there, says it's just appalling, because these women are forcing these images on people in the street when there are small children around.

They're insane, literally insane. They're total fanatics, and anyone who has seen them in New York understands what I was doing—I mean, to go up to them and yell at them, to force the cameras on them, and—suddenly—they're just cowards.

So this film, which has been shown at Sundance, the most prestigious film festival in the country, has been censored. It was suppressed by the New York Gay and Lesbian Film Festival. A film made on the streets of New York!

OBSERVER. What about self-censorship?

CAMILLE PAGLIA. This is my rebuke to the white middle-class, respectable feminist movement. When I was last over in England I threw one of your prominent feminists right out of an interview. They are so pompous, so respectable—so self-censored. This is why they do all this complaining: "Why is it that the American feminists get all the attention? Why don't we get any attention?" Why? Because you're boring middle-class ladies.

OBSERVER. Don't feminists censor like everyone else?

CAMILLE PAGLIA. There is absolutely totalitarian censorship of any divergent or dissenting opinions within the world of women's studies. I couldn't get a job anywhere in the Seventies. When I came on the scene, if you ever breathed one word against women's studies—just opened your mouth—you were tarred as a male-chauvinist pig, as a reactionary, as a neo-conservative.

OBSERVER. Really?

CAMILLE PAGLIA. I love the situation in England, where you have the Page Three girls. I adore that. The idea that you open up a family newspaper and see all those bare boobs. That's absolutely fabulous, it's unheard of in America—it would be absolutely impossible.

POP THEATER

WOODY ALLEN AGONISTES

Two weeks ago, the discreet twelve-year relationship between Woody Allen and Mia Farrow exploded into public attention in a media firestorm of charges and countercharges. Day after day, screaming headlines documented the revelations: Allen had filed for custody of the couple's three small children; he had been accused of molestation of one of them in Connecticut; he admitted a sexual liaison with Farrow's adopted Korean daughter, Soon-Yi Previn, whose age has been variously reported as nineteen or twenty-one.

After an initial period of confusion, most sensible people seemed willing to suspend judgment for the moment on the child abuse charge, in the absence of hard evidence. But on talk shows and in the print media, there was a thunderous chorus of condemnation of Allen for his relationship with Soon-Yi. Family therapists, feminists, and church-going conservatives called it callous, lecherous, incestuous, decadent. Woody Allen, one of feminism's great white hopes for the ideal "sensitive male," had flunked out. The lovable nerd was just another leering Nero.

This controversy is a perfect thermometer for taking the temperature of the American psyche. Twenty-five years after the sexual

[New York *Newsday*, December 2, 1992]

revolution, what have we learned about ourselves? Practically nothing. Contrary to feminist propaganda, we have not found the answer to any important sexual issue. In fact, as the century ends, we have barely begun to pose the questions correctly.

At his press conference two weeks ago, Woody Allen said there is "no logic" to falling in love. This ancient wisdom about the Dionysian irrationality of our emotional lives is documented in the earliest Greek and Roman love poetry. It is a great spiritual truth sadly missing from the ugly, clumsy ideology of current feminism, which is obsessed with social-welfare clichés of oppression, victimization and "care-giving."

Woody Allen is an artist. To whom does he owe ultimate responsibility? Since Romanticism, we have expected the artist not to celebrate God, king, family, and established values but to break taboos, to explore his or her deepest, most socially forbidden self. Though his films have weakened recently, Allen is one of the central analysts of contemporary American manners and sexual experience. It is outrageous that therapists, bystanders, and pundits of every stripe have used this painful crisis to strike hysterical poses of moral superiority over him.

Picasso, Elvis Presley, John Lennon, Madonna, Robert Mapplethorpe: during the past decade, each of these important artists has been denounced by holier-than-thou groups, from feminists to the Moral Majority, for their unsettling themes or bohemian lifestyles. This provincial American abuse of artists must end. Neither art nor the artist will ever conform to bourgeois decorum or tidy moral codes. Originality is by definition rule-breaking.

Allen's films, like *Bananas, Love and Death,* and *Annie Hall,* often show the comic inadequacy of words, reason, or good intentions to deal with the storminess of sex and love. In *Broadway Danny Rose,* he himself plays a gentle, earnest, compassionate bumbler overwhelmed by a flamboyant, vengeful Italian firecracker, wonderfully portrayed by Mia Farrow.

Farrow seems to have carried this unexpected flair for Italian theatricality into her present life drama, in which she has managed to exert maximum power while deftly avoiding overt public statements. Dispatching a host of adult and pint-sized proxies as skillfully as Shakespeare's volatile Cleopatra, Farrow has fused Puccini heroines: she is both the pining, abandoned mother, Madame Butterfly, and the tempestuous, jealous diva, Tosca, who uses any weapon that comes to hand.

There has been an undertone of perversity or kinkiness in Farrow's sexual personae from the start of her career. Her May/December marriage to Frank Sinatra still astonishes. Who can forget that first yacht-deck photo of the hard-bitten casino roué next to the androgynous gossamer waif? (Sinatra's ex, Ava Gardner, snapped, "I always knew Frank would end up with a boy.") In *Secret Ceremony* Farrow played a delusional girl-woman projecting a homoerotic incest fantasy onto a very patient Elizabeth Taylor. In *Rosemary's Baby* she fought for her pregnancy against the forces of darkness and oddly nosy neighbors on Central Park West.

Motherhood is a far more complex phenomenon than the current brand of neat-as-pie yuppie feminism admits. Motherhood may unleash primal instincts for possession and territoriality beyond morality. Hovering vulturelike over the whole affair is Farrow's dowager queen mother, actress Maureen O'Sullivan, hurling Junoesque thunderbolts at Allen (in her words, an "evil" man) from her stronghold on the West Coast. Farrow's sprawling, multiracial household is in its own way tribal and matriarchal.

Allen is being impugned as an "immature" satyr with a Lolita fixation, like those other small-statured collectors of nymphets, Charlie Chaplin and Roman Polanski. The pursuit of youth and beauty has also been an integral part of highly accomplished gay male life for centuries. Allen has the right to seek his muse wherever he may find her. The quiet, dreamy Soon-Yi, paternalistically trashed by the bleeding-heart commentators as "helpless," "passive," and "naive," may represent simplicity and emotional truth to Allen. Such insights, even if transient, are priceless to an artist.

Is it incest? Legally, no. Psychologically, yes. But incest is a universal theme in world mythology that we have never come to terms with. Doing the research for *Sexual Personae,* I was stunned at the frequency of incest in Romantic literature. And incest permeates the two greatest plays ever written, Sophocles' *Oedipus Rex* and Shakespeare's *Hamlet.*

Freud's theory of infantile sexuality is a century old, yet it remains unabsorbed. Most parents could not function at home if they fully accepted their children's sexuality. Our horrified fascination with the Allen/Farrow scandal comes partly from our own repressions. Similarly, the child-abuse witch-hunts focusing on day-care centers in recent years are baseless hallucinations, eruptions from our vestigial Anglo-Saxon puritanism.

Woody Allen's love life began in the shadow of the potent Jewish mother, then evolved through brunette and blonde shiksa goddesses to an Asian Mona Lisa. Thus it is ironic that he who moved so far romantically from his Jewish roots should still end up accused of incest. Like Oedipus, he could not escape his fate.

This sorry episode in the showbiz chronicles has much to teach us. Don't send your Valentines with a Betty Crocker stamp. Cruelty and brutality lie just beneath the surface of love. Intimacy and incest may be psychologically intertwined. Power relations may generate eroticism. Perhaps—bad news for sexual harassment rules—hierarchy can never be completely desexed.

At his press conference, Woody Allen looked haggard and rumpled, like a graduate student flushed out of an all-night study session. In giving anguished testimony about the mystery, compulsion, and folly of sexual attraction, he has recovered and renewed his cultural status: the artist as scapegoat, illuminating our lives through his own suffering.

OUR TABLOID PRINCESS:
AMY FISHER

Amy Fisher is America's Diana, our tabloid princess. Many people at first ignored the case of the "Long Island Lolita," the seventeen-year-old high school senior who shot the wife of her thirty-eight-year-old lover in the head. But those who dismissed it as too trivial or vulgar were forced to take a second look when three different TV movies on the scandal were broadcast in a single week earlier this month, to smash ratings.

Since it broke last May, the Amy Fisher story competed with the presidential campaign and threatened to upstage the inauguration itself. Faced with this mass phenomenon, the establishment press responded only with disdainful bewilderment or pious hand-wringing over the debasement of popular taste and journalistic standards. Enough crocodile tears were shed to float the African Queen.

Like the recent fiasco of Zoë Baird's failed nomination as attorney general, the Amy Fisher phenomenon dramatically demonstrates how out of touch the cultural elite is with popular thought. For years, mainstream feminists have shrilly hammered at us about date rape, sexual harassment, and child abuse. They have portrayed

[*San Francisco Examiner*, January 31, 1993]

life under "patriarchy" as a tear-stained melodrama of lecherous male tyrants and passive female victims.

The feminist inquisitors tirelessly pounce on whipping-boys-of-the-month—philandering Senator Bob Packwood is their latest demonic centerfold—but the popular imagination keeps stubbornly rejecting their simplistic sexual scenario and refreshing itself in tabloid truth. The instant myth of Amy Fisher turned feminist dogma on its head: as in the hit films *Fatal Attraction, Basic Instinct,* and *The Hand That Rocks the Cradle,* woman rules and destroys. The femme fatale is for real.

Early commentators on the Fisher case tried to reduce it to pat social-welfare formulas. There was the usual hunting-for-victims that has become such a tedious substitute for analysis in America. Was man-of-the-people Joey Buttafuoco the victim of a wily little tramp? Or was Amy the naive victim of a slick gigolo who had his jollies and got off scot-free, while the women suffered? And surely somewhere in Amy's childhood there had to be "abuse"—the feminist stock response to anything ambiguous in human behavior.

When long-haired Amy, spoiled only child, mall chick and part-time call-girl, mounted the Buttafuoco porch with a pistol in her pocket, every power play in the history of love was on red alert. It was high noon on a Tennessee Williams veranda. Though reviewers ineptly hailed the meandering ABC movie, starring scrumptious Drew Barrymore, as the best of the three, it was in fact only the first version, NBC's tightly paced "Amy Fisher: My Story," featuring the unheralded Noelle Parker, that got it right.

Amy vs. Mary Jo Buttafuoco on the porch was a trash tango, a clash of the female titans. Joey, the absent ostensible subject, shrank to nothing. He is a poof man, a stud muffin, a big calzone. Amy and Mary Jo faced off in a street fight, a territorial war for possession of sexual property. The NBC movie showed mutual insults escalating into clumsy violence, which exploded out of the normal and ordinary. It was terrifying.

In my opinion, the crucial element in this story is Mary Jo's refusal to leave her husband, despite her facial paralysis and the bullet now permanently in her head. People would long ago have lost interest without this detail, which is more unique and perplexing

than the standard mystery-tale motif of how-much-did-the-husband-know about the murder plot in advance.

Fresh from the hospital, Mary Jo, mouth distorted, harangued a mob of skeptical reporters on the porch, bitterly denouncing Amy Fisher and defending the virtue of her spouse. She even sang praises about their "better than ever" sex life on Howard Stern's radio show. It was an astonishing display of female triumph of the will. A betrayed wife had won back her man and defeated her younger competitor.

On the *Donahue* show a few weeks ago, Mary Jo sat serenely by her husband, who proclaimed his innocence against a hostile audience and the host himself, who called him "the most hated man in America." But Joey Buttafuoco is just a puppet maneuvered by a maternal dominatrix, who has pulled him back into the domestic orbit as the third of her children. Her head wound is the battle scar of a total victory.

At the end of the *Donahue* show, Mary Jo's Irish mother stood up and spat defiance at the crowd. Joey "wouldn't be sitting up there"—alive on this planet was the implication—if she thought he had hurt her daughter. Mother and daughter had eerily the same face, a grimly downturned mouth chiseled on a boxer's jaw. The feminist view of male oppression is naive. Woman is dominant.

The child-abuse obsession of the past decade, which plastered pictures of missing tots on milk cartons and now induces unknowns and celebrities to make public confessions of miraculously restored memories of ancient molestation, is predicated on a black-and-white paradigm of adult defilement of childhood innocence. The Lolita archetype is the fascinating heart of the Amy Fisher case. Lolita is not merely a male fantasy. A man—novelist Vladimir Nabokov—may have named her, but she is drawn from life.

Lolita melts the sexual borderline that society has artificially drawn between child and adult. She is as conscious, willful, and manipulative as any mature woman. In Amy Fisher we saw Lolita in action, spinning her erotic spells from the high-school girls' room to the auto body shop. More power to her. Sitting in jail, she is paying the price for her daring pirate raids on respectability and convention.

The Amy Fisher case shows the limitations of current feminist thinking about sex. Neither mainstream nor academic feminists are comfortable with the kind of aggressive, sleazy eroticism flaunted by Amy and her paramours. Genteel middle-class feminists cannot understand the cocky, swaggering, working-class masculinity of Joey Buttafuoco, which is far more important and universal than the cowed less-than-manhood of the polite white-collar wordsmiths who have swallowed the feminist line in academe and the media.

The official rhetoric of the cultural elite is completely out of sync with the actual evidence of experience. In sentencing her to five to fifteen years in prison for first-degree assault, the judge told Amy that she was "motivated by lust and passion" and had pursued Mary Jo "like a wild animal stalks its prey." The sex impulse, uncontrolled in its natural state, is barbaric. Feminism has got to look honestly at the animal savagery and lust in all of us and stop blaming men for the darkness of the human condition.

THE FEMALE LENNY BRUCE:
SANDRA BERNHARD

As a guest of the British Broadcasting Company, which is doing a documentary on her, I recently saw Sandra Bernhard's new show, *Giving Till It Hurts,* at New York's Paramount Theater. From its campy celebration of Jacqueline Susann's *Valley of the Dolls* to its prayer to San Francisco's late great Sylvester, the drag king of disco, I felt that I was seeing my own spiritual autobiography unfold before my eyes.

Bernhard's career has surged forward in the last two years after a long period in which she never stopped working but seemed to many people to be wasting her talent in erratic, self-indulgent displays of chic cynicism. Bernhard first gained broad public attention for her brilliant performance as a terrifyingly seductive sociopath in Martin Scorsese's *The King of Comedy* (1983), which earned her a permanent place in film history.

Like Jessica Walter after her dazzling performance as a violent erotomaniac in *Play Misty for Me,* Bernhard was shortchanged by Hollywood, which never came up with the kind of meaty *film noir* roles she deserved. Bernhard continued doing her strange brand of performance art in comedy clubs around the country, but unfortu-

[*San Francisco Examiner*, December 6, 1992]

nately the way she stayed in the national eye was through some two-dozen unsettling television appearances on the David Letterman show.

I happen to detest David Letterman as the essence of cheap, snide, adolescent, white-bread humor. At first, I forced myself to watch the show if Bernhard was on but, upset and horrified, finally gave up. Jittery and wild-eyed, she seemed to be on an express train to self-destruction.

In 1986, Bernhard began collaborating with writer-director John Boskovich, leading up to the first of her two shows, *Without You I'm Nothing*, which was made into a movie in 1990. During the show's six-month run in New York in 1988, Bernhard met Madonna, and the two cavorted around town as prankish "gal pals." Were they lovers or not? The tabloids had a field day.

In the past year Bernhard became a regular on *Roseanne*, the top-rated mainstream sitcom, but retained her on-the-edge flair by posing nude for *Playboy* and hosting a bizarre HBO party special with a garish Fellini decadence.

With her new stage show, Bernhard has emerged as a more mature and confident star. The undertone of bitterness and disillusion that ran through her early career seems gone. Her romantic disappointments have deepened her as a performer.

As a sexual persona, Bernhard is unique in the contemporary arts. She is completely American. No other country can produce this kind of brashly individualistic woman, harsh, aggressive, raunchy and physical, with an imagination drenched in thirty flamboyant years of popular culture.

My sense of identification with Bernhard's volatile worldview comes partly from a shared ethnic history. Suburbia, which flowered after World War II, is still insufficiently understood. It was here that the rich, ethnic, extended families collapsed into the tense, isolated nuclear family, which tried to sanitize itself into conventional American normality.

The repressions of suburbia have produced Bernhard, Madonna, and me. Half of us is a nice suburban girl; the other half is a raving pornographic maniac, the beast buried in the cellar.

Bernhard's creativity springs from these cultural conflicts. Her

Jewish family, with its East Coast sensibility, was transplanted from Michigan to Arizona. Like Bette Midler growing up in Hawaii, Bernhard was an alien.

Her geographical displacement was intensified by a gender displacement. In her new show, Bernhard speaks of her teen-age anguish over her period not beginning until she was seventeen. Too tall and neither blond nor cute, Bernhard was not destined for prom queen.

Bernhard's act is shot through with autobiographical musings, the seething longings and glamourous dreams of a prisoner in the pleasant suburban wasteland. Like Anne Sexton and Sylvia Plath, she is a Confessional poet. But Bernhard has turned Confessionalism away from suicide and toward comedy, a mode of survival and redemption rather than loss.

American stand-up comedy began in vaudeville and was transformed into social commentary by Lenny Bruce. There was a penetrating style of Jewish intellectuality, typified by Mike Nichols and Elaine May and the early Joan Rivers, that regrettably has gone out of fashion in comedy in the past fifteen years. Joy Behar, with her devastating Catherine Deneuve parodies, briefly revived it but seemed to lose interest.

Sandra Bernhard has Lenny Bruce's brooding menace and quick, razor-sharp mind. She re-creates the brainy neuroticism and earthy sensuality of Beatnik women, with their gloomy hipster realism. By her gutsy insistence on singing—in an ever-improving but often thin or fractured voice—Bernhard has rejoined stand-up to its origins in vaudeville, where music and comedy were brassily interwoven.

All musical styles of the past quarter century are evoked in Bernhard's shows: jazz, Broadway, country, rock, soul, Motown, disco, as ingeniously reinterpreted by a Jewish rapper. It's a vast aural spectacle. For my Sixties generation, cultural history *is* popular music, in a way incomprehensible in Europe.

Fragments of ads, brand names, movies, TV, and celebrity gossip float through Bernhard's routines. But her technique is not the tiresome sterile irony of postmodernist "appropriation." On the contrary, she daringly explores a raw, stormy emotionalism, sudden tantrums that repel or terrify.

The task of the artist and intellectual at the end of the century is to rework the discontinuities of our lives into new wholes. How can we clarify our thinking about this pagan Age of Hollywood? French and German theory won't do. We need a native language of sensory analysis.

Bernhard's operatic surrealism is a good start in this direction. She combines the modernist themes of desolation and abandonment with the spirituality of black music and the hostile but affirmative energies of rock. She has the sophisticated worldliness of gay men and the gorgeous theatricality of drag queens. With Boskovich, she is rescuing gay identity from its excessive politicization and reorienting it toward culture.

Above all, Bernhard is reinventing feminism. While the once-pioneering Lily Tomlin has become the high priestess of political correctness, Bernhard embraces the great female personae excluded by the prudish Steinem politburo: bitch, stripper, whore, lady, fashion model.

The evolved Bernhard is a wonderful influence on young audiences. Her new feminist is a powerful, self-reliant personality with a sharp, bawdy tongue. Like the drag queen, she can defend herself without running to grievance committees. Whether lesbian or bisexual, she accepts and respects male lust without trying to censor it. And she knows that comedy is the best road to truth.

BROOKLYN NEFERTITI:

BARBRA STREISAND

One of the supreme moments in recent popular entertainment was when Barbra Streisand sang "Evergreen" for Bill Clinton at his inauguration gala. All of her American fans were saying to ourselves: "Look at what we've missed for the past twenty-five years!" She looked spectacular, wearing a business suit with big padded shoulders and a long skirt slit up the thigh. I was delirious. She was all man and all woman.

It was a return to her roots, to the unconventional, somewhat androgynous persona she had at the beginning of her career in the early 1960s. She's gone full circle. There is a wonderful unity and simplicity about Streisand's current persona. Even her speaking style has been resimplified and become clearer and stronger. I love the fact that she's retaken the public stage as a political figure. Until a couple of years ago, when she made *The Prince of Tides*, many people were tired of her. I was impatient with her erratic productivity and the middlebrow drift of her taste. But now she is a splendid role model for women: a mega-celebrity who is also politically engaged.

[An interview with Rebecca Mead, cover story, *Sunday Times* magazine, London, May 30, 1993. Another article by Paglia on Streisand appeared too late for inclusion in this volume: *The New Republic,* July 18, 1994.]

Many people question her motives and find her posture ludicrous. They say that she's getting involved in politics for the sake of fashion, trimming her sails for the moment, that she's a White House sycophant and hanger-on. But in point of fact, her political commitment long predates the rise of Clinton. She is an authentic heir of leftist politics in America. Her beliefs can be traced to her origins in ethnic, working-class Brooklyn. She came out of the crucible of Jewish political activism.

Streisand's radical politics go back to the passionate Jewish liberalism that pervaded 1950s avant-garde circles and descended in turn from labor-union agitation in the 1930s. Greenwich Village in the late 1950s and early 1960s was seething with folk singers, and many of the populist songs being performed in coffee houses were labor protest songs of the 1930s. In a sense, Streisand is coming out of that. Even her crisp, emphatic diction is immediately recognizable as the old voice of Jewish political activism.

When she first exploded upon the world in the early 1960s in *Funny Girl,* what Streisand represented was an electrifying new individualism that looked forward to the Sixties counterculture. The nonconformism of her sexual persona was so radical compared to what we had been raised with for the prior fifteen years, with all those cheerful, sanitized blondes, such as Doris Day and Debbie Reynolds. There was a whole series of blonde nymphettes, such as Carol Lynley and Sandra Dee, prefiguring the Barbie doll. They were sweet, docile, winsome, harmless, very attentive and deferential to men.

What was so amazing about Streisand was her aggressive ethnicity. The Nose, which she refused to have changed, was so defiantly ethnic. It was a truly revolutionary persona. She was a brilliant new icon of modern womanhood. She was the first public figure to wear retro clothes from the 1930s. This "thrift-shop look" became a hippie style later adopted by Janis Joplin. Streisand made the cover of *Time* magazine as a gamine waifish outsider and then was treated mythologically by *Life* magazine; she posed as a haughty Nefertiti and as a Regency siren in Greek dress.

While in high school, I went through a rabid Streisand period, when I slept on giant rollers to get my hair like hers and had long nails with plum polish. Early Streisand remains for me the best

Streisand. She visibly seethed with emotion. When drag queens imitate her, it's always from that period, with that smooth, sleek helmet hair, when she was still singing in cabarets.

There has always been a conflict in Barbra Streisand, as in Oscar Wilde, between her populist politics and her aristocratic and tyrannical persona. In early pictures, with her hair swept back, she looks so grand, like a Russian duchess. This is what gay guys liked about her—the arrogant, monarchical divahood, which is definitely not democratic. Streisand has always been a kind of drag queen herself. That's true of Sandra Bernhard too, and it's true of me and of a lot of women who didn't feel particularly feminine when they were growing up. For women like that, by the time you figure out what femininity is, you've become a female impersonator.

I've written in *Sexual Personae* that all the great stars imitated by gay men—Mae West, Marlene Dietrich, Bette Davis, Diana Ross, Joan Collins, and Barbra Streisand—are androgynous. They are men-women, with this tremendous duality. That's why their romantic relationships are so bad, because they are autocratic and autonomous. As artists, they need no one else.

I was so excited when it was announced that Streisand would appear in male drag in *Yentl* (1983). But she pulled her punches, and I was disappointed. Amy Irving, playing the girl who fell in love with Streisand as the disguised yeshiva student, was meltingly sexual, but when it came to the kiss, Streisand shrouded it in shadow. She undercut her own persona. There is a male part of her that is palpably there, but she's unwilling to really go for it. Perhaps she is so uncertain of her sexuality that she fears compromising it.

Streisand's insecurity about her sexual attractiveness is probably one of the reasons she stopped performing live for two decades. Audiences had started to call her "cold" on stage. She always felt like the homely, cross-eyed child from Brooklyn. But how rare it was to have the nonconformist ugly duckling elevated to the central role of major Hollywood films. When Streisand appeared in *The Way We Were* (1973) with Robert Redford, people cattily commented on how much prettier the male star was than the female. Probably it was psychologically important for Streisand to withdraw in the 1970s and 1980s and become a hausfrau. She wanted to live like a real woman, and to be desired like one.

Unfortunately, she eclipsed her own persona in that domestic period, when she was constantly redecorating and meat-shopping and cooking for her man. It was embarrassing. She had reverted to convention and become what the 1950s wanted us to be, a housewife and mother. I suffered every time I saw her in that atrocious mop of curls. She looked terrible.

Her longtime boyfriend, hairdresser-turned-producer Jon Peters, first got to Streisand when he was visiting her house and said, as she was walking in front of him, "Nice ass." She was thrilled that a good-looking man was relating to her as a sexual being, because she was very insecure about this.

In terms of twentieth-century popular culture, Streisand is a unique sexual persona. Fanny Brice, whom she was playing in *Funny Girl*, was a superb stage comedian, but she never had the status of a sexual being. There are different ways to break conventions, of course. Jean Harlow did a slutty, trashy kind of thing: she had a working-class street sexuality that sharply contrasted with the elegant cosmopolitanism of her Hollywood contemporaries. Streisand's greatness is that she was able to inject the madcap Fanny Brice persona with all the sensuality and glamour of the great stars.

To me, Streisand is a duchess, a queen, a tyrant. That is the persona she created in Hollywood. She has a reputation for being a bitch because of her perfectionism and desire for total control over every production. She is like Catherine the Great, a woman of autocratic power, who ruled alone and was a shrewd political operator, intolerant of any invasion of her turf.

Streisand's craving for autonomy became a problem for her, since she never learned how to collaborate. The same thing has happened to Madonna. Such artists start out so individualistic, following their own instincts; but the point comes when they are so used to doing their own thing and not seeking advice from good people that they screw up. It happened with Madonna over the disastrous *Sex* book, and it happened with Streisand in *A Star Is Born* (1976)—a fascinating film but in many ways ludicrous; she was both the star and the producer.

Streisand is in the Katharine Hepburn/Bette Davis tradition of women who just spoke out and took the consequences. She is someone who is totally self-determined and doesn't care what people think of her. Streisand's on-screen persona is quite unlike that of either Hepburn or Davis, but the way those stars defined the Hollywood establishment in the 1930s and 1940s is very much like Streisand's independent off-screen persona. Streisand's predecessors are prewar; no one was behaving like that after the war.

While Streisand has to be respected for the genuineness of her political beliefs, one is entitled to be somewhat skeptical of any ambitions she might have for elective office (the rumors are inconclusive about this). The idea of Senator Streisand may be risible. At this point, it is absurd, inconceivable. She has not lived the political life and learned the skills of negotiation and compromise that you need to succeed in office and to communicate with ordinary people.

I think Streisand is a Jesse Jackson figure, someone who is not very good at the day-to-day grind and banal minutiae of being a politician but who has a gift for giving big, stirring, kick-in-the-ass speeches that move multitudes. Now, at midlife and seasoned by experience, Streisand has a great public role to play, even if you don't agree with what she is saying. For example, even those who support gay liberation, as I do, may not agree with her controversial call for a boycott of the entire state of Colorado because of an anti-gay law passed there.

Streisand has now become a grande dame, like Lady Bracknell in *The Importance of Being Earnest.* The thundering majesty of the Victorian dowagers has been sadly missing from women's sexual personae throughout the twentieth century. Streisand's imperious oratorical manner seems wonderful to me, as a feminist who has been trying to bury forever our Doris Day–Debbie Reynolds past.

LOLITA UNCLOTHED

A girl's hand drops a needle onto a spinning 45 rpm disk in a tiny box record player. Sarah Vaughan's rakishly flirtatious "Let's" begins to play, as the camera pulls back to show a pubescent blonde girl in denim pedal pushers, ankle sox, and ballerina slippers, leafing through movie magazines. Absentmindedly twirling her hair around her fingers, she lies on her stomach, with her feet up and her ankles fetchingly crossed. Perched on the open lid of the record player are a pair of red-rimmed, heart-shaped sunglasses. Cut to a darkened, shrine-like set hung with a large yellow painting of the face of an adolescent girl wearing the same sunglasses. Her eyes peer provocatively over the green glass, and there is a bright blue lollipop resting between her parted, sensuous, very red lips. Across the top of the painting, the name "Lolita" is scrawled like a signature, with a heart dotting the "i." CAMILLE PAGLIA, in black sweater and pants, steps out of the shadows and mounts the platform in a somewhat pugnacious manner.

CAMILLE PAGLIA: Nabokov's novel is a final corruption of the tradition of the veneration of the child that in fact was created by Rousseau and Wordsworth at the birth of Romanticism. The

[A Rapido TV production for *World Without Walls*, Channel 4, London. Produced and directed by Peter Stuart. Aired May 11, 1993.]

child was now considered sexless and saintly. Freud tried a hundred years ago to redefine the infant and child as fully sexual, but that idea has never taken. It is too *appalling* to most parents to really *imagine* that there's a sexual dynamic going on between themselves and their children. So this, as far as I'm concerned, this motif of childhood sexuality, *is* the last taboo.

(Cut to 1966 black-and-white film of a relaxed VLADIMIR NABOKOV, *wearing eyeglasses, dramatically reading from a copy of* Lolita *(1955), open on a table before him.)*

VLADIMIR NABOKOV: "Lolita, light of my life, fire of my loins. My sin, my soul. Lo-lee-ta: the tip of the tongue taking a trip of three steps down the palate to tap, at three, on the teeth. Lo. Lee. Ta."

(Cut to shot of the page, then back to PAGLIA *on set.)*

PAGLIA: "Lola" is traditionally a great name—as in Lola Montez—for a courtesan figure, going back to the nineteenth century and in fact earlier. "Lolita," the diminutive, already implies a kind of infantilization of this figure of adult sexuality. So I think there's a kind of child's play, a sort of breaking of the taboo, a profanation of childhood language, nursery rhymes even in the name "Lo-lee-ta" *(draws it out lasciviously)*.

(Cut to black-and-white newsreel footage of the premiere of the film of Lolita *in New York in 1961. Stentorian, Walter Winchell-like commentary by* MICHAEL FITZMAURICE *for* News of the Day. *Headline: "Lights! Cameras! Premiere in Manhattan." Pan of Times Square on a rainy evening. Under the huge marquee of Loew's State are crowds behind police barriers and surging photographers popping flashbulbs.)*

MICHAEL FITZMAURICE: Broadway at dusk! And as the lights go on, the *News of the Day* camera records the welcome for *Lolita,* the film the whole town's talking about! There is acclaim in the film world for Stanley Kubrick, director of *Lolita,* arriving with Mrs. Kubrick. *(Film of the Kubricks exiting their limousine. An umbrella is held out by a uniformed male usher wearing Lolita's heart-shaped glasses.)* And now, Sue Lyon and James Mason. The capable young actress, who was fourteen when she received the nod to play the title role in *Lolita,* shares the plaudits of the critics and movie fans with Mr. Mason, a veteran of many great starring performances. *(Sue Lyon, in a sensational platinum-blonde bubble hairdo, is paternally supported by the suave James Mason. Also visible are Joan Fontaine, in a chignon and fur stole, escorted by Robert Stack.)*

(Cut to stark black-and-white movie promo: "How did they make a movie of . . . Lolita?*" Collage of Sue Lyon-as-Lolita photos flash by. Cut to London journalist* SUZANNE MOORE.*)*

SUZANNE MOORE: When I think of Lolita, I always think of those heart-shaped sunglasses. When my young daughter wanted some sunglasses, we went into the shop, and they had all different shapes—they had heart shapes and star shapes, you know, for thirty pence, kids' plastic sunglasses. And I bought her— she was really little, about two or three, I think—these little heart-shaped ones, and this friend of mine said, "What are you *doing?* What are you *doing,* putting those on *her?"* Because for him it just signified so *strongly* a kind of sexual—a sexualization. It was the equivalent of putting a little girl in stockings or something. It just wasn't done.

(Cut to the most famous scene from the film, Lolita. *In a bikini, sunglasses, and huge sunhat, Sue Lyon is languorously stretched out on the lawn, reading while her transistor radio blares Nelson Riddle's "Lolita Ya Ya." The raucous voice of Shelley Winters as her landlady-mother is heard extolling the virtues of the establishment to a prospective tenant, James Mason as* HUMBERT HUMBERT.*)*

CHARLOTTE *(Lolita's mother)*: My flowers win prizes around here! They're the talk of the neighborhood. Voilà! My yellow roses, my—uh, oh—my daughter. Darling, turn that down, please. (HUMBERT, *startled and immediately transfixed, stares at* LOLITA. *Turning down the radio with a petulant moue, she returns his gaze unflinchingly, then slowly removes her sunglasses. They continue staring, as her mother chatters on.)* I can offer you a comfortable home, a sunny garden, a congenial atmosphere, my cherry pies—

HUMBERT *(dumbfounded)*: Well, uh . . .

(Cut to author ANNE RICE, *regally seated in a sumptuous green-velvet chair next to a fireplace with a crackling blaze.)*

ANNE RICE: What Lolita has become today is the image of the seductive young girl who is every man's dream of sensuality. That wasn't what the real Lolita was in Nabokov's novel at all. She was a very ordinary girl who didn't herself *have* profound sexual feelings and never really enjoyed the illicit relationship with Humbert Humbert, but that's been forgotten. When people speak of a Lolita today, they mean *(she grins)* a hot little number.

(Cut to a montage of art works showing blossoming young girls in subliminally or overtly provocative poses: Jourdan's The Young Sea Nymph *(1870), Bouguereau's* On the Bank of the Ruisseau *(1888), Mary Cassatt's* Little Girl in a Blue Armchair *(1878), Balthus'* Katia Reading *(1976).)*

PAGLIA *(on set)*: Culture seems to follow patterns of innocence and then cynicism. Because even in our own time there has been a great evolution in our attitudes toward what is now called child pornography. Many of the great art works of the Renaissance had kiddie porn elements, in particular the great *David* of Donatello *(statue shown)*, which today would get Donatello *arrested* and taken off in a *paddy wagon!* In the mid-nineteenth century there was a tradition of painters and photographers, like Lewis Carroll, for taking pictures of young girls totally nude *(a montage of seven photos)* or placed in historical situations, with costumes and so on revealing the nude body in ways that would seem to us today, after Freud, as enormously perverse and sexualized. But this is part of the tradition of Romanticism, of looking at woman and the female principle as being innocent and pure. It's part of the heritage of Rousseau and Wordsworth. Such things are *impossible* now, because we have so *resexualized* the image of the child. This is a *profound* cultural problem that we still are wrestling with.

(Cut to The Face *magazine cover of Kate Moss, proclaimed "This year's model." Cut to* KEVIN KOLLENDA, *model agent for Take 2.)*

KEVIN KOLLENDA: I think there is a definite Lolita syndrome we're seeing in fashion today. You're seeing an innocence reborn. It's the doey-eyed expression, the beautiful lips, the clear skin, the freshness. *(Magazine covers shown.)* And I think that's why the market's gone out after it—because it's a whole new approach. There are girls that nobody's ever seen before. *(Film of Jocelyn, a new "waif" model, at a photo shoot.)* There is the *woman* inside her that comes out. And I think that's *needed* in the photos, because otherwise it would look like a little girl wearing Mommy's clothes or wearing some older woman's clothes. There is the *knowing* in her eyes, the awareness of her womanhood, of her sexuality that I think is combined with her youthfulness. I think that's the magic of this whole look right now. It is quite virginal, the whole approach. It's very new; it's very clean. It's very moralistic—in a world that maybe right now is lacking in some morals!

(Cut to a bubbling bottle of Coca-Cola. The camera pans up to reveal moist red lips suggestively wrapped around a straw.)

PAGLIA: The 1950s were a period when young girls were expected to be virgins in America. Then *my* generation of the 1960s broke through and was overtly sexual. Now what's happened in the generation since the 1960s is quite remarkable. There has been a lowering of the age of overt sexuality in the personae of young women in America. There's a kind of shopping-mall style in junior-high-school and high-school girls that has led to the Amy Fisher case in this country.

(Cut to television news film of Fisher's 1992 sentencing.)

BAILIFF: All rise!

VOICE OF REPORTER *(ABC's Jeff Greenfield)*: When eighteen-year-old Amy Fisher was sentenced today for shooting the wife of her alleged lover, the judge acknowledged the obvious.

JUDGE: To some people, you have become a media celebrity.

PAGLIA *(on set)*: Amy Fisher, in her personal style—a kind of slutty, trashy shopping-mall style—absolutely embodies the American version of Lolita. Right from early on, headlines in America were screaming "Long Island Lolita." *(Front pages of New York*

Post, Daily News, *and* New York Newsday: *"Young Gun," "Laughing Lolita," "D-Day for Amy," "Why was I ever born?"*) It was an amazing resurgence of this image in popular culture here. I think what's so fascinating to *me* in the Amy Fisher case is the way you have this *face-off* on a porch between this seventeen-year-old girl and this suburban mother, and they were fighting, essentially, for territoriality over this *man*, all right? *(Film of Mary Jo Buttafuoco, the wounded wife, pressing through a mob of reporters in the courthouse hallway. Then Joey Buttafuoco cursing photographers outside his Long Island home.)* Every one of these great crime stories or great sexually sensationalistic stories is showing the actual *reality*—the *unstable* reality of human sexuality.

(Back to Fisher's sentencing. Somewhat rumpled and nervous, she listens to the judge's statement, her face a strange mixture of fear and fascination.)

JUDGE: Motivated by lust and passion, you were a walking stick of dynamite with the fuse lit.

(On screen: "Amy Fisher is serving five to fifteen years for attempted murder.")

PAGLIA: Nabokov's *Lolita*, which seemed *very* sensationalistic and out of sync with the times in the mid-1950s, now seems to be almost a documentary record of the kind of pornographic real-life cases that have spilled over into the media in the Nineties.

(Cut to amusing clip from the film Lolita. HUMBERT *is wedged between* LOLITA *and her mother in the front seat of a car at a drive-in, where a horror movie is playing. As screams peal from the screen, both women clutch at* HUMBERT's *knee* LOLITA *to her mother's surprise and annoyance—ends up with* HUMBERT's *hands sandwiched between her own.)*

ANNE RICE: Children are definitely sexual beings. They're sexual beings from the time they're little, bitty babies, and of course we have to protect them. We have to look out for them. We don't want to put them at the mercy of adult sexuality. That would be a terribly overwhelming and unfair thing to do. And there *have* to be laws to protect children, but to *deny* that they have any sexual feelings at all is *monstrous*. To talk to fifteen-and sixteen-year-old girls as if they have no desire themselves is perfectly insane! To lead them to believe that the appropriate role for them is that of a passive victim when they reach the age of seventeen and eighteen is *nonsense*.

(Voice of a contemporary actor reading an excerpt from Lolita, *while vintage Fifties film shows adolescent girls primping and preening amid sewing machines in home economics class and then modeling sports skirts in a fashion show.)*

HUMBERT: "Between the age limits of nine and fourteen there occur maidens who, to certain bewitched travelers, twice or many times older than they, reveal their *true nature*. The little deadly demon among wholesome children, she stands unrecognized by them and unconscious herself of her fantastic power."

PAGLIA: I think the Lolita story forces us to face the fact that the girl in these adult-child relationships may *not* be the innocent that she seems, that there is a complicated game being played under the surface. Because I have heard repeatedly from mothers that there are certain daughters born to them who learn how to twist Daddy around their little finger from the moment they can *walk*, all right? I think there may in fact possibly be even a flirtation gene. I myself was born without it!

(Cut to contemporary actors playing HUMBERT *and* LOLITA, *who is non-chalantly chewing gum. Obsessed, he stares at her, while she slowly blows a big pink bubble until it bursts with a pop. Cut to clip from Vincente Minnelli's film* Gigi *(1958). Dressed like a dandy with top hat and cane,* MAURICE CHE-VALIER *sits on a park bench in Paris, as Gigi (Leslie Caron) plays tag with other schoolgirls.)*

MAURICE CHEVALIER: This story is about a little girl. It could be any *one* of those little girls playing there. But it isn't. It's about one in particular—that one. Her name is Gigi . . . Gigi. *(Laughs suggestively.)* What you have to look forward to, Gigi! *(Chuckles and sings.)* Those little eyes so helpless and appealing/ One day will flash and send you crashing through the ceiling./ Thank heaven for little girls . . . "

PAGLIA: I don't think there is quite as sharp a borderline in France between childhood and adult sexuality as there is in England and America. It's therefore no surprise to me that the Lolita motif has continued as a French archetype all these decades after all this confusion for the last five years, where I felt that I had to constantly rationalize my work and my feelings about my children. *(Montage of her photos of her nude children.)* And there is a *huge* amount of *sensuality* in how I feel about them. But that *isn't sexual,* and I think that that's where the difference lies. And I *do* think that people have a lot of trouble with that hairline difference between sexuality and sensuality. *(She picks up a black-and-white photo of Daisy and Jesse, aged seven and nine, touching hips. Seen from behind, their backs and buttocks resemble those of marble Greek kouros sculptures.)* This image here, when this was exhibited, as part of a larger exhibition—I went to one of the exhibition organizers and said I thought that this would be a wonderful image for the poster. And she just completely freaked out and said that there was absolutely no way this could *ever* be used for a poster in *any* sense, and she mentioned the word "pedophilia." And I was really *shocked. (She picks up a photograph of Daisy, at eight, peering through tumbled hair half-obscuring her face.)* And another exhibition organizer looked at this one, and she'd been leafing through the photographs and saying that she liked them, and she said, didn't I think that I'd "constructed" this in a "Lolita-ish" way? And again, I was *completely* dumbfounded! I really didn't know what to say because it had *never* even *occurred* to me. I've had lots of comments about, you know—well, obviously you posed her with her hair over her eyes to make her look at the camera in a soft porn pose—which, to be honest with you, I mean, I *didn't.* It was a look that she *had* a lot of the time, and you can see it in family snaps—if you care to look through my family album! So I didn't have a problem with this image. And although I think that this one *(displays a photo of her son, in a dreamy pose, at ten)* could be misconstrued in exactly the same way, no one's ever mentioned a word about this one being a sexual image because, perhaps, of him being a boy.

ANNE RICE: I don't think there's any danger in using children in art. I think it'll always be confusing. There'll always be a heavy note of seductiveness in it, you know. And if you look at the old Pear's soap commercials with the beautiful little girl *(cut to Pear's advertisement),* that's a sexy little girl. Now there's nothing really since the period of Brigitte Bardot. *(Clips from early Bardot films,* I find very attractive in French culture the overt sexual grace and frank acknowledgment of sensuality in young French women.

(As a woman looks on, the ebullient, teenaged Bardot is whirled round in the arms of a brawny man, who carries her away.)

WOMAN: She's enchanting!

MAN *(domineeringly)*: She's—she's such a baby!

(Cut to film of seven-year-old blonde Bardot lookalike VANESSA PARADIS *singing on French television.)*

VANESSA PARADIS *(lisping charmingly)*: *Et même la lune . . . vivre avec nous la vie . . . (forgets words, trails off, and giggles).*

HOST: *Tu fais un peu de danse? Tu fais un peu de danse, non?* [You'll do a little dance?]

PARADIS: *Oui.* [Yes.]

ANNOUNCER: *De la dance classique?* [Classical dance?]

PARADIS: *Rhythmique.* [Modern dance.]

ANNOUNCER: *Fais moi voir commencer!* [Go ahead, show me!]

(Cut to moody, blue-toned music video of a fifteen-year-old Paradis, now with full-scale, petulant Bardot lips. She slowly washes her face with water from a basin, pats herself dry with a towel, and stretches out languidly on a bed.)

SUZANNE MOORE: Well, the last time I was in Paris, I just noticed everywhere images of nymphets, if you like, of people like Vanessa Paradis. I think French women often are kept in a very kind of infantile position within their families, and that's reflected in a kind of sexual imagery that you see there.

(Cut to NANCY HONEY, *photographer, in London.)*

NANCY HONEY: It was interesting that when I recently had an exhibition of a lot of different pieces of my work in France, they certainly had *no problem* when it came to how the images would be *read.* And I just thought that was so different and refreshing, dirty or ugly about that. It's beautiful. But she's cuddly, and she's sensuous, and it's a gateway to something. But, I mean, you're not meant to *open* that gate and go that way, you know? That's the idea. But if we get too puritanical and we try to stamp out any use of children in art, I think that would be a terrible thing. Children *exist.*

(Cut to photographs from Immediate Family, *Sally Mann's pictures of her children. One little girl, playing* Sorry, *has an off-the-shoulder blouse; another holds a pretend cigarette; another, clutching a doll, wears heart-shaped sunglasses. A half-nude boy gracefully poses with hand on bare hip; his wrist seems tied by black thongs. In the last picture, a girl who may or may not be nude stands in roller skates on a darkened porch, her hand falling near her crotch.)*

PAGLIA: I feel the function of the modern artist is precisely to shatter *all taboos* and that where the subject of the art work causes the most pain, that is where the artist is contributing the most to civilization.

(Cut to pastoral scene, Barley Splatt, Cornwall. Water spills into a stream, which mirrors the stone, fortress-like country home of GRAHAM OVENDEN, *artist.)*

GRAHAM OVENDEN: One of the great problems at the moment is the actual automatic association of sexuality with sexual abuse in children. (OVENDEN *is shown sitting in his studio among his paintings of nude prepubescent girls.)* I mean, it's just patent and complete and utter nonsense. I think that the two have become so ingrained in the popular imagery, in the tabloid imagery, it's going to be *very* difficult for children in fact to have *any* normal understanding of their sexual selves.

This conversation in Germany or France, in fact, would be a non-starter, because the problems and the neuroses which we are talking about is a peculiar Anglo-Saxon problem, as far as one can tell. *(gestures at two nude paintings)* This is a pair of commissioned portraits which I am working on at the moment, and they happen to be German girls. And they happen to come from one of the most famous German families! *(laughs)* I don't feel the slightest desire, in fact—apart from doing straight por-

traits—of doing nudes of children in Anglo-Saxon countries. I
suppose in a way one could say I'm being chicken by saying
that, but we've actually reached a point in this country where
it becomes equivocal whether in fact one is actually doing something legally.

The present morality is a very *cloaking* one. Instead of the
figure growing outwards in all its sort of state of grace, its clarity
and its purity, it is cloaked. It's taken *back* into darkness, into
the shadows. I mean, I don't bring nudity into it. *Nudity* is totally
immaterial, because nudity is actually a state of *purity*—an *absolute state. (The camera pans other of his paintings, where nude young
girls boldly fix spookily intense eyes on the viewer.)* This gaze, I mean,
this is one of the most precious and wonderful qualities which
you find in childhood. That stare, that *clear-eyed stare* in fact has
the universe in it. And there is that sort of emotional quality in
a child's look. I'd like on occasion to think of it as the child
staring out at you and saying, you know, "Beware. Do *not* corrupt me." Perhaps because people are generally, shall we say,
emotional cowards. It worries them, that stare.

(Cut to ANDREW SAMUELS, *Jungian analyst in London.)*

ANDREW SAMUELS: If you start to look at Lolita—the theme, the
syndrome, as well as the book—from the point of view of males
in crisis, then something new happens to our thinking. Let me
explain what I mean. If you look at Lolita from the point of
view of a clapped out, valueless, spiritually empty, middle-aged,
middle-class professional—people like you, me, and a lot of the
viewers of this program—then what you start to see is the way
Lolita, the image, carries a certain kind of hope. Hope for a
spiritual regeneration, hope for a connection with something
deeper.

(Cut to actors portraying HUMBERT *and* LOLITA. *As he leafs through a
magazine, she is chewing gum, toying with her hair, and scratching her shin.
Voice-over of extract from* Lolita.)

HUMBERT: "My innocent little visitor slowly sank to a half-sitting
position on my knee. Her adorable profile, parted lips, warm
hair were some three inches from my bared eyetooth; I felt the

heat of her limbs through her rough tomboy clothes. And all at once I knew I could kiss her throat or the wick of her mouth with perfect impunity. I knew she would let me do so, and even close her eyes as Hollywood teaches."

(Cut to KIM MORRISSEY, *author of* Poems For Men Who Dream of Lolita.*)*

KIM MORRISSEY: *Lolita* is a book where the fictional character of Dolores—Lolita—has no voice. And you never hear her side of the story. And so there's a great desire, I think, for women to have those voices that are traditionally left out of literature heard. When I wrote these poems, I wanted people to *never* be able to say the word "Lolita" again and use it in the clichéd way that we have. *(She reads from her book. Dreamlike footage of girl on a swing is superimposed on her face, accompanied by distorted playground shouts.)* "Stepfather, somewhere between the dark stain on the tiles and the towels heaped on the back of the toilet, you rest your case. I may leave if I want. Today you are giving me choices. I watch my head turn in the mirror, thin hair fingerbrushed back, tied low on my neck like a bow, taste your hair at the back of my throat, tightly wound wires riding the tip of my tongue. Today is a day we make choices. You or the foster home. You or the chair."

PAGLIA *(on set)*: I would maintain that the novel contains a cloaked incest drama. That in fact there is a masked father figure—Humbert—in this story that expresses the eternal conundrum of the incest taboo in our culture. We must recall that the two greatest plays in Western history, Sophocles' *Oedipus Rex* and Shakespeare's *Hamlet,* contain incest themes. We seem to be returning to this problem again and again.

(Cut to film clip from Lolita. *Sue Lyon as* LOLITA, *chomping crackers, is perched in a window, with her feet flirtatiously up on a table at which James Mason as* HUMBERT *is dolefully sitting.)*

HUMBERT: I will never give away any of your secrets.

LOLITA: You wouldn't?

HUMBERT: I promise.

LOLITA: Oh! Well for that, you get a little reward.

HUMBERT: Oh, thank you very much.

LOLITA: Here. *(She dangles a large slice of fish over his mouth.)*

HUMBERT *(fatigued, exasperated)*: Oh, no, please. No—Lolita. No.

LOLITA: Put your head back. Put your head back! Open your mouth. You can have *one little bite!* *(He suddenly grips her wrist and takes a big bite.)*

CHARLOTTE *(puzzled, then anxious at the foot of the stairs)*: Lolita! Lolita!

PAGLIA: We're faced with a conundrum, a paradox here at the end of the century. We want to draw the father *into* the family unit closer and closer. Fathers now freely push strollers in a way that would have been embarrassing for them in the 1950s. But *now,* how close is too close? *(Cut to contemporary reenactment of LOLITA clumsily applying lipstick in a mirror. HUMBERT hovers intently in the background of her reflection.)* Just *what* are the boundary lines of acceptable physical behavior between fathers and children?

NANCY HONEY: Lots of dads have actually told me that they now feel that they can't even *touch* their eight-, nine-, ten-year-old girls without feeling that somehow there's something *wrong* with it. And it's, I think, *more* dangerous to stop physical closeness for a father and daughter, or for a father and son, than it is to be so worried about it. *(Cut to intimate portrait of HONEY's husband and son)*

ANDREW SAMUELS: There *is* something mutually enriching and enhancing in the communications between father and daughter that stress, above all, the potential erotic liability of the daughter. What we're badly lacking, and urgently need to develop, are texts that stress *positive* aspects of the erotically charged relationship between daughter and father. *(Cut to reenactment of HUMBERT gently kissing LOLITA's forehead)* What *I* would want to do is to reconnect Lolita—and our worries about Lolita are justifiable and understandable worries about a veritable *explosion* of Lolita-ism in Western culture—I'd want to connect that *back* to ordinary benevolent erotics in the family.

(Cut to film of Nabokov in shorts, prowling mountain meadows with a butterfly net. He deftly traps a butterfly, inspects it, then releases it.)

PAGLIA: Nabokov's novel was like a hand grenade thrown into the middle of the 1950s, blowing apart this kind of tranquil, settled, unexamined relationship between parents and children. In *Lolita,* Nabokov created a character who would come to symbolize the removal, in the final decades of this century, of the line that history had drawn between childhood and adult sexuality. We are now in the center of a sexual storm. It remains to be seen whether that line, artificial and repressive as it was, was not in fact in the best interests of culture.

(Cut to logs of the girl in the opening scene. She is twisting her hair around her fingers. We hear Sarah Vaughan singing "Let's fall in love right here and now." The girl lifts the needle from the spinning 45, abruptly stopping the music. Cut to reenactment of HUMBERT *watching* LOLITA *blow an enormous bubble. It pops into a black-out.)*

MASTERS AND

MISTRESSES

DIANA REGINA

With the release of Andrew Morton's book, *Diana: Her True Story*, the decade-long Diana cult has become more than a sentimental fairy tale. Morton's book, first published in June, created a publicity storm unprecedented even for naughty, tell-all celebrity biographies. The June 7 edition of the *Sunday Times* of London, which contained the first serialized excerpt, sold a record number of issues, up 21 percent from the regular 1,143,000 sale. In the United States, the issue of *People* that contained the first excerpt for American audiences sold 4,001,100 copies, a record in the magazine's eighteen-year history. Simon and Schuster had to double its 200,000-copy print run of *Diana* within days of publication. The book flew to the top of *The New York Times* best-seller list, which also contains, at fifth place, a recent book by Lady Colin Campbell, *Diana in Private*, and at fifteenth, Nicholas Davies's *Diana: A Princess and Her Troubled Marriage*.

The book was shrouded in secrecy during production, but tantalizing tidbits began to leak out in the week before its serialization by the *Sunday Times*. The marriage of the Prince and Princess of

[Cover story, *The New Republic*, August 3, 1992]

Wales was over. Diana, weakened by bulimia, had tried to kill herself five times. Charles flaunted a mistress. There would be a divorce, a constitutional crisis, the collapse of the monarchy. The editor of the *Sunday Times*, denounced by members of Parliament and royalist hangers-on, stoutly defended the authenticity of the book, whose on-the-record sources are of unprecedented closeness to Diana, including her brother, Viscount Althorp. Because the book also uses a large number of unpublished family photographs, there was speculation that Diana herself had cooperated, however discreetly, with its production.

But as the American response to the news shows, the fascination with Diana is more than a British phenomenon. It is an international obsession whose scale and longevity show that it is more than high-class soap opera or a reactionary wish-fulfillment fantasy for American Anglophiles. Those who have never taken Diana seriously should take a new look. With this latest burst of press attention, Diana may have become the most powerful image in world popular culture today, a case study in the modern cult of celebrity and the way it stimulates atavistic religious emotions. It is increasingly obvious that Diana's story taps into certain deep and powerful strains in our culture, strains that suggest that the ancient archetypes of conventional womanhood are not obsolete but stronger and deeper than ever.

Cinderella. When we first met her, Diana was a shy, blushing teenager who had landed the world's most eligible bachelor, a dashing Prince Charming with a throne in his future. Morton's book reveals that Diana is Cinderella in more ways than one. Despite her privileged background, she had a desultory finishing-school education and earned money doing odd jobs as a charlady—"vacuuming, dusting, ironing, and washing." Bizarrely, we actually see her "on her knees cleaning the kitchen floor" as she chats with a chum about her weekend plans. The Cinderella analogy continues in the way Diana is pushed around and undermined by real and step relations: her bossy, fast-track sister Sarah, her ruthless, showy step-mother Raine, and the snippy female royals. She is stonewalled, outwitted, criticized, particularly by a stiff and censorious Queen Mother, who had been publicly portrayed during the engagement as Diana's benevolent elder mentor.

The betrayed wife. Morton's book confirms rumors that have floated around for years about Charles's long-term mistress, Camilla Parker-Bowles, whom Charles dated before her marriage in 1973 to an army officer who is now Silver Stick in Waiting to the Queen, a peculiarly suggestive Tudor honorific. We now learn that Charles hardly spent a moment alone with Diana during the engagement. She seems to have been selected with clinical detachment as a brood mare to carry on the Windsor line. Like Mia Farrow in *Rosemary's Baby*, tricked and maneuvered into impregnation by Satan, she is isolated and conspired against by a faithless husband in league with a secretive, coldly smiling coterie. Most intolerably, her suitability as a mate was approved by Camilla herself, who deemed Diana the least threatening of rivals. Charles even proposed to Diana in the Parker-Bowles garden, as if under his mistress's aegis.

We are certainly getting only one side of the story. It is unlikely that the mature, athletic, tally-ho Camilla, whom Diana cattily calls the "rottweiler," is as merciless and scheming as she is presented here. But the tales we are told—photographs of Camilla falling out of Charles's diary, Charles on the royal honeymoon sporting new cuff links from Camilla with two "Cs" intertwined, Diana over-hearing Charles in his bathtub professing eternal love to Camilla on his portable telephone, Camilla boldly presiding as hostess at the married Charles's country estate—inevitably make us sympathize with the young, fragile, and self-doubting Diana. Like Isabel Archer in Henry James's *The Portrait of a Lady*, Diana is an ingenue subtly manipulated by a cynical matron, a sexual sophisticate of insidious insideness.

The princess in the tower. Diana's story revives motifs of imperiled or mourning femininity that flourished in Victorian poetry and paint-ing but that one had thought long dead in this era of aggressively career-oriented feminism. Having discharged his princely duty to marry, Charles apparently cut himself off from Diana emotionally. She seems orphaned, abandoned. Her old friends, outside the moat, joke that "POW," Princess of Wales, really means "prisoner of war." Languishing in plush solitude, Diana resembles a whole series of melancholy pre-Raphaelite heroines painted by Holman Hunt and John Everett Millais: Tennyson's lovelorn Lady of Shalott caught in the threads of her loom, or his desolate Mariana, languidly stretching herself in her blue velvet gown; or Keats's half-mad young lover Isabella, watering the pot of basil with her tears. Like Andromeda chained to the rock—the theme of one of Burne-Jones's greatest paintings—Diana is both imprisoned and exposed. She is trapped in royal formulas of decorum, with the world's eyes upon her. Her immediate predecessor is another Diana: Julie Christie in *Darling* as a spirited young woman who leaves swinging Sixties London to become an Italian *principessa*, only to be buried alive in grandiose luxury and the unctuous obsequiousness of a hovering army of servants.

The mater dolorosa. Diana's children, William and Harry, give her image stature. Without them, and her widely noted physical tenderness toward them, her marital complaints would seem far more juvenile or petulant. It is ironic that Charles, who plucked Diana from obscurity and who has all the weight of rank and wealth behind him, seems helpless in the court of popular opinion against the ancient archetype of the sorrowing mother or *mater dolorosa*, which Christianity borrowed from the cult of Isis. Charles had sought and found, in Morton's words, "a virginal Protestant aristocrat to be his bride" only to discover that his philandering attempts to remain himself produced a new Catholic Madonna, a modern Mary with a taste for rock and roll.

"Diana in tears" was the caption on the June 29 cover of *People* magazine—the second cover story in a row—which reproduced a photo now seen everywhere of the Princess of Wales at her first official appearance several days after the *Times* serialization began. Head bowed and biting her lip, she seems visibly shaken, but no tears are visible. This did not stop an American supermarket tabloid from artificially adding a tear streak and enhancing the drops, so that Diana resembles a Spanish Baroque Madonna with precious crystal tears sparkling down her cheeks. Weeping Madonnas are considered miraculous manifestations in Catholicism; like Diana, they draw rapt and unruly crowds. Morton matter-of-factly reports several dramatic instances of Diana's prophetic power to foretell death or catastrophic illness. For example, she publicly predicted her father's massive stroke the day before it happened, and she said aloud, while watching Charles gallop on his horse, Allibar, that it was going to have a heart attack and die—which it immediately did.

With the painful revelations of this book, Diana now assumes the international position once held by Jacqueline Kennedy after the assassination of her husband. Suffering redeems, and the world honors grace under pressure. Diana's dislike of the sporting life at Balmoral, the royal family's hallowed vacation retreat in Scotland, recalls the soft-spoken Jackie's hard knocks in the early years of her marriage: trying to fit in with the hyperkinetic, competitive, roughhousing Kennedys, she broke her ankle in a touch-football game and never went that route again. The supreme moment of Jackie's public life was her dignified deportment at John Kennedy's funeral, where, draped in a misty black veil, she stoically stood with her two small children, gazing at the flag draped casket. In Morton's book, Diana is significantly shown alone with her children. Though she is smiling, the somber black-and-white of the photographs suggests her mourning for a dead marriage.

The pagan goddess. Diana's conflict with her husband's mistress has Greco-Roman echoes unusual for the British royal family: Diana, a fierce Italian goddess of the woods, versus Camilla, Virgil's Amazon, the militant Volscian horsewoman. A photo in Morton's book shows the young Diana Spencer dreamily reading a hunting magazine, *The Field: The Stalking Review,* with grazing stags on its cover. The caption informs us, "While she has a reputation for being unenthusiastic about blood sports, Diana does enjoy stag hunting." Throughout art history, the ancient Diana, hot on the chase with her dogs, is almost invariably depicted with a stag or doe. Do names contain their own fate?

The Hollywood queen. Morton tells us that Charles, exasperated by his wife's "histrionics," has often accused her of feigning "martyrdom." Indeed, in reserved upper-class British terms, Diana's behavior has an operatic Mediterranean theatricality. In her quarrels with Charles, the pregnant Diana threw herself down the Sandringham staircase, where she was found by the "Queen Mum," as the London dailies put it in June. On other occasions, she slashed her wrists with a razor blade, cut herself with a lemon slicer, stabbed herself in the chest and thighs with Charles's penknife, and hurled herself against a glass cabinet at Kensington Palace. These may have been, as the *Times* headline said, "Cries for Help" rather than serious suicide attempts, but Diana's lurid private exhibitionism, so different from her public introversion, is reminiscent not only of the sensually gory lives of the saints but of Hollywood at its garish high point, the era of the "women's pictures" of Lana Turner, Susan Hayward, and Jane Wyman, which featured flawed, gallant, tormented women loyal to gorgeous but callow men.

The old Hollywood studio system was like the Vatican in the way it manufactured stars and promoted its ornate ideology. The House of Windsor still functions like a studio in the way it sequesters its stars and subjects them to inhumane rules that make them more than human. Although she is still called "Di" in America, as if she were magically ever-virgin, Diana at her marriage ceased to be a private person and became Her Royal Highness, the Princess of Wales, one in a long succession of women holding that title. She merged with her function. Similarly, the movements of the royals are recorded daily in the *Times* under the rubric of their residences, as if the palace itself has a greater living authority.

Diana's enormous glamour springs from the tension between energy and structure. Going about her public duties, she radiates a magnetic power that is directly produced by her disciplined containment within class and rank. Her staggering worldwide popularity demonstrates the enduring power and significance of hierarchy, a power that fashionable academic paradigms—influenced by feminism, Marxism, Foucault, and the Frankfurt School—cannot understand and whose enduring mystique can only be explained by Roman Catholicism or Hollywood history.

Diana's sole contemporary parallel as an international pop diva is the second Madonna, who, like Diana, expresses herself best through dance, the universal language. Both Diana and Madonna have trouble with words, which fail them in public. Diana even stumbled over her wedding vows, when she reversed the order of Charles's names. It is remarkable how Diana has projected her personality without the use of words. Photographs and video footage are her medium. She may be the last of the silent film stars. Morton's book reveals Diana's secret private life as a solitary ballet dancer: we see her gracefully poised *en pointe* on the rotting stone balustrades at the "creepy" ancestral Althorp estate, which symbolize, as in *Last Year at Marienbad*, the ambivalent burden of history. Diana's classical dance training has given her an aplomb and distinction of carriage that make for great photographs even when she is simply getting in and out of cars—a talent conspicuously lacking in the lumbering, bottom-heavy Sarah Ferguson. Like the great stars of the Hollywood studio era, Diana exists for us as primarily a visul presence.

The beautiful boy. The stunning childhood color photographs in Morton's book, lavishly reproduced with the care normally reserved for old-master paintings, reveal an element in Diana we may have been only subliminally aware of: her boyish androgyny. With her refined Greek profile and ethereal expression, she looks remarkably like the seraphic Antinous. Staring vacantly at the television in a half-dozen different pictures, she has the eerie, blank, contemplative "Attic look" of Athenian divinities.

Charisma springs from a presexual narcissism that is both male and female. It is Diana's androgynous charisma that makes her so photogenic; the camera is picking up her perfect, glowing, self-enclosed childlikeness—not to be confused with childishness, a behavioral flaw. Morton's book provides startling new information to explain this phenomenon: "I Was Supposed To Be a Boy," reads one chapter title. A badly deformed male baby was born to the Spencers, after two healthy girls, and soon died. Diana, the third girl, born a year and a half later, disappointed everyone's expectations. The fifth child was the long-awaited male heir, christened with great fanfare in Westminster Abbey, with the Queen as godparent. Brought up with her brother in a divorced home, with her two older sisters soon off to boarding school, Diana seems to have merged with him in gender: standing in the photos next to his athletic, long-legged sister, he seems plump, girlish, and abashed.

Very beautiful people have an autoerotic quality plainly visible in the Diana pictures, which border on kiddie porn. The young Diana, in boots and creased, crotch-tight overalls, leans back against a fence rail in an attitude of solicitation normally associated with boy prostitutes. We see a good deal of the ample developing bosom and a great array of peekaboo shots in towels and bathrobes, including one in a Paris hotel bed. Aquatics offer all the charms of semi-nudity, and so we repeatedly watch Diana diving or posing,

with the precise leg position of Botticelli's Venus, at poolside. There
has been a persistent, half-conscious provocativeness in Diana's big
public moments. In her first candid photo session at the London
kindergarten where she worked, the newly engaged Diana was
caught against sunlight in a see-through skirt that revealed her willowy legs. For her first official appearance with Charles, she chose
a strapless, low-cut, lushly bust-revealing black ballgown that enamored the world but—we now learn—surprised and annoyed
Charles.

One of the principal, much-debated issues relating to the cult
of Greek youth was *paideia,* or education. Child-rearing emerges as
a major theme in Morton's book. Diana was raised with the "for-
mality and restraint" typical of British upper-class families. Her
brother never had a meal with his father until he was seven. The
kind of constant parent-child contact that is the norm, for better or
worse, in poorer, smaller homes was missing from both Diana's and
Charles's upbringing. Nannies, ranging "from the sweet to the sadistic," as Morton puts it, are the parent substitutes. One nanny
punished the Spencer girls by mixing laxatives in their food; another
beat Diana on the head with a wooden spoon. The children retaliated
by putting pins on the nannies' chairs or throwing their clothes out
the window. Privileged British children are soon packed off to boarding school, in an enforced separation from their homes that would
be considered cruel and traumatic in contemporary America. Diana
is determined to treat her sons differently: "I hug my children to
death and get into bed with them at night." Is this enlightened or
suffocating?

The book's striking dust-jacket photos illustrate Diana's duality.
On the front, she kneels in a fountain of white chiffon. She is wearing
what looks like a stripped-down wedding dress from which every
adornment has been torn, after battle on the field of love. The bodice
is daringly off-the-shoulder, in her usual unsettling subtext of sensuality. On the back, in her androgynous mode, Diana wears a
bohemian black turtleneck and pants. With her tousled hair, she
looks like the Beatles on their first album cover. This reminds us
that, with the failure of the Wales' marriage, the popular imagination
has suffered its bleakest awakening since the Beatles broke up.

Diana's multiple personae, from princess and mother to Greek ephebe, are rich and far-ranging but also mutually contradictory, and they are clearly consuming her. No one, least of all a nervous, vulnerable young woman, could sustain the voyeuristic laser beam of the world's adulation. Deification has its costs. The modern mega-celebrity, bearing the burden of collective symbolism, projection, and fantasy, is a ritual victim, cannibalized by our pity and fear. Those at the apex of the social pyramid are untouchables, condemned to horrifying solitude. There may have been many unhappy wives in royal history, but they did not have to live their emotions under the minute scrutiny of the telephoto lens. Mass media have made both myth and disaster out of Diana's story. We have created her in our own image. And, pursued by our best wishes, Diana the huntress is now the hind paralyzed in the world's gun sight.

TELEVISION AND THE CLINTONS

Television is America's kingmaker. The election of Bill Clinton to the presidency has finally demonstrated that television is not the crude, vulgar destroyer of political intelligence that so many commentators have claimed over the past twenty years.

The television eye does not lie. Ads can be manipulated, but the live camera, following candidates around the clock through the long, bruising primary and campaign seasons, lets the public scrutinize the field up close and personal. Jostled, harassed, and dog-tired, candidates eventually reveal their true nature, in all its quirks and strengths.

Policy alone is no way to pick a modern president. In the nineteenth century, before America was a world power, exhaustive three-hour debates of the Lincoln–Douglas kind may have been indispensable for proving fitness for office. But in today's intricate web of global telecommunications, unpredictable hair-trigger crises in remote, unstable places are a constant reality.

George Bush was right: character is the ultimate criterion for measuring political candidates. The man or woman who would be

[*San Francisco Examiner*, November 15, 1992]

president must have energy, stamina, good instincts, and steady nerves. Like an admiral or general under fire, the president must make snap judgments about confused, mercurial situations where information is scanty and the lives of thousands hang in the balance.

Clinton's positions on civil rights, the environment, and the economy were not enough to elect him if he failed the character test. Questions about his honesty and integrity hovered over him throughout the campaign. Zigging and zagging, he never gave fully satisfactory answers about his military draft history or alleged extramarital affairs. But popular support solidified enough to win him the White House. How and why?

The 1992 election was one of television's finest hours. Press reports have overstressed the unique television candidacy of independent Ross Perot, who used his billions to buy airtime in the canned style of late-night kitchen-gadget commercials. Television gave Perot national exposure, but it also undid him. Charmed at first by his brusque business sense and tart Texas talk, many people became disturbed by Perot's erratic glibness and mythomania, of which his bloody, elaborate, but totally uncorroborated dog-bites-terrorist-buttocks tale was the most grotesque example.

Television at first seemed to sink Clinton. His performance on *60 Minutes*—when he and Hillary evaded Steve Kroft's questions about Gennifer Flowers's claims of a long affair with Clinton—was weak. He was sheepish, ill-at-ease, abashed, like a schoolboy caught with his hand in the cookie jar. His wife was stronger, more resolute, mixing offense and defense with defiant bursts of vinegar and pepper. Hillary seemed fascinating and talented, but did one want to promote to commander-in-chief a man who came across as an overgrown mouse on his wife's leash?

60 Minutes was the valley of political death out of which Clinton climbed by his own persistence and effort. Week by week, he slogged along through the primaries, facing down snickering, insults, and slander. He seemed tireless. The exhausted press corps called him "Robo-candidate." This was Clinton's punishing rite of passage.

As the nation watched on television, bags sagged under his eyes, and his voice grew raspy. His goofy, overconciliatory manner disappeared. His temper flared. The moment in New York when he fiercely snapped back at a gay heckler was pivotal. Battleworn and peevish, the boyish Clinton found the stern masculine persona without which no one—male or female—can lead a nation.

Retaining his buoyancy and composure through adversity, Clinton grittily proved his character on television. It was also how he defeated a sitting president. By sheer brute physical vigor and endurance, Clinton forced a changing of the guard, a supplanting of one generation by the next. The fall of the elders before a young challenger is always a cruel moment in mythology or in wolf packs.

Throughout the campaign, Bush was vague, fumbling, fatigued. He who had finally emerged from Ronald Reagan's paternal shadow only four years ago now seemed antiquated, dispensable. Bush's waning was ironically intensified by the unexpected waxing of Dan Quayle, who in the twilight of the Republican dynasty suddenly gained a sharp combative voice and persona after his long purgatory of scathing mockery by comedians and pundits. Quayle's self-propulsion out of eclipse was also made possible by television.

The baby-boom generation has come to power in both parties with a surge of primal energy. Clinton has ignited the hopes and passions of the students of the Nineties in exactly the way John F. Kennedy did for us in the Sixties. I remember the breathless exhilaration I felt as a thirteen-year-old campaigning for Kennedy in 1960. The doldrums of the Eisenhower years were over. The whole future opened giddily before us.

The exuberant energy of the Clintons and Gores connects us again to what was best about the Sixties generation, which later defeated itself in so many ways. On the podium at the Democratic convention, Hillary Clinton and Tipper Gore held hands and jumped up and down in a victory dance of infectious glee. On stage at the governor's mansion in Little Rock on election night, Al Gore, kneeling and wildly shaking hands, had to be yanked back by the belt as he nearly toppled into the crowd.

Spontaneity, humor, fun: the Sixties, older and wiser, have returned. It's hard to imagine Nancy Reagan breaking into a jig to Fleetwood Mac. Sixties women are not afraid to break the rules or offend decorum. The Clintons as a shrewd power couple have forged a broad national coalition by breaking the sterile deadlock of liberal versus conservative that has paralyzed political thought for twenty-five years. They have taken the best from left and right to make a promising new synthesis that combines the moral quest for social justice with a respect for history and tradition, the virtues of the heartland.

But what happens next? To govern, one must command the stubborn machinery of Washington, which outlasts all presidencies and parties. One must prioritize, husband resources, quell the turf wars of subordinates and special interests, and keep the ravenous media at bay. And around the world a hundred sectarian pots threaten to boil over. If the new administration can find the right combination of courage, toughness, and patience, the Sixties will have truly matured.

KIND OF A BITCH:

WHY I LIKE HILLARY CLINTON

Many of us voted for the Clintons as a power couple. They complement each other, and neither is totally adequate as a leader alone. That, I think, is what is so new. They are a symbol of the new kind of feminism: woman as co-equal to man, and sharer of responsibilities. When conservatives maligned Hillary before the election as "The Lady Macbeth of Little Rock," the feminist establishment tried to claim that this was the sort of vulgar, derogatory talk always used by the patriarchy to cut down ambitious and competent women. I saw that the charge had some truth in it. I like Hillary because she's kind of a bitch. She has a quick, sharp tongue—which she managed to conceal for most of the campaign but which comes out periodically.

But what won Clinton the presidency—his buoyancy and his common touch—are things that Hillary Clinton lacks. I've been a public fan of Hillary's right from the start, but there has been wild overpraise of her by the feminist establishment, which has seriously overestimated her capabilities.

Normally in power couples, it's the man who is cold and realistic

[An interview with Rebecca Mead, cover story, *Sunday Times* magazine, London, April 18, 1993. Original title.]

and the wife who has feeling for children and likes to press the flesh. It's the opposite with the Clintons, a sexual reversal: he's the one who gets teary-eyed and is a sentimentalist, who is a sucker for ceremonial occasions and for kissing babies. She has much more of a legalistic and highly organized way of thinking. She has the more traditionally masculine mind, he has the softer heart.

There's something feminine about Clinton's sexual persona. He's the eternal boy, eternally optimistic, and that is extremely useful on the world stage. The boyishness of a leader is a gift, a charismatic quality. In *Sexual Personae* I concluded that true charisma is androgynous and that many important leaders have a subliminal androgyny appealing to and unifying the social classes. I think that Hillary Clinton acting as Lady Macbeth behind the scenes allows her husband to show his boyish side.

But such youthfulness can be extremely dangerous. It's a difficult problem when a leader's machismo is under challenge, as it is now with the controversy over gays in the military. Unlike most presidents, Clinton never served in the armed forces and was under a shadow during the campaign because of his alleged draft-dodging during the Vietnam war. Clinton needed to establish his authority immediately after his inauguration, and this is where Hillary complicated matters. We want a co-equal wife, and a woman who has her own career. But we cannot have a situation where the president is a wimp and his wife is a virago, an Amazon or Omphale figure.

Looking at it mythologically, I see a real danger of Hillary turning into the Omphale archetype, the woman who enslaved Hercules, the most virile man of antiquity. Omphale put Hercules into women's clothes and made him spin and do woman's work in her household. Hillary is an enormously powerful woman. We don't want the perception, or misperception, that she's controlling politics from the boudoir, from behind the throne. Otherwise he turns into a puppet dangling from the strings of a dominatrix.

To me there's a big question mark about what is going on sexually in that marriage. I have the feeling that the Clintons' publicly admitted marital problems came from Hillary's relapses into her hyper law-student mode, intense and bookish, which shuts off sexuality like a faucet. I wonder whether she has a problem—more common among women than is realized—of integrating sexuality with high intelligence and careerism. Pictures of Hillary in law school and her early career show that she was completely dowdy. This is also something I went through. In the 1970s I vowed I would never wear a dress again because it was a badge of servitude. I was determined to sabotage my own sexual persona, and that's what I think Hillary did too.

Hillary can be sexy, but it was amazing how, on inauguration day, there was an uncomfortable return to her dowdy persona. She had this dreadfully frumpy scarf pulled up to her chin and a stiff hat jammed down to her eyes, and she just looked stumpy and dumpy. It was a reversion under high stress to dowdiness, and I think we were seeing her truest, deepest nature.

The problems of the Clinton household are mirroring those of an entire generation. It seems to me that the Clintons represent the best of the Sixties generation, and the worst too. We had so many hopes and ideals, but we hit the wall of reality. Decade by decade, we of the Sixties have been forced to acknowledge that life is more complex and baffling than we thought. I am very uneasy when feminists and journalists overpraise Hillary and hail her as the supreme feminist woman, the supremely gifted one who will soon be running for president herself.

The toll taken on the Clintons' daughter Chelsea by their power-couple marriage seems to be obvious. The girl looks like an orphan. She looks abandoned, as if she's a castaway on a desert island, a hostage in the family. During the entire campaign she was kept from sight. There was all this pious talk from people that the Clintons were nobly shielding their child from the pressure of public scrutiny. The first time we got a look at Chelsea, just before the Democratic convention, it was a terrible shock. One felt she was a walking, talking demonstration of the internal problems of her parents' marriage. At the convention, Hillary was all turned out and stylish, but Chelsea seemed to be deliberately trying to upstage her mother by looking like a spinster in mourning. Her rebellion against her parents was painful to see; it sabotaged the public displays and protestations of family happiness. I think there's a combat going on between mother and daughter, even a kind of terrorism.

I'm not saying that Hillary should have stayed home with Chelsea. Feminism must move forward, and women must get what they can from both the career realm and from motherhood. But we must get over this naive optimism that everything will be just dandy, that you can succeed gloriously as both a mother and a professional without taking from either. Many of Hillary's problems came from this terrible dilemma facing modern women. The feminist establishment in America constantly insists that you can have it all. But I agree with Katharine Hepburn that you can't; something or someone will suffer.

Hillary's strength during the campaign was her shrewd ability to mask herself in a bland, centered, middlebrow American persona that was a kind of throwback to the 1950s. She consistently looked quite good. She was able to communicate to American women that she is someone who sympathizes and empathizes with the role of wife and mother and yet holds her own beliefs and is in no way under the male thumb. She seemed to be both an independent thinker and a conventional woman grounded in the family.

There was a pivotal moment in the campaign when Hillary said, in response to a nasty question about being a working mother: "Well, listen, I could have stayed home and baked cookies." Many people in America, especially women, did not like that at all. There was an outcry, and the campaign could have been lost at that moment. My admiration for Hillary Clinton is that she knew immediately that she had made a misstep and she deftly adjusted. You never heard that voice of hers again. People said: "Isn't that wrong, for her to retreat in the face of social convention?" I said no, no, no, on the contrary: this was a sign of Hillary's insight and political astuteness. She knew the progressive issues that she and her husband stood for—racial harmony, women's rights, toleration of gays— would benefit more from her husband's election than from her being able to be fully herself and do her own thing. She sacrificed her own self-expression for a great good. The reality principle triumphed.

At the peak of her campaign mode, Hillary was tapping into the power of the Southern woman, which she had learned after many years as the governor's wife in Arkansas. Southern women can be both earthy and glamourous. They are superb hostesses: they know how to flirt wittily with men. Down South the women are very potent. There's a way they can command men that Hillary learned when she arrived there from the North.

Over time, she became a Southern blonde, which I have learned to admire as a great sexual persona. Hers was a sober version of the Southern belle; there's no doubt that Hillary got a lilting cadence to her voice and a confident smile on her face from her experiences in Arkansas. Now, of course, she's in Washington, where people don't act like that, and she seems unfortunately to have lost the persona, since the models for it aren't around every day.

Part of the problem is that she's doing the circuit as head of the president's task force on health care, asking questions, amassing information, and so forth, and it's increasingly difficult for her to retain that light, warm, feminine manner that she sustained so successfully during the campaign. Now that she's deeply immersed in hard practical issues, the TV cameras catch that cool, disciplined personality that was hiding under the gracious Southern persona. Now we see the eager, earnest, conscientious law student coming out again. She's been forced into the public eye in her most limited, most cerebral persona. Meanwhile Clinton is floundering with the gays-in-the-military issue, which he mishandled from the start. Right now, as sexual personae, the Clintons are a disaster.

Hillary must very quickly recover that successful warm, calm persona she had throughout the campaign. The country cannot feel confident about leaders who look as if they're anxiously cramming for an exam.

I think there is a problem that the feminist establishment refuses to face: career women in the Anglo-Saxon world have desexed themselves. Latin countries still acknowledge and celebrate the sexual power of woman. There is a mystique about it which we do not have. Unfortunately, when women achieve high positions in Britain and America, it seems to be at the price of their sexuality. There is a bleached, sanitized, desexed, desensualized quality to Hillary's persona, even at her sexiest. In other words, Hillary Clinton shows all of the possibilities of the modern career woman, but also all of the dangers: at the executive level of the industrialized world, we may be cutting ourselves off at the neck. Our battle is not just with the male establishment but with ourselves: how do we keep mind and body together?

HILLARY IN THE SPOTLIGHT

From Crossfire, *CNN, March 8, 1994. Hosts: Michael Kinsley and Pat Buchanan. Guests: Democratic Party strategist Ann Lewis in Washington and Camille Paglia in New York. On Hillary Clinton and the Whitewater scandal.*

KINSLEY: We're going to get into that shredding in a little bit, but let me ask Camille Paglia. I don't know about you, but I encounter extraordinary antagonism towards Hillary Clinton, far beyond anything that could be explained by Whitewater or health care or anything like that, and I do think, it seems to me, that a lot of it at least is old-fashioned resentment of a successful, powerful woman. Now, isn't that fair?

PAGLIA: I don't agree with this, because I'm a Clinton Democrat. I *loved* Hillary during the campaign. I wrote articles about her. One appeared in England, a cover story, and so on, but I have been *bitterly* disappointed in her performance ever since they took office. I'm judging her not as a woman but as a *person* in the public life. I feel that she has *no* idea how to maintain herself in that high position. She just hides from accountability. I find her arrogant. I find her cold. I think that there was too much unctuous genuflection in front of her, that the liberal media had only one image of her for the last year, and they're starting to wake up to reality, seeing her in action here. I think she has fumbled and bumbled and shown a kind of lack of character. The first moment when I began to have a chill about her was inauguration gala night, when Clinton sat there enjoying himself, very effusive, very open, and she sat there with this like pursed expression on her face, very tight. I felt that they were a power couple, a great power couple. They made many, many serious mistakes. One of the first things they did wrong was to separate the two of them within days. I mean, the way she was suddenly unleashed within days of taking office. Their people should have allowed the country to get to know her for a few months. To put her in charge of health care—one of the most important issues facing the nation, a very complex matter—so early on, she began to look like a kind of worried student. She was always frowning—

KINSLEY: Now, Camille, if a man, say Pat Buchanan, to pick a man at random, had said that he was against Hillary Clinton because he didn't like the way she pursed her lips at the inauguration ball, he'd be savaged for sexism.

PAGLIA: As a woman and as a feminist, I can state that I am not critiquing her as a woman. I'm critiquing her as *a person in the public eye*. . . . What I'm saying is that week after week, month after month, her old reputation, coming from the far right, of being the Lady Macbeth of Little Rock, has proved to be *true*! . . . There *is* something manipulative, cold, and self-withholding about her that it has taken the liberal media a *year* to realize, and they—

LEWIS: Wait a minute—

BUCHANAN: All right. Let's get Ann Lewis back into this.

LEWIS: If we're going to talk about Hillary Clinton as a person, can't we just stop and look at the year she's had? I'm stunned to hear this kind of language being thrown around. Here is a woman who one year ago relocated her family, including a teenage daughter, and those of us with teenage children know that isn't ever easy to do, changed her job, left friends and her sort of support network behind—

PAGLIA: Oh, give me a break!

LEWIS:—moved to a strange city—

PAGLIA: Oh, what a sob story.

KINSLEY: Hold on, Camille.

PAGLIA: Oh, the violins, the violins!

LEWIS: I am going to finish my talking—

PAGLIA: What a sob story.

LEWIS:—moves to a strange city, her father dies—

PAGLIA: Oh, her father dies.

LEWIS:—her friends are under attack—

PAGLIA: Oh, please.

LEWIS: This has been personally very difficult—

BUCHANAN: Ann Lewis—

LEWIS: and to see her now criticized for what somebody remembers as an expression on her face—

BUCHANAN: Ann, excuse me—

LEWIS:—seems to me so grossly unfair, it's appalling.

PAGLIA: That is absurd—*ridiculous!*

BUCHANAN: Camille, can I get into this?

PAGLIA: They want *special standards for women!* *That's* what you're asking!

LEWIS: Camille, I'm asking for common standards of decency and human dignity.

PAGLIA: *Decency?*

LEWIS: I would extend it to anyone here on this stage—

PAGLIA: She's in the public eye.

LEWIS:—and that includes people who are in the public eye, because when you go into the public eye, you do not lose your humanity or your warmth—

BUCHANAN: Camille, I'm going to get in here.

PAGLIA: Oh, I've never heard such sentimentality—! Saccharine, saccharine sentimentality.

BUCHANAN: Excuse me, Camille. Ann Lewis, aren't you asking for something of a double standard here?

PAGLIA: Yes.

BUCHANAN: First you want her to be the super cabinet officer. She's got control of health care and all the rest of it. Along comes Whitewater-gate, she can't have a press conference. It's like, look, we want to go out and play with the boys, play touch football, they get knocked down, and you're crying and talking about how tough it was to relocate her family.

PAGLIA: Right. . . .

KINSLEY: Camille, isn't it a little tough on someone like Hillary Clinton to be accused essentially of being a false feminist because she really got her job through her spouse? What else can the spouse of the president do, even if it's a man? Can't really have a career of his own, can he?

PAGLIA: Even the way she handled the health-care thing I did not approve of. I felt that her performance on the Hill—she was always one step away, I felt, from saying, "You know, I'm *smarter* than you." There's something about her—

KINSLEY: You know, people say the same thing about you, Camille.

PAGLIA: I am not in public office! I am *outside* the political establishment—

KINSLEY: So I don't understand what your objection is. Your objection is that people of the public establishment shouldn't imply that they're smarter than other people but that you can?

PAGLIA: No, no, no. I feel there's a kind of secretiveness about her, even the way they handled the health-care thing. I have *not* been impressed with her performance over the last year, and it's taken people a long time to catch up with it.

KINSLEY: What are you talking about, secretiveness on health care? They produced a thirteen-hundred-page report. They're in trouble because it's so detailed.

PAGLIA: No, it was never clear how many people were involved in the whole procedure, who they were—

KINSLEY: Oh, Camille, who on earth cares about that? The fact is, Hillary put together, with the help of her task force, a thirteen-hundred-page plan which is now getting in trouble precisely because it's so detailed, whereas the rival plans are not.

PAGLIA: I'm sorry, no, no. They dug a hole for themselves, because when they started out, I was *behind* the Clintons—the idea of universal coverage and so on. As the year has gone on, I have systematically lost *confidence* in *her* and in *him*. I no longer believe *anything* they say. I believe *nothing* that comes out of that White House. They have a *terrible* staff. George Stephanopoulos is a complete incompetent. I don't know why he wasn't kicked out of there ages ago. . . .

KINSLEY: Camille Paglia, you told something to our staff that I just want to check out whether you really meant it. You criticized Hillary Clinton for taking sixteen days off from the health care task force to be by the bedside of her dying father, who did subsequently die. Gosh, at the end of a long life, sixteen days with your father is— What was wrong with it?

PAGLIA: She had just been put in charge of this enormously complex thing of health care, okay? Either we have to judge her as a *person* or judge her as a *public official*. If you're going to give yourself over to the public trust, there are certain private things you must sacrifice. I feel that in this age of jet planes it was absolutely ridiculous. I mean, to me that was not impressive. I do not feel this was a great demonstration of her filial feeling. On the contrary, I think she was getting out of Washington is what she was doing, and it was the same motif she's doing now:

hide, don't deal with the reality, don't learn! She's out of her depth.

KINSLEY: What was she trying to duck? Her popularity was terrific back then. She had no reason to want to get out of Washington. I mean, you're really attributing cynical motives to going to be by her dying father?

PAGLIA: Yes, I am.

KINSLEY: You wouldn't want a man or a woman to do the same thing?

PAGLIA: No, neither a man—which means *the same standard*.

KINSLEY: I agree with you.

PAGLIA: If you saw a *man* sitting by the bedside of his father for sixteen days, you would think there were possibly other motives involved.

KINSLEY: Maybe you would think that. . . .

LEWIS: And by the way, nobody has said that the brilliance of the White House in handling this—let's be clear, that's right. This is Whitewater, an issue around which there is no serious allegation of wrongdoing. Bill and Hillary Clinton in 1978—

BUCHANAN: No serious—

PAGLIA: Oh, God!

LEWIS: No serious allegation. When you take out a loan from a commercial bank, not a savings and loan, they pay commercial rates—

BUCHANAN: You don't think that rate—

LEWIS: They paid it all back, and all of a sudden, we're talking about it as if it were a big scandal.

BUCHANAN: I'll tell you what—

KINSLEY: Let me ask you—

PAGLIA: There was a *suicide*! There was a *suicide* in the White House, for heaven's sakes. I mean, what are they *talking* about? God!

KINSLEY: Camille, there was no suicide in the White House. The suicide had nothing to do with Whitewater—

PAGLIA: Oh, I don't believe that—oh, *please*!

KINSLEY: You don't believe that either?

PAGLIA: I don't believe that for *one minute*! . . . I came back from England in early January, and outside of America people see Hillary Clinton *much* more *clearly* than they do here, okay? That is, there's this kind of a *sanctimony* about her in the press for the last year. I really think that there is something *sexist* about all of the horror of us—of anyone—criticizing Hillary. People are acting as if we're contaminating the Madonna by daring to—

KINSLEY: Who's horrified? She's been taking a beating for the past week. I don't see anyone saying it's inappropriate. They say it's inaccurate, but they're not saying it's inappropriate.

PAGLIA: There's been a *year*, okay, of this lily-white reputation of her, *wild overpraise*, even of her performance on the Hill. People have been afraid to be called sexist and so on. So inside the Beltway, everybody's very accustomed to thinking of her as a kind of—you know, as Saint Hillary. . . . This is a woman who's out of her depth, a *person* who's out of her depth in the present position that she has.

LAYING THE GHOST

OF ANITA HILL:

BILL CLINTON AND PAULA JONES

From Larry King Live, *CNN Television, May 16, 1994. Host: Larry King.*
Guests with King in the studio in Washington, D.C.: Eleanor Smeal, president
of the Feminist Majority Foundation and former president of NOW; Katie
Mahoney, head of Christian Defense Coalition's Paula Jones Legal Defense
Fund. In Philadelphia: Camille Paglia, identified on-screen as "feminist com-
mentator."

[King questions Smeal about the reluctance of feminist groups to support former
state of Arkansas clerical worker Paula Jones in her charge of sexual harassment
against then-Governor and now-President Bill Clinton.]

LARRY KING: Camille, would you talk to Paula Jones?

PAGLIA: I sure would! I find her story pretty credible—in fact, much
more credible than Anita Hill's. I am delighted. I must say,
first of all, I'm a Clinton Democrat. I support ninety percent
of Bill Clinton's policies. I hope to vote for him again. But I am
the only leading feminist who went *against* Anita Hill, and boy,
I am so *glad* that you see NOW squirming on the hot seat, okay?
They are *such* hypocrites. Finally, they are being exposed to the
nation for the partisans that they really are!

SMEAL: We're not squirming at all. We're just not going to be baited—

PAGLIA (*with relish*): Oh, you're *squirming*! . . .

KING: Why do you seem to enjoy this?

PAGLIA: I am so happy that finally the Stalinist, p.c. feminist establishment is exposed for what it is. Instead of blaming David Brock [author of *The Real Anita Hill*] and the *American Spectator* [a conservative magazine], it's the media that was totally biased, that should have pursued these issues. They were so eager to get rid of Bush, they never pursued these issues in Little Rock. So now the chickens have come home to roost. This case is not just about Anita Hill. What about the [Mike] Tyson case?— where Tyson was *railroaded*—a similar case, where someone invited a woman up to his hotel room—

KING: Camille, you *are* a feminist?

PAGLIA: I am a committed feminist. I am a *dissident feminist* (*angrily stabs her finger at the camera*). And NOW does *not* speak for American women! NOW does not speak for all women or all feminists! . . .

KING: Camille, you are a Clinton supporter—a vibrant Clinton supporter?

PAGLIA: I am. In Europe, you see, the private lives of politicians are of no concern to their public behavior. I believe in moderate sexual harassment guidelines. If he was indeed her boss ultimately, as the governor of Arkansas, I think there might be a sexual harassment issue there. But just a man hitting on a woman and trying to have sex with women? I think we're a very puritanical country. I'm for a high libido president! I applaud him, if he goes out and picks up women. . . .

SMEAL [about the Jones case]: I think it's a put-up job by the right wing. . . .

PAGLIA: Oh, come *on*! The Anita Hill case was a put-up job by the feminist establishment. Why has the media and why have lib-

True

erals ceded over to the *right* the power of critique? Don't blame the people who are pushing Paula Jones forward. She needs all the support she can get. Her charges are *far* more serious than those of Anita Hill. . . . [King asks about the allegations of sexual harassment against Senator Bob Packwood.] I like the way the feminist establishment *used* Packwood until the election of Clinton, then they threw him to the *wolves!* What is this, the Soviet Union? If Packwood is accused, bring the women forward. Bring the accusers forward! Let's examine them in public.

SMEAL: They want to come forward. They've been demanding a hearing—

PAGLIA (*scornfully*): Nonsense! Oh, you people manipulate the news—

SMEAL: You're always attacking us—you're making a cottage industry out of it. That's all you're doing!

PAGLIA: Oh, you people are such Stalinists! You people are dishonest—you are manipulative. We are *sick* of you, NOW— sick of you, former leaders of NOW! We're *tired* of you! . . . I think most people in the country don't really care about Bill Clinton's private life. What we *do* care about is *honesty.* So I think that the White House should be much more up front and stop this stonewalling. Because you can't believe a single word that comes out of this White House. I'm behind Clinton's policies. I just think that he has very bad judgment about *staff.* A lot of this is just staff ineptitude. If he would just 'fess up and get *on* with it. He's not accused of anything that happened since he swore the oath of office, and that would be the grounds of impeachment. . . . Paula Jones should be given her day in court. I don't think we should believe *any* allegations until the evidence is put forward. Certainly that was not the case with Anita Hill! I'm just hoping it does *not* derail the Clinton presidency. I think the sexual peccadilloes of great men, of great politicians should be overlooked. I know I'm kind of on the radical extreme with *that* one.

Prescient!

MONA LISA IN MOTION:

JACQUELINE KENNEDY ONASSIS

The death of Jacqueline Bouvier Kennedy Onassis on May 19 was headline news in America and inspired testimonials of love and respect across all divisions of social class and political party. Jackie was the most famous woman in the world in a long period following that of the great stars of old Hollywood and preceding that of our own pop princesses, Diana and Madonna, both currently in semi-eclipse.

Merely as a paragon of high fashion and elegant good taste, Jackie could not have won the position she retained over several decades in millions of people's affection. It was her baptism by gunfire that deified her. Her extraordinary behavior during and after the assassination of her husband has given her a permanent place in history. In the blood-spattered limousine in Dallas, an archetypal *pietà* was forced on Jackie. Cradling the shattered head of the head of state in her lap, she became Michelangelo's grieving Madonna, caught between horror and admiration at the wounded body of her beautiful son. The Catholic Andy Warhol paid tribute to this aspect

[*The New Republic*, June 13, 1994]

of her in his Duccio-like checkerboard altarpiece of Jackie as national *mater dolorosa*.

Jackie's heroism was made possible, I submit, by a neglected element of her famous biography. Everyone knows about her athleticism and cult of fitness, her love of horses from childhood. What we are admiring in her deportment in crisis is dressage, the art of English horsemanship, an aristocratic style that descends from the pre-revolutionary *ancien régime* of the eighteenth century. When people say Jackie is "the closest thing to royalty" American democracy has ever seen, this is what they really mean.

Dressage is a form of radical minimalism, of hierarchical stillness and repose. The rider's signals to the horse are completely invisible. Jackie, masquerading as the perfect adornment, was a master of manipulation and control, not of the psychological realm, where she was at the mercy of adulterous men, but of the physical realm, which she brought to the highest level of refinement. From her renovation of the White House to John F. Kennedy's magnificent state funeral, she simplified, condensed, and reshaped, out of her powerful instinct for visual symbolism.

In ancient Greek culture, the image of horse and rider represented the victory of reason in the eternal battle of civilization with anarchy. Horsemanship had a spiritual meaning as the discipline of our animal impulses. As her parents' marriage disintegrated, the very young Jacqueline Bouvier found in the public ritualism of riding a life structure that served her well to the end. She became a custodian of the forms—posting herself at Lyndon Johnson's side as he swore the hurried oath of office on Air Force One, doggedly celebrating her son's third birthday party on the day of his father's burial. The educative paradigm in equitation—the patient process of "schooling" colts—was fulfilled in the success with which she reared two unpretentious children who have escaped the whirlwind of self-destructiveness that so often envelops the scions of celebrity.

Reflecting today on Jackie's stoical management of self and surroundings in the aftermath of the assassination, we may rue the disrespect with which my Romantic Sixties generation treated the artifice of etiquette. It was tradition and ceremony—a severe formalism of lamentation as in Aeschylus's *Libation Bearers*—that reordered the nation's blasted and scattered emotions after the shocking slaughter of its leader. As we fled the suffocating conformism of the Fifties, our indifference to the positive aspects of convention even-tually stranded us in the mawkish Great Wallow of victim culture. "Let it all hang out," we said, for which we are now paying the price. Jackie's classy grace under pressure, her cool rejection of complaint or self-pity demonstrate the redemption possible in repression, sublimation, and silence. _Generous._

As patron, connoisseur, and conservator of the arts, Jackie set herself apart from the ordinary run of socialite women of the horsey set, with their earnest, peppy, man-the-battle-stations bravado— good examples are Princess Anne or Prince Charles's mistress, Camilla Parker-Bowles—ironically, the style of the rambunctious Hyannisport Kennedys, whose mania for touch football broke the ankle of Jack's new bride. Balancing the contemplative with the active, Jackie rediscovered the Greek ideal in horsemanship.

And the sport gave her superb reflexes. One of the absurd claims in C. David Heymann's _A Woman Called Jackie_ (1989) is that when she scrambled up on the back of the limousine in Dallas, Jackie was fleeing in terror for her life. Apollo preserve us from bookworm biographers! Were Jackie seeking safety, the bred-in-her-bones, crouching "forward seat" in jumping horses would automatically have put her on the floor of the car. In lunging for a flying fragment of her husband's skull, Jackie placed herself directly in the line of fire, an act of great physical courage for which she has never been honored.

As a diva who enamored the world paparazzi, Jackie had interesting ambiguities. In _Sexual Personae_, commenting on her resemblance to perverse and perhaps hermaphroditic images in Aubrey Beardsley, I cited a diary entry where Cecil Beaton records Jackie's "suspicion of a mustache" and her "big boyish hands and feet" (apparently size 10AA). Unlike her romantic rival Marilyn Monroe, Jackie did not base her female power on an ample bosom. On the contrary, her mannequin's silhouette was linear, in the classical ballet style of Audrey Hepburn. A rigorous dieter, Jackie may have been one step from anorexic, but we never noticed it, because of her wide, serene moon face with its dreamy gaze and Mona Lisa smile.

In modern iconography, Jackie belongs to the Gene Tierney category of brooding brunettes, mysterious and withdrawn. The

Gene Tierney!

voice is undeveloped and whispery, the eyes wide and frightened. Such women often have a steely resolve or willfulness, all the more daunting because of their evasion of open confrontation. The passionately intelligent Jacqueline Bisset, playing Jackie in *The Greek Tycoon* (1978), never quite caught her unsettling ethereal quality, her misty clairvoyant aura. Jackie's influence as a trendsetter of modern female personae can be seen in Anouk Aimée, Mary Tyler Moore, Marlo Thomas, Barbara Parkins, and Stefanie Powers. It is a vibrant, mature heterosexual style, physically active and mentally alert, but without feminist stridency or anger. It is a still-attractive model of attentiveness to men without subservience to them.

Jackie's sophisticated stage presence and youthful *joie de vivre* were exhilarating, after the Mamie Eisenhower decade of bourgeois domesticity and chintz. Jackie was a transition toward a more assertive and politically involved First Lady, the constitutional desirability of whom we are still trying to assess. The dignity and restraint of Jackie's later years made us forget or forgive her shopaholic jet-set period, when she spun out of American orbit and married a Mediterranean Minotaur.

What is indelible now is Jackie's fortitude and valor as a survivor of the blood sport of male politics. Some strange law of retribution cut down the wheeler-dealers in Dallas and spared the women at their sides, as in a Greek tragedy like Euripides's *The Trojan Women*. The stained suit Jackie refused to change that day documented the polarities of womanhood: the pastel pink of girlhood and romance and the barbaric blood red of birth and death. That garment, like the Shroud of Turin, was a pictogram of her life story, with its failed pregnancies and widowhood. This was a woman who thought in universals: a rose garden, an eternal flame, a riderless horse, named for her father, whose skittishness in the funeral parade expressed uncontrolled male libido, the one beast Jackie never tamed.

MEMOIRS AND

ADVENTURES

1. The Saint. Brought from Italy by Felice and Vincenza Colapietro.
Photo: Dean Gazzo.

THE SAINT

For fifty years, a large framed print of an Italian saint hung over a bed in the house of my maternal grandmother, Vincenza Colapietro, in Endicott, New York. The identity of the saint was a mystery. A young man in his teens stands with hands piously clasped and gazes down at an image of the Madonna, her heart pierced by the daggers of the seven sorrows. He is wearing the cassock and heavy, sinister black cloak of the Passionist monks. A misty silver halo glows around his head. On the table next to Mary's picture is a crucifix and, in grisly brown-gold, a gleaming human skull, resting near a bouquet of lilies, symbolizing the Holy Mother's purity.

The saint's picture terrorized several generations of children, beginning with my uncle Bruno, who had to sleep beneath it. When his childhood bedroom eventually became the guest room, all my overnight visits to my grandmother's ended with me being laid down to sleep under the saint. As I usually stayed awake for hours, listening to the raucous hilarity of Italian voices and savoring the heady smell of strong coffee, whiskey, and anisette, I had a lot of time to stare at the image above me.

At first, the picture looks like a poster for a horror film. The blank walls and burnt sepia tones give it an aged, tomblike quality. The saint's rapt devotion to Mary is dreamy and hypnotic, both

obsessive and obsessing to a baffled child's eye. He is one of the
pretty boys who are everywhere in Italian art, notably in the creamy-
skinned, homoerotic Saint Sebastian and Saint Michael statues that
seemed to me, from my toddler's perspective in the church pew, far
more interesting than those of Jesus, Mary, or Joseph. My grandmother's saint locks eyes with the Madonna, typifying the intense
relations of mothers and sons in Mediterranean culture. As a monk,
he will not marry; like the priests of Cybele, he will remain the son-
lover of the goddess.

As the years passed, the saint's picture accumulated more and
more meaning. It became one of my personal icons, representing
not only the sacred omphalos-spot of my grandmother's house but
the essence of Italian Catholicism itself, which is both a religion and
the nation's cultural identity, descending from pagan antiquity. The
saint's quiet, cloistered contemplativeness symbolized for me the
beckoning life of the scholar, a vocation with monastic origins, particularly rich in my family's past because of the nearness of our
village of Ceccano to the great Benedictine abbey at Monte Cassino,
founded in the sixth century.

My disaffection from American Catholicism, which began during my adolescence in the late Fifties, was due partly to its strident
anti-sex rhetoric and partly to its increasing self-Protestantization
and suppression of its ethnic roots. Within twenty years, Catholic
churches looked like airline terminals—no statues, no stained-glass
windows, no shadows or mystery or grandeur. No Latin, no litanies,
no gorgeous jeweled garments, no candles—so that the ordinary
American church now smells like baby powder. Nothing is left to
appeal to the senses. The artistic education of the eye that I received
as a child in church is denied to today's young Catholics.

The polychrome images of tortured saints that are a staple of
Italian and Spanish Catholicism contain brutal truths about the
pagan realities of the body. Suburban American Catholicism, with
its soothing bourgeois banalities, has censored out all the horror and
ecstasy of human experience. The skull and lilies of my grandmother's picture are a Catholic version of the Hindu cycle of birth and
death, which we Westerners think we can transcend. As Frazer
showed, the resurrection story, the triumph over death, originated
mythologically in ancient nature-cults of the dying god.

Mediterranean culture is honest about death, which it does not sentimentalize or conceal from children. The skull over the cradle: Italian funerals feature open caskets and corpse-kissing, just as rural Italian families rear their young with useful life lessons of rough play. As a child, I learned to be wary about kisses from laughing old widows, who would give one a sharp nip in the ear lobe for fun. The first line of my autobiography would read: My people were nursed by the she-wolf. Ha!

In 1986, having survived my grandfather Felice for twenty years, my grandmother died at the age of ninety, and her house was sold. I took as my heirlooms my grandfather's battered chisel, which symbolizes for me the Italian love of labor and our genius for stonework and construction; a chipped carving knife, honed and dangerous as a scythe, souvenir of the kitchen, the center of domestic cult; the rusted clothesline reel that hung behind the house for fifty years, instrument of the old sun-blessed rituals of purification; and the gloomy saint's picture—which, quite understandably, no one else in the family wanted for a minute in his or her home. Intensely coveted but inherited by default, the picture is one of my most treasured possessions.

My grandmother never satisfactorily explained how our family acquired the picture in the first place. We suspect it must have come from a monastery high in the hills above Ceccano, on the road to Castro di Volsci, whose name ("Camp of the Volscians") recalls the region's fierce pre-Roman tribal history. As for the saint's identity, we assumed it was forever lost.

Five years after my grandmother's death, there was a burst of publicity in American newspapers about an Italian saint whom a Virginia man, an activist "defender of bearing arms," was nominating to be "the patron saint of handgunners." The saint, shown in a black Passionist cape with its big white heart-and-cross emblem, looked exactly like my grandmother's saint, now grown up. He was Francis Possenti, called Saint Gabriel of the Sorrowing Mother, who was born in 1838 in Assisi, died young of tuberculosis in 1862, and was canonized in 1920.

All my life, I had seen in the picture a meek, mild-mannered youth, studious, sensitive, and withdrawn. But astonishingly, the real-life Francis Possenti had been quite different. A wild teenager known for gambling, riding, and shooting, he decided to become a priest, against his wealthy father's wishes, after a near-fatal illness. While he was studying at the Passionist monastery at Isola, twenty bandits attacked the town, plundering and torching it. Possenti, armed with a pistol, faced down the marauders and demonstrated his marksmanship by shooting a lizard through the head. The bandits were shamed into surrendering their weapons. The town was saved.

Whether one believes in God or not, the lives and legends of the saints are a never-ending source of instruction and illumination. Saint Gabriel, with his skull, his lilies, and his pistol, is my ideal patron. The monks of the old country were a robust and fractious lot, alternating daily between the spiritual and practical lives. Religious and intellectual conviction should never be genteel. We must be ready to take to the streets to resist and expel the pillagers, even when they are of the town. I offer the persona of the pistol-packing monk to today's students, tomorrow's teachers.

MY BROTHERS IN CRIME:

BENDERSON, JARRATT, FELD,

FESSENDEN

Gay men have played a pivotal role in my personal and intellectual development. They shaped my aesthetic, expanded my world-view, sharpened my conversational style, and civilized my tomboy rowdiness. Through them, I completed my break from American Catholicism, under whose capricious rules I had been seething since adolescence.

Women who consorted with gay men used to be called "fag hags." The term was dismissively applied to a certain kind of hovering, heterosexual mother figure, disappointed in love, who indulged and coddled her charges and listened and worried without blaming or shaming. That wasn't me. My rough manner and ambiguities of gender and sexual orientation made me the comrade of gay men, not their nurse. Together, we defied bourgeois convention and moral law. Like the Romantics, we were brothers in crime.

Six gay men were central to my life. Robert Caserio has been my loyal friend, intimate confidant, and professional ally since graduate school at Yale. Kent Christensen has been my colleague, advisor, and consultant in all things cultural for the past ten years at the University of the Arts in Philadelphia. Both are lifelong political liberals and, at the same time, gentlemen in the traditional sense: courteous, cultivated, humanitarian.

This essay is a portrait of the other four, whose sexual personae broke the rules and whose refusals and rebellion belong to the public record of my generation. Bruce Benderson, a childhood friend, introduced me to Stephen Jarratt and Stephen Feld during my first year (1964–65) at Harpur College, at the State University of New York at Binghamton. The three became my coterie, the only group I have ever happily flourished in. Their contributions to the creation of the campy, semimythic diva and deranged gender-neutral entity, "Camille Paglia," are immeasurable.

In 1972, the philosopher James Fessenden and I, both fresh out of graduate school, met as young faculty members at Bennington College. We immediately became constant companions. Like Caserio and Christensen (and another of my Bennington friends, Richard Tristman), Fessenden had attended Columbia University, whose sweeping history-of-ideas curriculum seemed to produce minds peculiarly sympathetic to my own. It was Fessenden with whom I was in most sustained contact throughout the long process of writing *Sexual Personae*. For twenty years, until his death from AIDS in 1992, we were a festive, competitive symposium of two.

BRUCE BENDERSON

I met Bruce Benderson after my family moved to Syracuse in 1957, when I was ten. My father, a high-school teacher in rural Oxford, New York, had enrolled as a graduate student in Romance languages at Syracuse University. We lived in graduate student housing, a crowded complex of dilapidated army barracks spread on rolling drumlin hills. Bruce's family situation was quite different. His father was a prominent attorney; his mother, a Democratic activist, was the most famous woman politician in upstate New York. The Bendersons lived in Bradford Hills, as exclusive a residential area as I had ever seen, though by today's lavish standards, their house was relatively modest.

From the start, Bruce questioned the security and affluence of his upbringing. He was the first of the contemporaries of my acquaintance to "protest," to go against the grain, to put himself on the line for a political ideal. The 1950s have been grossly sentimentalized by recent popular culture. Far from being the carefree

"Happy Days" of hamburg joints, convertibles, and sock hops, the period could be a living hell for nonconformists and minorities like blacks, Jews, or gays. As a nonathletic, intellectual Jewish boy, Bruce suffered endless rejections and humiliations in a schoolyard world that worshiped WASP good looks and social success, the values of the fraternities, sororities, Protestant churches, and country clubs that ruled Syracuse life.

Partly inspired by his Russian immigrant mother's liberalism, Bruce identified with the underdog and all victims of tyranny. My early encounters with him were not always pleasant. Bruce resented and denounced my rude impatience with passive, clingy classmates, whiny girls whom I reduced to tears. Later, he realized that, clumsy and brutal as I was, I was reviving feminism in a period when it was totally dormant. And I was to realize that Bruce's compassion for the outsider and the loser belonged to his larger critique of bourgeois society and political oppression. I also came to appreciate Bruce's extraordinary intuitive understanding of the complex psychology of the wounded, suffering, or masochistic woman—typified by Marilyn Monroe, whom he took seriously long before anyone else.

Bruce was the only visible beatnik on the cultural landscape in junior and senior high school in Syracuse. He was the first person who knew about Bob Dylan or read French avant-garde literature. He was "arty" without being effete. Bruce is large, robust, tending toward corpulence. His peasant vigor, so much like mine, still draws us together. There was always a satirical zest to his esoteric interests. For example, in high school he somehow got hold of a battered department-store mannequin, which he christened "Nadja," after André Breton's novel. This led to a long-running joke, which I rehearse to this day with our friend Ann Jamison (whom Bruce, in a desperate stab at normalcy, took to the senior prom for forty fiasco-filled minutes). "Nadja!" we shout, "your *bust* has arrived and is *banging* its *boobs* on the *door!*" Probably inspired by *The Twilight Zone,* we had re-created the comic surrealism of Buñuel and Dalí's *Un Chien andalou* without having heard of it.

When Bruce and I ended up at the same college, we discovered the full extent of our mutual intellectual and artistic interests and forged a permanent bond, preserved, even when we have lived hundreds of miles apart, by long, intense phone calls at any time of day or night. In thirty years, I have never had a conversation with Bruce in which I did not learn something new. He is the most original thinker I have ever known. Bruce has the aggressive verbal and analytic style of the Talmudic tradition, combined with the hipster slant of modern urban Bohemia. With his voracious appetites, humorous lewdness, and polymorphous-perverse body language, he reminds me of Allen Ginsberg, one of my heroes. His discourse, a synthesis of psychoanalysis, literature, and politics, parallels that of another of my heroes, Norman O. Brown. But Bruce, consistent with my generation's multimedia ambitions, has added film, pop culture, and the visual arts to the mix.

Like me, and no one else we knew, Bruce was passionately committed to becoming a writer from adolescence on. While I was drawn to both scholarship and journalism (I was editor of our high school newspaper), Bruce had no interest whatever in nonfiction, a choice I continue to lament today, since I know his amazing aptitude for cultural commentary. The short story and novel forms have been Bruce's primary focus. In college his experiments in poetry were disastrously terminated when an eminent creative writing teacher, in a private office conference, expressed disgust at the homosexual content of his work, a traumatic moment still painful to Bruce after all these years. But at Harpur there was a literary ferment going on outside the classroom. Our group was reading Baudelaire, Rimbaud, Mallarmé, Lorca, and Genet, as well as contemporary American poets.

After graduation, Bruce lived in New York during the period of the Stonewall riots and then, with Stephen Jarratt and Stephen Feld, moved to San Francisco, the capital of the counterculture. There he began to read Robbe-Grillet and Nathalie Sarraute as well as the French poststructuralists, whom he absorbed and admired before their usurpation and distortion by American academics. Bruce traces his writing aesthetic to three influences: decadent French Romanticism, from Baudelaire to Huysmans; the American Beat movement, notably William Burroughs, John Rechy, and Hubert Selby, Jr.; and the French *nouveau roman* of the Fifties and Sixties. Bruce has always found in French culture greater intellectual freedom as well as a Mediterranean pleasure principle missing from America, with its

Puritan heritage. He visited France for long periods and ended up translating or co-translating a series of French authors, including Philippe Sollers and Pierre Guyotat. The Sollers translation was done in collaboration with Ursule Molinaro, a French-born avant-garde novelist who became Bruce's mentor and muse.

Despite every discouragement, Bruce pursued his writing in a period when publishing became increasingly commercial. He burst out irately to me, "I can't look at *The New York Times Book Review* more than once every two years without going to New York Hospital with a false heart attack!" When he left San Francisco for New York in 1974, he chose to live on the Lower East Side, which was in a shambles. As a writer, he felt a special rapport with heroin addicts, the homeless, and the mentally ill, all of whom were invisible at the time to American journalists and politicians. Visiting Bruce, I would pick my way in horrified exasperation past the derelicts and the garbage. It was many years before I fully understood what he was doing by settling in that neighborhood and opening a dialogue with the people of the street. He was determined to isolate and explode the repressed assumptions of bourgeois culture, and in this enterprise he has been my most important guide. The insights of his rigorous class-analysis were crucial in my guerrilla warfare against establishment feminism, which had made such a reactionary retreat from Sixties values.

Despite the boldness with which he had asserted the right to homosexual love in college, Bruce did not feel comfortable with the new gay activism that followed the Stonewall rebellion in 1969. He found, to his discomfort, that he did not get along with many gay men, and the feeling was mutual. He was bored by the middle-class complacencies of the gay bar scene, disguised under unconvincing costumes of denim and leather. He loved drag queens, without being attracted to them, and loathed the way post-Stonewall gays rejected the queens and everything effeminate. Strong-willed straight women, in the model of his celebrated mother, remained his principal confidantes. He has always been comfortable with what he calls his "heterosexual component" and has slept with dozens of women, with sometimes complicated results. He speaks of the "lure and excitement and power" that women have for him, even though his overwhelming interest has been men.

today, this same complacency is "disguised" by body piercings + overlarge clothes (1998)

Bruce's love life began to center more and more on the dangerous streets between Times Square and the Hudson River. He became a regular at seedy bars frequented by teenaged Puerto Rican hustlers, most of whom are straight but who survive by selling their sexual favors to men. He began to befriend ex-convicts and visit prisoners. Our conversations would be interrupted by emergency collect calls from inmates at Attica or Rikers Island. Like most of Bruce's friends, I was highly apprehensive about all this and direly predicted he would be robbed, injured, or worse. After several years, we stopped nagging him, since he seemed remarkably sure-footed in that unstable underworld. There were incidents and imbroglios, but he escaped serious harm. His discoveries were of the highest social significance: for example, the radical differences of worldview between the industrial working class and the so-called underclass, the "people of the rain forest," who, he said, "faced life and death issues with cavalier machismo." And he had a materially positive effect on several cherished hustlers. One in particular, who eventually left the street life to obtain his high-school diploma, became like a son to him. When Bruce took me to his favorite dive on 46th Street (the evening ended in turmoil, as the bouncer ejected a gun-waving patron), we met a magically beautiful blonde transsexual nodding out on heroin on a tottering bar stool and dreamily reminiscing about the final hours of her "friend," Marilyn Monroe. We kissed and caressed her soft hand in tribute.

Bruce's writing increasingly drew on his first-hand experiences with male prostitutes, transvestites, convicts, and drug addicts. As American culture changed, after the materialistic era of the Seventies and Eighties, his work began to find a more receptive audience. By the late Eighties, his stories were appearing in various arts magazines and were eventually published as a collection, *Pretending to Say No* (Plume Books, 1990). His second book is his first novel, *User* (Dutton, 1994). Bruce also cowrote the screenplay for *My Father Is Coming* (1991) with the German director Monika Treut, a sexual freethinker who was equally tired of gay and feminist orthodoxy. Meeting me at Bruce's apartment, she was struck by my bizarre brand of comic Amazonism and put me carrying on with Bruce in her next film, *Female Misbehavior* (1992). Treut, who obtained her doctorate with a scholarly study of sadomasochism, has become my most important ally in the international movement for a progressive pro-porn, anti-dogma feminism.

After AIDS was identified and had claimed hundreds of lives in New York and San Francisco, Bruce went through a period of severe anxiety, in which the slightest symptom seemed a harbinger of death. He was scrupulous about practicing safe sex with hustlers, not so much to protect himself from them as vice versa. He applied a ritualistic standard of cleanliness to his sexual encounters. In all moral dilemmas or debates he explicitly invoked the standards of "the ethical Jew," here above all. As the years passed, he showed no signs of illness and remains healthy today. But I will never forget a daffy exchange in 1984 as I drove him from Manhattan to Syracuse for our twentieth high-school reunion, the first time we had seen our WASP sirens and tyrants since graduation. Somewhere between Albany and Utica on the Thruway, I tried to distract him from his obsessive examination of his dry skin patches and minutely swollen armpit glands. Listening to the radio, I vaguely asked him, apropos of nothing, "Did Pat Benatar have a nose job?" He peevishly shot back, "Does she have a face? They don't operate on *mice*."

Bruce and I carry each other's complete biographies in our mental data base. We have listened to and harangued each other and mutually processed every item of our respective romantic odyssey and creative quest. I listen with exquisite attention to what he says, since I have learned that wherever Bruce is, the culture will be five years later. This was most striking in his fascination with Japan in the early 1970s. He traveled to Tokyo, decorated his apartment with kimonos and a massive shoji screen, and learned to prepare sushi—a delicacy totally unknown to me that enamored me for life. I remember sitting with glassy-eyed astonishment, staring at the supple bamboo sushi molds, as Bruce exuberantly described the critical step of fanning the hot rice—as if it were a fainting Southern belle. Five years later, Japan, as a trade rival, had moved massively into American consciousness.

An enormous part of my friendship with Bruce has been our love of movies, in particular the "women's pictures" of the Hollywood studio period. We spend hours on the phone discussing Lana Turner, Jane Wyman, Carroll Baker, Ann-Margret, or his specialty, Joan Crawford, never a favorite of mine until I heard Bruce's bril-

liant dissections of her mature sexual persona. We constantly exchange showbiz minutiae and arcana, a gay male expertise I have
never found, to my despair, in lesbians. For many years, Bruce
assisted his friend the Argentinean novelist Manuel Puig (in exile
in Rio de Janeiro) by systematically videotaping the most obscure
vintage B-movies that turned up on New York television in the
middle of the night. I love to command Bruce to recite whole passages of dialogue from our cult films, particularly those in female
voices, which he imitates with fiendish facility. With his raucous,
disruptive humor and gift for mimicry, he could easily have been a
radio disk jockey or stand-up comedian.

Our relationship has usually been one of warring siblings. As
we chat about people, art, or current events, each of us struggles for
interpretative dominance. When one is subsequently proved wrong,
the other never forgets it. We crow over victories, recite past triumphs, and are generally insufferable. There has been an odd ethnic
cross-identification in us from the start. Bruce is fascinated by
Roman Catholicism and collects sacred memorabilia: hanging on
his wall is a large, doleful stone relief of one of the Stations of the
Cross, taken from a demolished church. I, in turn, was always drawn
to Judaism and, in junior high school, was curtly overruled by my
parents when I wanted to join the Jewish Community Center. My
mentors, such as Milton Kessler and Harold Bloom, have always
been Jews—the only people, I've joked, who can stand me. Bruce's
favorite saint, as I learned at grisly length, is Lydwine of Schiedam,
whose picturesque mortifications (fasting on a drop of wine per day
and counting her giant, worm-filled abscesses) were catalogued by
our revered French Decadent oblate, Huysmans.

Bruce and I are often at swordspoint on questions of morality,
which despite his bohemianism, he cannot fully renounce. He believes not in God or religion but in social justice, though, like me,
he detests the condescending paternalism of victim-oriented social-
welfare workers and bourgeois philanthropists. He is baffled by the
Italian clan mentality and its savage code of vengeance. The Greco-
Roman strain is very pronounced in me; I see the vendetta as jolly,
historical, knee-in-the-groin sport. But of course athletics is foreign
to Bruce ("I hate projectiles!" he booms). The same thing with cars:
I adore them; Bruce loathes them. He is a lover of cities, in all their

grime and decay; his hatred of suburbia is due partly to its bland sanitization and partly to its dependence on driving. He feels agoraphobic in vast parking lots. I, on the other hand, can breathe free only in wide-open spaces under a big sky. And my car is my masculine, mobile superself, transcending the here and now.

One of my principal bonds with gay men is our love of pornography, which we see as liberating and never, in the standard feminist way, as degrading. The pro-sex feminists I have encountered are rarely as raunchy and ribald as gay men in their taste for porn. Bruce's lusty appreciation of the most extreme forms of pornography was crucial as I developed my theory of the unity of art and pornography for *Sexual Personae*. The libidinal is Bruce's great ideal. He despises all ideology that kills libido—in gay activism, feminism, or organized religion. The ultimate Sixties principle in his philosophy of life is his Romantic view of the interpenetration of energy and eroticism.

STEPHEN LEON JARRATT

If Bruce Benderson, with his excesses and assertions, is a Baroque personality on the grand scale, Stephen Jarratt is a cool mathematical grid of abstract minimalism. The contrast between these two friends could not be more marked. Bruce would devour an entire package of chocolate Oreo cookies at a sitting, while Jarratt (as we called him, to distinguish him from Stephen Feld) nourished himself through his job at the college snack bar by consuming pickle chips and soda water all day. Bruce physically resembles stout, mischievous Bacchus figures like Federico Fellini or Zero Mostel, while Jarratt, with his tall, slim frame, dusky skin, handsome, craggy features, and diffident reserve, looks like a melancholy Heathcliff or brooding Byronic poet. He is given to long silences, from which you expect him to say, "Call me Ishmael."

Bruce, Feld, and I grew up in immigrant families, so we had a very clear sense of Jarratt's WASP heritage and its centrality to American culture. At the same time, we saw how this had marooned him historically and how we were somehow more active, more optimistic, freer. Jarratt was like Poe's Roderick Usher, the last of an ancient dynasty, trapped in his own solitary imagination. His family was from Missouri and Kansas, in the traditional, conservative Midwest. His father was an Air Force officer who moved from post to post. Jarratt's residence abroad, including a pivotal year and a half of adolescence in Morocco, gave him a discernible air of cosmopolitanism. His spiritual struggles as a gay man were intricately involved in his antipathy to the militarism of his background. Like Jim Morrison of the Doors, whose father was a naval officer, he rebelled against his father's concept of masculinity. Ironically, with his perfect manners, graceful gestures, deep, mellifluous voice, and matinee-idol good looks, Jarratt was most women's dreamboat ideal man. There is something of Jarratt's manner and appearance in Mark Frechette's oblique performance in Antonioni's *Zabriskie Point* (1970), whose female lead, Daria Halprin, beautifully captures the electric intelligence and sensuality of Sixties hippie girls.

Our generation was in open revolt against the conformism and careerist regimentation of the Fifties, symbolized by the film *The Man in the Gray Flannel Suit* (1956). Jarratt's mode of resistance was passivity and paralysis, which he eloquently articulated with dry black humor, punctuated by his characteristic long pauses. His refinement and stoic withdrawal were like those of Huysmans's aristocratic Des Esseintes. As a consummate aesthete and connoisseur, Jarratt represents for me the highest development of modern gay culture. His eye for color, line, and form was exquisite, an innate talent that cannot be explained by social conditioning. His discourse on color tones—in films, paintings, fabrics, or sunlight—was spellbinding. The shadings of red, blue, violet, green: Jarratt made us see them as material presences in the world.

For Jarratt, perception was everything. He moved in an envelope of Zenlike stillness, which caught up and tranquilized even manic creatures like me. Jarratt seemed the real-life embodiment of Walter Pater's doctrine of pure contemplativeness. This visionary aspect of the psychedelic Sixties has been too much ignored in retrospective surveys by the media. The Vietnamese war was only one element in that turbulent decade and has been overstressed, because it and the demonstrations against it were photographable, while individualistic inwardness was not. Jarratt read widely but left little mark in the classroom. Authenticity resided for him in quiet reflection and the sharp, truthful observation, shared with friends. His psycholog-

Untouchable—I picked this up from then

ical sense was acute and bonded him to women, whom he treated
with a mixture of caution and respect because of his ambivalent
relations with his powerful, opinionated mother.

If Jarratt was my priest of perception, the cinema was our
church. We worshiped the screen with religious fervor. No one has
adequately documented the revolutionary impact of art films on my
generation. From the moment I saw Roman Polanski's unsettling
Knife in the Water in my first week of college, I was enslaved and
enamored. At Harpur, moviegoing had cult status. My group in
particular believed that avant-garde thought was being created,
frame by frame, in and through film. When Antonioni's languorous
L'Avventura was shown, the crowded college auditorium emptied
within twenty-five minutes—except for a scattering of holdouts, including my three friends and me. Monica Vitti's beaky nose and
windswept hair shot this way and that on a rocky island—superb!
Jean Cocteau's eerie *Orphée*, with its angelic poet, leatherboy mo-
torcyclists, and dominatrix of death, nearly gave us cardiac arrest.
When Andy Warhol's *Harlot* was shown, again the theater emptied,
and again we were virtually alone, this time in the front row. An
expressionless drag queen, ringed by an imperceptibly shifting honor
guard, slowly peels a banana and eats it, as gossips chatter offscreen.
It takes twenty long minutes. We were ecstatic and stayed for a
second showing. Midway through each, Bruce wandered up on stage
and did an absurdist mime in front of the screen, to protest the
audience's restlessness and to signal our connection with Warhol's
vision.

There are two commercial films I associate with Jarratt, since
we saw them together at their release in downtown Binghamton.
One was Joseph Losey's *Secret Ceremony* (1968). In an essay on Elizabeth Taylor, I have described the moment when Jarratt and I cried
out simultaneously, as the star abruptly appeared in a violet suit
and turban against a wall of sea-green tiles. It was one of the high-
lights of my life, an aesthetic epiphany in which joy and pain were
equally mixed. Losey, a gay leftist expatriate, was Jarratt's favorite
director, and we tracked his films for years, sharing information,
hunches, and insights. Thanks to Jarratt's tutelage, I absorbed Losey's decadent scenarios and suave formalism into my philosophy
of art, as it was to be elaborated in *Sexual Personae*.

The other commercial film was *Valley of the Dolls* (1967), where, at an afternoon showing in the near-deserted Binghamton theater, Jarratt and I made unforgivable spectacles of ourselves. Crippled with helpless laughter, we were literally on the floor. At every glimpse of a female forearm sporting a clunky, futuristic wristwatch, Jarratt had convulsions. I was dazzled by the trashy dialogue and spacey Courrèges costumes. *Valley of the Dolls*, which quickly disappeared, remained one of my all-time favorite films, and I followed it avidly when it resurfaced long afterward in shortened, censored form on late-night TV. Its West Coast resurrection and restoration in the late Eighties as a gay male classic stunned and delighted me. But why was I surprised? I seem to have the soul of a gay man.

Certain music reminds me of Jarratt, such as Lotte Lenya's classic versions of the ironic Weill-Brecht Berlin songs, then widely available in an elegant double album. Jarratt loved Peggy Lee's "Is That All There Is?," with its brittle, boozy, devil-may-care litany of life's sorrows. He played Ravel's "La Valse" for me, and after some initial impatience, I marveled with him at its escalating cacophony and apocalyptic rhythm, its *danse macabre* of cultural breakdown. Erik Satie's witty, aimless piano pieces and Ravel's and Debussy's rich, sinister string quartets were central to our coterie. At the off-campus Binghamton house Bruce shared with Feld, the unfurled album cover of Bob Dylan's *Blonde on Blonde* hung like a hazy icon on the wall. It was there that I first saw the artful tangled-hair cover of the Beatles' *Revolver* album and listened to its glossy music in mute wonder. The Doors' moody *Strange Days* encapsulated our alienation in the depressing pre-Stonewall gay world. Jarratt remembers the "grim," shabby Binghamton bar where gays congregated. Visiting Greenwich Village, we had to knock with trepidation on a tiny barred door on pitch-black Barrow Street to be gruffly admitted to a sterile, cramped space lurid with dim red light. It was like a circle of Hell. The theme music for that bleak period in our lives is the first Velvet Underground album and Bob Dylan's "Ballad of a Thin Man" and "Desolation Row." Those songs hauntingly express our crushing sense of isolation and abandonment as citizens of Sodom.

Jarratt was a collector of neuroses, his own and others'. Part of the beatnik heritage of the Sixties was the fashion for quirky neuroticism, a badge of personal style—quite unlike today's boring generic categories like "incest survivor" or "child of alcoholic parents." Jarratt was the first person I knew who had "anxiety attacks." His modernist moods always had a metaphysical dimension. He was like a psychic barometer of Blake's "invisible worm that flies in the night in the howling storm." Jarratt's first Harpur roommate, who suffered from a tyrannical father and was under psychiatric care, dreamed every night that he was dribbling oranges down an allwhite basketball court. Working with Jarratt at the snack bar was a large, plump, warm-hearted but compulsive girl who snacked nonstop on hamburgers fried in butter and who one day plucked out all her eyelashes and eyebrows in a fit (they took a year to grow back). Another high-strung girl, a pioneer of the then-unknown malady of bulimia, screamed uncontrollably at her Jewish refugee parents in ways that were unthinkable in Italian terms. I overheard Jarratt, sighing, say to her over the phone as they chatted about friends, "I know. It's hard to talk to people who are very happy." Jarratt loved Antonioni's *Red Desert* and identified with the tortured Monica Vitti in it. "Certain combinations of colors would fill her with dread," he said to me recently. "She looked so glamourous in her free-floating anxiety." Like Bruce, he saw and honored the martyrdom in the great female stars. As he once remarked, "No one can wring a tear like Susan Hayward."

After graduation, Jarratt and I corresponded regularly. His letters were instantly recognizable in the mail by their sepia ink and bold italic script, executed with an Ozmiroid art pen. The first major incident I had to endure without my gay legionnaires occurred in the summer of 1968, when I ran smack into Catherine Deneuve on Fifth Avenue. She was my current obsession, and no one had a clue she was in America. I omit the extraneous details—a Janis Joplin concert at the Fillmore East, a boy on a bicycle run over by a bus, my pursuit of Deneuve to the glove department of Saks. Suffice it to say that, as the violet sky crackled with thunderbolts in the humid air, I fled wildly up the avenue looking for a phone booth and hysterically called Jarratt from the St. Regis Hotel. He was then working in a Binghamton laundromat (where, he likes to say, he

learned *never* to put the clothes in until the detergent has dissolved).
I felt like I was on another planet, walking among the gods but
bereft of my boon companions and soulmates.

Like many of the most talented members of my generation,
Jarratt shunned the professions and took only subsistence-level
jobs—cleaning houses in San Francisco or working for many years
for a costume jewelery importer. As sexual personae, we were on
reverse tracks. Galled by the low status of women in the domestic
Fifties, I wanted passionately to achieve in the cultural realm. Ambition was my leading trait. Renunciation was Jarratt's. Where he
was passive, I was audaciously active. The militarism that he rejected in his father he accepted in me, as an androgynous Aries
warrior. For example, I struck one of the first blows for contemporary
feminism in 1966, when, in the middle of the night on a deserted
Binghamton street, I rescued a tiny female acquaintance of ours
from molestation by young drunks by smashing a captor's mouth
against his teeth with a lucky hit from my gloved hand. He had to
be helped away, bleeding profusely.

After several years in San Francisco, Bruce and Feld moved
back to the East Coast. Jarratt stayed. The avant-garde city by the
bay, a Mecca of sexual liberation to so many gay men, was to be
one of the hatcheries of AIDS. Jarratt saw firsthand the destruction
of our generation's hopes. When he was diagnosed with the disease
in 1989, after being hospitalized with an episode of pneumonia, he
bore it with his customary dignity, stoicism, and gallows humor.
The form his illness has now taken is cytomegalovirus retinitis, a
degeneration of the retina. It is a cruel fate for the aesthete who
lived by his eyes. But Jarratt's vision transcends the physical. He
has been a witness to the whirlwind of the *fin de siècle*. As both
Sagittarian humanist and devotee of beauty, Jarratt embodies an
ideal synthesis of philosophical detachment with sensory responsiveness. His somber perceptions and vibrant imagination continue
in the friends whom he altered and educated.

[On February 2, 1994, two months after this essay was completed, Stephen Jarratt died at forty-seven in San Francisco. He was
totally blind.]

STEPHEN HOWARD FELD

As an adolescent in Syracuse, I found a secondhand copy of a book called *The Epigrams of Oscar Wilde*. It became my bible. I memorized its phrases and repeated them until they became part of my brain chemistry. Wilde's voice, malicious, incisive, insouciant, broke into the provincial circuit of school, church, and home in Fifties America like Radio Free Europe. Wilde—followed a few years later by Simone de Beauvoir—was my first model for radically independent thought, for cold, clear mind unencumbered by religious morality or social convention.

When I met Stephen Feld, thanks to Bruce Benderson, in college, I was amazed to hear him speaking with Wilde's voice. I automatically gravitated toward him and became his unembarrassed fan. I followed him around like his kid sister and watched and listened to him raptly, remembering his witticisms and recording them in a notebook in my room. Feld was the real-life model for my extended analysis of Oscar Wilde in *Sexual Personae*. His everyday conversation was my key for understanding the brilliant rhetoric and dramatic dynamics of *The Importance of Being Earnest*.

Feld was gregarious, brash, and wickedly funny. A Jewish prince from Long Island, he had been the apple of his vivacious mother's eye. His glasses and thinning black hair gave him an intellectual look, but he was well-built, with a solid, agile frame. Feld's confident, casual, lordly manner attracted people. He was popular with everyone, gay or straight. While Stephen Jarratt, like Wordsworth, was most himself when alone, Feld was literally "the life of the party"— a term I had never fully understood before. Flinging himself down at the piano, he would bang out medleys of Broadway show tunes in his muscular manner, singing at the top of his voice. His sense of fun was infectious. When we rendezvoused at the college dining hall, Feld, at my request, would do cartwheels and handsprings across the full length of the entry lounge. He made his own rules, and the world applauded.

Virginia Woolf identified the inaugural moment (in 1908) of the irreverent Bloomsbury world of modernist literature and art: the

young Lytton Strachey, arriving for a visit, pointed to a stain on her
sister Vanessa's white dress and exclaimed, "Semen?" Wrote Woolf
long afterward, "Can one really say it? I thought & we burst out
laughing. With that one word all barriers of reticence and reserve
went down." Victorian propriety was over. Sophisticated women of
the Twenties and Thirties often had a freedom of speech and manner
that was lost in the enforced hiatus of the gruelling Second World
War. Middle-class girls of the Fifties were raised by the prudish,
conservative code of Victorian respectability. My generation found
many ways to rebel. Gay men were my liberators. Stephen Feld,
above all, did for me what Lytton Strachey did for the Stephen
sisters. His scathing wit and bold, bawdy talk broke me out of the
jailhouse of gender.

While he was warmhearted and generous as a host and *bon vivant*,
Feld was intolerant of any kind of false sentimentality. He was far
more accepting than I of different kinds of people, with all their
flaws, yet he had a fearsome talent for unnerving and disorienting,
for doing the unexpected, even if it gave pain. Hurrying to class one
bright winter's day, he and I rounded the outer corner of a dorm
and encountered a long-haired sylph whom I happened to have a
crush on. I became breathless and tongue-tied, as usual, while Feld
drolly leered. Fleeing in haste at the sight of us, the girl slipped on
the ice and went sprawling, her books skidding ten feet in front of
her. Feld openly laughed—the cruel Homeric laughter of Greek
princes at the drubbing of Thersites.

I was mortified at the girl's embarrassment yet stunned with
strange admiration at Feld's shattering of bourgeois etiquette, his
rejection of "niceness." It was a form of truth-telling, a frank ad-
mission of human aggression without the mask of piety. Pre-Stonewall gay men had an astonishing sense of masks, their own and
others'. They willfully violated every politically correct tenet—including compassion for the handicapped, who became "criplettes."
Whatever was forbidden had to be done or said. For our era of
Romanticism, taboo-breaking remains the route of the heroic.

Feld had a way of sharply rebuffing confidences at tender moments. The pattern was inconsistent, so there was always surprise
but not necessarily displeasure. It was conversation as rough play.
My favorite incident dates from 1974, when I enthusiastically told

Cunningham, Cage

Feld that my Yale friend Bob Caserio had spotted him recently in
New York but that he had disappeared into a building. Feld haughtily replied, "My dear, I never disappear into buildings. I always
linger in the doorways." End of exchange.

Feld's brusque response fascinated me, and I thought about it
for years. It ended up verbatim, with four pages of analysis, in the
manuscript of *Sexual Personae,* one of the passages Yale Press cut for
space at production deadline. There I had spoken of Feld as a
practitioner of what I called Wilde's *monologue extérieur,* the poetry
of the English epicene. In this particular conversation-stopper I saw
evidence of Decadent termination or closure, the Apollonian swerve
from Dionysian empathy, the aristocratic refusal to be drawn into
any philanthropic sense of community. I also dwelled on Feld's use
of the doorway as a framing device and of his self-positioning on the
vanishing point. I detected a form of ritual display in which there
was a paradoxical conflation of exhibitionism—even solicitation—
and ritual sequestration, an invocation of the visual in order to
frustrate it. When.

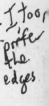

I felt that Feld's arch riposte proved the oral continuity of the
Wildean tradition over a hundred years and demonstrated the cold
aesthetic formalism in modern male, as opposed to female, homosexuality. A Yale editor raised the question of legal repercussions
from publishing such personal material. When I conveyed this, Feld
declared, "Tell her: I've always lived my life in as public an eye as
possible," and "I am only concerned that there is not *enough* about
me." Though he offered to sign a release, the editors relegated him,
as he gloomily put it, to "the cutting-room floor."

Like many gay men and unlike, alas, most gay women, Feld
had a sophisticated instinct for fine food, interior decor, and fashion.
He owned (and used as a room-dominating coffee table) a Louis
Vuitton trunk before the line went broadly commercial, and he
preached the doctrine of Bloomingdale's before the store became a
fad. At dinner, he spoke to me severely about the way I ate my
buttered bread wholesale, instead of breaking it into delicate pieces.
It was Feld and Jarratt who showed me that good manners were
suprasexual civilized forms and not just, as I had fiercely thought,
a plot by the authorities to feminize and control women. I became
much less of a rambunctious hellion after my contact with them.

What few feminine attributes I may now appear to have were absorbed from them, which is why many people who hear me speak have reported that, at hallucinatory moments, there seems to be a gay man behind the microphone. *I find you a hot, experimental hetero*

At parties, Feld would gather together a huge variety of people whose only common denominator was him. The moment he would step away, we would fight like cats and dogs, but his mere presence seemed to have a magical unifying effect. A girl in our larger college circle tartly remarked, "Feld has to be surrounded by people. If he doesn't have an audience, he doesn't exist." This was true in the best sense: Feld was a theatrical animal, at a time when theater and dance were redefining American culture. Life itself was a performance art for him, as for Bruce. At Harpur, I was active in my own one-man style of surreal psychodramas and happenings—forty elaborate pranks that landed me on probation.

Feld, who played the lead in the campus production of Ibsen's *Rosmersholm,* seemed to be considering a career in some area of show business. With his ingenuity, panache, and facility for making things happen, he belonged to the great age of vaudeville or Tin Pan Alley. Feld's friendship with Bruce, which had its ups and downs over the decades, was closest when they had common artistic interests. Their difficulties mirrored the conflicts in American Jewish culture, as portrayed in Philip Roth's *Goodbye, Columbus,* made into a wonderful film (1969) starring Ali MacGraw and Richard Benjamin. Bruce was like Benjamin's pensive character, drawn to the dispossessed and resisting the natural impulse toward materialism and security of a people, his own, who had just escaped persecution. Feld's Long Island, from which so many Harpur students came, was like a nation unto itself, a vast paradise of middle-class comforts. When I visited his home in Westbury, he and his mother took me to Fortunoff's, a fabled nearby store, to experience the human tidal wave of the suburban marketplace. Befuddled by the mad din, I clung to Feld's sleeve as we forced our way through the throng. It somehow made perfect sense that the next day, as I drove Feld and his mother through town, my radiator exploded, and we were stranded.

After graduation, Feld followed the open-ended Sixties pattern of odd jobs. Returning from San Francisco, he worked for several years for travel agents in New York. Postcards would arrive from

I too have to escape

Which I appropriated/ late as usual, way in the '80s

South America or India, where he led tour groups eleven times—
Around the World with Auntie Mame, we joked. In his late twenties,
Feld began a stable relationship (now twenty-one years old) with a
research biologist, Peter Hollander. They took an Upper East Side
apartment and acquired two tiny, frenetic shih tzu dogs, whom
Feld named Margot (after Margot Fonteyn) and Tallulah (self-
explanatory). In their late twenties, both men returned to school to
study medicine. Peter became a radiologist and Feld a very successful
Park Avenue psychiatrist, an ideal profession for someone with such
a quick take for character and such a gift for putting people at ease.
When the pair went shopping for a weekend country house in the
northern Hudson River Valley, nothing would do, until the weary
realtor said, "There *is* something *you* might like"—an old town
grange. Feld walked in, took one look at the platform, and cried,
"At *last,* my very own stage! We'll take it!" The remodeled grange
of course became a showplace. Feld has, in a sense, reimagined and
reworked the stable married life of his parents' world. But underneath it all, his Wildean elitism remains: he subscribes to *Royalty,* a
British monthly that chronicles the doings of world aristocracy.

In college, my coterie and I were Mods and beats rather than
hippies. Feld cut a striking figure on campus in his green-vinyl car
coat, a badge of British dandyism purchased on Carnaby Street and
"coveted" by Jarratt. It was an exact copy, Feld boasts, of the one
worn by Julie Christie in Paris in *Darling,* a favorite film of ours. I
affected men's ties, paisley Tom Jones shirts, Edwardian pin-striped
bell-bottoms, naval pea coats, and antique jodhpur boots. My favorite piece of everyday clothing, however, was Feld's khaki jean
jacket, which I appropriated like a family hand-me-down and wore
for several years. Hard as it may be to understand now, since the
style has become universal, it was a radical gesture for a woman
then. Hippie girls did don their boyfriends' jean jackets, but only
with reinforced feminine iconography—long, flowing hair, peasant
blouses, dirndl skirts. I aggressively wore Feld's jacket with cropped
hair and trousers (as can be seen in a period photo reproduced in
my *Vanity Fair* profile of September 1992). The hippie clique who
ruled the student-center scene didn't like it one bit, as I certainly
heard while traversing the snack bar on the way to class.

Feld remains for me the symbol of modern gay men's extraordinary power of personality. His aplomb, audacity, and whiplash one-liners—delivered with perfect comic timing and his characteristic European shrug—made him the perfect companion and tutor for a raging young woman in flight from bourgeois conformism. I can still hear his inimitable voice twenty years later, in episode after episode from our lives.

Discussing a friend of his, I asked, "Does she have a good sense of humor?" Feld replied, "Not really. But she laughs at all my jokes. I consider that the highest form of humor." When he complained about the vast amount of information he had to master in medical school, I said it was well-known that the brain has large numbers of unused cells. Feld shot back: "*My* brain is full. Every time I memorize a medical fact, I forget something about a Betty Grable movie."

Of a stylishly eccentric college friend of ours who had played Death in Lorca's *Blood Wedding*, Feld said to me half a decade after graduation, "Leona has tried for years to look like everyone else, and she's finally succeeded." Of her and another Harpur original, a voluptuous blonde hippie nymph who became one of the organizers of the People's Park protest at Berkeley, Feld sighed, "My dear, we are the only ones who have retained our mythic stature."

In 1976, when he and Peter were visiting me in Bennington, Feld described a recent visit to a gay bar in Boston: "We were wearing jeans and a shirt, and we were overdressed. You had to have grease on your hands to get in." The next year, while I was breakfasting at his mother's house, my eyes quizzically met his as he poured salt profusely over his plate. He defiantly proclaimed, "I'm on a salt-free diet. I use salt freely." It was impossible to corner or capture him. He was as elusive as the Scarlet Pimpernel. With a wisecrack and a toss of the head, he would have kept the Spanish Inquisition at bay.

Bruce Benderson, Stephen Jarratt, and Stephen Feld were the crucible of consciousness out of which *Sexual Personae* was born. They directly inspired many of my images and ideas, and they embodied an avant-garde philosophy of life based on free speech, intellectual curiosity, sexual adventure, and theatrical individualism. As I lecture at colleges and universities across America, I am distressed by the banal sameness of so much student life. Different races, ethnic-

ities, social classes, and speech patterns have been systematically
dissolved into a bourgeois blandness that I thought we got rid of
after the Fifties. I feel fortunate in my friends, who in the Sixties
way dared to think and act on a grand scale. For me, creative
enterprise began at home, with my adoptive family of the mind.

JAMES LANDRUM FESSENDEN

James Fessenden, like Stephen Jarratt, came from conservative Protestant Midwestern stock, centered in Indiana and Illinois. His British roots were well-documented: the Fessenden family tree was
centuries old and was outlined in a privately published volume that
Jim paid no attention to. When I first met him in 1972 as a fellow
new colleague on the Bennington College faculty, his outlandish
Sixties costume made him look like a sybaritic eighteenth-century
squire: knee-high crimson-suede lace-up boots, crushed-velvet trousers, mutton-sleeve silk shirts, military greatcoat, and long, curly,
unkempt dirty-brown hair hanging to the waist, as thick as a periwig.
With Jim's chubby cheeks and heavy eyeglasses, it made a strange
effect.

Fessenden, as I tended to call him except in our private moments, was tall (6'4"), strong, and broad-shouldered. He was made
for football, but he despised athletics and took no exercise except
walking. His body language was languid, luxurious, half-female, like
that of Delacroix's lounging Sardanapalus. Like me, he was an Aries
and an only child (my sister was born when I was 14, after my
personality was, for better or worse, fully formed). We instantly
recognized each other as fellow aesthetes, passionate devotees of the
religion of art and admirers of Friedrich Nietzsche.

Naturally, I wanted to integrate Fessenden into my college circle
of gay men. But my first efforts were disastrous, and I gave up. At
a restaurant dinner I arranged in New York, Bruce Benderson and
Fessenden bristled at each other, and the evening ended in open
hostility when Fessenden showed undisguised interest in meeting
Bruce's current flame and housemate, a gorgeous Japanese youth
named Nobuo. I remember thinking to myself, gay they may be but
men they still are, with all the snorting, hoof-stomping territoriality

of bison. Bruce was indignant for years afterward. The two never met again.

Fessenden initially came to Bennington to fill in for a year, while an elderly woman philosopher was on leave. He ended up staying longer but was finally terminated because, it was rumored, there had been complaints that to win entrance to the in-group of philosophy students, one had to take drugs with the two young male teachers and hang out at their on-campus faculty houses. There may have been some truth in this. Fessenden and his best friend, an analytic philosopher and straight fellow student from Columbia University who affected a rock-star look (tall and gaunt, with long, curly black hair and motorcycle sunglasses indoors and out), set a style of hip, loitering indifference that may not have profited the already undisciplined children of the rich and famous who were Bennington's stock-in-trade.

At the start, we brash young Turks offered a serious challenge to the Bennington establishment, which was mired in a genteel liberalism long on paternalistic sentimentality and short on political realism. There were many gradations of left-wing to centrist thinking among us: my close friend, Richard Tristman, for example, had been fired just before the uprising at Columbia when he gave all his students A's as a protest against the academic system. Many of the faculty who went directly from graduate school to Bennington in the charged late Sixties and early Seventies were heady with a sense of destiny. We had all the arrogance of youthful talent. We felt intellectually superior and didn't hide it. We thought we could change the world overnight. Life was to teach us otherwise.

Fessenden was politically radical throughout our friendship. He hated authority and the corporate values represented by his businessman father. Though personally kind, he was contemptuous of the namby-pamby civilities required for college meetings and committees. He categorically refused to play the career game required for advancement in academe. His nemesis was the senior woman philosopher, who flirted with retirement but returned to dislodge him. Socially well-connected and married to a trustee of the college, she was competent but undistinguished and far from informed about recent issues in her field. Fessenden came to hate her as a symbol of the old guard, of power and position unjustly attained.

She blocked him, and she defeated him. I felt even then that Fessenden, in his justified sense of his own merits, was unnecessarily cruel to her. To the end of his life, he never admitted any fault in his handling of that first career crisis—which proved to be his last, since he never completed his doctoral dissertation on Nietzsche or found another academic job. The ferocity with which he darkly remembered his opponent eventually made me think she was a shadow of his own frigid, manipulative mother, who put the screws in, one Christmas in the mid-Seventies, by giving him a leatherbound book embossed with the title *Nietzsche* and as the author's name, "James Fessenden." The pages were blank.

Fessenden was the most comprehensively learned person I have ever known. Richard Tristman, trained in literature, is also a polymath, with special knowledge of philosophy, theology, science, and medicine. But Fessenden's breadth of interest extended beyond the library from intellectual history to the visual and performing arts and popular culture. He had considered becoming a classical pianist. As a small child, he studied at the Eastman School of Music in Rochester. (When asked, on the entrance application, the title of his favorite composition, he replied, "The prelude to the third act of *Die Walküre*"—i.e., the wild "Ride of the Valkyries.") Music suffused all one's encounters with Fessenden. He received visitors to his faculty house—or later his dingy, cramped, cell-like apartment near Columbia on New York's Upper West Side—in a magic envelope of sound. He was particularly expert in opera, whose librettos he minutely studied in their original languages and whose performance history he catalogued as an avid collector of records and tapes.

Fessenden adored dance, classical ballet above all. He never missed a major production in Manhattan. A dedicated visitor to museums and galleries, he read deeply in art history, ancient to modern, and followed the latest developments in contemporary painting and sculpture. He haunted bookstores, monitored recent releases, and had a wide-ranging appreciation of great poetry, drama, and novels, which he cited with ease. He devoured biographies and always had some fascinating detail to relay. Like me, he was a movie fanatic who loved both the Hollywood studio era and European art films of the postwar decades. He was an aficionado of Alfred Hitchcock; both of us were crazy about Bernard Herrmann's

Hitchcock scores, particularly *Vertigo*, of which Fessenden possessed a prized early recording. Our ultimate personal film as a duo was Jacques Rivette's surreal, three-hour, Alice-in-Paris saga, *Céline and Julie Go Boating* (1974), which we saw together and discussed with cultic fervor for years.

Although he had no interest in television, Fessenden knew and respected popular music. One of our few quarrels was over the Rolling Stones' great album *Aftermath*, whose rich sonorities were destroyed, I insisted, by the new compact disc reissue that Fessenden was playing with pride for me. The artist I most associate with Fessenden is David Bowie, who was in his orange-haired, extraterrestrial, transsexual Ziggy Stardust phase during our early years at Bennington. The *Aladdin Sane* album, with its eerie half-embryo/half-mummy cover photo and its brilliant Scriabin-like piano interlude on the title song, is pure Fessenden for me. "All the Young Dudes," the ominously elegiac song that Bowie wrote for Mott the Hoople, always reminded me of Fessenden, even more so since his death. It was a dirge for the new dandyism.

The Sixties cultural revolution, which failed to transform the academic or literary worlds as it should have, was contained in the eclectic, interdisciplinary mind of James Fessenden. Discourse with Fessenden was an extraordinary experience. He brought to bear on the moment not only his profound philosophic knowledge but his linguistic and etymological skills. While I never showed work in progress to him (or to anyone), Fessenden was my primary partner in dialogue and debate throughout the period when I was writing *Sexual Personae*. As I bounced ideas off him, I marveled at the combination of precision and flexibility in his thinking. He caught the finest shadings of every syllable. He understood the traditional systems and the warpings I was performing on them. It was a kind of music: Fessenden heard the dissonance and the jazzlike improvisations I made. Never in my life, before or since, have I been so blissfully relaxed in serious conversation. Fessenden's consciousness, both reflective and perceptive, seemed to float like a hawk. He was a superb audience, goading one to supreme efforts, which he rewarded with his characteristic guffaw, handclap, or glance of arch bemusement.

A shared taste of ours that ended up writ large in *Sexual Personae*

was the beautiful boy, whom I traced from Greek sculpture to Flor-
entine art and Wilde's Dorian Gray. Only one other woman of my
acquaintance—the London art historian and curator Kristen Lippincott, then my student at Bennington—has ever been equally
entranced by this archetype. The Luchino Visconti film of Thomas
Mann's *Death in Venice* (1971) had just been released. We went bon-
kers over the publicity still of the seraphic, long-tressed, blonde Bjorn
Andresen as Tadzio. Fessenden had his own Tadzio, or what I was
to call "the beautiful boy as destroyer." He was a heartstoppingly
handsome Italian youth named Raffaello, whom I knew only through
a snapshot. A decade later, I asked Fessenden how long his pursuit
of Raffaello had lasted and what it had led to. "Two years," he
glumly replied. "It led to light bulbs being thrown at me by a
transvestite ballerina."

   This was all I ever learned. I assume Fessenden was referring
to his involvement with a downtown troupe of New York dancers
who performed classical ballet in drag. Bitter rivalries split the en-
semble into the Ballet de Trocadero and the Ballet de Monte Carlo,
the latter going on to international success. The founder and star,
Anthony Bassaë, known as Karpova, was a close friend of Fessenden's who lost control of his own company. He was stocky and round-
faced, with the caramel skin of his native Caribbean. He had a
magnetic presence. When Tony died in New York, an early victim
of AIDS, Fessenden visibly mourned. There was now a permanent
undertone of melancholy in him.

   Another, even earlier loss from Fessenden's inner circle was
Lance Norebo, a strange creature with the height and lanky physique
of a basketball player but the haughty manner and carriage of a
fashion model. He had neither home nor possessions. He belonged
to the drag queen underworld of Harlem, the phantasmagoric
"house" culture that produced the notorious dance craze called
"vogueing." Lance, with his skull-like chiseled cheekbones, seemed
Asian but was apparently at least part Portuguese. He looked as
spectral and menacing as one of Melville's harpooneers. He was a
mysterious resident of Fessenden's apartment, coming and going at
will. The two were not involved; Fessenden simply admired Lance's
freedom and style. Lance scorned me as a noisy little woman—until
I sent him a glamourous old newspaper photo of two of his heroines,

Maria Callas and Merle Oberon, striding in matching gaucho hats and boots out of a lunchtime New York restaurant. My stock rose enormously after that.

Once, in midafternoon, while Lance was still sleeping, his friend Gaga, a fellow drag queen, telephoned. Fessenden could not rouse the drowsy, snappish Lance. "Well," sniffed Gaga, "just tell her it's *Audrey's birthday*"—and hung up in a huff. The words were barely out of Jim's mouth when Lance leaped from bed like a comet, flung on some clothes, and raced frantically out of the apartment. Audrey Hepburn, thanks to *Breakfast at Tiffany's*, was a principal divinity among queens, and her birthday was a high holy day. Lance ate next to nothing—"a few grains of rice" per day, with a cup of tea, according to Fessenden, who attributed Lance's lack of resistance to the AIDS virus to this monkish abstemiousness. When he fell ill, Lance was camping in an abandoned building on the Lower East Side, to which he had pursued a romantic interest. A month later, he was dead. Only afterward, as he was trying to locate Lance's relatives, did Fessenden realize, to our shock, that "Norebo" was a pseudonym: "Oberon" spelled backwards. Both Fessenden and I revered and honored drag queens for their power of imagination and imperious rejection of banal reality.

Fessenden had returned to New York, after being forced out of Bennington, at exactly the moment gay bathhouse culture was moving into high gear. I was used to accompanying my male friends to their bars and vice versa, a vestige of the pre-Stonewall era when provincial cities usually had just one gay bar, in which the sexes mingled. I remember when the doors of the men's bars closed in my face. It was probably 1974; the hostility to a female presence was palpable. The reason: pitch-black orgy rooms and sex shows— chained men sodomized in slings—were coming into fashion. Upset at this divorce from my friends, I tried to pass in drag. An amused Stephen Feld loaned me his battered leather aviator's jacket and smuggled me, hair slicked back, into a crowded New York bar, where I tried to blend. But mannish as I am, I made an unconvincing male and aroused notice. I had to accept the fact that, as a woman, I was persona non grata in the new gay garden of earthly delights.

With his indolence, nocturnal habits, and voyeuristic tastes, Fessenden took to the bathhouse scene immediately. He was generally secretive about his sex life, but he told me enough of his experiences there—seeing a naked, well-endowed Rudolf Nureyev, for example—to whet my appetite and envy. It was a realm, based on nudity and gargantuan promiscuity, that I obviously could never enter, even in drag. Fessenden's standards of hygiene were never that strict to begin with—another of his eighteenth-century traits, which worsened as the years passed. The degeneration of his apartment, uncontrollable as he became ill, is unimaginable in female terms. I often wonder whether the health risks in that hot, humid bathhouse underworld of thrilling sexual adventure would have been more obvious to women than to the men who, for complex reasons they never faced, shut women out.

My epitaph for Fessenden: He lived, and he died. I mean by this that he lived life fully, sating himself on the pleasures of the mind and the pleasures of the body. He was not prudent. He postponed no gratification. He spurned the caution and frugality of his Protestant ancestors. Like so many members of our generation, he chose sensuality and the quest for truth over pensions, security, materialism. With his slow, grand movements and dreamy contemplativeness, he seemed to view each hour as a crystal goblet to be filled with rare wine. Of all my friends, he was the most inveterate drug-taker—marijuana and later cocaine, which surely (though he never admitted it) had something to do with the gold plate surgically installed to fill a hole in his sinus. Cocaine for him, as for Freud, gave clarity and command: thinking was his deepest self. At the end, he was making huge withdrawals for drugs from a large cash reserve unwisely deposited in a non-interest-bearing checking account. It was the remnant of his inheritance from his dead parents. His luxury, excess, and solitude reminded me of the extravagant, impacted language of Gerard Manley Hopkins poems I loved in high school. As adolescents marooned in the provinces, Fessenden and I had had the same longing for sophistication and beauty.

While our romantic lives were separate, there was one area of pleasure we ardently shared: food. My friendship with Fessenden was a symposium in the original Greek sense: we ate, drank, and talked ideas for hours on end. The electric connection we were trying to establish, as Sixties rebels, between thought and sensation was reified in our conduct. Eating and drinking, rather than drug-taking,

have always been my Mediterranean mode of testing and pushing
my own neurotransmitters. Fessenden and I were systematically
exploring the brain. It was a psychedelic undertaking. My generation
treated inner like outer space, which *Star Trek,* our symbolic saga,
calls "the final frontier." In the theoretical terms of *Sexual Personae,*
Fessenden enjoyed unusually close communication between his
Apollonian and Dionysian sides. He fulfilled in his own being the
dual consciousness I see as crucial for intellectuals of the twenty-
first century.

My substitute for LSD was Indian food, to which Fessenden
introduced me and which became a constant theme of our exchanges.
It began in 1973 during a short visit to Bennington by the brilliant
British philosopher Gillian Rose, the last woman Fessenden (as a
graduate student) had dated. She concocted a fantastic Indian soup,
golden-mustard in color and silty with twelve fresh-ground spices.
It packed a wallop: I was hung over for two days. In New York,
Fessenden took me to his favorite restaurant, the hole-in-the-wall
Bit of Bengal on upper Broadway, where I had my first ultra-hot
lamb vindaloo, a seductive culinary rut I have never escaped, no
matter how resolutely I scan the rest of the menu. There Fessenden,
languorous as Lewis Carroll's hookah-smoking caterpillar, ordered
my first ambrosial, rust-red mulligatawny soup and educated me
about its proper ceremonious consumption. "*Really,* Camille," he
thundered, as I gulped it down. Obscure Indian restaurants all over
New York became the scene of my spice-triggered psychedelic
"trips" with Fessenden. After our mammoth feasts, I would smoke
a cigar as, gorged and happy, we strolled the streets.

It was for another Indian sojourn that I rendezvoused with
Fessenden at the big black cube sculpture on Astor Place in May
1989. The dinner was to be celebratory: the edited manuscript of
Sexual Personae, after endless headaches, conflicts, and white-knuckle
negotiations, had just gotten the go-ahead for production at Yale
Press. I had visited Fessenden only a month before, so I was not
prepared for what I saw. His classic expression of casual, smug
confidence was completely gone (and never to return). He looked
sweaty and distracted. I saw desperation and fear in his eyes. The
shock took my breath away. Earl Mountbatten said of the sudden,
premature death of his wife, "It was a poleax blow." I knew my life

would never be the same. A picture of my future isolation, like a desert landscape, flashed before me.

Fessenden curtly fended off my concerned queries about how he was feeling—"too many drugs," he claimed and never budged from that story. He had always refused to discuss health matters, even bad colds, with me. We were fraternal Aries warriors; he had the stubborn pride and victor mentality of an athlete. Thus began the charade we played to the end. The word "AIDS" never passed between us, except about others. Before dinner that evening, we stopped for an errand at the apartment of one of Fessenden's musician friends, who was traveling abroad. Sitting down at the magnificent grand piano, Fessenden began to play from memory—Chopin and Liszt. I had never seen him so open or vulnerable. Lost in thought, he was literally playing his heart out. I knew it was his anguished leave-taking, his farewell to what might have been. Lying on the Oriental carpet, I was oppressed by a sense of the tragic waste and self-destruction of my generation.

At the tiny table in the dark restaurant on 6th Street, I gave an award-winning performance. I chattered, gossiped, entertained, and gobbled paratha bread and lemon pickle as usual. Pointedly spearing and devouring delicacies near or on Fessenden's plate, I tried to suggest he had nothing to fear from admitting his condition; he would not be ostracized as dangerous or contaminated. It was a gruelling, futile effort. His mood remained grim. Driving back to Philadelphia after dinner, I sped into the first rest stop on the New Jersey Turnpike and frantically telephoned Bruce Benderson to pour out my grief and anxiety. It was one of the worst days of my life. Exultation had turned to horror. "Count no man happy," says Greek drama.

Several years passed before Fessenden's illness, heralded by bouts of pneumonia, was obvious to others. By the fall of 1991, he was barely leaving his apartment. Since he had no family left, aside from a few elderly Midwesterners he had lost contact with, an ad hoc group, half dozen in number, of Fessenden's friends, ex-students, and protégés began to confer about him. Gillian Rose and her mother, an AIDS volunteer, visited from London to assess and significantly improve the situation. Roger Kimball, who had studied with Fessenden at Bennington and toward whom I had always been unfairly hostile, proved himself a man of honor and integrity by taking charge of Fessenden's legal and financial affairs and bringing in expert help to untangle the mess.

Fessenden's primary malady was a massive overgrowth of fungal microbes in his body, crippled by autoimmune deficiency. Little showed externally, except for a severe weight loss. His mind began to slow, and he became progressively less responsive, indifferent to conversation or even music. I regularly telephoned semiweekly but could see him rarely. While he was hospitalized in the spring of 1992, Lauren Hutton, who had expressed a desire to meet him, accompanied me on a visit. In May, at the conclusion of her semester at the University of Sussex, Gillian Rose flew to New York. It was as if, she later said to me, Jim had waited for her in order to die. She was in the hospital with several others as he began to fail. They sat for hours in the corridor until, at 1 A.M., the doctors informed them that Jim had died. Gillian immediately called me in Philadelphia with the news.

The prognosis had been so pessimistic for so long that there was neither surprise nor shock in Fessenden's passing. And there had been such a transformation and reduction of him, physically and mentally, that the real Fessenden seemed to have vanished. Most of us felt relief that the towering intellect he had been would have to endure no more humiliations to his frail shell of a body. My worst moment had been the first stunning revelation at Astor Place. After that, I had made a fatalistic adjustment to reality. It was, I liked to think, the steely pragmatism of the soldier.

Three weeks after Fessenden's death, I was in London for the release of the Penguin paperback of *Sexual Personae*. As I was fielding questions from the stage of the Institute of Contemporary Art, with Gillian Rose in the audience, I began to describe the painful, lonely childhood of sensitive and artistic gay men in macho America. To my astonishment, huge tears began to stream down my face. Why only in public? Because it was the public realm where Fessenden belonged. And because his failure to enter it was partly due to his noble refusal to deform the philosophic quest by concern for money, status, or power. The audience I addressed was rightfully his.

The Fessenden who will live on for me is the one who, after meeting her in London, was a devoted fan of Ava Gardner, whose wildcat temperament seemed to express what he could not assert in reality. There was a trace of this in his attitude toward me. All of my gay male friends treated me with the same blend of amused exasperation and affection; they saw my absurdity at the same time as they admired my pugnacious energy. In a way, I was their proxy for conventional masculine action. Fessenden enjoyed my scrapes and scandals at Bennington, which ranged from a public ass-kicking to claims of clairvoyance to fisticuffs at a college dance, the latter of which led, after a clash of lawyers, to my departure. In my processing of Sixties politics, disruptive behavior was a form of civil disobedience. Matured by disaster, I ended up with more respect for institutions and their needs than did Fessenden, who never turned his aggression directly on his oppressors.

Fessenden's campus house at Bennington, Ludlow Studio, was the site-of-origin of my beloved cat, Numa Pompilius, an elegant blue-gray stray who had been hanging around for months until I adopted her. Numa, who had a distinct and well-deserved superiority complex, was my inseparable companion for fifteen years, throughout the writing of *Sexual Personae*. She was the model for my autocratic portrait of cats and their mystic symbolism in Egypt. For many years, Fessenden owned a shaggier gray-and-white cat, similarly from the Bennington countryside, whom he named Camille.

I also associate Fessenden with Yasmin Aga Khan, who became, as our friend Karen Colvard put it, my "hobby." Though we never spoke, I became fascinated with Yasmin when, during my first week at Bennington in 1972, I caught what appeared to be a beautiful Arab boy staring at me across the mail room. The more florid Spanish features of her mother, Rita Hayworth, only came out in Yasmin long afterward. Hayworth, looking regal in a muted beige dress, was in attendance at Yasmin's senior recital in 1973. Fessenden and I were loud and obnoxious at the reception.

Back in New York, Fessenden whiled away his slow hours at the police archives (the improbable job he had until the end) by culling piquant items for me from the tabloid gossip columns. His envelopes bore the return address "Celebrity Service," which eventually turned into an allegorical personage, "Célébrité," my satirical nickname for him. Thanks to the vigilance of Célébrité, we zestfully followed Yasmin (or, as Jim called her, "Yasmaga") through her many adventures, from Margaret Trudeau to various globetrotting

suitors and husbands. In the late Seventies I had a close encounter
with Yasmin, an astrakhan-clad woman friend, and a visibly shaky
Hayworth in, of all places, the glittering Islamic Rooms of the Metropolitan Museum of Art. I was thunderstruck but for once had the
sense to leave them alone.

Throughout our friendship, Fessenden and I discussed French
literature and culture, a subject in which I felt at home, since my
father taught French and had brought back from a year at the
Sorbonne, when I was a toddler, many books about the Louvre,
Versailles, and Fontainebleau that had a great impact on me. Fessenden and I admired the Roland Barthes of *Mythologies* but were
less enthusiastic about his later development. We liked Gilles Deleuze's book on masochism but again felt the sequel was lacking.
Expert in German, Fessenden enjoyed reading the poststructuralists
in French, though he never overestimated their importance as did
American literature professors, for whom he had withering scorn.

From our first acquaintance, Fessenden kept telling me that
what I was doing in English was very similar to what Lacan was
doing in French, but I found Lacan boring, pompous, imprecise,
and ahistorical. We often argued about Foucault, whom Bruce
Benderson was also fond of. Many years of bickering and stalemate
skirmishes passed before Bruce had a key epiphany: he finally admitted, under Amazonian pressure, that Foucault's cold, invigorating discourse was refreshingly woman-free. I never pressed this point
with Fessenden, since I knew in my bones it was too true of him
and his attraction to Foucault.

In the spring of 1993, at a panel discussion on political correctness with Robert Hughes in Washington, D.C. that was filmed
for British television, Edward Said congratulated me on the stand
I had taken against New Historicism, with its bourgeois assumptions
and vulgar inaccuracies. I told him that his intellectual successors
were not the opportunistic mediocrities who have won tenure at our
major universities but rather the authentic leftists of my generation
who rejected the sycophancy of the career system and drifted out
into the general culture. I passionately declared, "Your heir is
dead—James Fessenden," whose mentor and dissertation advisor
had been Arthur Danto, Said's friend and colleague at Columbia.

When I descend like a demon on Harvard or any other university where I lecture, it is Fessenden whom I am avenging with my wrath. The most fêted names of our generation of humanities professors are a callow lot, unlearned and uncultivated. America deserved better. By recovering what we can from the ruins of the Sixties, we can help the next generation to learn from our mistakes. This is our legacy.

DR. PAGLIA

PART ONE OF *FEMALE MISBEHAVIOR*

A FOUR-PART DOCUMENTARY BY MONIKA TREUT

Pan of 42nd Street, New York City on a rainy night. Traffic noise. CAMILLE PAGLIA *strolling past the porn theaters and adult bookshops. Voiceover of* PAGLIA *conversing with* BRUCE BENDERSON.

PAGLIA: I was so miserable here, twenty-five years ago.

BRUCE BENDERSON: Really?

PAGLIA: Yes, in graduate school. You remember.

BENDERSON: Mmmmm . . . vaguely.

PAGLIA: I still have no sex life. But even then it was very intense. My hormones were at their *height*.

BENDERSON: I do remember sitting on a rock here waiting for a go-go dancer that I knew to come and meet you for the afternoon. I was trying to fix you up with a female go-go dancer.

PAGLIA: Yes, *there's* an example! There's an example of the misery of my life. My sex life has been a *disaster*.

[Produced and directed by Monika Treut. Volcano Pictures for Hyena Films. Filmed in Philadelphia and New York, November 1991. Released in 1992.]

BENDERSON: Yeah.

(Shot of PAGLIA *and* BENDERSON *sitting on couches in the Helen Hayes Suite of the Milford Plaza Hotel, overlooking 8th Avenue. There is a lavish spread of food on the table between them.* PAGLIA *eats constantly as she speaks throughout the film.)*

PAGLIA: I mean, every time I try, like, to seduce a woman, I've just been . . . hopeless. It's like people can't take me seriously! I mean, I think that—I don't know—

BENDERSON: I think that you unconsciously subvert it, in many cases.

PAGLIA: What *is* it then? What do you think it is?

BENDERSON: You get to the point of consummation, then something in you says that it's wrong, and you make sure that it doesn't happen.

PAGLIA *(perplexed)*: I don't know what it is.

BENDERSON: It's the Catholic part of you.

PAGLIA: You think?

BENDERSON: Yes!

PAGLIA: But, you know, *I* think it's something else. I think on some level that I'm slightly *absurd*. I'm an absurd, rather comical person.

BENDERSON: Well, I agree with *that! (They laugh.)*

PAGLIA: No one can really take me seriously. *Men* can take me seriously as a sex object because, you know, I have tits and ass, like *that.* And I *do* feel the *lust* between men and women.

BENDERSON: Oh yeah, we *love* those tits and ass, babe!

PAGLIA: Yeah! And so—

BENDERSON: Shake 'em!

PAGLIA: Right!

BENDERSON: Go ahead! Yeah!

PAGLIA *(laughing)*: Right! Shake it! But the thing is that women don't take me seriously at all as, you know, as a seducer. I'm just *ridiculous,* and so, I mean, I've *never* succeeded.

(Cut to Fifties footage of typical mother in heels and plaid summer dress fussing over small daughter with blond ringlets on their stoop. Voiceover begins of PAGLIA *at the Egyptian gallery of the University Museum of the University of Pennsylvania in Philadelphia.)*

PAGLIA *(with air of disgust)*: As a child in the early 1950s in America, I was being asked to identify with bride dolls, things like this. There would be, like, these lacy images of *brides.* I was expected to collect these dolls and so on. It was the period of Debbie Reynolds and Doris Day and these sorority queen blondes. Girls were supposed to be "nice" and feminine and so on, and instead I was identifying with things like *this* from Egyptian culture. *(Gestures toward black stone object next to her.)* And here we have, like, a *tombstone,* okay?—or in some cases a stele that could just be a monument commemorating something that happened during a king's reign. You see, everything about this, to me, was *anti* the 1950s, *anti* the bourgeois culture of that period, because you have these mystic images, cryptic signs. Here we have a rapacious falcon or hawk, all right? I've always identified very strongly with carnivorous kinds of animals. I'm a kind of dominating, aggressive woman who just was totally out of sync with culture at that time.

I suppose one could say that it *(indicating the object)* has a hard phallic quality, but the *monumentality* of Egyptian culture, its imperialistic statements, its *assertiveness* attracted me *enormously.* Plus the idea of cryptic signs and so on. I've always been fascinated by visual emblems, and I find an exact correlation between something like this, which I could not have understood as a child, and advertisements of the period. I couldn't read as a small child, but I would see images and people doing strange things—you know, people holding a box, or holding a box out like *this (she demonstrates in the 1950s style of Betty Furness),* which later I could read—TIDE SOAP. So I felt since earliest childhood that advertisements were never something that was just popular culture and not to be taken seriously. But rather right from the beginning I saw that there was a connection between ancient pagan culture and the popular culture all around me which, let's say, my parents would not take seriously. My parents were very against commercialism and advertisements and so on. I had a kind of stubborn interest in the cryptic signs of advertisement. So for me the Egyptian hieroglyphics and advertisements are in the same line. And it's *true*. As I went on, I learned that the great pharaohs were *advertising* themselves. That's what they were *doing*—"I am the greatest, I am the most fabulous." Which they've done now. Five thousand years later, we're still reading their signs

(Cut back to PAGLIA *and* BENDERSON *in the New York hotel.)*

PAGLIA: Being a strong woman, okay, a strong sexual woman, is an absolute *horror*—because there are very few things that you can *do*, okay? *Really*, the number of opportunities for sexual adventurism available to men—it's just *appalling*—through history!

BENDERSON: Well, I believe that's true image-wise, but I don't see why you have to follow all these social rules.

PAGLIA: It's *undignified!*

BENDERSON: But—

PAGLIA: It's *sleazy!* It just *is!*

BENDERSON: Well, I—

PAGLIA: When Cher—look—Madonna is also in a similar situation apparently. She's at a point where there's no man as strong as she is, right? And so she has this problem. And now the rumors are, in these new biographies, that she takes the limousine, picks up Hispanic, you know, beautiful Latino youths off the street, has sex with them in a limo, deposits them off! *(Laughs.)* I mean, that seems to me a very good reconciliation—

BENDERSON: Oh, so you're worried about press coverage.

PAGLIA: No, no! It's a matter of dignity. She retains her dignity by having her limousine, and doing it in the limousine.

BENDERSON: Darling, dignity is—oh, she *maintains* her dignity—

PAGLIA: Yeah, she maintains her dignity. I fail to see how—

BENDERSON: Well, all we need is a limousine for you.

PAGLIA: Right. My Pontiac Grand Am isn't quite as, uh, dignified.

BENDERSON: All right. We'll rent a limousine for you next time.

PAGLIA *(thoughtfully)*: Yeah, yeah. 'Cause, see, I *like* sex with men.
I have no problem with that. I mean, I can't stand these lesbians
who get on talk shows and say, "Oh! Oo! Oo! Men don't do
anything for me," or "Penises are ugly," or things like that. I
have no problem with that, okay, at *all*. It's just that men . . .
men . . . once you get beyond the level of their sexuality, then
you get into this political area. You know, they have to compete.
My crushing intellect becomes a problem to them.

Not true.

BENDERSON: I agree. One should never get beyond the level of
sexuality with men.   *Oh really.*

PAGLIA: This is the point.

BENDERSON: They're totally uninteresting.

PAGLIA: Exactly. Yes, yes. And then, when I say this, the feminists
accuse me of treating men as if they were merely *bestial* or as if
they were incapable of an emotional life—

BENDERSON: Oh, you're exciting me!

PAGLIA: —when in fact my entire book is about the emotional life
of men. What?

BENDERSON: You're exciting me.

PAGLIA: How? About what?

BENDERSON: Talking about bestiality in men.

PAGLIA *(sighing)*: I know. At least you've *had* some bestiality.

*(Cut to vintage Wild West footage of leering cowboy mauling and bussing a
frantic young woman. Cut to PAGLIA sitting on the floor with MONIKA
TREUT in the University Museum in Philadelphia.)*

PAGLIA: What I'm opposing is the anti-intellectualism of contemporary feminism. Feminism in its current phase began as a movement of eccentric individualists, but it has really rigidified into a kind of cult. They're like Moonies. They are really religious thinkers who usually have separated in some way from their religious background or their cultural background. They are people looking for an identity, okay? And such people are absolutely—They have not really examined their own assumptions. They're not intellectuals. So as a consequence, when you challenge them, they become very emotional, because they have no equipment for responding to you. Feminism today in America has become simply a series of rote, learned, jargon phrases. So if you try to critique their view of rape, let's say, they get very angry, and all they can do is parrot back to you something they've learned—a statement like *(imitates droning computer voice)* "Rape is a crime of violence but not of sex." They're like robots, okay? They've been programmed. Or they'll say something like "No always means no." Not true.

Now, both these statements are *stupid.* They absolutely are meaningless, all right? And what I'm doing is I'm going around as an intellectual, not just as a feminist but as an intellectual, and I am seizing on and attacking each of these jargon phrases and exposing them, and I'm doing it by shock tactics. For example, this business about snuff films, all right, which is like, oh, snuff films, this huge nightmare vision of contemporary anti-porn feminists. And so I'm doing things like saying, "Let snuff films be made!" Now I don't mean, of course, a film in which a *real* woman is killed. When we go to a mystery story, we don't want to see a real woman, a real *person* being murdered. When we go to *Hamlet,* we don't want to see, like, ten people being killed by the end—the same thing with the *Oresteia* or anything else. But I'm saying that whenever there's a taboo, it's the absolute obligation of the artist and intellectual to *seize* on that taboo and to *shatter* it. In other words *(cut to vintage footage of plump, middle-aged women being punched and pummeled by early exercise equipment),* all these tender places in the contemporary ideology—we must *push* on them, *palpate* them, make people *squeal,* okay? So I'm doing that also for things like the battered wife motif, the battered woman. People are always, like, you know, wringing their hands and sobbing over these victims.

I *hate* the victim-centered nature of contemporary feminism! It's *loathsome* to me. I believe woman is the *dominant sex*, okay? And that everyone knows this, *everyone* knows throughout world culture that woman *dominates* man. Everyone but feminists knows that! And I think that it's absolutely perverse and neurotic to insist that history is nothing but male oppressors and female victims. This is *ridiculous*, all right? They want to make women small! *(She angrily gestures with thumb and index finger.)* Is this *feminism?* To make women *small*, to make them into victims? This is *absurd!* What I see is going on between the sexes, you see, is war. I'm an Aries. I have no trouble with war. I'm a combative personality. I believe that war and combat are the way that we form our identities. All great artists have in some sense warred with their religion, with their culture, with their family, with others, with the artists who came before them. And so conflict and aggression are at the center of my system. *(Cut back to PAGLIA and BENDERSON.)* I've seen a film of a female cat mating, breeding, and I identify with it so powerfully.

BENDERSON: Oh, yeah, I've seen that.

PAGLIA: Because the cat is an isolated animal, like me, a solitary animal, and you can see that she's driven by these hormones to mate, to breed—

BENDERSON: *Yes.*

PAGLIA: —but she's *angry* at having to submit. *Why must it be submission?*

BENDERSON: *Yes!*

PAGLIA: And you have this war going on between this male cat and this female cat, and *(imitates growling and scratching cat)* she's, like, clawing him, okay? And he's waiting, waiting. *Eleven times* he may penetrate her with this kind of penis that has a hook on it that injures her.

BENDERSON: Yes! It's very hard and bony.

PAGLIA: Yes. And I identify with that so powerfully. And I say, yes, that's *me*. I am like this completely carnivorous, solitary, self-ruling animal, like a cat.

BENDERSON: Right.

PAGLIA: You know? And I want to mate, and nature pushes me very powerfully to mate, but then I wanna *kill*. See, I hate this sort of, to me, saccharine or cloying intimacy—I don't mean to characterize *you!*

BENDERSON: Oh *do,* please!

PAGLIA *(laughing)*: No, no, I'm not categorizing you! But I'm in flight from this thing in the American bourgeoisie. Which is this thing of being *nice,* making *nice,* and nurturing, coddling and so on. I just can't do that. That's my problem with relationships, that I can't do it.

BENDERSON: I don't totally believe that, because you're very nurturing to me sometimes, over our long relationship.

PAGLIA: That's to my friends. That's to my immediate friends.

BENDERSON: So you can't give some of this *abbondanza* around, you know, sort of spread it around outside of your circle of friends?

PAGLIA: I have trouble getting it together with sex. When I get that with someone, the sex seems to leave. That's my problem. *Hm.*

BENDERSON: Really? How interesting.

PAGLIA: Yeah. As a woman, I just can't get nurturance and sex together. I cannot.

BENDERSON: To other women you can, though.

PAGLIA: Well, yeah. Susie Bright criticized me, you know, for saying that I feel we need less intimacy, not more, with sex. I think that intimacy kills sex. *Hm.*

(Cut to technicolor footage of formally dressed Fifties couple toasting each other with clinking coffee mugs. A lush soundtrack swells. Cut back to PAGLIA *and*

TREUT *sitting on the museum floor.* PAGLIA *makes wild Italian gestures throughout this scene.)*

PAGLIA: Now feminists today, as I see it, are the heirs of Rousseau. They believe *(imitates prissy woman with singsong voice)* we're born naturally good and whatever is *nasty* about us, we got that from an unjust social system. So if there's rape, why, *no one* would ever rape *naturally.* It must be coming from *pornography!* Yes, pornography! Men are taught to rape by pornography! *(With disgust)* This is so stupid. Rape has occurred everywhere in history, okay? Rape is simply a brutal form of the will to power, okay? Men are *taught* not to rape. The idea that feminism *discovered* rape, that feminists *alone* are the ones who have decried the violence of rape . . . *absurd!* Feminism—it is *mired* in the shallow present, it is so *ignorant* about culture! Men throughout history have condemned rape. Ethical men have *always* done that, for heaven's sakes. *(Angrily)* I mean, the fall of the tyrants in Rome was because of the rape of Lucretia by Tarquin, right?

So we teach people by ethical rules of society—whether it's through morality in religion or by just the rational code of ethics—not to murder, not to steal, not to rape. Now, feminism is focusing on rape at the college level, at the freshman year. *(Imitates breathlessly posturing Joan of Arc feminist)* "We can stop rape by passing grievance committee rules!" Is this stupid? Is this ignorant? I mean, first of all, my generation of girls, we were raised in the Fifties, where you had to be a virgin, okay? We arrived in college in 1964, and we were kept in all-girl dorms, locked at eleven o'clock at night. We had to sign in. *My* generation's the one that broke through that in America and said, "No more rules!" We said to the colleges, "Get out of our sex lives! Let *us* have the freedom to *risk* danger, to *risk* rape. *Get out,* okay?" Now today, feminism is so stupid, it wants authority figures *back into sex!* It wants authority figures *(imitates unctuously paternalistic bureaucrat)*—"Okay, what happened on this date? Oh, he put his hand on your left breast? Oh, that was wrong, wasn't it? *Punish him!"* *(Slaps her own hand)*

This is *ridiculous.* Women must take *full responsibility* for their sexuality. I'm saying to women not to stay home, all right, but

That's what they asked for, then retracted

This is what they few it then even know it

rather, *accept* the idea of sex. Every time you go on a date with a man, the idea of sex should be *in the air*, okay? If it's not in the air, if you're not understanding that, why are you going on a date? These feminists seem to think that dating was something created on Mount Sinai, that God handed down the Ten Commandments *(imitates divine table-inscribing)*: "And then, you shall *date!*" This is absurd. Unchaperoned dating is something very recent in history. It's confined to the industrialized democracies. Even in Germany, I understand, this idea of dating, as understood here, this great thing you do—you get up *(imitates primping and flouncing)* and get all ready to go out on a date—this is something very *new*. It's *absurd!* These feminists who think that they can totally reform the way men relate to women by focusing in on college dating, they are *so* parochial, *so* provincial! Now, *my* view of sexuality—*(jump cut back to* PAGLIA *and* BENDERSON*)*—Because I do believe in *telling all,* and I don't believe in playing games, and that's one of my problems. I think that sex is a game—and I have a great trouble flirting and playing the game.

BENDERSON: Exactly.

PAGLIA: Because I'm too simple. I'm an Aries. I'm absolutely simple—and simplistic, even.

BENDERSON: So you think it's because you're not holding anything back that you eventually turn the woman off? *Me, too. Let's get to*

PAGLIA: I feel this is the intimacy problem again. You keep on saying we should have intimacy, and I feel that *my* error has been maybe to, like, put too much intimacy into the sex connection. You know, maybe I should be treating it more cerebrally, more abstractly. *int. imay now, that my motto.*

BENDERSON: That could be. *I me, neither!*

PAGLIA: See, I don't exploit people. I'm *terrible* at that. And so, I think that in some sense sexual contact is—there's a *self-withholding* going on in it that I'm not capable of. And you're right, I think I just show too much.

BENDERSON: Right. A good hunter is self-possessed. Is that what
you mean?

PAGLIA: Hmmmm. I think there's a predatory aspect to sexual con-
quest that I *completely* lack. *(Ruefully eating)* I don't know, I mean,
I'm in my forties now, and people still think I'm very youthful.
You know, I get along great with children. There's something
about me that's presexual. It's like I never got over my what
Freud calls polymorphous—you know, the pansexuality—polymorphous perversity. But in certain ways, I don't think I've
ever progressed into the dating stage yet! *Dating* is still something
very difficult to me.

BENDERSON: Well, do you feel sexual towards children?

PAGLIA *(pondering it)*: No, but I feel absolutely at one with children.
Children between the ages of three and eight. And I feel *that's*
where I sort of have *stopped*. And so I feel totally sexual in a
kind of whole-body way, but I find it difficult coupling. *Coupling*
is very difficult to me. I mean, I think that most powerful and
talented women—I mean, *really* powerful women like *me*—have
had some sort of difficulty with sexual adjustment in ways that
very powerful men don't necessarily have. *Some* powerful men
have had these problems, but I think that every very, very
talented woman in some way has difficulty in how to relate
sexually to other people. And that's been my problem.

*(Cut to vintage footage of crone shooting pistols at lightbulbs and other targets
held by women or small children. Cut to PAGLIA standing beneath large, pink-
granite pharaonic sphinx at the University Museum. She addresses the camera.)*

PAGLIA *(sternly)*: I have *never* identified with Christianity. The only
elements in it that I identified with are those in Roman Catholicism that *I* have identified in my writing as pagan, the
pagan elements in it. Whether it's the sexual personae of the
martyred saints . . . Saint Sebastian, with the arrows sticking
out of his body—he's a kind of parallel to the beautiful boys of
Greek art and so on and so forth. There was just something in
the *humbleness* of Christianity, Saint Joseph and Mary and the
baby and so on, that I *absolutely rejected*. I just felt like such an

alien, not only a sexual alien but a <u>social alien,</u> in my own time. So dreaming about ancient Egypt and studying it was my escape, you see, from what I regarded as *(disdainfully)* the humiliating simplicities and humbleness of Christianity that we were being taught. Turn the other cheek and all that. Well, I don't believe that for a minute. I don't think any Italian really does. We believe in *war!*

(Jump cut to PAGLIA *and* BENDERSON*)*

PAGLIA *(laughing)*: Well, I'm a bisexual lesbian who's also monastic, celibate, pervert, deviant, voyeur.

BENDERSON: Are you masochistic?

PAGLIA *(pondering it)*: No, I don't think I'm masochistic. I don't think at all. Because I'm very self-preserving. I don't like suffering. I don't think I'm masochistic.

BENDERSON: Right! Well, masochists are very self-preserving. That's the mechanism of self-preservation in their masochism.

PAGLIA *(still pondering)*: I really don't think I'm masochistic. I don't.

BENDERSON: They're masochistic in order not to feel something *worse.*

PAGLIA: I don't see it, except in, uh, the sex act. *(Smiling sheepishly)* I enjoy being on the bottom. ~~I thought so.~~

BENDERSON: Oh, tell me *more* about that!

PAGLIA *(shrugging)*: No, it's true. I mean, I'm a butch bottom. Susie [Bright] was right.

BENDERSON: Would you like to be tied up?

PAGLIA *(emphatically)*: No, no. I wouldn't like, I don't think, the idea of powerlessness—

BENDERSON: Would you like to have your nipples tortured?

PAGLIA *(indignantly)*: No!

(Cut to vintage footage of voluptuous, raven-haired woman throwing knives at a tiny, beatifically smiling girl, as a crowd of children watches. Cut to PAGLIA

and TREUT *sitting on the museum floor. More agitated Italian gesticulation by* PAGLIA.*)*

PAGLIA: Because I'm criticizing liberalism, people automatically call
me a conservative. This is *madness!* The idea that somehow one
cannot critique liberalism from the left, from the left wing of
liberalism. I mean, *how* can people be so stupid? *How* can they
be so naive? I am on record—I'm constantly on record in all
my interviews as well as in the book—as being pro-prostitution,
pro-pornography, pro-abortion, pro–legalization of drugs, pro-
homosexuality, pro–drag queens. Now, *how* is that neo-conservative? The people who are saying this are *so* idiotic! We are
dealing here with *such* simplistic minds. I mean, there's no point
in even *listening* to such people!

See, the value of my work is not just what I am *saying* but
rather that I am breaking up all these bunkered positions. Many
people are condemning themselves out of their own mouths. I'm
sort of like this race boat that goes zooming by, okay? And it's
as interesting in the *wake* of where I've been as what I'm doing
myself. That is, people everywhere, in university departments
or in downtown New York or in San Francisco, are getting
apparently into huge arguments about my work, and it's being
very, very useful. For example, you have people who've been
claiming to be cutting edge and avant-garde, people who are
interested in *(contemptuously)* Lacan, Derrida, and Foucault. For
the first time, in their inability to *deal* with my ideas, inability
to even read my book accurately, they are being revealed in
their university departments as, in fact, completely stereotyped
thinkers. The impoverishment of their minds, the smallness of
their imaginations is slowly being revealed to *others* in their
immediate circles.

So, I'm a very powerful weapon, okay, being used *not* by the
right against the left but rather by people who are *liberal* thinkers
who have been enslaved by these poseurs, these racketeers, people who are pretending to be liberal but who are in fact just
naive politically. I have been congratulated by women—people
rush up to me at the end of my lectures—women of my age,
women who are younger, who are *so sick* of being bullied by

these sanctimonious *puritans* who call themselves feminists. I'm a feminist, but I am liberating current feminism from these false feminists who have a death grip on it right now, who are anti-porn and so on. I'm bringing, like Madonna, a sense of beauty and pleasure and sensuality back into feminism. Because, you know, feminism's main problem for the last twenty years has been that it is incapable of appreciating art, okay? There is no aesthetics in feminism. All there is, is a social agenda. Art is made a servant to a prefab social agenda. So what I'm doing is allowing feminism to take aesthetics into it, and also psychology.

(Cut back to PAGLIA *and* BENDERSON.)

PAGLIA: If people could see the inside of my brain, I would be in *prison!* (BENDERSON *laughs uproariously.)* In other words, I get away with *murder!* I get away with murder, okay? Because I think that men are constantly being arrested and taken away in paddy wagons for things that I'm doing in my *mind,* you know? That's why I can understand the way men's minds work, because the way I look at women is absolutely lascivious. It's what feminists call "the male gaze." But obviously it's *not* "the male gaze" because, honey, I am *using* it! I have been doing it for many a decade.

BENDERSON: Oh, well, I don't know. Maybe you have a testosterone imbalance.

PAGLIA *(gravely)*: Yes, I think I do have a hormonal imbalance. I surely do. But I'm hairless! You'd think I'd have a beard or a mustache, but I don't!

BENDERSON: Well, perhaps you have an excess of both hormones. Too much testosterone *and* too much estrogen.

PAGLIA: Yes, yes, this may be the case. I certainly feel at the mercy of my hormones. It's, like, every week, it's something different with me. Some weeks of the month I feel very female, others very male. I feel I have a sex change every month. (BENDERSON *laughs loudly.)* It's *true!* I feel it. Sometimes I desire a man, sometimes a woman, you know. It just goes back and forth. I mean, it never is the same with me. Never for a minute.

BENDERSON: Well, maybe you can chart it, and then you could be at the right place at the right time.

PAGLIA *(laughing)*: Oh, I'm enough for myself. I'm in love with myself. It's the romance of the century!

(Cut to PAGLIA *on 42nd Street scrutinizing movie posters of blonde porn stars. Her finger trails languidly across their glossy breasts and buttocks. Cut to her drifting into a neon-lit porn emporium and then to a video booth, where she gleefully watches a pantingly explicit hardcore film. Cut to* PAGLIA *and* TREUT *sitting on the museum floor.)*

PAGLIA: Feminism does not realize—contemporary feminism—the degree to which it has *silenced* dissenting women and men. It does not realize. And so it's completely off in an ivory tower, and it's *shocked* when it goes into the outside world and says, "What, what? You don't agree with us? Then you must be a *backlash* to *us!* Yes, you must be having a backlash to us because of our *success.*" When, in fact, feminism has to open its eyes and realize that it's made not a *dent* in anything outside a small group of white, upper-middle-class men. These are the *only* men who have changed, okay? Now in the law office, a man can't say to you, "Hey, babe! You got great tits!" That's the *only* change that has been made. It's made not a *dent* in the outside world. Construction workers don't listen, working-class men don't listen. The entire world is *unchanged* by feminism.

So my feminism is calling for strong men, strong women. And also we must take all of the aspects of sexuality into ourselves. We can no longer say, "This is good sex." Anything that is not, that is dark or violent or abusive or hot, or anything like that . . . oh, that's "bad" sex! I mean, this is unbelievable, what's going on. Contemporary feminism has simply relapsed into the puritanism of seventeenth-century New England here. It's appalling, okay? I'm simply bringing a world sophistication to sexuality, and it's obvious by the enormous surge of popularity of my book that people are listening because they are sick and tired of being *sermonized* to by these women!

These women are absolutely *(grimacing)* . . . it's *pathetic!* Young women are being trained to look at fashion magazines and see nothing but . . . you know, like you'll see a beautiful woman's face, and it'll be "decapitation," "mutilation," "amputation." It's *loathsome* what's going on, okay? So I don't *care* what these women say. I mean, these women are losers. They're gonna lose to me. My victory over them will come decade by decade by decade, okay? Their *punishment* for maligning me now is to see the triumph of my work. Ha! *(Cut to* PAGLIA *looking directly into camera and jabbing her finger at the audience.)* Let them suck raw eggs and *eat my dust!*

SEX WAR

A SHORT FILM BY LUCA BABINI

LAUREN HUTTON *and* CAMILLE PAGLIA, *in a black Gaultier corset dress, seat themselves at opposite ends of a Renaissance banquet table crowded with food, fruit, and wine goblets. Next to each of their chairs, a large TV screen shows a live image of the other woman. Amid the forest of studio lights are racks of votive church candles. Cameramen circle and roam throughout the film.* HUTTON *and* PAGLIA *talk at top speed, constantly interrupting each other in overlapping dialogue.*

LAUREN HUTTON: Okay. One of the things that I knew very, very clearly from the first time I was trying to get into boys' gangs as a young preadolescent—because it seemed that boys and woods were much more interesting with their houses that said, "No Girls" than girls playing with dolls, so I always wanted to be out with the boys because it looked like more fun to me. But I always knew that they were *very* alien creatures, and quite dangerous. You could feel it, you know? It was like being around with like a really bad alligator snapper, which is something that could take you off a hand, down where I grew up.

[Excerpted. Directed by Luca Babini. Allied Species, Inc. and Trouble-maker's Film, Inc. Filmed in New York on February 1, 1992.]

CAMILLE PAGLIA *(laughing)*: Right!

HUTTON: And because early feminists were so frightened that they weren't as smart as men—because we were taught that—it seems like now they've taught young women to think that in fact men are not different and they're not dangerous. I believe that they're outright savages! *(PAGLIA laughs.)* That men are savages and that *our* business is to civilize them.

PAGLIA: I agree with that.

HUTTON: And in a good way, not an emasculating way, which sucks. But in a decent way. So you said that, um, what'd you say? You said that we must have a common-sense attitude toward rape. You have twelve tequilas at a fraternity party and go up to a guy's room, and you're surprised when he assaults you.

PAGLIA: Yeah. That's right.

HUTTON: And girls right and left, over and over and over you see them, going up to somebody's room in the dead of the night and not understanding that men are not the same as us in sex. And *that's* what's exciting. Male lust.

PAGLIA: Right. That's what's exciting.

HUTTON: That's what I fantasize about.

PAGLIA: That's what I think is wrong in the feminist rhetoric right now, because I think we don't want to curtail or to castrate—

HUTTON: Yikes! No!

PAGLIA:—male sexuality.

HUTTON: That's what's interesting.

PAGLIA: Yes, that's what's interesting. I think it's for the good of the species. You want to keep men *hot*, okay? All right?

HUTTON *(laughing)*: Keep 'em *hot*, absolutely!

PAGLIA: So my motto for men is going to be this, "Get it up!" That's my thing. "Get it up!" And now my motto for women: "Deal with it."

OFFSCREEN MALE VOICE: Say that again? *(HUTTON laughs.)*

PAGLIA: I'm saying for men, get it up and keep it up. Get it up! And I'm saying for women, *deal* with it. *Deal* with it! *Not* cut it off, not like, you know *(imitates panicky spinster),* "No, no, no, no!" Not lecturing to men, okay? It's up to women to realize that there's this dangerous force—

HUTTON: I think I like this.

PAGLIA:—in male sexuality, in the force of nature, and again, it's for *the good of the species.*

(Cut to new segment.)

HUTTON: I think rape is up. You say no, right?

PAGLIA: *No,* absolutely not. I mean, I feel that the frequency—

HUTTON: Have you seen statistics on this, or are you just—

PAGLIA: The frequency of *reporting* is definitely up, okay?

HUTTON: Yes. But why wouldn't rape *itself* be up, since girls go—

PAGLIA: It isn't up.

HUTTON: I mean, in the Fifties, boy, you did not go to a guy's room who was, like, much bigger than you. And never with a guy you had just met, and you had ten tequilas, and in fact unless you were looking to be—you know—

PAGLIA: In point of fact, I knew many examples. I mean, I knew examples in high school and in college of girls who had been raped who wouldn't *dream* of reporting it. As a matter of fact, as the years have gone on, I have known fewer and fewer women who are raped, all right? I think it's probably going *down* because women are more *together.* I think that women, in general, are wiser. There are a lot of *stupid* women who are out there who become these date-rape heroines. They make me so *sick.* They get on TV, they're on the cover of *People* magazine, all right?

These stupid girls on the cover of *People* magazine, whenever it was. The girl, you know, at Colgate University. There's an advertisement: oh, yes, "Come and spend the weekend at the fraternity house, we *guarantee* your safety." Now, what kind of *dope* do you have to be to spend a weekend at a fraternity house and think your safety's guaranteed? And she gets drunk. Oh, her grandmother had died recently. So she gets drunk.

HUTTON: Young male lust. Hmm.

PAGLIA: And at something like three in the morning—after she drank too much—three men come into the room, and she's *surprised?* And now she's a heroine on the cover of *People?* These are *stupid girls, stupid women!*

HUTTON: Well, maybe in fact they're victims of this sort of early feminist idea that men and women are the same—

PAGLIA: That's *absolutely it.*

HUTTON:—that we have the same brain, and the girl thinks, "Well, I'm not gonna jump a guy and throw him on his back and absolutely out-and-out rape him." Although there *were,* there *were* three women in Kansas City that raped that guy. Did you ever see that?

PAGLIA: No, I didn't.

HUTTON: It was fabulous! They raped him and threatened him with a hammer. He reported them. *(PAGLIA laughs.)* And the cops made a lot of fun of him in Kansas City, I think.

PAGLIA: Now see, I look at movies. There's so many movies that show the delirium of gang rape and how men can goad each other into a gang rape and abuse a woman and not realize that she's a person, okay? How many movies do you have to see like *Death Wish?* Or *Where the Boys Are.* I mean, there are so many of these movies. How *dumb* can you *be?* See, what women don't understand is that it's possible for men to have sex with an inert object, okay?

HUTTON: A watermelon, perhaps. Or anything, yeah.

PAGLIA: Well, even a watermelon! But I think even a drunk woman, a woman who's comatose.

HUTTON: Yeah. Inert objects, yeah.

PAGLIA: Women can't imagine that, okay? That actually men could enjoy having sex, group sex, with a drunk and, you know, passed-out girl. I can understand it. From my male brain, whatever it is. I think I have the brain of a rapist. Actually, that's the *truth*, okay?

HUTTON: Can you speak into the mike? *(Laughs)* You have the brain of a male rapist?

PAGLIA: I can *understand* rape, okay? As a woman who's been very frustrated by other women's attitudes toward *me*, I can *absolutely* understand it. I *totally* understand it.

HUTTON: And what is it? Let's get it down here. Is it an idea of naked dominance?

PAGLIA: No. What it is is that women *have* something you *want*. You wanna get in there. They seem to be like citadels, all right?

HUTTON: Citadels.

PAGLIA: And they *close* the door against you, and you have this rage, and you *want* to get in there, okay, and also you have this sense of *honor* which women don't understand. A sense of *pride*. And what I have had happen to me, okay, where girls and women have said to me, "You think I'm leading you on?" And when in fact, her behavior had been, like for forty-eight hours, *outrageously* leading on! *Outrageously* provocative! I think half the time women don't know what they're doing, okay?

HUTTON: Or we're taught to relate almost only sexually quite often, you know, with daddies first and then—

PAGLIA: But I believe there's a kind of autoerotic quality to women's sexuality and that men are aroused by it. That it is the vibrations or the signals being sent out, okay? And that women do *not* understand the signals they're sending *out*. They do *not* understand the inflammatory nature of those signals. And that I, as a lesbian or as a bisexual woman, *absolutely* understand it, okay? I understand the *lust* that men have for women, the *rage* that men have toward women. And the way it can turn into rape. And the only reason I think I have never raped anyone is because I'm a *woman*. I can't possibly, you know? I can't take any satisfaction, physical satisfaction, in an inert object. I could not do it.

HUTTON: Well, it's probably more interesting in fantasy than the actual thing, too.

PAGLIA: No, I don't believe that's true.

HUTTON: You've never found that out?

PAGLIA: No.

HUTTON: You've never experienced that? Where something that was erotic in a fantasy, when it was actually carried through was sort of . . . well, squeamy?

PAGLIA: In studying the images of rape in literature and art, and also the fantasies of rape, I feel that—

HUTTON: It's sort of heroic in a way.

PAGLIA:—I feel I understand it. And that the feminist discourse on rape is totally wrong and it's putting women in *danger*, okay? They do not—

HUTTON: Yes, I agree with *that*, absolutely!

PAGLIA: They do not understand, okay? They do not understand what lust is, from the male point of view.

HUTTON: Or the *glory* of male lust.

PAGLIA: The glory of male lust, yeah.

HUTTON: Or, in fact, how interested we *are* in it.

PAGLIA: Yeah. I want to fan the *flames* of lust—

HUTTON *(thoughtfully)*: Fan the flames . . .

PAGLIA: Fan the flames of lust, that's my aim.

HUTTON: Good. Deal with it.

PAGLIA: Deal with it. *(HUTTON laughs.)* All right. Get it up and deal with it. Right.

HUTTON: Okay. Male lust and the rock and roll strut!

PAGLIA: Right.

HUTTON: OK, so why are there no female—

PAGLIA: Well, I think that rock and roll is basically male lust, right at its peak, okay? Because it's a teenage male activity. And I as a great rock fan—and I've been listening to it for thirty-five years—I have to remark on the fact that there are no great women lead guitarists in the *world*, okay? Anyone who knows about rock *has* to admit this. I mean, it's not that women don't have *access*. That's *bullshit*. They now have access to guitars, they now have all-women bands. They have for *years*, right? Not *one* great woman [hard rock] solo has been done—

HUTTON: Why?

PAGLIA:—in the twenty-five years of rock. Because I believe it's all about lust. It's all about aggression, male aggression, all right? That kick-ass, you know, knock-the-door down, in-your-face thing.

HUTTON: Oooh!

PAGLIA: Yeah. It's male. You see? And I've *got* that. That's what I'm doing in my book. That's the sound in my book. *(Smacks her fist into her hand.)* That high-impact sound. That is the sound of the guitars, all right? Now, I'm doing it in *words*—

HUTTON: You've never met a guy who's tougher than you?

PAGLIA *(long pause)*: Uh . . .

HUTTON: And smart at the same time?

PAGLIA: Oh, no, no, not smart. But there are men who are. When I'm in the presence of real male dominance, I can feel it. I can feel it, and I enjoy it. It's rare, but it's there, okay? But who could get along with me, you know? You see, my grandmother said—

HUTTON: What do you mean, "no"?

PAGLIA: My grandmother said to me in Italian—

HUTTON: "No," what?

PAGLIA: My grandmother said, "If you were married, your husband would either beat you or kill you!" Okay?

HUTTON: Oooh. So granny scared you. That's scary.

PAGLIA: No, she didn't scare me.

HUTTON: So then you wouldn't mind being beaten?

PAGLIA: No, no! She was saying that I'm such an obnoxious personality that it would be almost impossible to have like a couple—

HUTTON: I don't think you're obnoxious. You're pretty ridiculous on your— Never mind! (*Laughs.*)

PAGLIA: But to live with it on a day-to-day level—it's nice to visit, but to live with it? I mean, you know, this is a vacation. This is recreation. Can you imagine day after day after day?

HUTTON: Oh, I bet you'd calm down.

PAGLIA: Oh, *please!*

(*Cut to new segment.*)

PAGLIA: See, my theory is that in the last hundred years we've seen a collapse of the great extended families, the tribal extended family—the tribal family would be what you saw in Africa— into this nuclear family.

HUTTON: Very dangerous. Very dangerous.

PAGLIA: And maybe that the nuclear unit perhaps is an artificial and oppressive construction—

HUTTON: Absolutely.

PAGLIA:—and is like a pressure cooker of incestuous feeling.

HUTTON: Yeah. Yeah. Good thinking! So you're saying that it's absolutely out-and-out breeding and there's no outlet for it. Because you don't have aunts and uncles and grandparents and neighbors sitting around saying, "Oh, Dad's completely nuts today, watch out!" or "Mother's riding the rag and she's doing this and that." Kids think that the parents are in fact the entire world.

PAGLIA: Right. Right. That's *exactly* it, and they have no wise elders to help them, okay? And you have this awful— It's like a prison! It's leading to anorexia.

HUTTON: Yeah, absolutely.

PAGLIA: Anorexia to me is one of these disturbances when the daughter tries to stop her sexual maturation. It's because she's responding, I think, to the incestuous currents going on in the nuclear family.

HUTTON: Yeah. It serves a point.

PAGLIA: I think that homosexuality is also coming from this. That is, if you have no other form of relatedness, these two parents alone cannot *possibly* help you to understand the world. You need the entire *tribe* to help you understand the world. You need *rites de passage*. And the schools have failed, the Church has failed, and so on. The kids' culture is TV, it's popular culture.

HUTTON: We're a society in deep chaos, no? Deep shit!

PAGLIA: We're in a period of sexual crisis, absolutely. I don't think that feminism's helping right now.

HUTTON: No.

PAGLIA: I think feminism's obstructing and forcing—

HUTTON: No. It's making bigger enemies of us than we were.

PAGLIA: It's making bigger enemies of the sexes.

HUTTON: And it's making young girls unsafe because they don't understand that they're dealing with a very potent savage and spectacular animal. Men.

PAGLIA: It's also alienating women from their own bodies—

HUTTON: Yes. Yeah.

to share!

PAGLIA:—because they don't understand that in their bodies they
have something which men *want*, okay. So they're encouraged
to interpret all male lust as oppressive and victimizing and
negative, instead of seeing that it is up to them to husband this
flame. They have a flame, and it's enormously powerful, all
right? For example, Francesca Stanfill, who interviewed me for
the *New York* cover story a year ago—she's a novelist, she has
two children, she went to Yale and so forth—she said *nothing* in
her Yale education prepared her for being a mother.

HUTTON: Right. Yeah.

PAGLIA: That's very interesting. *Nothing* helps a woman to understand what she is as a natural being.

*Or a man with his
flame.*

HUTTON: That's it.

PAGLIA: Nothing in our culture will help.

(Cut to new segment.)

PAGLIA: I think the problem with our culture is that we seem to be
living in an urban technological society in which we are in, you
know, air-conditioned offices with sealed-in windows, working
with machines all day long. We're forced to be very limited
Apollonian personalities in the day. Therefore it's all the more
important that, at night, we go back to recover the Dionysian
other self which has been repressed.

HUTTON: Amen.

PAGLIA: For that, we need *more* lust, not *less* lust! Feminism is totally
out of sync with what is *needed* now, OK? We want *more* pornography, *better* pornography. Pornography everywhere! Not in
the *office*, necessarily—

HUTTON: Have you tried writing some pornography?

PAGLIA: I did! I mean, my book.

HUTTON: Women write pretty good pornography.

PAGLIA: My book is the most X-rated academic book probably ever written.

HUTTON: Mmm. Right.

PAGLIA: Ha! A hundred nuns with dildos? That was Harold Bloom's favorite line in that book.

HUTTON (laughing): Oooh—I missed that part.

PAGLIA: Yeah, well, that's the Marquis de Sade chapter. The orgy in the convent.

HUTTON: I don't know if that's so incredibly attractive. A hundred nuns and— Oh! I'd be running.

PAGLIA: The Marquis de Sade wrote that scene.

HUTTON: Why do you like him so much? Well, never mind. I don't even want to talk about why you like him. Tell me about this. You said that male culture created western technological tradition that gave you—

PAGLIA: Western technological tradition created the modern, capitalistic life that has allowed the emergence of the feminist. Our feminist culture at the present moment is *completely* dependent on *capitalism*. My grandmother was still scrubbing clothes on the back porch on a *washboard!* My ability to *write* this book came from this society which men have created. *No* other culture has produced feminism but ours. The idea that western culture is evil—!

HUTTON: Men. Great men. So how do we tamp down this sort of *war* that's going on here? First, women need to be sort of secure. You said that on some level men understand that women are—

PAGLIA: Dominant! Woman is the dominant sex.

HUTTON: Yeah. But yet we believed our grandmothers' stories that, in fact, *men* are dominant. So we bought our own conspiracy.

PAGLIA: Men are dominant in society, okay? And it is the mission of feminism to seek the full political and legal equality of women.

We must win the entrance of women into the social realm. What I'm saying in my work is that we are much bigger than merely social selves. That there's a social sphere of life, but there is also a sexual or emotional sphere that overlaps the social sphere but is not identical to it. So I'm saying that, in the sexual and emotional sphere, woman is *dominant* and men *know* it on some deep level. They remember having emerged from this huge, matriarchal, goddesslike, shadowy figure from which they struggled for identity. Yes. They were inside the woman's body for nine months, and they struggled for identity out away from her—in the early years of life in which the woman is completely, you know, overmastering them.

HUTTON: So how do we do that? How do we in fact deal with it?

PAGLIA: Well, I'm saying we must accept sexual difference and *understand* what is going on. What is going on is *sex war*, and all the things that are going on—the turbulence between the sexes—may be a *permanent condition*. We must seek for understanding. *I wish it weren't so. I work for equality. But*

HUTTON: Well, to some degree it would keep things interesting, right? So you need that sort of flame. *women can't deal with it!*

PAGLIA: To keep it interesting. But we shouldn't be blaming men.

* * *

PAGLIA: Nature has a plot, a plan for women to reproduce, all right? And then if you don't want to reproduce . . . like I have absolutely no interest in having children. And I have been at total war with my body—

HUTTON: Amen.

PAGLIA:—for thirty years.

HUTTON: Do they sneak up on you? Dreams? Do you suddenly dream that some witch is throwing a baby and you've got it caught in your arms and you've got to like take care of it? And the witch is gone—

PAGLIA: Is *this* a dream that you *have?*

HUTTON: You bet. *(PAGLIA laughs.)* I have all versions of that. Or I *had* them. Fortunately the eggs are gone.

PAGLIA *(laughing)*: You have baby-throwing dreams?

HUTTON: Yes, absolutely, at different times. You haven't hit them yet? You should have hit them.

PAGLIA: No, I don't have baby dreams.

HUTTON: What? How do you have them?

PAGLIA: I have nature dreams. I have big nature dreams.

HUTTON: You never actually . . . It doesn't actually spring out? The idea—

PAGLIA: Uh uh.

HUTTON:—of having a baby doesn't come undisguised into your dreams?

PAGLIA: That would be a terrible nightmare to me. I think that's a *waking* nightmare to me. I—I — It has never happened in my dreams.

HUTTON: It's a nightmare for me, too.

PAGLIA: Yeah, yeah.

HUTTON: I mean, I actually *raised* some babies, so I know what a nightmare it is!

PAGLIA: You raised babies?

HUTTON: My mother's, yeah. It's a very hard and big deal.

PAGLIA: Oh, all right. No, it would be a horror to me. But I have big dreams. Big nature dreams. Like about fire, flood, you know, that sort of thing. Storms. That's my cup of tea.

HUTTON: Mmm hmm.

PAGLIA: But you have dreams where babies are *flung* at you, and they—

HUTTON: I did. I don't have them anymore. I don't have them anymore because I'm almost out of eggs.

PAGLIA: How many babies are being flung at you at any given time?

HUTTON: Only one at a whack. *(Laughs)* Thank God.

PAGLIA: Oh, one at a *whack?* All right. *(They laugh.)*

(Cut to new segment.)

HUTTON:—but I don't think they [feminists] like men. Everybody used to say to me, was I a feminist? I mean, I had decided at thirteen that I would never, ever be supported by a man, because I'd seen, you know, my mother and many other women in deep trouble because of that. And I never have been. So in that sense, that's feminist. And I certainly believe that everybody should have the same money for the job. But it seemed that they didn't like men. And as angry as I was and became at men, I certainly felt they were the *job.* I mean, they are *it.* That's what we've got. It's men. They're the most interesting *game.*

PAGLIA: Anyway, what women conceal from men, you know, is the degree of men's dependency on women. I think that part of the maternal love that a woman has for a—

HUTTON: Say it again. I'm sorry. Women conceal from men—

PAGLIA: Women conceal from men the degree of men's dependency on *them.* I began to see it's a *game* being played.

HUTTON: Ah! So it's like pushing the young—the son—out.

PAGLIA: It's an actual *game* being played, okay, *by women.* Because I began to see that the heterosexual love that a woman has for her husband is in fact *maternal.* And *that's* what I lacked. That's what I lacked. I lacked maternal feeling. *Not true.*

HUTTON: It's not all maternal.

PAGLIA: No, but I had lust for men, but I don't have the maternal feeling for men. I mean, I don't want to stroke men—

HUTTON: They'll stroke you back, you know.

PAGLIA: No, you know what I mean—psychologically. I began to see that men had these, like, *spasms of ego,* okay? And then it's followed by *relapses.* And that women are constantly in this kind of medical relationship and nursing relationship to men. I began to see that the most successful heterosexual women that I knew were in fact *nursing.* THAT's because they've not learned to share equally!

HUTTON *(laughing)*: Nurses.

PAGLIA: It's nursing. And it's a version of the maternal function, all right? And I began to see there's a kind of soothing, stroking thing that the successful heterosexual woman has—and that men are not necessarily looking for tits and ass, okay, in the long run. They're looking for nursing.

HUTTON *(pondering)*: Looking for nursing.

PAGLIA: Yes.

HUTTON: You don't think that men ever get past that stage?

PAGLIA: No. They sink further and further. Not true for me.

HUTTON: I've decided that I'll go to my grave alone, if I can't find a man that will accept me not as a mother or daughter and that I don't have to be a mother or a daughter to. I mean, once in a while we all relapse into those roles, because that's who we are and that's a nice thing to do every once in a while. But there must be a way of— There must be a place where it's an equal cross.

PAGLIA: Alas!

HUTTON: Or is that where you're talking? Alas?

PAGLIA: Alas! I think that in late life it's even *more* obvious that the woman takes over the relationship. I see it all the time in the shopping malls— *(Offstage laughter from the crew.)*

HUTTON *(big laugh, as she slaps the table with both hands)*: Oh, *stop!* We're not living our lives in shopping malls!

PAGLIA: The woman is dragging the guy around, and he wants a hot dog: "You can't have that!"

HUTTON: Those are people who probably never, ever became alive. I call them "the undead." They're like people who just go from, you know, *their* parents having sucked all the life out of *them* when they were children to *them* pumping out children, so they can *suck* the life out of them. That's the only life there ever is. In fact, they're people who never had ideals, gave up what ideals they had and have been old from birth. You know, going through school, more than half your class was old, right? They were *old kids*. I'm younger than most of the twenty-year-olds I know. *Me, too.*

PAGLIA: This is true. Right.

HUTTON: That's why I'm not particularly worried about age.

PAGLIA: Hormonally, suddenly women's estrogen—women's female hormones begin to lapse, and therefore their male hormone becomes more powerful. At midlife, men's *male* hormones begin to lapse, all right? So the woman becomes *more* powerful in later life. That is the men's fate. Men have a *brief moment of power*, okay, when their hormone is at its *height* in their late teenage years and in their twenties. *That's it*, okay? That's *it!* *No, that's only part of it.*

HUTTON (*laughing*): Camille! Get back! Get down!

PAGLIA: I'm saying that men go from control by their mothers to control by their wives, and that is the horror of men's life. And that feminism refuses to see this.

HUTTON: So this is why you say that young or any gay male is a heroic symbol and free.

PAGLIA: Yes! Gay men are *heroes* to me!

HUTTON: Because they stand against this bullshit.

PAGLIA: Because they stand against control by women. *I stand against that control, too, but I'm*

HUTTON: Yes, yes.

PAGLIA: And they alone are preserving the masculine impulse today. Feminism is doing everything it can to destroy masculinity. *straight,*

HUTTON: So you don't believe in *love*.

PAGLIA: Oh, I *do* believe in love.

HUTTON: I mean, maybe *none* of us sort of think it's possible, but it must be. Don't you think? Heterosexual love? Must be.

PAGLIA: I believe in love. Love's an *illusion*, I think. I think there's sexual *passion* under the surface of it, and then there's a nesting instinct. I think that women really do nest.

HUTTON: Yes, but we're different.

PAGLIA: And that men *shrink*.

HUTTON: We can learn from them and they can learn from us—

PAGLIA: The husbands *shrink*.

HUTTON:—so why shouldn't, as we go on in life and learn more and more, why shouldn't we in fact be able to be alongside someone who's showing us a different view of what it is?

PAGLIA: Well, you have a wish of what would be *good* about life. I am just trying to, as an objective observer, record—

HUTTON: Well, I don't go in shopping malls hardly *ever!* I stay *out*. I go in them, I go *nuts!*

PAGLIA *(laughing)*: The shopping mall is the *center* of American culture!—as Martha Stewart knows.

(Cut to new segment.)

HUTTON: The state of the sex wars, okay? The sex war is heating up. You said you think that in fact sex is getting less interesting. And do you think this is because women—because we decided that we have the same brains? So people don't allow for this sort of different—

PAGLIA: Well, I think that feminism's gotten very shrewish, all right?

HUTTON: Shrewish.

PAGLIA: And there's a lot of lecturing and sermonizing about sex today. All these *rules*. And that you should behave in *this* way and *that* way and there's only one kind of pornography or erotica and you should not be pornographic, et cetera, et cetera, and don't do things that are demeaning to woman. And I feel there's been a *terrible* backsliding from the Sixties, when there really *was* a kind of liberated sexual imagination. There were porno books that were, like, very high-class porn books done often under a nom de plume by well-known writers. There were sex magazines. There was a kind of feeling of experimentation, fun, and so on, vivacity, that's *completely gone*.

HUTTON: Yeah.

PAGLIA: And I think we have an overpoliticized sexual realm right now, where even the alternative press—*The Village Voice, Mother Jones*—is taking the most reactionary political positions about what's tolerable in sex.

HUTTON: It seems to me it goes back to the Sixties when we thought this whole new world was going to come when we were young. And we thought we were taking over. We were going to come up with love and honor and political . . . to bring America back to America being what it was supposed to be.

PAGLIA: Paradise now.

HUTTON: Paradise now.

PAGLIA: Right.

HUTTON: I remember I was on my way to Berkeley. Because basically I became politicized when I saw—for me, the Sixties started, the Sixties opened for me when I picked up a newspaper and on the front page—this was in Tampa, Florida; usually we had kittens on the front page—suddenly, on the front page was a girl who was, you know, approximately my age. She had long black hair, still left over from beatnik fashion, long black stockings, dirndl skirt, I think. She was being dragged by her hair down a bunch of steps. She had long black hair, she was on her back, and it was a long shot of a very large, fat cop trudging down the thing with all his equipment and dragging this girl, my age, down the steps on her back. And I thought, "In *America?* Are they out of their *mind?*" And it was the beginning of the

Free Speech Movement. And she was being dragged down because a bunch of kids had gotten together on the steps and said
they were gonna stand there and talk until, you know, they got
freedom of speech and freedom of—what's it called?

PAGLIA: Assembly.

HUTTON: Yes. Freedom of assembly. So I immediately packed up
and got ready to go to Berkeley and then got, uh, snafued and
waylaid in New Orleans. Couldn't, couldn't, couldn't make it.
But in fact the D.A. who ordered that—that pulling kids, girls,
eighteen, by their hair down the steps—was Edwin Meese.

PAGLIA: Whoa!

HUTTON: He was from Oakland, and he was the youngest D.A. in
history. He ordered that. He then became the brains for—brain
for—Reagan. I mean, he was the Reagan brains, since that was
a totally empty skull there. And all our heroes, in fact, were
silenced or shot. And kids now—I mean, we had a lot of heroes.
When we were kids, when we were in our early twenties, in our
late teens, we had a lot of heroes. We had both Kennedys, who
in fact were heroes at the time. We had Malcolm X, we had
Martin Luther King, we had Margaret Mead. She came out
and said, "I tried some grass. I liked it. It's pretty nice." *(Laughs)*
We had lots of them.

PAGLIA: Well, *she* didn't get shot! *(Laughs.)*

HUTTON *(laughing)*: No, she didn't get shot, but we haven't heard
from her lately! It seems to be a very sad time with no heroes
and no one in our generation speaking up, because in fact—

PAGLIA: We have to acknowledge, though, that what happened was
that our generation was guilty of excesses and of impatience and
lack of practicality in presenting a program of practical—

HUTTON: Yeah. They didn't know what they were doing or where
they were going.

PAGLIA: They didn't know—right. It's sort of like, "Let's levitate
the Pentagon."

HUTTON: Yeah. And they were throwing bombs like assholes without even knowing for what.

PAGLIA: But the conservative reaction of the Seventies and Eighties has got to be understood. Our generation made many fundamental errors of strategy and judgment that *led* to that reaction, okay? The idea that all of our problems today are because of the conservatives—*no*.

HUTTON: Mmm.

PAGLIA: Our problems are because we *rebelled* but we had no program to put in the *place* of that particular structure. And so, once there were the days of rage and riots in the street, People's Park, okay, which was just a—

HUTTON: I remember People's Park.

PAGLIA:—a kind of childish, you know, running around playing games.

HUTTON: Well, they were kids. So how could you have a plan when you're twenty years old and you haven't lived or seen anything or done anything?

PAGLIA: That wonderful film *Berkeley in the Sixties* shows documentary film footage—shows the way in the beginning you had these often Jewish, very passionate social activists involved in civil rights at Berkeley. And the way it changed and altered, okay, this film shows. People talk about it—like one of the people in it, the professors in it say the minute it got out that Berkeley was the place to be, suddenly you began to get every lunatic in the country going there—

HUTTON: It was coopted.

PAGLIA:—and then you begin having the psychedelic drugs, okay? It suddenly became a psychedelic scene. And the minute it got into drugs, people lost the ability to *see* social reality for what it *is*, all right? And, you see, those early Jewish activists were very practical—they were grounded in the study of economics, their parents were refugees of the Holocaust, and so on.

HUTTON: They were also the same people that asked for the lifting of all codes and rules and regulations on colleges, right?

PAGLIA: Mmm hmm.

HUTTON: So that now you can graduate from Princeton and get absolutely no classical history, no math. I mean, you know, basket-weaving.

PAGLIA: Right.

(Cut to new segment.)

HUTTON: I think probably the reason men are so bad to each other is that we are in fact not protective of something in there that we tolerate between women.

PAGLIA: I don't think *any* of us are fully civilized beings. You see, I think that there's a barbaric undertow to all of human life and it's out there. It's like the passion of sex and aggression is always ready to break into open sight.

HUTTON: Right.

PAGLIA: And I think that's what crime is. Crime is basically a kind of regression. You know, in terms of, like, serial murderers—we've talked a little bit about this. I mean, I think that there are different parts of the brain and one is the reptilian brain, the part that's the most—

HUTTON: Back.

PAGLIA:—primitive.

HUTTON: Back brain.

PAGLIA: And that these are the impulses, amoral impulses toward sex and aggression.

HUTTON: So is that original sin? Our back brain?

PAGLIA: Yeah.

HUTTON: Our reptilian brain?

PAGLIA: Yes. Yes, I think it is. It's like a serpent. It's the serpent within us. And it's there in all of us. I don't think we're born good. See, feminism believes, with Rousseau, that we're born good and that bad social signals turn us bad.   *We're born with both.*

HUTTON: Mmm.

PAGLIA: Like pornography makes men rape. This is *ridiculous!*

HUTTON: Yeah.

PAGLIA: What I'm saying's the *opposite.* I'm saying, like the Catholic thing, we're born *bad.* We're born with an impulse toward—

HUTTON: We're born animals.

PAGLIA: We're born animals.

HUTTON: And hopefully we grow up.

PAGLIA: And rules *civilize* us. Society *civilizes* us. Society is women's protection against rape. It trains men *not* to rape, all right? And I mean, all throughout history, rape has been condemned. The idea that feminism discovered rape is *absurd,* okay? Ethical men throughout history have been on the record about this—that rape is a form of brutishness that has never been tolerated in any civilized community. And so the date-rape thing—this is out of control. I have to explain to foreign reporters the date-rape thing. They never can understand it. They say, "What is this?" When I enunciate common-sense principles of female behavior, I'm abused. I'm called "anti-women" and "pro-rape." I mean, it's *insane* what's going on now! Again, it's the feminist attempt to gain control of sex by politicizing it and hammering it to death with dead rhetoric. *Yes.* It's *jargon!*

HUTTON: You're talking about European people coming and asking you this, right? They've had time to grow an aristocracy. We haven't had that. We changed every single generation.

PAGLIA: Well, they have a more sophisticated view of sex. What's permitted on Italian or on British TV in terms of sex is extraordinarily more adult and mature than what we are permitted

here. And everyone knows that we are allowed more violence
than the British or—

HUTTON: Ooh! Tell me about the breasts of—who? You said I get
to pick a saint's name since I became a Catholic.

PAGLIA: Oh, Saint Agatha.

HUTTON: Saint Agatha.

PAGLIA: Saint Agatha had her breasts cut off and served on a platter,
apparently, or at least exhibited on a platter. And so when it
comes time for your confirmation, since you're going to be an
honorary Catholic, you *must* pick a saint's name.

HUTTON: There's an Italian bonbon, you said, that's shaped like
Saint Agatha's breast?

PAGLIA: Yes, apparently an Italian bonbon of white chocolate, I
think it is—

HUTTON: White chocolate.

PAGLIA:—yes, that's shaped with a little nipple—

HUTTON: A cherry stem nipple?

PAGLIA:—with a little nipple in white chocolate, I think. I'm not
sure. I have never had one, so I can't really give any firsthand
account. (HUTTON *laughs*.) But there's Saint Agatha. That's a
very colorful saint to be, you know.

HUTTON (*smacks her forehead and laughs*): These Eye-talians. I tell ya!

PAGLIA: Yeah. Well, we have an instinct for sex and violence. That's
what I'm saying in my book, that in Italian culture you see a
residue of the ancient pagan past. And that's why I have such
a bizarre mentality. Because of being Italian.

*   *   *

HUTTON: I think you can't have just male, you can't have just hunter
intelligence, and you can't have just caretaking intelligence. Like
you say, we'd still be in grass huts!

PAGLIA: Mmm hmm.

HUTTON: But if you'd just have men, they're going to be burning down the grass huts. Which is what they're doing now.

PAGLIA: Yeah, unfortunately, this has been the evidence through history, okay? But my theory is that one day people from outer space will appear *(HUTTON laughs)* and that suddenly the entire human race will see that it has more alike, more in common than with these, these jelly-like creatures with, like, one eye in the middle of their forehead. This is what *I* believe will unify the world eventually. But it may take a long time.

HUTTON *(smiling, looks at watch and up at sky)*: What time is it? Getting late!

PAGLIA: Yeah, yeah. But actually, you know, again as someone who has studied history *(Director Luca Babini is seen here at PAGLIA's side, as he aims his camera at HUTTON)*, I have to tell you I don't have this gloomy view of the contemporary world that many others do right now. I just do not because I have seen what the past has been like, where you have banditry and war and starvation and so on.

HUTTON: Yeah, no. God knows a lot of things are a lot better.

PAGLIA: The condition of the world is certainly not at all— I don't see any decline. People who are always wringing their hands about the way we're going and how we're living in the most corrupt . . . they have no knowledge at all of the corruption of the past and the venality of the past. For example, to appreciate America you have to go, let's say, to Italy. Like my father was thinking of retiring to Italy because we're Italian, and the difficulties over there that he had merely even making a *phone call* *(HUTTON laughs)* so enraged him that he realized what an *American* he is and how we don't even realize the conveniences and pleasures of America, the efficiency of America, because we take them for granted. YUP,

* * *

HUTTON: I had a great time. Thanks.

PAGLIA: Goodbye. Goodbye, George! Goodbye, Gracie! *(They laugh.)*

(As credits roll, cut to HUTTON *applying lipstick brush to a squirming, protesting* PAGLIA *in the makeup session preceding the filming. Gabriele Vigorelli had just done* PAGLIA*'s hair.)*

HUTTON: Calm down! Nice, full sensuous Italian lips!

PAGLIA: You're giving me bigger lips than I *have!*

HUTTON: These are nice Italian lips.

PAGLIA: Well, these lips are too big—

HUTTON: Calm down. Think of Rita Hayworth.

PAGLIA: Rita Hayworth had her—

HUTTON: Sshhh! *(They laugh.)*

2 & 3. Stills from *Sex War*. Lauren Hutton (above) and Camille Paglia (below). Hutton in mirror (right) and on monitor (left), being filmed by Luca Babini (rear center). Photos: Allied Species, Inc.

4 & 5. The filming of *Glennda and Camille Do Downtown*. Glennda Orgasm and Paglia crossing Sixth Avenue (top) and in front of Stonewall Inn (bottom). Photos: Tracy Tippet.

GLENNDA AND CAMILLE DO

DOWNTOWN

A sunny spring Saturday in New York's Washington Square Park. As rock music blares on the soundtrack, GLENNDA ORGASM, CAMILLE PAGLIA, *and her two leather-clad bodyguards, the* CENTURIONS, *stroll through the crowds toward the fountain.* GLENNDA *is wearing dramatic Cleopatra makeup, a blonde Sixties "flip" wig, and a gold ankle-length gown glittering with sequins and ivory beads.* PAGLIA *is in blue jeans, black jacket, and a white Keith Richards T-shirt trimmed with a dagger-pierced heart. Since* GLENNDA *is 6'1" and* PAGLIA *5'3", the mismatched pair look like Mutt and Jeff.*

GLENNDA ORGASM: Here is this week's very special guest: my favorite feminist scholar, Camille Paglia. Hi, Camille!

CAMILLE PAGLIA: Hi, Glennda. It's wonderful to be here.

GLENNDA: Isn't it nice? It's gorgeous weather.

PAGLIA *(surveying the lounging New York University students)*: It's fabulous. Very Sixties! Glennda, I want to introduce you to my

[Produced and directed by Glenn Belverio (Glennda Orgasm). Filmed in New York City on May 15, 1993. Aired June 14 and 17 on Manhattan Cable Public Access Television. A shortened version premiered at the 1994 Sundance Film Festival.]

Centurions, my bodyguards. *(Two brawny African-American men wearing dark glasses and grave expressions loom into camera view.)* Rennard Snowden and Brian Roach. These are my men.

GLENNDA: Hi!

RENNARD SNOWDEN *(formally shaking* GLENNDA'S *hand)*: How are you?

PAGLIA: They accompany me everywhere. They're very famous. Their image has gone around the world.

(The stern, silent, unsmiling CENTURIONS *flank* PAGLIA, *as* GLENNDA *admires them.)*

GLENNDA: Wow! They're beautiful!

PAGLIA: Aren't they gorgeous?

GLENNDA: They're great!

PAGLIA: They're my Egyptian warriors.

GLENNDA: I feel safe. I feel much safer.

PAGLIA: *I* feel like a *girl* when I'm around them! Thank you, thank you, guys! *(The* CENTURIONS *return to their outlying positions.)*

GLENNDA: Thank you! Okay. So Camille, what's the concept? What are we doing today? What is this video?

PAGLIA: Well, we're here to trash, essentially, the feminist establishment, all right? And all anti-sex porn-phobes!

GLENNDA: Oh, it's getting so *moralistic* these days. I feel like I can't make a move without someone beating down on me saying, "You're being too sexy!"

PAGLIA: Oh, absolutely. No, it's absolutely horrible. Catharine MacKinnon's everywhere. *(looking around)* We could see her at any moment, popping out of a bush with Barbara Walters! Really! This is an Anti–Andrea Dworkin Day, all right?

GLENNDA: Yes, a Dworkin-Free Zone! *(They laugh.)* What's the name of the video, Camille?

PAGLIA: Well, we're calling this *Glennda and Camille Do Downtown,* and we're imitating the famous *Debbie Does Dallas.*

(Cut to footage from the 1979 porn classic, Debbie Does Dallas. *Cheerleaders bob, and football players scamper. Debbie peels off her shirt and soaps her breasts in the locker room.)*

GLENNDA: Oh, wow, that's a great movie.

PAGLIA: Yes, it is. And, and of course, I *love* all early porn. I *love* that period when women's bodies were lush and sensual and untoned.

GLENNDA: Right.

PAGLIA: So, um, *lewder.*

GLENNDA: It's a form of art, and people don't like to say that it's a form of art.

PAGLIA: It *is* art. Pornography and art are identical for me, absolutely.

GLENNDA: Absolutely. I agree.

PAGLIA: I think Michelangelo is a pornographer.

GLENNDA: Well, I think a day without pornography is like a day without sunshine!

PAGLIA *(laughing):* I agree with you completely. The *Pietà* is to me a piece of pornography.

GLENNDA: Absolutely. And Michelangelo was a pornographer.

PAGLIA: He was. And the Pope is a collector of porn.

GLENNDA: Wow! He's the biggest porn collector in the world!

PAGLIA: He is. The Vatican Museum—

GLENNDA: The Vatican!

PAGLIA:—is filled with nudes, you know?

GLENNDA: Wow! Wait 'til Gay Pleasures finds out about this!

PAGLIA: I know. So, here we are in Washington Square Park, and we just feel like it's the middle of—

GLENNDA:—the Sixties.

PAGLIA: The Sixties. Yeah, it's like your handbag. Show your handbag, Glennda!

(The camera zooms in for a close-up of GLENNDA's *large, square faux-leopardskin purse.* PAGLIA *fondles it appreciatively.)*

GLENNDA: This is a very Sixties handbag.

PAGLIA: Is this fabulous?

GLENNDA: That was your generation, your generation of the Sixties.

PAGLIA: I am of the Sixties, that's right.

(Cut to news footage of stoned Sixties hippies moving and grooving at an outdoor rock festival.)

PAGLIA: And so many of us, you know, blew our brains out on acid. Not me!

GLENNDA: Oh. That's good.

PAGLIA: Because I'm addicted to my own hormones, Glennda.

GLENNDA: But how do you feel? You know, a lot of Sixties fashion has come back into style, like Sixties and Seventies into the Nineties. But do you think it's brought in the same kind of values, or is it a more sanitized version of the Sixties and Seventies?

PAGLIA: Well, when anything returns, it's always ironic. It loses some oomph. I mean that's a lesson of history. But essentially, I do feel the kids of the Nineties have moved backward and are looking to Sixties idealism again. It's such a change, and a blessed one, from the kind of Rolex, you know, BMW, Seventies–Eighties materialism. (GLENNDA *groans.*) I hated that period— Michael Milken, the Wall Street crap. I hated that.

GLENNDA: White middle-class mechanisms.

PAGLIA: Yeah. So the Nineties are—it's the period of the drag queen. Drag queens are the dominant sexual personae of this decade, in my view.

GLENNDA: Well, you know, Camille, there's been a lot of talk about 1993 being the "Year of the Drag Queen." How do you feel about that?

PAGLIA: Oh, I think it's so true. And I have modeled *so* much of my personality on drag queens. I mean, I learned how to be a woman from drag queens. There's no doubt about it.

GLENNDA: Wow.

PAGLIA: I was not happy with my sex role. I was, you know, butch for decades, and now I know how to put on a dress, Glennda.

GLENNDA: Absolutely. Well, you know, a lot of feminists accuse drag queens of mocking women. Have you ever heard them say that?

PAGLIA: Oh, God! Oh, they're so naive. *Please!* Drag queens have preserved the *power* of woman! I call my feminism "Drag Queen Feminism."

GLENNDA: That's great. *Men who can't feel power as such!*

PAGLIA: See, because I feel that drag queens have a better, more historical sense of sex roles than do feminists, all right? They understand the *power*, the *glamour*, the *glory* of woman! I mean, in putting on a dress, putting on high heels, you are *fabulous!* It goes back to *Babylon*. It goes back to ancient *Egypt*. I'm so *tired* of this kind of yuppie feminism, white bourgeois feminism with the attaché case. Oh! The kind of Susan Faludi, Naomi Wolf boring crap! That's so white bread—you know, white bread and mayonnaise, that's all it is.

GLENNDA: Well, you know, what I like about drag is we have these extremes. You can be ultra-butch, and then you can be ultra-feminine. And I think sometimes feminism tries to push everyone into the middle and say, "No, we have to whitewash everyone," and everyone has to be, like, kind of unsexy and androgynous.

PAGLIA: Yeah.

GLENNDA: Androgyny *can* be sexy. But I think they want a kind of unsexy state of androgyny. *Bingo.*

PAGLIA: This is exactly right. Right now in the Ivy League, okay, there's a lot of talk that the prominence of drag queens right now is due to the new interest in androgyny, the dissolution of sex roles. Now I think that's *wrong*. The drag queen flourishes in periods when sex roles are actually very *firm*. Like the Fifties, okay?

GLENNDA: Right.

PAGLIA: That was a great period of drag. Drag went underground. It fell apart in the Seventies and Eighties. So *I'm* saying that the dominance of the drag queen now in the Nineties is due to us looking *again* for what is it to be a man, what is it to be a woman. And we're looking historically again. We no longer like the kind of Mao suit, unisex look. That's *tired!* That's *stale!* Androgyny is *dead!* Drag queen–ism is in!

(Cut to GLENNDA and PAGLIA now seated on a park bench near the triumphal arch.)

PAGLIA: You're, like, part Italian, right? You're half Italian?

GLENNDA: Yes. I'm half Italian.

PAGLIA: Yes. Do you feel this? Do you feel the Italian energy?

GLENNDA: Yes, yes! It keeps me going. Motivation. Absolutely.

PAGLIA: Yeah. I mean, you see these little widows—they're like eighty-year-olds—Italian widows running around. You know, they outlive their husbands by thirty years. This is me. I wasn't married, but I'm like a widow. You know, it's the same thing. I'm like a widow or a nun.

GLENNDA: Yeah. I know Italian women—they would come to work, they'd be in their eighties, and they'd still come to work. Every single day to work. Work, work, work.

PAGLIA: Right, right.

GLENNDA: They're so determined.

PAGLIA: Yeah. And don't get in their way! They'll put— *(makes twisting gesture of putting the screws in)* They're mean. They're mean. They'll push you out of the way. *(laughing)* They're vicious! They're vicious! An eighty-year-old Italian widow? Don't get in her way!

GLENNDA *(laughing)*: Well, I knew this Italian woman that worked for my father, and she used to say, "The Mafia is beautiful." *(PAGLIA cackles.)* And she used to whistle *The Godfather* theme all the time.

PAGLIA: Oh really? Well, my grandmother used to say, you know, Mussolini was beautiful—"*bello*"!

GLENNDA: She carried a knife, too.

PAGLIA: Oh, I do, too!

GLENNDA: Yeah? That's what I thought.

PAGLIA: Yeah! You wanna see my knife?

GLENNDA: Oh, wow! We're gonna see Camille's knife!

PAGLIA *(rummaging through her handbag)*: This is my knife, all right? This was actually given to me by— Oh, no, that's my mascara! Wait!

GLENNDA *(laughing)*: Now, *that* could be a deadly weapon.

PAGLIA: I'm so split! I'm so split—my personality. Oh, *here* it is. *(She unsheathes the slim silver blade and displays it to GLENNDA and the camera.)*

GLENNDA: Wow. Wow! It's very compact. It looks like a nail file. It's beautiful. Wow.

PAGLIA: My friend, Bruce Benderson, the writer, gave this to me. It's a Ninja knife from 42nd Street. He knows 42nd Street intimately. It's probably illegal, but I'm not sure. I don't care.

GLENNDA: Oh, who cares?

PAGLIA: Yeah, who cares? Right.

GLENNDA: We're breaking the rules today.

PAGLIA: Whenever I sign books, I have my men next to me, you see, and I have my Ninja knife, and I fear nothing.

(Cut to Fifties footage of a curvaceous Miss America. Cut to GLENNDA *and* CAMILLE, *standing in front of a lifesize cutout of Betty Grable in an 8th Street shop window between Fifth and Sixth Avenues.)*

GLENNDA: You know, there was a documentary about Miss America pageants, and Miss Americas in the 1950s were voluptuous, with big hips. And now they're— I like the Miss Americas better in the Fifties and Sixties.

PAGLIA: I agree.

GLENNDA: They're, like, white bread, and they all look the same. They all have the same hairdos. *(*PAGLIA *laughs.)* It's just not the same. I mean, the feminists complain about, "Oh, it's exploiting women." I just think it's banal, what's happened.

PAGLIA: Right. Well, you know, this idea that somehow beauty contests are a way to make women into meat or to turn them into just objects—that is absurd. The idea of the beauty contest goes all the way back to ancient times. The judgment of Paris, you know—where Paris had to judge the three goddesses, and he awarded the apple, the golden apple, to Aphrodite, and she gave *him*, in turn, the most beautiful woman in the world, Helen of Troy. Which started the Trojan War. You know, it caused problems.

GLENNDA: Absolutely.

PAGLIA *(ruefully)*: It caused problems. But—

GLENNDA: It caused a lot of problems.

PAGLIA: Yeah, a lot of problems. But the point is the idea of judging beauty seems to me, you know, just part of our tradition, and I just refuse to take it that seriously. I mean, I'm not someone who is a compulsive shopper or dresser, but I *love* watching the beauty shows. I *always* did. Right from the start, I've never regarded them as sexist.

GLENNDA: They're amusing. You know, I saw this great documentary where this feminist was protesting, and she dressed in a meat dress, a dress made out of lamb chops and hamburger patties.

PAGLIA *(whooping)*: That's *great!*

GLENNDA: And even though she was, like, an extreme feminist, I just thought her *style* was amazing. She just seemed so unconscious of the style that she had—the meat dress. And she was wearing high heels, and she was yelling, "Judge meat, not women!" But she was still fabulous. I loved her.

(Cut to 1985 news footage of spike-heeled protester in mini-dress at Miss California pageant shouting, "Judge meat, not women!" Cut to GLENNDA *and* PAGLIA *crossing street at 8th and Sixth Avenue. They bear down on a curbside table staffed by two dour women aggressively wielding blow-ups of pornographic photos. It is a protest by WAP [Women Against Pornography], who have forced these photos on pedestrians around New York for years.)*

GLENNDA: Wow! Oh, lookit, Camille, look!

PAGLIA *(imitating Roseanne Arnold through much of this scene)*: Oh, my *Gawd!*

GLENNDA: It's *Hustler!*

PAGLIA *(archly)*: It is. Let's look. What are—who are these people?

GLENNDA *(with feigned innocence)*: What is going on over here? Look!

PAGLIA: What are they doing?

GLENNDA: Wow! *(Reads one of their signs)* "PORN IS WOMAN HATE."

PAGLIA *(heavily Roseanne)*: Oh, my *Gawd!*

GLENNDA *(posing Socratic questions)*: Camille, what is going on here?

PAGLIA *(with feigned wonder)*: They're anti-porn feminists!

(The scene degenerates from this point on. The protesters yank away the posters or flip the backs to the cameras. One woman strikes at the camera with her poster. The film crew angrily protests. There is pushing and shoving and a general melee. The CENTURIONS *move in, as a large crowd quickly gathers. The husky torsos and arms of* RENNARD SNOWDEN *and* BRIAN ROACH *are glimpsed protecting the camera.)*

GLENNDA: Wait, wait, I wanna see the picture!

PAGLIA *(archly)*: Oh, my *Gawd!*

GLENNDA AND CAMILLE *(simultaneously reading the sign and chanting together like Oscar Wilde's Gwendolen and Cecily)*: "FEMINISTS FIGHTING PORNOGRAPHY"!

OFFSCREEN PROTESTER: We don't want our picture taken.

GLENNDA: Look at this. *(reading)* "PORN DEGRADES WOMEN."

PAGLIA *(reading)*: "PORN DEGRADES WOMEN."

GLENNDA *(feigning wonder)*: This is unbelievable! Can we see the pic—wow! Look, Camille, look at the pictures!

PAGLIA: What? Oh, my *Gawd!* Look!

GLENNDA *(lustily)*: It's *hot!* Wow! Bondage!

PAGLIA: That is *hot!*

GLENNDA: Where can we *get* some of that?

PAGLIA *(with delight)*: Bondage! Oh, *my!* *(glancing at the protesters)* They seem very phobic, don't they?

GLENNDA: I don't think they like us, Camille.

PAGLIA *(dreamily)*: I don't think they do.

GLENNDA: Wait, what's going on?

PAGLIA: Isn't that amazing? They don't want their pictures taken.

GLENNDA *(addressing the protesters)*: What does the petition do? What is it for?

OFFSCREEN PROTESTER: No, I don't want it for you.

PAGLIA *(Roseanne again)*: Oh, my *Gawd!*

GLENNDA: It's not for us? Why? We're Americans.

PAGLIA: They don't want us. They don't—

OFFSCREEN PROTESTER: Identify yourselves.

PAGLIA: My name is Camille Paglia—

OFFSCREEN PROTESTER: Oh, *no!*

PAGLIA:—and this is Glennda Orgasm!

GLENNDA *(laughing)*: I'm Glennda Orgasm.

PAGLIA: And we *love* pornography!

GLENNDA: We love it.

PAGLIA: And we want sex! We are tired—

GLENNDA: *More sex!*

PAGLIA:—of the anti-porn feminists and their *bad attitudes!*

GLENNDA: A day without pornography is like a day without sunshine!

PAGLIA: Oh, my *Gawd*—yes! I can't believe you're on the street just when we're filming our thing. Oh, my God, look at them.

(The protesters whisper to each other while shielding their posters from the cameras.)

ONE PROTESTER TO THE OTHER *(aghast, gesturing toward* PAGLIA *as if she were Satan)*: I'm glad to know who it is!

GLENNDA: Do you have any gay pornography?

PAGLIA: Look at them.

GLENNDA: Do you have any lesbian pornography?

PAGLIA *(eagerly)*: Do you have lesbian pornography here? Do you have any s & m pornography?

GLENNDA: They have—look—that's—

(Crowd mills about, as one protester again tries to interfere with the camera by striking at it with her poster.)

MALE VOICE IN CROWD: Keep your hands off my First Amendment!

PAGLIA *(to film crew and bodyguards)*: Watch out! Watch the cable!

OFFSCREEN PROTESTER: We don't want our pictures taken!

GLENNDA *(to the protester)*: What? Oh, come on! It's a photo op! It's publicity!

PAGLIA *(to the protester)*: Well, they're *not*. They're photographing *us!*

GLENNDA: They don't want the publicity!

PAGLIA: They don't want the publicity. They're afraid! You're afraid! You're afraid! You people are afraid. You've got no guts!

GLENNDA: Come on! Publicity!

VOICE IN CROWD: It's Camille!

PROTESTER *(to film crew as she snatches away her flailing poster)*: Get your hands off of my property!

PAGLIA *(starting to get angry)*: You don't own the street corner, honey!

GLENNDA *(laughing)*: Yeah! Come on, this is a—

PAGLIA: Yeah, you guys are real tough, aren't you, when no one is contradicting your ideas. You people are *hypocrites!* You people are *phobes!* You people are *puritans,* okay?

GLENNDA *(sternly to protesters)*: What do you think you're doing?

PAGLIA *(building up to high pitch of Italian fury)*: And now we are *here,* okay? Your opponents are *here!* Instead of your usual bullying, okay, you have some people who can *oppose* you, okay, who know something about *art!* Who aren't so fucking phobic as *you* are, okay?

GLENNDA: Pornography is art. Why don't they know that?

PAGLIA: You people are like mental defectives as far as I'm concerned, okay? You finally have someone who can deal with you, and you're *shrinking!* You people are *wimps!*

GLENNDA: Oh, they're having a conference.

PAGLIA: Wimps!

GLENNDA: They're having a conference.

PAGLIA: Granola lesbian wimps! Okay, alright? *(Shouting)* Anti-*art*, anti-*sex*, anti-*everything!* You people can go to *hell!* OK? Camille Paglia is here—in your *face!*

PROTESTER *(to* PAGLIA*)*: Why did you lose your job teaching at Bennington College?

GLENNDA *(groaning with exasperation)*: Ohh!

PAGLIA *(infuriated at this reactionary appeal to authority, leaps two steps toward the flinching protester.)*: Because I am, like, an *in-your-face* feminist, okay? And I got in a *fistfight!* Okay? *(Applause, whistles, and shouts of approval from the crowd, whom* PAGLIA *now turns to and bellows at.)* The feminism of the twenty-first century will be *pro-art!* Pro-*sex!* Pro-*porn!*

GLENNDA: More porn! More porn!

PAGLIA: Yes, *more porn!*

GLENNDA: More porn!

PAGLIA: We're *tired* of you guys! The *backlash* is against *you* people! *You* guys have caused the backlash—

GLENNDA: It's true!

PAGLIA:—with *your* bad attitude! Get real! *Get real!*

YOUNG FEMALE ONLOOKER *(stepping out of the crowd and pointing toward* PAGLIA*)*: So why don't you put on some nipple clamps?

PAGLIA: Get into the new age! Okay? *Grow up!* Grow up!

FEMALE ONLOOKER: Why doesn't she put on nipple clamps and, like, get on her knees then? *(sarcastically)* Okay, it'll be real artful.

PAGLIA: Oh, wow! Yeah! Why don't you read a book, honey? You obviously haven't read something recently, okay?

FEMALE ONLOOKER: Oh, please!

PAGLIA: Go buy a book. Go buy a book. *(looks theatrically up and down the street)* Where's a bookstore? *(points to onlooker)* Send this woman to a bookstore! *(points to protester)* Send *this* woman to an art store! Go look at a *painting!* Go look at Caravaggio, Michelangelo! Look at *Greek art!* Okay? This is, like, so fucking puritanical. Go to *India! Pro-sex Hinduism!* This is *bullshit! Bullshit! (makes aggressive Rolling Stones toss of the mike) You people SUCK!*

FEMALE ONLOOKER: So are you saying that it's okay to degrade a woman?

PAGLIA *(impatient)*: Oh, honey, go read a book!

FEMALE ONLOOKER: Go read a book yourself!

PAGLIA: You're *into* your "degradation"!

FEMALE ONLOOKER: No!

PAGLIA: You are in a *mind-set!* You have been *brainwashed!* You have been *programmed!*

FEMALE ONLOOKER: No, no! I'm all for sex. I love sex.

PAGLIA *(suddenly noticing the animated onlooker's very appealing dusky skin and large breasts, bursting out of a tight, sleeveless olive-green military shirt)*: Uh uh. No!

FEMALE ONLOOKER: I love sex, okay?

PAGLIA *(softening slightly because sensually distracted)*: Honey, go to a museum!

FEMALE ONLOOKER: I love sex.

PAGLIA *(pulling herself together)*: Oh, *right.* Yeah, except when it involves ideology, you love sex. Okay, let's move on to our next stop, Glennda.

GLENNDA: Yeah, I think we should.

PAGLIA *(cheerfully)*: Bye now!

GLENNDA *(laughing)*: I think we've made our mark here.

PAGLIA: Have a happy day!

(Cut to GLENNDA *and* PAGLIA *ten minutes later, standing in front of a restaurant and bar on Christopher Street, in the heart of Greenwich Village.)*

GLENNDA *(sighing with relief)*: Whew! Here we are, Glennda and Camille, and I'm still *overheated* and trying to calm down from our encounter with the WAP women—Women Against Porn. Wow! That was quite a ruckus!

PAGLIA: Those people were wimps! They had *nothing!* I mean, they're so used to bullying and harassing people on the street. When they had someone to contradict them, they just absolutely, you know, fell apart. And not only that, but their fascist attempt to shut off the cameras! They want to stand there and scream but not appear on camera. These people are hypocrites! These people have no courage. They're just like little schoolyard bullies.

GLENNDA: Well, you know, I feel like we're safe now. We've found refuge. We're at Stonewall. Stonewall—

PAGLIA *(in mock surprise)*: No, no! *(raises her hands like an ecstatic Baroque saint)*

GLENNDA:—where the revolution started. Yes!

PAGLIA *(looking at the bland facade of the renamed bar)*: This can't be Stonewall. Is this really Stonewall?

GLENNDA: Yes. This is Stonewall.

PAGLIA: Well, if it's really Stonewall, then, like the Pope, I have to kiss the ground.

GLENNDA: Okay.

PAGLIA: All right. *(She falls to her knees, kisses the pavement, and bows in Islamic obeisance.)* Ah! Stonewall!

GLENNDA *(laughing)*: Wow. That was amazing. *(In the background, the* CENTURIONS, *quaffing Evian, solemnly peruse the street.)*

PAGLIA: Where the drag queens revolted.

GLENNDA: Yes. And you know what we should talk about now, Camille? Actually, you need your microphone. *(A crew member hands a mike to* PAGLIA.*)*

PAGLIA *(brightly, like TV host Bob Barker)*: Thank you!

GLENNDA: The march on Washington. The [April 1993] gay march on Washington.

PAGLIA: Yeah.

GLENNDA: Do you know, I saw a lot of news. I couldn't go, because I was too busy. As you were, too. We were just too busy.

PAGLIA: Well, I was boycotting it, because I hate those people who run that. You know, they certainly did not open up the podium to anyone who did not agree with their views.

GLENNDA: Right. The thing is there was a lot of focus *away* from drag queens. Because they were interviewing people on MTV, and everyone was saying, "Nope, no drag queens here! Look, no drag queens, just normal folks. Just white middle-class Americans, and we just want our rights, and that's what it's all about!"

PAGLIA *(nodding in agreement)*: Actually, the C-Span cameras kept on showing a kind of huge sea of white middle-class people. It was like a *shopping mall!*

GLENNDA: A sea of white faces.

PAGLIA: Yes. And it was very discouraging, in many ways. It was sort of, like, you know, what's the point? These people are demanding their rights? They look like they *have* their rights. Just a bunch of privileged people who just wanted to party. There was nothing particularly marginal, you know? People on the podium, *claiming* marginality, when in fact there were hundreds of thousands of shopping-mall people there!

GLENNDA: Well, to be fair, there *were* a lot of drag queens there, but this group called the Gay and Lesbian Alliance Against Defamation—the leaders sent out press releases saying "Please" to the general media, "Media, please do not focus on the drag queens and the leather people, because they're a bad representation for our community."

PAGLIA: Oh, it is disgusting. Oh, it is yuppification, yuppification! This is not the Sixties, okay? I mean, I *hate* this.

GLENNDA: That's not revolutionary, to hide the drag queens.

PAGLIA: That is not revolutionary, no, no.

GLENNDA: You know, next year is the anniversary. Twenty-five years since the death of Judy Garland and the Stonewall Rebellion.

PAGLIA: Oh, my God. Unbelievable. See, Stonewall—I mean, it was the *drag queens* who pulled up paving stones and fought back against the police. The *drag queens* were the ones who had the balls to fight. It wasn't the yuppified, white bourgeois gay guys who did any fighting! Okay? So the drag queens were at the start of the revolution. How *easy* it is for people to forget that!

GLENNDA: Mmm hmm.

PAGLIA: Exactly. See, I feel that the problem with gay activism right now is that it's too ghettoized. It wants special rights for one group. I feel the true Sixties revolution is about arguing for the protection of all nonconformist behavior of *every kind*.

GLENNDA: Right. Absolutely.

PAGLIA: Homosexuality is only *one* area within that, okay? And I think that that is the terrible flaw of gay activism. And so I don't get along at *all* with the gay activist establishment. It's that there's no philosophical perspective, there's no real *vision* in them. They're just a bunch of people who are totally insular. They hate *me*. They call *me* homophobic. Oh, right, with *my* history, I'm "homophobic," honey! *Yeah*, like I'm—

GLENNDA: "Self-hating."

PAGLIA:—I'm "misogynist" and "pro-rape." That's another one I hear.

GLENNDA *(laughing)*: Pro-rape!

PAGLIA: Right! And so the drag queens fit directly into such an argument. I mean, what could be more nonconforming than a drag queen?

GLENNDA: Well, it's unfortunate that this gay rights movement has caused more marginalization of other groups—drag queens and cross-dressers, straight and gay cross-dressers, and people who are into the s & m lifestyle and fetishes. Those people are being pushed further into the margins, instead of, you know, a more inclusive—

PAGLIA: Yeah. *My* thinking is that we need a libertarian philosophy that argues for the civil rights of all acts in the private realm. That's what I'm arguing for. And we cannot just have a sort of gay versus straight dichotomy. *(angrily)* Right now, the gay activist establishment is a bunch of sanctimonious, pious people up on a pulpit. I have never heard such dogma, except from the *feminist* establishment—that's the only one that's worse, you know?

GLENNDA: A lot of feminist rhetoric trickles down into the gay movement, I've noticed.

PAGLIA: That's *right*. And in my opinion, anyone in the gay activist movement who adopts feminist rhetoric *is* misogynist, because feminist rhetoric is based on the victimization of woman. \

GLENNDA: Mmm hmm.

PAGLIA: Woman as victim. *Drag queen* philosophy is based on the idea of woman as dominatrix of the universe! *Ruler* of the cosmos! All right? That's why I follow the drag queen philosophy and *not* gay activist or feminist philosophy.

(Cut to GLENNDA and PAGLIA amid the crowds at the annual Christopher Street Fair. Behind them, a handsome young gay man with a studded black-leather band around his biceps is vigorously pummeling a woman on a large wooden massage rack.)

GLENNDA *(with feigned innocence)*: Camille, what's going on?

PAGLIA *(gleefully)*: Someone is being tortured.

GLENNDA: Wait—no, no, Camille, it's massage.

PAGLIA: Oh, deep massage!

GLENNDA: *Deep* massage.

PAGLIA: Interesting how massage and torture look so similar.

GLENNDA: I thought we had stumbled upon an s & m street fair!

PAGLIA: You know, I have heard of all kinds of massage rituals where people walk on backs and crack their back and so on. I mean, you know, Swedish massage is very close to s & m.

GLENNDA: There's a very sadistic and masochistic relationship there.

PAGLIA: There is. In fact, in old Hollywood movies there was the motif of the kind of big, burly woman who was the Swedish masseuse, you know?

GLENNDA: Yeah. A big butch woman.

PAGLIA: A big butch woman. And she would, like, hammer on you and so on. *(beaming with delight)* I think that this has not been really fully considered—the connection between Swedish massage and s & m!

GLENNDA: But I like seeing it out in the open. It's nice. Look! Look at him go! It's amazing.

PAGLIA *(laughing)*: Isn't that incredible!

GLENNDA: Wow.

PAGLIA: Now, you know, I think a lot of this is a kind of substitute for the old rituals of the Catholic Church, where you would beat yourself, flagellate yourself—

GLENNDA: Oh! But do you think it has pagan roots as well?

PAGLIA: Well, I think all abuse of the body has pagan roots, yes. But the mortification of the flesh in the Middle Ages—you would atone for your sins by beating yourself till you were bloody. In fact, such excesses were forbidden at one point by the Church, because—

GLENNDA: Are those the monks that whip themselves? *(Imitates self-flagellation)* I've seen—

(Film of Eastern Rite monks whipping their bloody backs.)

PAGLIA: Monks and nuns were getting very carried away. There were little tiny whips with hooks on the end.

GLENNDA: Wow.

PAGLIA: Yeah. So a lot of the rituals of the Catholic Church have strong s & m components.

GLENNDA: Do they still do that?

PAGLIA: Well, the modern Church frowns on it, because it understood the kind of perverse sexual pleasure, apparently, that some monks and nuns were getting from it.

GLENNDA: Whoa!

PAGLIA: But Robert Mapplethorpe certainly realized this connection. And my friend Bruce Benderson has often loved French decadent literature for its strange perverse Catholicism, an obsession with s & m motifs. I feel there is a deep undercurrent of sadomasochism in the Catholic Church. Especially the Mediterranean or Spanish versions of Catholicism.

GLENNDA: Maybe that's what that gay Catholic group is all about.

PAGLIA *(pursing her lips)*: Oh—

GLENNDA: There's a gay Catholic group.

PAGLIA: I know, but Dignity is a little bit too white-bread for me!

GLENNDA *(laughing)*: They are.

PAGLIA: They're too—they're a bunch of yuppies.

GLENNDA: They are.

PAGLIA: Really. No, I don't want to condemn them, but *(grinning and smacking her lips obscenely)* I want to put some *blood* into that little sect!

(Cut to GLENNDA *and* CAMILLE *standing outside Gay Pleasures, a bookstore on Hudson Street.)*

GLENNDA: Camille, let's go shopping for some good old-fashioned gay male pornography!

PAGLIA: Yes, let's look for porn!

OFF-CAMERA VOICE: Come on in!

*(*GLENNDA, CAMILLE, *and the* CENTURIONS *enter Gay Pleasures.)*

PAGLIA: Oh, I *love* it!

GLENNDA: Wow! We're here at Gay Pleasures.

PAGLIA: Oh, my gosh. *(picking up a book) Anal Pleasure and Health!* I love it. *(picking up another one) Dream Stud!* Look at these fabulous— now, you would never find such fabulous things in a *(sarcastically) les-bi-an* book store.

GLENNDA *(laughing)*: Oh, could you imagine? At Judith's Room [a lesbian bookstore]?

PAGLIA: Oh, no-o-o. Oh, my God! *(laughs)* Oh, look, look! *(plucks from a rack a postcard of David Sprigle's stylish nude photograph of a nonchalant, princely black man with a spiked silver collar and large erect penis)* Now, see, if this were of a woman, you would have them carrying on about how it's degrading and exploitative—

GLENNDA: Right.

PAGLIA:—but they refuse to consider the realities of gay male porn, which is *fabulous.*

GLENNDA: I never hear feminists talk about gay male porn.

PAGLIA: They don't.

GLENNDA: Why is that?

PAGLIA *(heatedly)*: They don't *want* to *admit it,* because it disproves their theory that all porn is about the degradation of women, you see? And *I'm* saying I've learned an *enormous* amount from gay male porn! It's the *hottest* porn that there is! There's nothing *better*.

GLENNDA: This is true.

PAGLIA: Because, you see, right now, heterosexual porn, it's really *not* that interesting, because you've got just a lot of very experienced, professional actresses who fake orgasm. Now, with men, you *can't* fake orgasm—

GLENNDA: It's true.

PAGLIA: I mean, it's either *hard* or it *isn't* hard, okay? (GLENNDA *laughs.*) So this is why I love gay male porn, and I think many other lesbian and bisexual women do as well, because it just is *hot.* It's totally *hot!*

GLENNDA *(looking at the displays)*: They have a lot of vintage stuff— old things from the Fifties.

PAGLIA: Yes. I love things that come from a repressive past.

GLENNDA: Like look at this—*Boys in Leather*.

PAGLIA: Oh, right. Or this, with its kind of Greek motif—*Trim*. Not only that, but gay male porn is *honest* about the sexual allure of young people, okay?

GLENNDA: Mmm hmm. Right.

PAGLIA: And you'll notice that when there are boys of indeterminate age, and even when there are boys who are the correct legal age, they're made to look *below* the age, right?

GLENNDA: It's a cult of youth and beauty.

PAGLIA: It's a cult of youth and beauty. And I think that's absolutely correct, and it's one of the great repressed subjects of right now, okay? Because we're into this child abuse hysteria right now. Everyone's hysterical about it.

GLENNDA: And it's killing sexuality.

PAGLIA: Killing sexuality, okay? The Lolita syndrome is one of the few examples of it in a heterosexual context. And I think we're

\ ripe for a revival of Lolita. Certainly we saw with Amy Fisher,
, okay, the "Long Island Lolita"—

GLENNDA: "The Long Island Lolita." There's a musical called *The Amy Fisher Musical*. Did you hear about it?

PAGLIA *(dishily, like Joan Rivers)*: I heard about it! Yes, I saw a little bit of it. I love it. I mean, on TV, I saw a clip.

GLENNDA: It looks like *Funny Girl*—the sign. *(GLENNDA demonstrates.)* Like, for *Funny Girl,* and she's pointing a gun.

PAGLIA *(pointing to another magazine)*: Look! *Hand Jobs. (camera catches the cover in closeup)* Now, you see? Look how *frank* everything is here! I mean, the *frankness*—

GLENNDA *(laughing)*: It's out in the open.

PAGLIA: With gay men, the frankness of sexual desire is *admitted!* I mean, there is no fooling around. There's no pretending it's like this emotional thing.

GLENNDA: Ideology and theory.

PAGLIA: There's no ideology.

GLENNDA: Books of theory that you have to read!

PAGLIA: It also avoids the sentimentality, the hand-holding, the pretending that it's all about, you know, *(imitates prissy, WASPy female voice)* love and nurturing. *(switches to raunchy Big Mama voice)* There's *no* nurturing, okay, *at all!* (GLENNDA *laughs.)* I *love* it! It's like just get it *hard,* you know, get it *out* there, stick it through a hole, you know, get it *off!* I love it!

GLENNDA *(guffawing)*: Great. That's it, absolutely.

PAGLIA: Yeah! So a lot of my theories about sex and pornography come from gay men, and this is the *great, invisible subject.*

(Cut to shot of nearby magazine rack with magazines titled A Hard Lesson, Black and Proud, Black Pharaohs, *and* Penis Coladas.*)*

GLENNDA: Why do you think there's such a vast amount of gay male pornography but not an equal amount of lesbian woman-on-woman porn? Why is that?

PAGLIA: Well, my observations of this confirm what Masters and Johnson found. That is, on the track of sexual frequency, they found that the individuals with the most sexual experience and activity were gay men. Next down the line were straight men. Next down the line to that were straight women. The group of human beings with the least frequency of sexual activity were *(trumpeting derisively) les-bi-ans,* okay?

GLENNDA *(laughing)*: Is that why it's hard for you to get a date?

PAGLIA *(ruefully)*: I get no dates. My life has been a ruin.

GLENNDA: Oh!

PAGLIA: I'm just an old nun. What can I say? No, it's true. Not only that, but there seems to be evidence that men are more visually stimulated towards, you know, sexual desire. Now, I'm just a kind of mutant, obviously, because I have always been highly interested in visual things.

GLENNDA: But some days you feel like a man, right? Are there some days you wake up and you feel like a man?

PAGLIA: I began as a man, and I'm turning back into a man at the end of my life, I'm afraid. As menopause approaches, I'm turning back into a man, I think, yeah.

GLENNDA: It's part of this abstract transsexualism, I've noticed.

(Cut to Fifties footage of a muscular, oiled man lying languorously on his stomach with bare buttocks prominently aloft. He is skimming through a paperback called I Can Take It All.*)*

GLENNDA: You have like this transsexual streak.

PAGLIA: Mmm hmm. Oh, I do. I absolutely do. I love it. *(picks up a copy of a magazine called* Stroke, *with a cover photo of a nude man acrobatically performing auto-fellatio)* Look at this! Look at this! Fabulous.

GLENNDA: Those are the expensive ones. I always buy them when they're on sale.

PAGLIA *(reading the cover headline)*: Oddities and Atrocities.

GLENNDA: But look—fifteen dollars. But they're good.

PAGLIA: Oh, my God! That is great. That is absolutely great! *(like a kid in a candy store)* Oh, *look* at all this fabulous stuff! *(leafing through another paperback)* Oh, see, men in uniform! I love things with men in uniform. I love Tom of Finland. He's a great favorite of mine, and Robert Mapplethorpe loved Tom of Finland too.

GLENNDA: He's great, yeah. *(still looking at* Stroke*)* Well, I like that this says *Oddities and Atrocities*, because so many people try to normalize gay sex. It's like, "It's normal, it's just like anything else." I don't *want* it to be normal, sometimes!

PAGLIA: That's right, that's right. Exactly.

GLENNDA: It's on the *edge*. It's *outlaw*.

PAGLIA: Well, I feel that all sexuality makes use of the taboo. In *any* culture, okay, if something is taboo, it becomes erotic. For example, women's ankles were invisible throughout the nineteenth century, so the mere glimpse of a woman's ankle caused people to go into a *frenzy* of eroticism, you see? And so, yes, I *love* the title *Oddities and Atrocities*. I may take that for my next book!

GLENNDA *(laughing)*: That could be the subtitle for *Sexual Personae*, Part Two!

PAGLIA: I'm looking for a title for my next book, my next essay collection. *(joking)* We may have *found* it, Glennda, right here! *Right here!*

GLENNDA: We found it at Gay Pleasures. Oh, my God! Right here at Gay Pleasures!

PAGLIA *(addressing the camera confidentially, imitating Sandra Bernhard)* Right here at this moment, you *saw* it!

(Cut to GLENNDA *and* CAMILLE *leafing through another bin of magazines and books.)*

GLENNDA: We're looking through some old 1950s . . . this one's called *Tomorrow's Man*, and that one's called—what is it called?

PAGLIA: *Vim!*

GLENNDA: And the thing is, in the Fifties they sort of masqueraded these magazines as muscle builders, body builders, so that they could get away with selling them. But they're really, you know, for certain gay men to read and enjoy—

PAGLIA: All kinds of bulging crotches.

GLENNDA: Some of them have women in them. Like this one—the two bodybuilders holding up a sexy woman.

PAGLIA (showing a photograph): Or this large bosom here.

GLENNDA: Which I think is great, because I think a lot of modern gay porn doesn't. I like to see women in it sometimes, because I think there's something really hot to just have a woman there sometimes. It's like bisexual and—

PAGLIA: I feel that's the revolution, Glennda!

GLENNDA (nodding): Yeah.

PAGLIA: I feel the revolution is for us to totally extend the level of our responsiveness in a bisexual direction. Whether we actually are bisexually active or not.

GLENNDA: Right. It's your sexual imagination.

PAGLIA: Sexual imagination!

GLENNDA: It should, if you can include that and see sexuality as a continuum, rather than gay over here or straight over there.

(Cut to GLENNDA and CAMILLE bathed in late afternoon light, as they stand near the splintered piers on the West Side Highway at 11th Street, near the old site of the Anvil, a notorious Seventies-era gay bar.)

GLENNDA (like Judy Garland as Dorothy): Oh, my God, Camille! We made it all the way over to the piers. I didn't think it was gonna happen, but we're here. We made it!

PAGLIA (like Dame Edna Everage): We have really been walking our little legs off today!

GLENNDA: And this is as far west as you can really go. I mean, we're at the West Side, the Hudson River, and we're by one of the piers. But look—look at this pier, Camille.

PAGLIA: It's amazing.

GLENNDA: It's very postapocalyptic.

PAGLIA: It really is. The pier is in a complete state of ruin.

(Cut to pan of pier.)

GLENNDA: You know what they call this pier? This is "The Sex Pier." People come here to have sex, late at night, during the day. Sexual outlaws come here—gay sexual outlaws.

PAGLIA: That is so great.

GLENNDA: And, you know, people fall in the water during sex or during their orgasm. Didn't Freud call the orgasm "The Little Death" . . . petite . . . petite—

PAGLIA: Well, that goes back centuries, actually, that idea.

GLENNDA: Oh, so he got it from somewhere else.

PAGLIA: Yes. You really risk death *here*. The timbers seem *shattered* with the force of so many orgasms!

GLENNDA: But that's the thing that gay men understand—the *risks* that you take sometimes in these public situations, that there's a little bit of a thrill. And maybe it's irresponsible, but if that's what you're *into*, you know, you have a *right*, if you want to come out here.

PAGLIA: Mmm hmm.

GLENNDA: Maybe you'll fall in the water, maybe you won't!

PAGLIA: That's exactly right, Glennda. This is what I'm always saying about the feminist problem with date rape, okay? That gay men understand there is risk and danger in sexuality, particularly the outlaw kind. I've learned so much from gay men. I'm sick and tired of women *whining*. They go on a date, they get in this car with a stranger, go to a man's room, and then they're surprised when something happens, you know? I mean, I love the gay male attitude, which is to go out into the dark, have anonymous sex. Right from the period of the Roman Empire—under the arches of the Colosseum—people understood that you go out on a sexual adventure as a gay man, you may not come home again. You may get beaten up. That's one of the *thrills*. That is the *aura*. It's sort of the erotic aura that's around outlaw sex. So again I feel that gay men have so much to teach establishment feminism about what sex *is*.

(Cut to GLENNDA *and* CAMILLE *at another pier, with the World Trade Center towers in the distance behind them.)*

GLENNDA *(addressing the camera)*: Camille and I have finished our tour! It's the end of *Glennda and Camille Do Downtown.*

PAGLIA: It's been a wonderful day, Glennda!

GLENNDA: It was beautiful. Of course, we learned a lot. We talked about a lot of topics. *(to the camera)* And just keep tuning in to the show. *(to* PAGLIA*)* Maybe we'll do another show.

PAGLIA: This is fabulous!

GLENNDA: Or two.

PAGLIA: Maybe this'll be a series!

GLENNDA: Yeah—*Glennda and Camille . . . The Series! (They laugh.)* Thanks for tuning in. Bye!

PAGLIA *(waving cheerfully to the camera like the Beverly Hillbillies)*: Bye, now!

(Loud rock music as credits roll over montage of the day: the CENTURIONS *stopping traffic at the arch,* PAGLIA *castigating the WAP women and kissing the ground at Stonewall,* PAGLIA *showing off a Keith Richards graphic on the back of her T-shirt,* GLENNDA *and* PAGLIA *doing a hip-bumping boogie. Cut to* GLENNDA *and* PAGLIA *snickering on 8th Street, when they first spot the women protesters half a block away.)*

PAGLIA *(yelling with delight)*: Hey, bitches! *(lewdly sticks out tongue)*

GLENNDA *(giggling)*: Let's tip their table over!

PAGLIA *(laughing and cupping hand to mouth)*: Feminist bitches!

ON LITERATURE

AND ART

GYPSY TIGRESS:

CARMEN

Georges Bizet's *Carmen* (1875) is the first music I remember hearing as a child. It remains for me the definition of what music is and what it should be—brilliant and passionate, overwhelming the senses with its directness and force.

I was mesmerized by a picture of Risë Stevens as Carmen in the album notes. For some reason, the fiery, laughing lady with piercing eyes had a rose between her teeth. It seemed savage and strange, an unsettling symbolism I never understood. In my parents' opera book was a colorful drawing of the toreador Escamillo parading in his glittering suit of lights. I loved his arrogance and glamour. And so at age six in 1953, I was Escamillo for Halloween. There is a photograph of me beaming in my black satin outfit trimmed with red and posing with a furled umbrella in lieu of a sword.

We are in a period where it has become fashionable to attack the great classics of art. A debunking cynicism passes for sophistication these days. "Misogyny," "male domination," and "phallic violence" are everywhere, we are told, in nineteenth-century opera, with its suffering heroines. The ravishing music merely masks the

[*Stagebill*, August 1992]

"oppression" for a callous bourgeois audience. Carmen, for example, is a "male fantasy," and the opera is, at heart, a "snuff film."

Well, Carmen is no male fantasy, for she was my fantasy too. Bizet's heroine, even more imperious than her somewhat rough and uncouth gypsy forebear in Prosper Mérimée's original novella (1845), is a spectacular sexual persona, a charismatic dominatrix possible only in Western culture, which gave birth to the independent, strong-speaking woman. The role has been treated in a variety of ways by different singers, whose voices range from throaty low mezzo to soprano. Some Carmens are cool and detached; others are earthy and tempestuous.

The most famous American Carmen was Risë Stevens, whose hot-blooded, highly physical, and knockabout version was first performed at the Met in 1943. Maria Callas never appeared onstage in *Carmen* but made a much admired studio recording in Paris in 1964. The theme has been a favorite in movie history ever since the first silent versions were filmed in France (1909) and Spain (1910). Theda Bara, Pola Negri, Dolores Del Rio, and Rita Hayworth have starred in the title role. Dorothy Dandridge was superb in Otto Preminger's modernized *Carmen Jones* (1954), with its all-black cast. Marilyn Horne provided the vocal track.

The plot of *Carmen* has important precedents in Western literature. The officer Don José lured away from his military duty by the temptress Carmen recalls Aeneas delayed by Dido's sensuality and Mark Antony throwing away the world for Cleopatra. In a Greek myth, the hero Hercules, enslaved to Omphale, actually dons women's clothing. All these stories ask questions about love and manhood. Sex contains many dangers. There is the risk of loss of identity. Shakespeare's treatment of the Antony and Cleopatra saga is complex and profound: he shows how Antony is enlarged by love but finally destroyed by his reckless disregard of his public obligations as a man. This is also José's fate.

Carmen is secondly a work of Romanticism. The gypsies, with their mysterious nomadic past, represent life in nature, an energy wild and free. As thieves and smugglers, they are outcasts and outlaws, rebel personae celebrated by the Romantics. Don José, the deserter joining the gypsies, is a runaway and dropout, a motif familiar to us from the 1960s counterculture. He turns his back on respectability, career advancement, and social acceptance. But he puts all responsibility for his identity on Carmen. He makes himself passive to her and thereby loses her interest. When she leaves him, he is nothing. Hence his rage and despair. The opera is a tragedy for both the central characters.

One of the most Romantic elements in *Carmen* is its interest in intense emotion, which defeats reason, prudence, and common sense, the balanced, moderate values of eighteenth-century neoclassicism. The opera is a case study of jealousy, which swallows José up in mad excess. Like Othello, he destroys the thing he loves. We are currently amidst a national debate over rape and its motives. Bizet's *Carmen* compellingly shows how a gentle, unassuming man can be swept toward violence and murder.

José's psychology is expertly drawn. He is deeply attached to his mother and native village. Micaela, his pious, mild-mannered fiancée, comes to him as his mother's ambassador. Like Shakespeare's Octavia, Micaela represents conventional womanhood, a simplicity, innocence, and purity. She offers her man the quiet devotion of a lifetime. Carmen, on the other hand, like Cleopatra, is a brawler and tawny-skinned tigress, overtly sexual and rapacious. José is fascinated by Carmen's egotism and flamboyance, her brassy brio and malicious sense of fun. Like Cleopatra, she has the many moods of a woman but the aggression and drive of a man.

But what attracts José to Carmen is also what is dangerous about her. Loving her is a gamble, and José loses. His simple idealism about women, whom he identifies with his saintly mother, does not prepare him for a monumental natural phenomenon like Carmen, with her unbridled appetites and volatility. He is naive, sentimental. When Carmen coldly spurns him, his childishness and dependency return. His personality is not strong enough to withstand rejection. He murders her as a way to preserve their connection. And his horrified lament over her body immediately snaps back into a yearning for maternal consolation, as if he has been suddenly orphaned. Perhaps this vocal passage is harmonically unresolved because man's relation to woman can never be resolved. *Hm.*

Carmen is no helpless victim. It is simply untrue that the opera misogynistically condemns a woman to death for wanting a modern sexual freedom. As one of the great *femmes fatales* of nineteenth-century art, the voluptuous, bewitching, promiscuous Carmen has an inner perversity and, at times, a cruelty bordering on the sadistic. She first flirts with José merely because he is ignoring her. She enjoys the challenge of seduction but becomes quickly bored. She keeps trading up the male hierarchy, going after Escamillo because he is the hottest new property. She uses and dumps José, insulting and humiliating him unnecessarily and finally obliterating his identity. He is conquered by Escamillo as much as by Carmen. Psychologically castrated, he avenges himself with the phallic knife.

Carmen is structured very much like Euripides' *Bacchae*. The working-class gypsy is, like the populist god Dionysus, an anarchic alien associated with magic, dance, and the pleasure principle. Both Carmen and Dionysus lure a representative of the social order away into the archetypal forest, where they cavalierly deconstruct his masculine personality. Throughout the opera, the pagan elements of Western culture are still at war with Judeo-Christianity, whose calm, ascending, hymnlike measures Micaela and José use in vain against Carmen's frenzied, escalating, percussive dance accents.

It was Bizet's riveting Spanish dance music that first seized my attention as a child. I now see it pointed toward my generation's domination by rock, which is energized by African-American dance rhythms. *Carmen*'s romantic story line, climaxing in a murder, is itself a kind of bohemian apache dancing, a bruising courtship ritual. The toreador too is a dancer who flirts with death.

The finale is brilliantly staged. Mérimée's Carmen dies in the forest, but Bizet ends his story as he began it, in a public square, the symbol of José's lost social status. Alienated, solitary, he tries to stop Carmen from entering the arena where the bullfight is about to begin. The roaring crowd, hailing his rival Escamillo, is the community from which José is now severed. A dark, eerie, sinister music wells up, like an earth tremor or rising storm wind. It is the shadow of Fate as well as the raw, elemental power of sexuality that Carmen has aroused but cannot control. We feel someone will die, but it could as well be José.

In this parallel performance outside the arena, Carmen taunts and goads José as if he were a bull. Trying to pass him, she is gored.

She dies in the dirt, in squalor. But her last moments are those of heroic defiance, as she chooses freedom above surrender. She refuses to whine, cower, beg, or plead. She has acted, and she accepts full responsibility for her actions. Capricious, carnal, greedy for life, she has played the dangerous game of sex by her own rules. Death is merely her final adventure.

ALICE AS EPIC HERO

"Lewis Carroll" was the pen name of Charles Lutwidge Dodgson (1832–98), a mathematician and Anglican deacon who spent his entire adult life as a sheltered fellow of Christ Church College at Oxford University. Dodgson belongs to the history of literature, rather than mathematics, because of his two masterpieces, *Alice's Adventures in Wonderland* (1865) and *Through the Looking-Glass* (1871), which were inspired by Alice Pleasance Liddell, young daughter of the dean of Christ Church.

The *Alice* books are the greatest examples of the crowded genre of Victorian children's literature, which sprang from the new Romantic vision of the child. For Rousseau and Wordsworth, children have a primal innocence and purity; they are saintly and sexless ambassadors of nature, untouched by corrupt society. Throughout Victorian literature, including the classic novels of Charles Dickens, the orphaned girl-child is the supreme symbol of profound emotion and beleaguered virtue.

Carroll's Alice, one of the outstanding characters of world literature, is not an orphan, but in her stories she is mysteriously

[Introduction, Lewis Carroll, *Alice in Wonderland* / *Alice Through the Looking Glass*, Book-of-the-Month Club, 1994]

parentless. We hear of a sister, a nurse, and three cats, but the entire adult world has been obliterated. It exists as empty architectural spaces, as in eerie De Chirico paintings—a schoolroom or a drawing room with a stone mantel, clock face, and mirror, through which Alice steps into another dimension. The invisible hierarchical system of social and familial authority has been re-created instead in the "wonderland" of the unconscious, our fascinating, baffling dream life that Carroll, before Freud, was the first to systematically explore.

The *Alice* stories are modern psychological fairy tales but also clever mock epics, like Pope's *The Rape of the Lock*. A seven-year-old girl is the intrepid protagonist, embarked on the archetypal journey of myth and legend that represents life itself. It is inquisitiveness, a "burning" curiosity or thirst for knowledge, that plummets Alice into her adventures in both books. Alone and lost, she shows courage and resourcefulness. Strange, menacing beings and disorienting alterations of space and time beset her. But she survives by her wits, reasoning her way through each problem and struggling to maintain the imperial British code of good manners amid confusion and chaos. On her heroic quest, normally the province of male warriors, Alice is forever the outsider, the alien, rebuffed by hostile cliques and quarreling in-groups, from the Mad Tea Party to the Garden of Live Flowers.

On her travels over the meadows and through the woods, Alice never turns into Huck Finn, a smudged vagabond scamp. She remains the well-bred young lady, her crisp apron and pinafore undisheveled even when she falls into a pool of tears or rockets up and down, bizarrely changing size. After Bloomsbury, we have been too ready to see male oppression in the nineteenth century. Alice's resilient femininity shows the power of Victorian womanhood. Rarely fearful and never frail or hysterical, Alice reflects Carroll's real-life adulation of little girls as superior to boys, whom he loathed and avoided.

The circumstances surrounding the composition of the *Alice* books would, in today's climate of sexual suspicion, get the author into very hot water indeed. On July 4, 1862, two bachelor clergymen, Carroll and Robinson Duckworth, took the three Liddell sisters on one of many private boating parties on the Thames, which at various times ended in the group hiding from the summer sun under a hayrick or getting soaked to the skin from a thunderstorm. On this particular day, Carroll, entertaining the children with his usual extemporaneous tales and riddles, created a fantasy starring his special favorite, Alice, which was so mesmerizing that she pleaded for him to write it down. The first manuscript was called *Alice's Adventures under Ground*.

A lifelong celibate, Carroll had no known romances with adults. Quiet, awkward, and introverted, he was afflicted with a bad stammer that disappeared only in the company of children, whom he loved to entertain. While traveling, he carried a black bag of games, tricks, and puzzles to pique the attention of little girls. Carroll's intentions were probably not overtly physical, like those of Humbert Humbert in Nabokov's *Lolita*, but perhaps it is naive to deny there was an element of sublimated, voyeuristic eroticism in his attraction to girls, with whom he may have secretly identified. As an amateur portrait photographer of considerable distinction, Carroll took a series of nude or seminude pictures of girls, many of which were later destroyed, at his instructions. It appears that Mrs. Liddell, the Dean's wife, disliked Carroll's loitering persistence, though he was tolerated as a harmless, if tiresome, eccentric.

Games the Liddell sisters were learning—first croquet, then chess—shape the two books. Carroll's vivid characters are often game pieces come to life—the furious, stentorian Queen of Hearts and her playing-card children, trembling gardeners, and loyal soldiers, who bend double to serve as croquet arches; or the pursed, dictatorial Red Queen and kindly, untidy White Queen, whom Alice, in her female rites of passage, encounters on the testing ground of a vast geographical chessboard. Game motifs are also present in the Dodo bird's tumultuous, circular Caucus-race and in the fierce ritual combats of Tweedledum and Tweedledee, the Lion and Unicorn, and the Red Knight and maladroit White Knight. We know that Carroll, a workaholic, obsessive-compulsive organizer and chronic insomniac, used puzzles, math problems, and quirky mental inventions to get himself through the night and to drive away irreverent or impure thoughts. He was an early speculator in symbolic logic: one of his academic books is called *The Game of Logic*.

But beyond this, Carroll sees all of life as a game, whose rules we must learn by comic trial and error. Despite our best intentions, reality often proves refractory or rebellious, as when Alice, earnestly trying to play croquet, finds her mallet, a live flamingo, twisting itself upward to stare her in the face. Many Freudian interpretations of the *Alice* books treat them in distressingly reductive terms as neurotic manifestations of a social misfit. But it is equally possible to see Carroll's maimed isolation and detachment as the inspiration for his coolly scientific view of society as a webwork of conventions. The best examples are his tea-party and courtroom scenes, with their elaborate ceremonial formalism. Critics have rightly noted Carroll's prefiguration of Kafka's *The Trial* and *The Castle*, modernist portraits of amoral, arbitrary authority.

There are analogies to the then-developing discipline of anthropology. Alice visits culture after culture, meeting their despotic rulers, learning their foods, customs, and languages, and inadvertently violating their surprising taboos. For instance, she finds herself in a Cyclops-like cave, the dusky shop of the curt, taciturn knitting Sheep, with its porous shelving and uncooperative floating curios and magic transformation into a stream lined with scented rushes. There may also be influences from Darwin's natural history: Alice confronts a host of familiar and exotic animals, insects, and plants, who deem themselves quite equal and even superior to mere humans. Each being has its own story, poem, or song, lengthy spiritual autobiographies or genealogies which Alice listens to with polite patience that wears thin as the day goes on.

Carroll's anthropomorphism is never coy or sentimental, in the standard Victorian way. The *Alice* books have the uncanny animism of primitive religion; these daunting creatures are bold, brash, and sharp-tongued. Even a pudding comes alive and indignantly berates Alice ("What impertinence!") for cutting a slice of it. Tooth-and-claw Darwinian themes of violence and carnivorousness abound: Alice is always catching herself as she carelessly or, as Freud would say, perversely mentions a predator (cats, humans) to its prey (mice, birds, fish). And she herself has a quite un-Wordsworthian spirit of sadistic mischief, as when she frightens her old nurse by shouting in her ear, "Nurse! Do let's pretend that I'm a hungry hyena, and you're a bone!" Carroll systematically subverts Victorian moralism by making didacticism synonymous with humorlessness and sterility.

The aggressive voices of Carroll's characters are unique and unforgettable. As in the great tradition of British drama (Carroll's childhood love of the theater was squelched by his clergyman father), personality is created by the power of language. Animals or objects burst into speech and hector Alice, who holds her own in scuffling fencing-matches of prickly dialogue. Carroll's meditations on language anticipate twentieth-century literary theory. Both the Gnat and Humpty Dumpty speculate about the relativity of names, and the Cheshire Cat makes a philosophical argument for radical subjectivity in our perceptions of the world. The ersatz Anglo-Saxon poem "Jabberwocky" uses punning "portmanteau" words simultaneously to intensify meaning and to break it down into Carrollian "nonsense" or absurdity. There is a persistent oscillation between language and silence, as the seething, quarrelsome characters suddenly stop and stare at each other, mute and stunned.

The dramatic panache of the *Alice* books was appreciated early on: a stage version of *Alice in Wonderland* appeared in London in 1886, while Carroll was still alive. There have been three movies (released in 1933, 1950, and 1972) and an animated Walt Disney musical version (1951). However, the most indelible images remain those created by Sir John Tenniel, a brilliant illustrator who labored under Carroll's vexingly punctilious supervision. The Tenniel Alice with long blonde tresses was based on another Carroll intimate, Mary Badcock, rather than slim, dark-haired Alice Liddell, whose connection to the first book was prudently obscured.

But it is surely Alice Liddell's personality that draws us in and charms us. "Who am I?" Carroll's Alice asks, like Odysseus, Oedipus, and Hamlet, as she makes her way past the Elysian throngs of boors, bores, and bullies, the meddlers, dandies, raconteurs, monomaniacs, melancholics, tricksters, sophists, gurus, gluttons, loafers, ninnies, male bunglers, and female termagants. The *Alice* books are a Saturnalian dream-within-a-dream, a sequence of surreal cinematic episodes linked by the melting transitions and misty amnesia of our innermost stream-of-consciousness. "I've a right to think," Alice defiantly declares to the ugly Duchess. In Carroll's panorama of the mind, where Romantic imagination and Enlightenment intellect join, Alice is our proxy in stubbornly making sense out of the flux of time.

LOVE POETRY

In evaluating love poetry, we must first ask whether the language is private and original or formulaic and rhetorical. Is the poet speaking for him- or herself, or is the voice a persona? The poem, if commissioned by friend or patron, may be a projection into another's adventures, or it may be an improvised conflation of real and invented details. A love poem cannot be simplistically read as a literal, journalistic record of an event or relationship; there is always some fictive reshaping of reality for dramatic or psychological ends. A love poem is secondary rather than primary experience; as an imaginative construction, it invites detached contemplation of the spectacle of sex.

We must be particularly cautious when dealing with controversial forms of eroticism like homosexuality. Poems are unreliable historical evidence about any society; they may reflect the consciousness of only one exceptional person. Furthermore, homoerotic images or fantasies in poetry must not be confused with concrete homosexual practice. We may speak of tastes or tendencies in early poets but not of sexual orientation: this is a modern idea.

[*The Princeton Encyclopedia of Poetry and Poetics,* Alex Preminger and
T. V. F. Bogan, 3rd edition, 1993]

Love poetry is equally informed by artistic tradition and contemporary cultural assumptions. The pagan attitude toward the body and its pleasures was quite different from that of Christianity, which assigns sex to the fallen realm of nature. The richness of Western love poetry may thus arise in part from the dilemma of how to reconcile mind or soul with body. Moreover, the generally higher social status of women in Western as opposed to Eastern culture has given love poetry added complexity or ambivalence: only women of strong personality could have produced the tormented sagas of Catullus or Propertius. We must try to identify a poem's intended audience. In antiquity the love poet was usually addressing a coterie of friends or connoisseurs; since Romanticism, however, the poet speaks to him- or herself, with the reader seeming to overhear private thoughts. We must ask about pornographic material in love poetry whether it reflects the freer sensibilities of a different time or whether the poet set out to shock or challenge his contemporaries. Much love poetry is clearly testing the limits of decorous speech, partly to bring sexual desire under the scrutiny and control of imagination. In the great Western theme of the transience of time, vivid sensuous details illustrate the evanescence of youth and beauty; the poet has a godlike power to defeat time and bestow immortality upon the beloved through art. Romantic impediments give the poem a dramatic frame: the beloved may be indifferent, far away, married to someone else, dead, or of the wrong sex. However, difficulty or disaster in real life is converted into artistic opportunity by the poet, whose work profits from the intensification and exploration of negative emotion.

The history of European love poetry begins with the Greek lyric poets of the Archaic age (7th-6th centuries B.C.). Archilochus, Mimnermus, Sappho, and Alcaeus turn poetry away from the grand epic style toward the quiet personal voice, attentive to mood and emotion. Despite the fragmentary survival of Greek solo poetry, we see that it contains a new idea of love, which Homer shows as foolish or deceptive but never unhappy. Archilochus' account of the anguish of love is deepened by Sappho, whose poetry was honored by male writers and grammarians until the fall of Rome. Sappho and Alcaeus were active on Lesbos, an affluent island off the Aeolian coast of Asia Minor, where aristocratic women apparently had more freedom than later in classical Athens. Sappho is primarily a love poet, uninterested in politics or metaphysics. The nature of her love has caused much controversy and many fabrications, some by major scholars. Sappho was married, and she had a daughter, but her poetry suggests that she fell in love with a series of beautiful girls, who moved in and out of her coterie (not a school, club, or cult). There is as yet no evidence, however, that she had physical relations with women. Even the ancients, who had her complete works, were divided about her sexuality.

Sappho shows that love poetry is how Western personality defines itself. The beloved is passionately perceived but also replaceable; he or she may exist primarily as a focus of the poet's consciousness. In "He seems to me a god" (fr. 31), Sappho describes her pain at the sight of a favorite girl sitting and laughing with a man. The lighthearted social scene becomes oppressively internal, as the poet sinks into suffering: she cannot speak or see; she is overcome by fever, tremor, pallor. "This description of the symptoms of love had the most persistent influence over more than a thousand years" (Albin Lesky). In plain, concise language, Sappho analyzes her extreme state as if she were both actor and observer; she is candid and emotional yet dignified, austere, almost clinical. This poem, preserved for us by Longinus, is the first great psychological document of Western literature. Sappho's prayer to Aphrodite (fr. 1) converts cult-song into love poem. The goddess, amused at Sappho's desperate appeal for aid, teasingly reminds her of former infatuations and their inevitable end. Love is an endless cycle of pursuit, triumph, and ennui. The poem, seemingly so charming and transparent, is structured by a complex time scheme of past, present, and future, the ever-flowing stream of our emotional life. Sappho also wrote festive wedding songs and the first known description of a romantic moonlit night. She apparently invented the now-commonplace adjective "bittersweet" for the mixed condition of love.

Early Greek love poetry is based on simple parallelism between human emotion and nature, which has a Mediterranean mildness. Love-sickness, like a storm, is sudden and passing. Imagery is vivid and luminous, as in haiku; there is nothing contorted or artificial. Anacreon earned a proverbial reputation for wine, women, and song:

his love is not Sappho's spiritual crisis but the passing diversion of a bisexual bon vivant. Love poetry was little written in classical Athens, where lyric was absorbed into the tragic choral ode. Plato, who abandoned poetry for philosophy, left epigrams on the beauty of boys. The learned Alexandrian age revived love poetry as an art mode. Theocritus begins the long literary tradition of pastoral, where shepherds complain of unrequited love under sunny skies. Most of his *Idylls* contain the voices of rustic characters like homely Polyphemus, courting the scornful nymph Galatea, or Lycidas, a goatherd pining for a youth gone to sea. Aging Theocritus broods about his own love for fickle boys, whose blushes haunt him. In his *Epigrams*, Callimachus takes a lighter attitude toward love, to which he applies sporting metaphors of the hunt. In Medea's agonized passion for Jason in the *Argonautica*, Apollonius Rhodius tries to mesh love poetry with epic. Asklepiades adds new symbols to love tradition: Eros and arrow-darting Cupid. Meleager writes with equal relish of cruel boys and voluptuous women, such as Heliodora. His is a poignant, sensual poetry filled with the color and smell of flowers.

The *Greek Anthology* demonstrates the changes in Greek love poetry from the Alexandrian through Roman periods. As urban centers grow and speed up, nature metaphors recede. Trashy street life begins, and prostitutes, drag queens, randy tutors, and bathhouse masseuses crowd into view. Love poets become droll, jaded, less lyrical. Women are lusciously described but given no personalities or inner life. Leonidas of Tarentum and Marcus Argentarius write of voracious sluts with special skills; Antipater of Thessalonika coarsely derides scrawny old lechers. For the first time, love poetry incorporates ugliness, squalor, disgust. Boy-love is universal: Straton of Sardis, editor of an anthology of pederastic poems, celebrates the ripening phases of boys' genitals. By the early Byzantine period, however, we feel the impact of Christianity, in more heartfelt sentiment but also in guilt and melancholy.

The Romans inherited a huge body of Greek love poetry. Catullus, the first Latin writer to adapt elegy for love themes, is obsessed with Lesbia, the glamourous noblewoman Clodia, promiscuously partying with midnight pickups. "I love and I hate": this tortured affair is the most complex contribution to love poetry since Sappho, whom Catullus admired and imitated. The poet painfully grapples with the ambiguities and ambivalences of being in love with an aggressive, willful Western woman. He also writes tender love poems to a boy, honey-sweet Juventius. There is no Roman love poetry between adult men. Propertius records a long, tangled involvement with capricious Cynthia, a fast-living new woman. There are sensual bed scenes, love-bites, brawls. After Cynthia dies (perhaps poisoned), the angry, humiliated poet sees her ghost over his bed. Tibullus writes of troubled love for two headstrong mistresses, adulterous Delia and greedy Nemesis, and one elusive boy, Marathus. In Vergil's *Eclogue 2*, the shepherd Corydon passionately laments his love-madness for Alexis, a proud, beautiful youth; the poem was traditionally taken as proof of Vergil's own homosexuality. Horace names a half dozen girls whom he playfully lusts for, but only the rosy boy Ligurinus moves him to tears and dreams. In the *Amores*, Ovid boasts of his sexual prowess and offers strategies for adultery. *The Art of Love* tells how to find and keep a lover, including sexual positions, naughty words, and feigned ecstasies; *The Remedies for Love* contains precepts for falling *out* of love. The love-letters of the *Heroides* are rhetorical monologues of famous women (Phaedra, Medea) abandoned by cads. Juvenal shows imperial Rome teeming with effeminates, libertines, and pimps; love or trust is impossible. The Empress prowls the brothels; every good-looking boy is endangered by rich seducers; drunken wives grapple in public stunts. Martial casts himself as a facetious explorer of this lewd world where erections are measured and no girl says no. The *Dionysiaca*, Nonnus' late Greek epic, assembles fanciful erotic episodes from the life of Dionysus. Also extant are many Greek and Latin *priapeia:* obscene comic verses, attached to phallic statues of Priapus in field and garden, which threaten thieves with anal or oral rape.

In medieval romance, love as challenge, danger, or high ideal is central to chivalric quest. From the mid-12th century, woman replaces the feudal lord of the militaristic *chansons de geste*. French aristocratic taste was refined by the courtly love of the Occitan (Provençal) troubadours, who raised woman to spiritual dominance, something new in Western love poetry. Amorous intrigue now lures the hero: to consummate his adultery with Guinevere, Chrétien de Troyes' Lancelot bends the bars of her chamber, then bleeds into her bed. The symbolism of golden grail, bleeding lance, and broken sword of Chrétien's *Perceval* is sexual as well as religious. Wolfram von Eschenbach's German Parzival is vowed to purity, but adulterous Anfortas suffers a festering, incurable groin wound. Sexual temptations are specifically set to test a knight's virtue in the French romances *Yder* and *Hunbaut* and the Middle English *Sir Gawain and the Green Knight*. The adultery of Gottfried von Strassburg's *Tristan and Isolde*, with their steamy lovemaking, helped define Western romantic love as unhappy or doomed. The Trojan tale of faithful Troilus and treacherous Cressida was invented by Benoît de Sainte-Maure and transmitted to Boccaccio and Chaucer. Heavily influenced by Ovid, *The Romance of the Rose* (Guillaume de Lorris and Jean de Meun) uses dreamlike allegory and sexual symbols of flower, garden, and tower to chart love's assault. The pregnancy of the Rose is a first for European literary heroines. Abelard wrote famous love songs, now lost, to Heloise. Dante's youthful love poems to Beatrice in the *Vita nuova* begin in troubadour style, then modulate toward Christian mysticism. In the *Inferno*'s episode of Paolo and Francesca, seduced into adultery by reading a romance of Lancelot, Dante renounces his early affection for courtly love. Medieval Latin lyrics express homoerotic feeling between teacher and student in monastic communities. There are overtly pederastic poems from the 12th century and at least one apparently lesbian one, but no known vernacular or pastoral medieval poetry is homosexual. The goliardic *Carmina Burana* contain beautiful lyrics of the northern flowering of spring and love, as well as cheeky verses of carousing and wenching, some startlingly detailed. The French *fabliau*, a ribald verse-tale twice imitated by Chaucer, reacts against courtly love with bedroom pranks, barnyard drubbings, and an earthy stress on woman's hoary genitality. Villon, zestfully atumble with Parisian trollops, will later combine the devil-may-care goliard's pose with the fabliau's slangy comedy.

Renaissance epic further expands the romantic element in chivalric adventure. Boiardo, Ariosto, and Tasso open quest to an armed heroine, a motif adopted by Spenser, whose *Faerie Queene,* emulating Ovid's *Metamorphoses,* copiously catalogues incidents of normal and deviant sex. Petrarch, combining troubadour lyricism with Dante's advanced psychology, creates the modern love poem. His Laura, unlike saintly Beatrice, is a real woman, not a symbol.

Petrarch's nature, vibrating to the lover's emotions, will become the Romantic pathetic fallacy. His conceits, paradoxes, and images of fire and ice, which spread in sonnet sequences throughout Europe, inspired and burdened Renaissance poets, who had to discard the convention of frigid mistress and trembling wooer. Ronsard's sonnets, addressed to Cassandre, Marie, and Hélène, first follow Petrarchan formulas, then achieve a simpler, more musical, debonair style, exquisitely attuned to nature. In the *Amoretti* Spenser practices the sonnet (introduced to England by Wyatt and Surrey), but his supreme love poem is the *Epithalamion*, celebrating marriage. Like Michelangelo, Shakespeare writes complex love poetry to a beautiful young man and a forceful woman: the fair youth's homoerotic androgyny is reminiscent of Shakespeare's soft, "lovely" Adonis and Marlowe's longhaired, white-fleshed Leander, romanced by Neptune. Richard Barnfield's sonnets and *Affectionate Shepherd* openly offer succulent sexual delights to a boy called Ganymede, a common Renaissance allusion. The traditional allegory, based on the Song of Songs, of Christ the bridegroom knocking at the soul's door, creates unmistakable homoeroticism in Donne's Holy Sonnet XIV, George Herbert's "Love (III)", and spiritual stanzas of St. John of the Cross. In ardent poems to his fiancée, later his wife, Donne, with Spenser, demonstrates the new prestige of marriage: before this, no one wrote love poetry to his wife. Furthermore, Donne's erudition implies that his lady, better educated than her medieval precursors, enjoys flattery of her intellect as well as of her beauty. Aretino's sonnets daringly use vulgar street terms for acts of love. Marino's *Adonis* makes Baroque opera out of the ritualistic stages of sexual gratification. Waller and Marvell use the *carpe diem* argument to lure shy virgins into surrender; the Cavalier poets adopt a flippant court attitude toward women and pleasure. Carew's *A Rapture* turns Donne's ode to nakedness into a risqué tour of Celia's nether parts. Libertines emerge in the late 17th century: Rochester, a Restoration wit, writes bluntly of raw couplings with ladies, whores, and boys. Milton's *Lycidas* revives the classical style of homoerotic pastoral lament. *Paradise Lost*, following Spenser and Donne, exalts "wedded Love" over the sterile wantonness of "Harlots" and "Court Amours" (4.750–70).

The Age of Reason, valuing self-control and witty detachment, favored satire over love poetry. Rousseau's delicate sentiment and pagan nature-worship created the fervent moods of "sensibility" and woman-revering Romanticism. Goethe, identifying femaleness with creativity, writes of happy sensual awakening in the *Roman Elegies* and jokes about sodomy with both sexes in the *Venetian Epigrams*, with its autoerotic acrobat, Bettina; withheld pornographic verses imitate ancient *priapeia*. Schiller dedicates rhapsodic love poems to Laura, but his hymns to womanhood sentimentally polarize the sexes. Hölderlin addresses Diotima with generalized reverence and reserves his real feeling for Mother Earth. Blake calls for sexual freedom for women and for the end of guilt and shame. Burns composes rural Scottish ballads of bawdy or ill-starred love. Wordsworth's Lucy poems imagine woman reabsorbed into roiling nature. In *Christabel* Coleridge stages a virgin's seduction by a lesbian vampire, nature's emissary. The younger English Romantics fuse poetry with free love. In *Epipsychidion* Shelley is ruled by celestial women radiating intellectual light. Keats makes emotion primary; his maidens sensuously feed and sleep or wildly dance dominion over knights and kings. Byron's persona as a "mad, bad" seducer has been revised by modern revelations about his bisexuality. In the "Thyrza" poems, he woos and changes the sex of a favorite Cambridge choirboy; in *Don Juan*, his blushing, girlish hero, forced into drag, catches the eye of a tempestuous lesbian sultana. Heine's love ballads are about squires, shepherd-boys, hussars, and fishermaidens; later verses record erotic adventures of the famous poet wined and dined by lady admirers.

French Romantics, turning art against nature in the hell of the modern city, make forbidden sex a central theme. Gautier celebrates the lonely, self-complete hermaphrodite. Baudelaire looses brazen whores upon syphilitic male martyrs; sex is torment, cursed by God. Baudelaire's heroic, defiant lesbians are hedonistically modernized by Verlaine and later rehellenized by Louÿs. In *Femmes* Verlaine uses vigorous street argot to describe the voluptuous sounds and smells of sex with women; in *Hombres* he lauds the brutal virility of young laborers, whom he possesses in their rough workclothes. He and Rimbaud co-wrote an ingenious sonnet about the anus. Mallarmé's leering faun embodies pagan eros; cold, virginal Herodias is woman as castrator. In contrast, Victorian poetry, as typified by the Brownings, exalts tenderness, fidelity, and devotion, the bonds of married love, preserved beyond the grave. Tennyson and the Pre-Raphaelites revive the medieval cult of idealized woman, supporting the Victorian view of woman's spirituality. Tennyson's heroines, like weary Mariana, love in mournful solitude. His *Idylls* retell Arthurian romance. *In Memoriam,* Tennyson's elaborate elegy for Hallam, is homoerotic in feeling. Rossetti's sirens are sultry, smoldering. Swinburne, inspired by Baudelaire, reintroduces sexual frankness into highbrow English literature. His Dolores and Faustine are promiscuous *femmes fatales*, immortal vampires; his Sappho, sadistically caressing Anactoria, boldly proclaims her poetic greatness. Whitman broke taboos in American poetry: he names body parts and depicts sex surging through fertile nature; he savors the erotic beauties of both male and female. Though he endorses sexual action and energy, Whitman appears to have been mostly solitary, troubled by homosexual desires, suggested in the "Calamus" section of *Leaves of Grass*. Reflecting the Victorian taste for bereavement, Hardy's early poetry features gloomy provincial tales of love lost: ghosts, graveyards, suicides, tearful partings. Homoerotic Greek idealism and epicene *fin-de-siècle* preciosity characterize the poems of Symonds, Carpenter, Hopkins, Wilde, Symons, and Dowson. Renée Vivien, the first poet to advertise her lesbianism, writes only of languid, ethereal beauty.

Love poetry of the twentieth century is the most varied and sexually explicit since classical antiquity. T. S. Eliot diagnoses the sexual sterility or passivity of modern man. Yet Neruda writes searing odes to physical passion, boiling with ecstatic elemental imagery. D. H. Lawrence similarly roots the sex impulse in the seasonal cycles of the animal world. Recalling long-ago, one-night pickups of handsome, athletic youths, Cavafy declares sex the creative source of his poetry. For Yeats, woman's haunting beauty is the heart of life's mystery; in "Leda and the Swan," rape is the metaphor for cataclysmic historical change. Rilke contemplates the philosophical dilemma of love, the pressure upon identity, the tension between fate and freedom. Valéry makes language erotic: the poet is Narcissus and, in *La Jeune Parque,* the oracle raped by her own inner god. Éluard sees woman erotically metamorphosing through the world, permeating him with her supernatural force. Lorca imagines operatic scenes of heterosexual seduction, rape, or mutilation and in "Ode

to Walt Whitman" denounces urban "pansies" for a visionary homosexuality grounded in living nature. Fascinated but repelled by strippers and whores, Hart Crane records squalid homosexual encounters
in subway urinals. Amy Lowell vividly charts the works and days
of a settled, sustaining lesbian relationship, while H. D. projects
lesbian feeling into Greek personae, often male. Edna St. Vincent
Millay is the first woman poet to claim a man's sexual freedom: her
sassy, cynical lyrics of Jazz Age promiscuity with anonymous men
are balanced by melancholy love poems to women. Auden blurred
the genders in major poems to conceal their homosexual inspiration;
his private verse is maliciously bawdy. William Carlos Williams is
rare among modern poets in extolling married love and kitchen-
centered domestic bliss.

For Dylan Thomas, youth's sexual energies drive upward from
moldering, evergreen earth. Theodore Roethke presents woman as
unknowable Muse, ruling nature's ghostly breezes and oozy sexual
matrix. Delmore Schwartz hails Marilyn Monroe as a new Venus,
blessing and redeeming "a nation haunted by Puritanism." The free-
living Beats, emulating black hipster talk, broke poetic decorum
about sex. Adopting Whitman's chanting form and pansexual theme,
Allen Ginsberg playfully celebrates sodomy and master-slave scenarios. In "Marriage," Gregory Corso imagines the whole universe
wedding and propagating, while he ages destitute and alone. The
Confessional poets weave sex into autobiography. Robert Lowell lies
on his marriage bed paralyzed, sedated, unmanned. Anne Sexton
aggressively breaks the age-old taboo upon female speech by graph-
ically exploring her own body in adultery and masturbation. Sylvia
Plath launched contemporary feminist poetry with her sizzling ac-
counts of modern marriage as hell. With its grisly mix of Nazi fantasy
and Freudian family romance, "Daddy," after Yeats' "Leda," may
be the love poem of the century. John Berryman's *Sonnets* records a
passionate, adulterous affair with a new Laura, her platinum hair
lit by the dashboard as they copulate in a car, the modern version
of Dido's dark "cave." *Love and Fame* reviews Berryman's career as
a "sexual athlete" specializing in quickie encounters. The sexual
revolution of the 1960s heightened the new candor. Hippie poetry
invokes Buddhist avatars for love's ecstasies. Denise Levertov and
Carol Bergé reverse tradition by salaciously detailing the hairy, mus-

cular male body. Diane di Prima finds sharp, fierce imagery for the violent carnality of sex. Charles Bukowski writes of eroticism without illusions in a tough, gritty world of scrappy women, drunks, roominghouses, and racetracks. Mark Strand mythically sees man helplessly passed from mother to wife to daughter: "I am the toy of women."

The 1960s also freed gay poetry from both underground and coterie. James Merrill, remembering mature love or youthful crisis, makes precise, discreet notations of dramatic place and time. Paul Goodman, Robert Duncan, Frank O'Hara, Thom Gunn, Harold Norse, and Mutsuo Takahashi intricately document the mechanics of homosexual contact for the first time since Imperial Rome: cruising, hustlers, sailors, bodybuilders, hikers, leather bars, bus terminals, toilets, glory holes. Gay male poetry is about energy, adventure, quest, danger, beauty and pleasure amidst secrecy, shame, and pain. Lesbian poetry, in contrast, prefers tender, committed relationships and often burdens itself with moralistic political messages. Adrienne Rich and Judy Grahn describe intimate lesbian sex and express solidarity with victimized women of all social classes; Audre Lorde invokes African myths to enlarge female identity. Olga Broumas, linking dreamy sensation to Greek sun and sea, has produced the most artistically erotic lesbian lyrics. Eleanor Lerman's *Armed Love*, with its intellectual force and hallucinatory sexual ambiguities, remains the leading achievement of modern lesbian poetry, recapitulating the tormented history of Western love from Sappho and Catullus to Baudelaire.

TOURNAMENT OF
MODERN PERSONAE:
D. H. LAWRENCE'S
WOMEN IN LOVE

The two deepest thinkers on sex in the twentieth century are Sigmund Freud and D. H. Lawrence. Their reputations as radical liberators were so universally acknowledged that brooding images of Freud and Lawrence in poster form adorned the walls of students in the Sixties. Yet the voluminous and complex works of both men were swept away by the current women's movement, when it burst out in the late Sixties and consolidated its ideology in the Seventies. Whatever their motives, the first feminist theorists acted as vandals and Bolsheviks. The damage they did to culture has in the long run damaged the cause of feminism. Perhaps

In the late Seventies and early Eighties, a diluted and censored version of Freud began to dribble back into academic feminism from two directions, one French Lacanian and the other American psychiatric, but it remains the case that very little Freud is directly read in women's studies and that a majority of feminists, in and out of academe, are hostile to Freud and refer to him with cheap derision. The situation with Lawrence is even more extreme. As far as women's studies is concerned, he has ceased to exist. A horde of minor, politically correct women writers has replaced him in the curriculum.

Many of our most talented women students are graduating from college without having read not only Freud and Lawrence but other major figures like Ernest Hemingway, Henry Miller, and Norman Mailer. An embarrassed student recently asked me hesitantly whether I permitted papers to be submitted on Hemingway. When I enthusiastically assented, she said she had hidden her interest in Hemingway for years and that close friends at once-distinguished Vassar College were viciously negative about him—without, of course, ever having read him. This is scandalous. Hemingway virtually invented modern American prose, the lingua franca of journalism; his style develops and strengthens you as a writer. What have we done to young women in the name of feminism?

In my original projection, the first volume of *Sexual Personae* was to end with Lawrence and Woolf. The latter material was contained in a mammoth 160-page seminar paper, "Male and Female in Virginia Woolf," which I obsessively produced for my last graduate seminar at Yale in 1970. But the Woolf boom in feminism happened shortly afterward and sent many a Woolf admirer running for the hills. As for Lawrence, the abundant Anglo-American literary criticism on his work was already excellent. There was no need for the kind of sexual rescue operation that I eventually performed, for example, on the admired but defanged Emily Dickinson.

Times have changed. Twenty-five years later, theory has supplanted literature, and criticism has degenerated into moralistic text-trashing. Those who love Lawrence, or any of the other ritually abused dead white males, must speak. I will focus here on *Women in Love* (1920), one of my book of books and a key to my sensibility. When I first read it in 1969, it seemed thin, tinny, strange, but it began to work on me subtly and became a profound influence on my thinking as I was designing *Sexual Personae*.

The most startling effect was that *Women in Love* collapsed in my mind with Edmund Spenser's *The Faerie Queene* (1590), which I was studying at the time and which was suffering from a grotesquely sanctimonious criticism of paralyzing dullness. Two authors more apparently dissimilar than Spenser and Lawrence could scarcely be imagined. But the representational style and sexual vision of their major works seemed parallel to me. Iconography and epiphany: In *Women in Love*, as in *The Faerie Queene*, aggressive, highly ornamented personalities burst on the eye in quick passages of ritual combat. Sex seems to ebb and flow in manic peaks and velvety lows of sadism and masochism, an oscillation of violent energy and torpid self-obliteration.

Women in Love, with its poetic language, mythic archetypes, and eerie occultism, is more a Romantic than a modernist or realist novel. Its theme is both nature and culture—the primal Dionysian forces within us and the rational Apollonian structures we have devised against our chaos. Each principle is shown moving toward its point of excess: the Dionysian spinning into barbarism and the Apollonian hardening into fascism.

Partly because of his proletarian roots, Lawrence is hypersensitive to social class and documents working-class experience without sentimentalizing it. Contemptuous of bourgeois niceties, he is conscious of his complicity, as a writer, with middle-class experience. Wealth and aristocracy appear in his work as artifice and mannerism, a glamourous imprisonment of mind and body. Hermione Roddice, the eccentric, somnambulistic socialite based on Lady Ottoline Morrell, is his most extravagant example of class as burden and destiny.

Women in Love analyzes industrial capitalism with harsh Blakean metaphors that dissolve the psychological into the economic. Greed and lust fuse, as in *The Faerie Queene*'s catalog of deranged appetites. A coal magnate, Gerald Crich, is Lawrence's incarnation of the European will to power; he is an idolator of the machine and of a rapacious phallicism. Exploitation is dissected as a dynamic of compulsive, self-consuming desire. The novel contains a far subtler and more revolutionary critique of Western sexuality than anything in academic feminism or poststructuralism. Rupert Birkin, its brooding, author-identified protagonist, is a nonconforming male, pale and sensitive, who seeks sensory modes of knowledge outside the iron frame of the West's imperialistic abstractions.

Lawrence sees the social spectacle with more completeness than do the usual glum puritans of the Marxist school. Only Arnold Hauser, in his vast Marxist masterwork, *The Social History of Art*, has integrated aesthetic values with class analysis as successfully as Lawrence in *Women in Love*. Fashion here is as signficant as economics. Body language, costume, speech, artistic tastes: for Lawrence, culture is a public theater of symbolic action.

In *Women in Love*, anthropology is a subset to zoology. Lawrence's radical new perspective introduces to the genre of the social novel Sadean and Darwinian perceptions about the continuum of humanity with the animal world. In her lavish getups of velvets and feathers, Hermione seems like a gigantic partridge on the prowl. The Brangwen sisters' yellow, rose, and emerald-green stockings are emblematic, in the Spenserian sense, and also sexually coded, the paradings of provocative mating display, appreciatively registered by men in the street. For Lawrence, society is a carnival of the animals. Instinct drives us in ways philosophy fails to acknowledge and science still cannot fully explain.

Women in Love is structured by a series of close encounters with animals, objects, persons, even plants. There are chattering canaries, a drowsy lap dog, a bullying tomcat, a terrified, rearing horse, and a "great lusty rabbit" who, "magically strong," goes wild in Gudrun's grasp. In a brilliantly original scene, bizarre, impressive, and ludicrous all at once, Gudrun taunts a herd of long-horned cattle with "palpitating" eurhythmic exercises, avant-garde and yet archaic, a modern bull-dancing.[1]

Goaded beyond endurance by Birkin's officious preaching, Hermione smashes at his skull with an oppressively vivid lapis lazuli paperweight, the blows falling with hypnotic slowness. Fleeing to the woods, Birkin purifies himself by rolling naked in the wet grass and stinging his flesh with sharp boughs and needles. The tactile sensuality of his ravishing embrace of vegetable nature is rivaled in Romantic literature only by cardinal passages in Keats, Whitman, and Christina Rossetti. Like Rousseau, Birkin escapes from mankind to wed himself to his origins.

Later, the emotion is reversed: rebelling against the omnipotence of woman, symbolized by the Magna Mater, Birkin crazily attacks and shatters the moon's reflection in a pond. But the "heaving, rocking, dancing" fragments magnetically rejoin; the "luminous polyp," with its "arms of fire," inexorably recovers and triumphs, mocking man's pretensions and conceit.[2] Lawrence's precursors in the dazzling execution of this savage scene, with its uncanny luminescence and dark psychic turbulence, are Coleridge and Melville, visionaries of uncontrollable nature.

While the close encounters of *Women in Love* are all highly ritualistic, those with objets d'art are overtly cultic. The novel has three sculptures, each representing a major region of the world. The first, a wood-carving from the West Pacific, is of a naked woman crouching in the agonies of childbirth. The "transfixed, rudimentary" face suggests "the extreme of physical sensation beyond the limits of mental consciousness." In the chapter called "Totem," Birkin defends the statue to a "shocked, resentful" Gerald, who denies it can be art.[3] This is the period when Picasso's generation of artists in Paris was being influenced by non-Western tribal artifacts.

The second sculpture is a "tall, slim, elegant figure from West Africa in dark wood, glossy and suave." Contemplating its "crushed tiny" face and heavy "protuberant buttocks," Birkin realizes that there are "great mysteries to be unsealed," expressing something "far beyond any phallic knowledge, sensual subtle realities far beyond the scope of phallic investigation."[4] Lawrence sees the human body in holistic or yogic terms: energy is released or blocked by cultural assumptions. Each organ or muscle group has symbolic corollaries and is a source of special insight. *Women in Love*, in a manner too easily ridiculed, is full of lush references to "loins," the complex pelvic area that Lawrence rightly sees as withered and demeaned in the West.

The third sculpture, a bronze statuette by a cynical, troll-like Austrian artist, is of a small, naked adolescent girl perched on a massive, "rigid," straining stallion, her legs dangling "pathetically" and "childishly."[5] Whereas the Oceanic and African sculptures show woman sacred and solitary, paradoxically dominating through her passive experience of brute nature, the European art work is predicated on a misunderstanding of sexual physics. Masochistically dependent, the woman has surrendered her mythological power to the male, who becomes a tyrannous phallic fetish. Lawrence is suggesting that when woman rejects her special intimacy with natural process, she trivializes and diminishes herself and guarantees male hegemony. This difficult lesson has yet to be learned by contemporary feminism.

Lawrence's use of the close-encounter format in *Women in Love* is almost masquelike, as in the episodic vignettes of *The Faerie Queene*. The plot is literally a process of looking for meaning, as life offers random experiences and frustrations. Things appear and disappear, after highly charged confrontations and conflicts. Momentary revelations explode at Lawrence's characters in ways their Western mental categories can't quite contain or order. The effect is almost elemental, like squalls, cloudbursts. Indeed, the baffling frenzy of the rabbit is described as a "black-and-white tempest," a "thunderstorm."[6]

One of Lawrence's major insights, a basic principle of Hinduism and Zen Buddhism, is that words cannot possibly correspond to or fully convey ultimate truths about life or the universe. By rhythmic repetition, surreal imagery, and heightened, operatic phrasings, Lawrence uses language to break through language in ways far beyond French poststructuralism, with its bourgeois pendantry and preciosity. The characters of *Women in Love* struggle toward understanding, their rational and verbal resources overwhelmed by the influx of unsorted sensory data and by eruptions of amoral unconscious impulses.

"Water-Party," a chapter that is nearly a self-contained Noh play, stunningly illustrates Lawrence's technique of illumination through disintegration. As darkness falls, strings of paper lanterns, like "ruddy creatures of fire," hover on boats over the lake. The scene is exquisitely beautiful. Birkin, with his usual mix of the oracular and the pompous, is discoursing to Ursula Brangwen about "the silver river of life" versus "the black river" of dissolution, "our real reality": Aphrodite represents not just love and sex but "the flowing mystery of the death-process." Myths are alive, changing as we change.

As Birkin and Gerald warily court Ursula and Gudrun, the tranquil mood of tingling erotic expectancy is suddenly shattered by "a confusion of shouting" and churning water across the lake. What has happened? To whom? How? Fear, helplessness, uncertainty, as the lovers, rushing to help, seem as frail as the glowing lanterns. Through the darkness come snatches of broken speech and a girl's shriek, almost like a stammer: "Di—Di—Di—Di!" Gerald's teen-aged sister Diana, heedlessly dancing on the roof of a party cruiser, has gone into the water; her rescuer, a young doctor, has not resurfaced.

Shortly afterward, numbed by futile dives into the icy water, Gerald sits "black and motionless," "his head blunt and blind like a seal's, his whole appearance inhuman, unknowing." He is defeated. Even the most imperious will is rebuffed by material limitation. The unknown world is always greater than the known. The entire episode is a paradigm of the novel as a whole, which endorses descents to levels of experience too remote for articulation. Beyond the heaving foreground of human agitation stretches the infuriating calmness of nature, blank and indifferent.

The lake's sluice-gate is opened; all night the "terrible crushing boom" of the water goes on, like the roar Wordsworth hears above the clouds on Mount Snowdon. Near dawn, the bodies are found: "Diana had her arms tight round the neck of the young man, choking him. 'She killed him,' said Gerald." Such refusal to sentimentalize is one of the most startling qualities of *Women in Love*. Birkin too says, even before the lake is drained, "What does it matter if Diana Crich is alive or dead?"[7] Gudrun is shocked, but Birkin's curtness is a philosophical detachment like Mrs. Moore's stern withdrawal in Forster's *A Passage to India*, where Western and Far Eastern conceptual categories clash after a mysterious occurrence in the heart of nature.

Like Freud, Lawrence strips away the false frills of Victorianism, the lugubrious pieties of institutionalized humanitarianism, which have sprung to renewed life in our own time. Because he has no illusions about our innate altruism, Lawrence is a keen analyst of criminality, which, again like Freud, he sees simmering in all apparently civilized people. In a typical conversation in *Women in Love*, jolts and surges of hostility and aggression go on just beneath the surface. The subtext is far more primitive than in Henry James, since Lawrence has taken our unruly carnality into the purview of his fiction. Sexual attraction is shown as an unstable complex of love-hate, a war for individuality and survival.

Lawrence's descriptions of criminal violence arising out of ordinary events—sex-tinged attempted murders by Hermione and Gerald—are chilling and compelling, in the tradition of Poe and Dostoyevsky. They were pivotal to my understanding of the psychopathology of rape, which mainstream feminism has reduced to naive, simplistic formulas. A superb example of Lawrence's command of the subliminal is the rabbit scene, where Gudrun's arm is scratched: seeing the "deep red score down the silken white flesh," "the long red rent of her forearm," Gerald absorbs the wound in erotic terms, as in the dream process or the metaphor-making poetic mind.[8] Lawrence constantly shows the mutuality and complicity of sexual response on the nonverbal level—precisely what is missing from the current clumsy date-rape discourse.

Though he has a reputation as a misogynist, Lawrence's picture of modern sexual relations is highly accurate. Like Blake, he shows the difficulty of heterosexuality, the anxieties men suffer as they try to escape the shadow of their mothers, who rule their lives in ways most feminists fail to see. To what degree should men obey or defy women? How far can a man develop himself emotionally before losing the respect of other men? What is masculinity for middle-class men divorced from the daily labor of their forefathers? How much of sexual desire comes from nature, how much from culture? Who is our ideal mate? Should love challenge us or put our questions to sleep?

The episode in which Gerald, haunted by the ugly death of his ailing father, tramps through muddy fields to invade Gudrun's bed-chamber should be basic reading for every student of sex. Yearning, coercion, and lust intermingle, as in life itself. What do men want from women? It's all here. Gerald's convulsive orgasm exorcises his anguish and tension—but at the cost of infantilization. Ironically, his phallicism makes woman a goddess and him a "child."[9]

Lawrence shows the unstable dynamic in heterosexuality, which swings man from conqueror to slave in the drama of arousal. Satisfied, Gerald sinks into delicious, healing sleep, like an infant "at its mother's breast," but Gudrun "lay wide awake, destroyed into perfect consciousness"—one of the novel's most terrible moments. It is a brutal modern version of Botticelli's *Venus and Mars,* borrowed by Spenser for a pornographic vampire scene of *The Faerie Queene.* Spenser, Blake, and Lawrence all show fallen sexuality as a cruel cycle of dominance and submission, where male power and male neediness are identical and where woman drinks man's energy as he spills it.

Throughout *Women in Love,* an unmistakable emotional and sexual attraction crackles between bookish Birkin and macho blonde Gerald. In the chapter called "Gladiatorial," the two lock themselves in a room and wrestle in the nude, their bodies amorously intertwined, till one collapses half-conscious on the other. They clasp hands, compliment each other's physical "beauty," and share a whiskey and soda.

We are in a period where homoeroticism of this kind is automatically interpreted as homosexuality, which I think is wrong. Birkin seeks *"Bruderschaft,"* blood-brotherhood with a male, a desire so significant that Lawrence ends the novel with it. After Gerald is found frozen to death in the snow (an Apollonian ice-sculpture, the novel's fourth objet d'art), Birkin tells Ursula that she is "all women" to him, his eternal mate, but he wanted "eternal union with a man too." Ursula, piqued, insists he can't have "two kinds of love."[10] Like *A Passage to India,* the novel ends with union between men defeated.

Despite the bisexual implications in *Women in Love,* I am skeptical about whether Lawrence would endorse full sexual relations between men. Surely, erections are missing from the wrestling episode, as part of the novel's questioning of phallicism. Western athleticism, which still overwhelmingly centers on the pitting of male against male, may be a structured positioning of homoeroticism in culture. That is, it is not a concealed or displaced homosexuality; instead, homosexuality may be a ritualized compromise for a *Bruderschaft* not otherwise obtainable. Though both *The Rainbow* and *Women in Love* (its sequel) explicitly address male fear of woman, Lawrence suggests that woman must be dealt with in all her natural power. Those who do less have narrowed their vision.

Lawrence was writing at a sea-change in sexual history. Gudrun Brangwen is a new kind of woman, confrontational and demanding; her speech is nervy, abrupt, and exclamatory. Seventy-five years later, it still sounds fresh and contemporary. The slow, majestic Hermione Roddice, with her aesthetical ambitions, remains the grand lady, bridging the period between Henry James and Bloomsbury. Virginia Woolf, for example, despite her feminist ideals, projected a public persona closer to Hermione than to Gudrun. As a woman, Gudrun shatters tradition and decorum; exuding aggressive sexual energy, she wields her sarcasm like a weapon.

When I first read *Women in Love,* I was drawn to Gudrun and resented the way Lawrence treats her as a foil to Ursula, whose serene, patient, self-effacing motherliness toward men seemed like everything my generation was rebelling against. Over time, however, the enduring truth in the contrast of sisters became clear. I used to be troubled by Lawrence's belittling remarks about feminists, whom his collected works portray as shrill, humorless, and desexed.

I now realize that Lawrence was accurately recording the fanaticism of a political movement in its late phase. The major thrust of nineteenth-century feminism was winning women the right to vote, which was achieved, in nation after nation in Europe and North America, in the early twentieth century. But major innovations, including the birth of artistic modernism, psychoanalysis, and Hollywood, were also changing attitudes and behavior and, in fact, overtook feminism and passed it. The sexual revolution of the Twenties was not produced by feminism. On the contrary, aside from Margaret Sanger's controversial birth-control movement (courageously supported by Katharine Hepburn's parents), too much feminist energy was diverted to moral-welfare causes such as the drive to ban liquor and prostitution. Fourteen years of Prohibition, and the spread of organized crime, were the result.

Lawrence's caricatures of feminists seem realistic again, since the current reborn women's movement similarly veered toward fanaticism, not just among the anti-pornography and anti-beauty ideologues (today's Carry Nations) but among mainstream activists whose obsession with feminist rhetoric has supplanted all larger philosophical or cultural concerns. I now recognize in the dissatisfied, word-obsessed Gudrun Brangwen the bright, perfect, brittle, overcontrolled women careerists of the legal, corporate, and academic worlds who have risen to prominence in the last twenty years and who coolly schedule their delayed pregnancies and professional childcare by time clock. Their destined mate is Gerald Crich, the ultimate capitalist manager, patron of the body reduced to a machine.

At a time when gender theory follows either strict social constructionism or a sentimental cult of benevolent nature, Lawrence's insights are of utmost importance. He sees humanity as unevolved, our ideals in daily conflict with animal urges we wrongly ignore or denigrate. Inspired by Frazer's epic prose-poem, *The Golden Bough*, Lawrence wants to recover our sense of primal mysteries, long lost in the West. He protests against the tyranny of abstractions, a product not only of reactionary institutions but of bourgeois liberal ideology.

Lawrence's importance for the Sixties was not just as a prophet of sex but as an expander of consciousness. For him, love in the Western sense is not enough; he would reject today's idolatry of "relationships" as parochial and limiting. As a Romantic, he exalts profound understanding over politics. In *Women in Love*, modern personalities clash in the new arena of sex, their words splintering and smashing like the lances of Spenser's knights. At the end of the century, the sexes are still at war. But there is a dawning sense that we must look back to nature to find out who we are.

1. *Women in Love* (New York, 1960), pp. 232, 159.
2. Pp. 239–40.
3. Pp. 67, 71.
4. P. 45.
5. Pp. 419–20.
6. P. 232.
7. Pp. 164, 181, 177.
8. Pp. 234–35.
9. Pp. 337–38.
10. Pp. 472–73.

BREVIARY OF THE NUDE:

KENNETH CLARK'S *THE NUDE*

One of the most influential books of my career was Kenneth Clark's *The Nude: A Study in Ideal Form*. Published in 1956, it was an expanded version of the six A. W. Mellon Lectures in the Fine Arts that Clark gave three years earlier at the National Gallery of Art in Washington, D.C.

My paperback edition of *The Nude*, small and compact as a breviary and tinted a cool blue-gray, is inscribed "1971." It was my third year of graduate school at Yale, and I was in the process of writing my doctoral dissertation, called *Sexual Personae*. I was scouring the great collections of Sterling Library, looking for ways to break through the academic disciplines, which had become too narrow and restricting. Revolutionary synthesis was needed.

The Nude came into my hands at a time when the most shrewdly ambitious graduate students were drifting toward Paul de Man, Derrida, Lacan, and Foucault, all of whom struck me as colossally uninteresting. In this, his greatest book by far, Kenneth Clark shows the broad learning, cultivation, emotional engagement, and passion for detail that are completely missing from the muddy maze-makers of soggy, foggy poststructuralism.

[*Times Higher Education Supplement*, London, December 10, 1993]

Boldly crossing 2,500 years of Western art, Clark assimilates and reorganizes an astounding wealth of material about the representation of the male and female figure. He avoids the convenient format of strict chronology and creates, in the core of the book, a brilliant series of meditations: "Apollo," "Venus," "Energy," "Pathos," "Ecstasy."

The Nude teaches us how to see. Anyone who has studied its 298 ravishing illustrations and been guided by Clark's elegant, nuanced prose will be blessedly impervious to current feminist cant about "the male gaze"—that puritanical superstition cooked up by ideologues with no instinct for art. Clark's interpretative style is simultaneously deeply sensual and crisply intellectual. Few scholarly books have so successfully combined seduction and instruction.

Clark's categories of the Crystalline and Vegetable Aphrodites, partly inspired by Plato, impressed me immediately, and I used them to analyze everything from Spenser's *Faerie Queene* to Hollywood movie queens. Body type and personality are naturally and theatrically related, though you would never know it from today's slag-heaps of bombastic, Foucault-inspired rubbish that predicate the body as passive to a lumpish something called "power."

Like Sir James George Frazer's *The Golden Bough, The Nude* melts the images and objects of culture into a strange, majestic dream, an epic landscape of the mind. The ancient and archaic come alive, or rather they prove they were never dead. In sharp, striking phrases, Clark reanimates academic discourse: the Venus de Milo is like "an elm tree in a field of corn"; the hand of Ingres's Thetis is "half octopus, half tropical flower"; Michelangelo's nude Sistine youths are "high-strung to the point of hysteria."

If ever I was in love with a book, it was with this one. *The Nude* taught me how to lure and jab, refine and condense, dispatch and recall. It has its weaknesses, notably in Asian and abstract art. But Kenneth Clark's masterwork is a monumental achievement, marrying connoisseurship to historicism.

THE ARTISTIC DYNAMICS OF

"REVIVAL"

The Modern Review faxed Camille Paglia to ask whether she had anything to say on the subject of revivals.

Thank you for your inquiry about "revivals" in cultural history. It is certainly revealing about the sorry state of Anglo-American intellectual life that this question—one of the most interesting yet posed to me since the publication four years ago of *Sexual Personae*—has issued not from any university faculty or scholarly journal but from *The Modern Review*.

Today's trendy theorists, with their jargon-infested, choke-a-horse style, are incapable of dealing with this issue, since they have foolishly committed their careers to the passé poststructuralist hypothesis that history is fragmented and meaningless and knowledge futile. The last major work animated by that idea was *Waiting for Godot*, by Foucault's idol, Samuel Beckett, who no longer speaks for anyone but morose somnambules like Susan Sontag. Since *Godot*, popular culture has exploded onto the world stage and, by its titanic assertions and vulgar vitality, shattered all the effete, elitist assumptions of literary modernism.

[*The Modern Review*, London, March 1994]

From childhood, when I became obsessed with the twin pagan phenomena of Hollywood and ancient Egypt, I have been passionately convinced of the continuity of Western civilization, which rises and falls with strange, haunting regularity. Recovery and revival seem built into our mental system. In "Junk Bonds and Corporate Raiders," I rejected the currently fashionable faith in the relativity and therefore nullity of value judgments in canon-formation: "The mythic pattern of Western culture is Greek revival: again and again, objects are lost and refound, overvalued, devalued, then revalued. But the classics always remain." Our rich popular culture, with its speeded-up revivals, has simply inherited the deep structure of classicism.

Throughout the sterile era of French theory, I clung to my belief in the great narratives of cultural history and the periodicity and organicism of artistic style. My influences here were, first, Vico, Spengler, and Yeats, whose vision of cataclysmic 2,000-year cycles was drawn from pagan astrology, of which I was a Sixties convert. Second, Mircea Eliade, who examined the motif of recurrence, or the "eternal return," in world religion.

Third, Heinrich Wölfflin, whose analysis of early, high, and late styles in painting beautifully applied, I immediately saw, to the career of the Beatles, from the rough vigor of "Boys" and "Chains," through the shapely perfection of "Day Tripper" and "Ticket to Ride," to the disintegrating sophistication of the studio-bound *Sgt. Pepper* and "White Album." At the end of that tripartite pattern, major artists revolt, resimplify, and return to the start, as we see with Donatello and Picasso, as with John Lennon, Bob Dylan, and David Bowie. We are all waiting, with some impatience, for Madonna to get around to this. Ever since she shucked her brash, streetwise, disco-tart persona, out of which she made her best music, her career has been built entirely on revivals, from Monroe to Dietrich.

Postmodernism's mingy synthetic substitute for revival is "appropriation," which usually means an artist of limited talent jumbling together, without insight, ironic references to great works of the past. I despise it, since I admire grandeur and expressiveness, whether in Bernini's revival of imperial Roman style; the marmoreal, neoclassic Federal architecture of Washington, D.C.; the ersatz Oxbridge Gothic spires of Yale; or Great Britain's extraordinary blues revival of the Sixties, which brought back to American shores, via the Rolling Stones, a raised consciousness about our black musical heritage.

Appropriation and pastiche are misconceived notions, promulgated by English-department drones with no sense of history. In point of fact, we belong to an Alexandrian age of syncretism, in which multicultural allusions fuse to make eccentric new wholes. I call our time decadent—but in *Sexual Personae* I argued that decadence is a complex historical mode, a thrilling, sensationalistic late phase of culture dominated by themes of sex and violence. In decadence, the major revival is of the primitive, which is juxtaposed with the supersophisticated. We see this pattern in Nero's cruel banquets, in Swinburne's poetry, and in the recent popularity of sadomasochistic regalia and tribal body-piercing. "Archaizing"—a term used by scholars of classical art—is infinitely preferable to the snide, competitive, destructive "appropriation." Archaizing is still reverent; it stitches the present to the past; it says nothing is ever lost.

Popular culture is a splendid laboratory to study the artistic dynamics of revival. Paradoxically, it forces a reassessment of high culture at a moment when we are crushing the heads of the serpents of theory. To consider influence and tradition brings one back to the canon, which is simply the body of work that other artists—not just critics and professors—consider the touchstone for creation and innovation. When Lenny Kravitz does his florid homage to the brilliant Jimi Hendrix, we see canon-formation in action, which all the gripes of generic Nineties grunge bands cannot stop. Revival means the dawning recognition of a timeless element in a work or style that seemed dated, confined to, and limited by a particular period. Therefore revival is crucial to the process of defining greatness in art, a responsibility shirked by too many of the lightweight luminaries of current academe.

SONTAG, BLOODY SONTAG

When I was in junior high school, *Women's Day* magazine, to which my mother subscribed, published a satirical memoir of a woman's disconcerting chance encounters with several famous people. My favorite was her adventure in a ladies room with Tallulah Bankhead, who mistook her for an old friend and delivered a long monologue from inside the toilet stall. A cartoon showed a fur-clad Tallulah hanging over the saloonlike swinging door and gesturing languidly at the stunned but fascinated writer, who never did get a word in edgewise.

I guess Susan Sontag is my Tallulah. The paperback edition of Sontag's first essay collection, *Against Interpretation,* appeared in 1967, while I was in college. It was among a dozen books that defined the cultural moment and seemed to herald a dawning age of revolutionary achievement, by students of the Sixties as well as by Sontag herself. Unfortunately, things did not turn out that way, and we're still trying to figure out why. Sixties thinkers lacked staying power. Like the Romantics, they seemed to spend themselves with their early efforts.

Against Interpretation was the high point of Sontag's reputation. Its importance at the time was its constellation of subjects: literature, film, theater, philosophy, anthropology; the artistic avant-garde (happenings); the sexual avant-garde (camp, drag). Sontag was learned yet anti-academic. Her essays, accessible to an educated general audience, helped to break the stranglehold that the over-professionalized universities had on "serious" thought in America. The glamourous dust-jacket photo imprinted Sontag's sexual persona as a new kind of woman writer so indelibly on the mind that the image still lingers, wraithlike, and makes criticism of her very difficult. She was the dream date of bookish men and the chic Deirdre-of-the-Sorrows alter ego of educated but genteel, white, middle-class women, the latter of whom emerged as and remain (surely not to her satisfaction) her primary audience.

I admired *Against Interpretation* for three reasons. First, it dissolved the disciplines in a way that was crucial for the future of intellectual life in America. As a college student, I fiercely opposed the rigid departmentalization and overspecialization of academe. Since she had been pursuing graduate work in philosophy and comparative religion, I expected Sontag would soon turn her attention to the American university and use her sophisticated rhetorical skills against it. But when her dissertation did not materialize, she drifted from academe and affected snobbish scorn for it without trying to change it.

As happened to the scintillating Germaine Greer, Sontag's separation from the university weakened her work over the long haul. The discipline of academic scholarship can kill and deaden but also refine and strengthen major talents of Greer's and Sontag's dimension. Harold Bloom scribbled in the margin of a draft of my dissertation in 1971, "Mere Sontagisme!" It saddened me, but I knew Bloom was right. Sontag, who should have been Jane Harrison's successor as a supreme woman scholar, had become synonymous with a shallow kind of hip posturing.

Reexamining Sontag's work for passages to cite in my dissertation, I was dismayed and frustrated. There was a line-by-line evasiveness in the same essays that had seemed so stimulating in college. I found no argument, only collage. Many of the generalizations or rapid-fire summaries now seemed, on the basis of my further study, questionable. Sontag seemed more and more a literary journalist rather than a philosopher or intellectual. But this was a period when first-person journalism was a performance art: I was avidly following the media adventures of Norman Mailer, Gore Vidal, and Jill Johnston.

The second reason I admired *Against Interpretation* in college was its frank interest in popular culture, with which I had been obsessed since childhood. I had never made the slightest distinction of value between the brilliant images of classical art and archaeology and those of Hollywood, television, advertisements, and pop music. What I thought I saw in Sontag was a fellow pop devotee, someone equally determined to smash the false dichotomy between high and low art. Sontag's "The Imagination of Disaster," a deep-structure analysis of science-fiction films, remains one of the best things ever written about popular culture. It is required reading in my "Mass Media" courses. This lucid, funny, ingenious piece should have started an entire school of pop criticism. Alas, academic commentary on popular culture lurched in another direction and ended up deep in the postmodernist morass. It is surprisingly difficult to find lively, accessible, jargon-free readings in popular culture to assign to undergraduates. "The Imagination of Disaster," in content and form, is an excellent model for speculative student essays.

Unfortunately, Sontag herself abandoned what she had started. Defending pop culture was highly controversial at that time. One could not be taken seriously as a thinker if one's remarks jumped so easily into hot copy in the glossy magazines. Sontag buckled under the abuse. She began to distance herself not only from pop but from American culture itself. Saturnine European writers—mostly male—soon dominated her work. Sontag made herself the hand-maiden of esoteric theory. At first her championing of Roland Barthes kept her ahead of academe, then in the doldrums of late New Criticism. But poststructuralist theory became a global industry in the Seventies and made Sontag irrelevant. Her career as a cutting-edge commentator and tastemaker has never recovered.

Sontag's calculated veering away from popular culture is my gravest charge against her. When in a 1988 profile in *Time* magazine, she denied she had ever been that interested in pop ("It isn't as if I wrote an essay on the Supremes") and boasted that she did not even own a television set, I was appalled and disgusted.[1] Not having a TV is tantamount to saying, "I know nothing of the time or country in which I live." Television *is* America, and year by year it is be-

coming the world. Sontag's betrayal of pop, to one who has never
lost the faith, is unforgivable, since as a graduate student and young
teacher, I shoved my pop acolytism down people's throats and took
the career hit for it. Yup.

The third reason I admired *Against Interpretation* was simply for
its public theater, its thrilling debut of an *au courant* woman intellectual. As an adolescent, I had fixed on Dorothy Parker and Mary
McCarthy as the only available female role models in the literary
life. I loved their tough realism, bare-knuckles pugnacity, and witty
malice. Like my idols Amelia Earhart and Katharine Hepburn, they
had the feminist freedom and adventurous cosmopolitanism of the
Thirties. Women in the placid, boy-chasing Debbie Reynolds/San-
dra Dee era seemed bland and timorous. As for Simone de Beauvoir,
whom I admired enormously after reading *The Second Sex* in 1963,
her rigorous intellectuality did not allow for humor or the irrational,
and her world was sternly pre-pop. With *Against Interpretation*, Sontag
revived and modernized the woman of letters.

The Romantic ideals of individualism and freedom that inspired
Sixties political protest also energized women to take their place on
the cultural stage. When the women's movement became a national
force late in the decade, that individualism began to be redefined in
narrowly feminist terms. Here is where Sontag, as the nation's premiere woman intellectual, could and should have played a leading
role. In 1972 she wrote a sensible article on women and aging that
implicitly acknowledged the new feminist agenda but then pulled
back, perhaps because of a mandarin disdain for the increasing
vulgarity and (as she put it in a withering 1975 exchange with
Adrienne Rich) "anti-intellectualism" of feminist rhetoric. Ironically, this was precisely when her infatuations began with European
male writers—who seem to be substitutes for the lost father figure
she admits she has always mourned.

Sontag's cool self-exile was a disaster for the American women's
movement. Only a woman of her prestige could have performed the
necessary critique and debunking of the first instant-canon feminist
screeds, such as those by Kate Millett or Sandra Gilbert and Susan
Gubar, whose middlebrow mediocrity crippled women's studies from
the start. It was Sontag who should have risen to the defense of
aesthetics, as feminism careened off on its Stalinist, anti-art track.

And with her expertise in French theory, it was she who could have exposed Hélène Cixous, Luce Irigaray, and their legion of Anglo-American imitators for the sloppy, third-rate thinkers they are. No patriarchal villains held Sontag back; her failures are her own. We have all, Greeks and Trojans alike, paid the price for Sontag's lounging in her tent.

Arriving at my first teaching job at Bennington College in 1972, I was still fully supportive of the women's movement and confident that it could correct its own errors and excesses. I was determined to be an uncompromising role model for young women and to put the radical new ideas about gender and sexual orientation into circulation on campus. My major courses—"Aestheticism and Decadence," "Women Writers," "Bloomsbury"—focused on deviant sexuality but always promoted the dignity and independence of art. With the students, I organized a women's film festival and wrote the program notes for movies (*Born Yesterday, Adam's Rib*, etc.) that illustrated modern female archetypes.

As chairman of the speakers committee of the Literature and Languages Division, I resolved to bring women of achievement to Bennington, despite the limited budget of an impoverished art school. Susan Sontag was my leading candidate, but it was a struggle to get the proposal accepted, partly because of her high fee. Not everyone thought as highly of Sontag as I did, and inviting a speaker merely because she was a woman was not yet socially acceptable. On April 9, 1973, in my second semester at Bennington, I drove two hours to Dartmouth College in New Hampshire to hear Sontag speak and, if I could, to pitch the idea of a visit to her directly.

An unseasonable snowstorm on that dark spring day made travel slow and perilous. Parking in haste to rush to the lecture, I left my headlights on. After her presentation, I spoke to Sontag at length and did interest her in coming to Bennington, though sufficient funding was iffy. Returning to my now moribund car, I realized (after terrifying fireworks caused by a bumbling mechanic blowing out the solenoid) that I would have to stay overnight in Hanover. Racing back to campus, I intercepted Sontag, who asked a lecture organizer to put me up for the night on her couch.

The car crisis gave me more time to converse with Sontag and observe her in action. It was the period when she was directing films in Europe, and she had a very stylish, lean look—boots, trousers, turtleneck sweaters, big belts, flowing scarves. Neither Mary McCarthy nor Simone de Beauvoir had such a persona or would have been able to carry it off. Though she denies it now, Sontag has always been hyperconscious of her theatricality and used it to great effect. I was excited by her performance at Dartmouth, since it convinced me that I was right to press for her invitation to Bennington and that she would make a spectacular impression on the students and convert the male faculty doubters.

Negotiations began in earnest to bring The Visit off. There was resistance in many quarters, but I won the support of the new college president, Gail Thain Parker (who had been hired at 29, in what may have been the last gasp of Sixties youth cult).[2] All available money was pooled: it was twice what Bennington had ever paid any speaker. But the total was still only half of Sontag's normal fee. Though her publisher, acting as her agent, opposed her accepting that amount, Sontag nonetheless agreed to come as a favor to faculty member Richard Tristman, a friend from graduate school at Columbia.

In the melancholy postmortem, I saw that the seeds of disaster were already sown in that preliminary agreement. Bennington, paying twice its normal amount, expected double the quality. Sontag, accepting half her fee, planned to exert half her normal effort. As Oscar Wilde said, "When the gods wish to punish us, they answer our prayers." The great day arrived: October 4, 1973. I blanketed the campus with posters and flyers announcing, as per our negotiations with her, that Sontag would speak about general cultural issues and answer questions afterward. I whipped up my students to bring all their friends for this extraordinary experience.

Sontag was scheduled to arrive from New York in late afternoon, go directly to the president's house to freshen up and chat, then be picked up by me for dinner with faculty at the Rain Barrel, a French restaurant in North Bennington. After that, we would go directly from dinner to the lecture site, the quaint old Carriage Barn. The appointed time of Sontag's arrival came and went. Like a lonely lookout in a Western potboiler, I tensely waited at the top of the great drive that sweeps up from the college gate. At last a car, and at last Sontag, nearly two hours late, fast asleep in the backseat and

looking as rumpled and haggard as a derelict. Horror and apprehension swept over me as she finally arose, puffy, groggy, and dis-
oriented, to return my greeting.

Civilized relaxation at the president's house was now impossible,
so after a quick hello there, it was lickety-split to the Rain Barrel,
where time seemed to stop. Sontag refused to be hurried. With a
sonorous flourish, she ordered steak *au poivre*, which seemed suitably
grand and exotic. Conversing aimlessly with the other guests, she
proceeded in a maddeningly leisurely manner through the various
courses and wines. I felt we were in hellish slow motion.

The start time of the lecture floated by. Emissaries began arriving from the Carriage Barn: it's full; it's been full for an hour;
the crowd is impatient; the crowd is angry; the crowd is fit to be
tied! Nothing I did or said budged Sontag in the least. Frantically
gulping wine, I realized, by the time she was ready to move, that I
was drunk but blessedly glad of it. Fortunately, it was a short drive
up the hill to the Carriage Barn which, as we entered, was tangibly
simmering with hostility.

In photos of Sontag and me standing before the crowd as I
introduced her, I am waving my arms around in what was certainly
a grotesquely unnecessary manner. Bacchus knows what I said, but
I do recall bounding around the centuries and invoking the *salon*—
as in "not since the female savants of the *ancien régime*," blah, blah.
Clearly smiling somewhat incredulously in the photo, Sontag
stepped up to the podium and said good-naturedly, "That was the
most . . . *unusual* introduction I have ever received!" This brought
down the house. It was the last light moment of the evening.

Collapsing onto a chair, my duty over, I prayed Sontag would
now dazzle the multitudes with the free-form cultural commentary
for which she had been billed. Instead, she removed a thin set of
folded sheets from her jacket and began to read from them. It was,
she said, a short story she had recently written. My heart sank.
Much as I admired Sontag's essays, I thought that her two novels
were awful and that she had little talent for fiction-writing. Bennington was known for its creative writing program; several of the
prominent writing instructors had been among the most openly dismissive about a Sontag visit.

A pall settled over the crowd. The story was bleak and boring.

It was, of course, about nothing, in the *nouveau roman* way. Inertia and spleen. The packed Carriage Barn was half asleep, half hissy. I avoided the glaring eyes and ominous signals of my students, perched on the balcony, and tried to ignore the smug, "I-told-you-so" expressions on faculty faces. I fantasized about having a heart attack and being carried out feet first. Finally, mercifully, it was over. There were some half-hearted questions and flat, desultory responses. But it was very late and the unhappy crowd restless. The applause was perfunctory. We decamped.

Then the reception. It would have made sense to hold the party on campus, but Bernard Malamud, Bennington's semi-resident star (and general pain in the ass), had insisted on giving it at his house. So everyone had to pile into cars and parade several miles to town. As I drove Sontag, I was surprised to learn she and Bernard had never met. What exactly happened at the party, I don't know. But one thing was crystal clear: Malamud—probably with his usual intolerable air of pious paternalism—shot something nasty at Sontag, and she was fuming. "He invites me to his house to insult me!"— she repeated this several times in my car on the way back to campus afterward. She said that Malamud's wife, greeting her at the door, had stammered, "Hi, I'm Ann Ma-Ma-Malamud." Sontag snorted, "I should have known what kind of man he is by the fact that, after thirty years of marriage, his wife still can't say his name!"

Sontag's fury seemed to energize her, and our conversation became lively. After we pulled up to the president's house, where she was staying the night, she sat slouched in her seat and talked for almost an hour. What struck me immediately was that, while at Dartmouth and for the entire evening at Bennington, she had been "Sontag," cool, detached, austere, and lofty, she now turned in the blink of an eye into "Susan," warm, gossipy, and distinctly Jewish in speech and manner. The transformation was startling. Hence I reject Sontag's present claims that it was the media or the misogynous establishment that, because of its discomfort with women thinkers, projected a false bitch-goddess persona onto her. Sontag, who was schooled in Los Angeles, created a high-profile property and sold it. Mazel tov! We need more women stars who can run their own studios.

Sontag spoke freely about her life. She told me about her friend, the actress Nicole Stephane, the gorgeous young girl in Cocteau's *Les Enfants terribles*. Stephane had recently broken an ankle and was confined by her doctors to her chair; since she was physically active, this was torture to her. Whereas, said Sontag with a smile, she herself had always been physically inert and would welcome as a dream come true doctors' instructions to sit in a chair and do nothing but read for six weeks! We talked about other beautiful women—for example, Adriana Asti, whom she had cast in her own film, *Brother Carl*.

At one point, I gently chided Sontag about her lateness and brought up the unplanned reading of the short story, both of which, I said, had put me in a bad position as her sponsor and host. She explained her being dead asleep in the car this way: she was, she claimed to me, "lazy," and her method of doing her essays was to "stay awake for two weeks." Hence her fatigue on arrival in Vermont. I thought to myself: "Well, now I know why her essays seem so disorganized."

Naturally, I avoided giving my real opinion of the vapid short story *du jour*. But my attempts at praise of Sontag's early essays were strangely rebuffed. About the famous "Notes on Camp," she gruffly declared to me: "Oh, I don't care about camp or homosexual taste any more. Once I write about a subject, I lose interest in it." Popular culture: equally boring, except for her own films. (I lauded the striped furniture in *Brother Carl*. She was pleased; she had chosen the fabric.) I grew more and more aggravated by her arch indifference to everything she had glorified in *Against Interpretation*. Piqued, probably, by Richard Tristman, an early supporter of mine, she asked about my own work, the then-in-progress *Sexual Personae*. I replied, but our minds did not connect. Something was missing.

My impatience, after that long, stressful day, became overt. Finally, she asked, half irritated, half amused, "What is it you *want* from me?" I stammered, "Just to talk to you." But that was wrong. I wanted to say, "I'm your successor, dammit, and you don't have the wit to realize it!" It was *All About Eve*, and Sontag was Margo Channing stalked by the new girl. In the car, Sontag and I pleasantly dished like yentas but made no contact on any other level. It was many years before I realized what the primary problem was. Though only fourteen years separate us, Sontag belongs to the generation before World War II. Born in 1947, I'm a pop culture baby. My brain, for better or worse, is completely different from hers. Her mind moved too slowly, because my generation's synapses are electronic and our circuitry hyperkinetic.

The next day, and for weeks afterward, I had to endure a chorus of derision about the Sontag visit. It had been a debacle. Never again could one argue for major funding for a megastar. A year later, I brought Elizabeth Hardwick to campus for a minimal sum, but that was it. The Sontag visit assumed legendary status as a low-water reference point. It became an inside joke at Bennington about any dreaded drudgery: "Well, at least we don't have to listen to a Susan Sontag story!" It took me years to live down. Two decades later, when I began to be invited to lecture around the country, I remembered the lessons of that night. I have kept my speaker's fees unusually low, and I try to give maximum energy and effort to my performances.

While liking several pieces in Sontag's second essay collection, *Styles of Radical Will* (1969), I became increasingly critical of her work in the Seventies. *On Photography* (1977, first serialized in 1973–74) seemed thin and forced, exposing an unfamiliarity with art history and, oddly, a lack of instinct for visual images. *Illness as Metaphor* (1978) was clumsy and ponderous, like a graduate-school seminar paper. I hated Sontag's silence about homosexual issues in the twenty years following Stonewall. By the time she played catch-up in her wobbly essay on AIDS (1989), she was rightly clobbered by the gay-activist establishment, with whom I normally disagree. *On Photography* made me begin to see that Sontag's learning, aside from philosophy and religion, is almost exclusively concentrated in the modern period. Her pedestrian novel, *The Volcano Lover* (1992), and her corny playlet about Alice James and Emily Dickinson, *In Bed with Alice* (1993), demonstrate Sontag's incomprehension of any era before her own.

Sontag belongs to the Age of Beckett, in the aftermath of the Waste Land. There her position is secure. She is the successor to Mary McCarthy. She is more original and versatile than Julia Kristeva. She was born with as much talent as Simone de Beauvoir but did not develop it with the same tenacity; hence nothing she has done approaches the monumental achievement of *The Second Sex*. As much as the Foucault-obsessed New Historicists, she rejected and squandered her own great heritage of profound Jewish learning. Because of her European pretensions, she held herself back from American culture and has not had the influence she should have. She made herself an expatriate in her own land. But we are in a period of reassessment and recovery of reputations. With all her limitations, Sontag deserves to be read on campus far more than the imposters and double-dealers who run women's studies. At her best, Sontag represents independent thought and lifelong engagement with artistic and intellectual issues.

Now for the campy denouement. There is no doubt my attitude toward Sontag hardened during the long period when I could not get published. Throughout the Seventies and early Eighties, the material from *Sexual Personae* was uniformly rejected by scholarly journals and literary magazines. Only two excerpts (on Spenser in 1979 and Wilde in 1985) were printed before the completed manuscript was accepted by Yale University Press, the eighth publisher to look at it. I found particularly galling the wholesale rejections by *Partisan Review* (which had "discovered" Sontag) of the copious material on popular culture.

I began to see Sontag as queen of the cliquish New York literary establishment. Like Gloria Steinem, she became the consummate insider posing as an outsider. Sontag's gassiest effusions were treated as holy writ by *The New York Review of Books*. By the end of the Seventies, she had long lost her cultural centrality, but people could only whisper it; no one dared commit such an assertion to print. Sontag's royal insulation from reality was bad for her and catastrophic for American literary life.

By the time *Sexual Personae* finally appeared in 1990, I viewed Sontag and her coterie as fossilized petty tyrants. Interviewing me for the cover story, "Woman Warrior," for *New York* magazine (March 4, 1991), Francesca Stanfill heard the complete saga of my early admiration for Sontag, with the subsequent disillusionment. In the article, a photo of Sontag and me at Bennington was mordantly captioned with my bitter résumé of our encounter: "I thought she was going to be this major intellectual."

From the moment *New York* hit the newsstands, I became an unwelcome hot topic in Manhattan literary circles. The Yale edition of *Sexual Personae* had already been out for a year and had been dramatically featured in local bookstores. For example, Brentano's commissioned a giant blow-up of the cover and devoted an entire Fifth Avenue window to the book for a week. Tower Books, in Sontag's domain of downtown New York, installed a *Sexual Personae* electric-lightbox display that loomed over the entry staircase for two years. Nevertheless, Sontag would deny that she had ever heard of me.

Once *Sexual Personae* went into Vintage paperback in September 1991 and became a national bestseller, followed by the release a year later of *Sex, Art, and American Culture*, another bestseller, one might have expected some faint sign of recognition from Sontag. She could scarcely retain her claim to intellectual preeminence while not having heard of a controversial woman thinker of my international standing. A perhaps apocryphal story circulated that Sontag had once been amused, at a party, by a male writer who had been deeply influenced by Gertrude Stein replying to a question about Stein, "Who is that?"

Much of my residual respect for Sontag disappeared during the blitz of American publicity for *The Volcano Lover*. Cover stories for *The New York Times Magazine* and *Los Angeles Times Magazine* were uncritical, unctuously flattering, and deficient in basic matters of fact, notably about Sontag's political history.[3] Open warfare with the Sontag camp broke out that month. James Wolcott's profile of me in *Vanity Fair* ended with my Homeric boast, "I've been chasing that bitch for twenty-five years, and I've finally passed her!"[4] In the same article, Sontag's son, David Rieff, made a series of disparaging remarks about me and my work— surprising, since his mother was claiming she never heard of me. After this piece was published, reporters could not get him to comment further.

Shortly afterward, in the course of speaking about another matter to "Page Six," the famed gossip column of *The New York Post*, I expressed my outrage about Sontag's kid-glove treatment by *The New York Times*. "Page Six" turned the affair into its lead story:

> **Camille Paglia** has come not to praise **Susan Sontag** but to bury her. The fast-talking feminist has mounted an all-out attack on the modernist, claiming she's passé and "the

ultimate symbol of bourgeois taste." . . . "Sontag's been playing the intellectual bully, the intellectual duchess. I feel I am the avenger," Camille told us by phone. "I was an early admirer and now I'm her worst nightmare." . . . "Sontag has been defunct as an intellectual presence for 20 years," Paglia says. "She's been utterly reactionary in the fields of pop culture, feminism, gay activism, and French theory. I am the contender challenging the heavyweight, and I believe that with my new book I have emerged victorious."[5]

The article reported that Sontag was in Barcelona and that neither she nor her publisher would comment on my charges.

Within days, Sontag surfaced in Manhattan at the official book party for *The Volcano Lover,* which seethed with deliciously catty gossip about the Paglia–Sontag contretemps. Later that week, Sontag appeared on national cable for what was probably her first-ever live-television call-in show. The very first caller, apparently inspired by the prankish gods, asked about me. Hesitating for a moment, Sontag said "I don't know who she is." After her somewhat meandering reply to the next question, the host cut to a commercial, as Sontag appeared to make comically exasperated gestures.

The program was aired live on a Friday night. When I saw it rebroadcast Sunday afternoon, I was exultant. With my instincts as a counterpuncher (acquired from a lifetime of watching boxing and other sports on television), I sprang into action. By that night, I had talked to "Page Six." The next morning, before people even arrived in their offices for the start of the work week, the article appeared:

> Feminist **Camille Paglia** thinks she has author **Susan Sontag** spooked. [Here followed a description of the television program.] Paglia laughs that Sontag can "no longer separate illusion from reality. . . . She either has to acknowledge my ideas, or lie. She's a poseur. She's never had a challenger and she can't handle it. The empress has no clothes."[6]

Few things in my career have given me more pleasure than the lightning speed with which I was able to counterattack on that occasion. It was the revenge of pop, which Sontag had abandoned. The logy barons of the incestuous New York literary world were helpless against this kind of guerrilla warfare by gossip column. As a worshiper of old Hollywood, I felt that the combative spirit of Hedda Hopper was with me.

It had been twenty years since America's last big literary feuds. I loved watching Norman Mailer and Gore Vidal go at it. And there was Mary McCarthy versus Lillian Hellman, and Truman Capote versus Jacqueline Susann, a favorite diva of mine. Indeed, *New York* had prophetically called for a return to "literary pugilistics" in an article titled "The 1992 Literary Olympics," where Sontag and I are imagined "mixing it up."[7] I am a believer in pagan public spectacle, which simplifies and clarifies through dramatic symbolism. In my psychology, as in William Blake's, aggression heals repression. The sheer entertainment value of trashy literary feuds was demonstrated by the speed with which *Entertainment Weekly* picked up the story. Our photos were captioned: "Pugnacious Paglia and Silent Sontag." When asked what would happen if our book tours crossed, I replied, "We would slap each other silly."[8] I delighted in booting Sontag into a magazine she would normally scorn.

That fall, when she appeared on *Christopher Lydon and Company* on Boston public television, Sontag evidently realized it would be wise to show some signs of connection with life. Now she admitted that yes, she had heard of Camille Paglia, but it was only very recently—"two and a half weeks ago"(!). And it was through some newspaper clippings "a stranger" had kindly sent her. She indicated no awareness that I had written any books or that she had ever seen them, even through a telescope. When an incredulous Lydon pressed her on this point, she became haughtily snappish. Lydon printed a partial transcript of the exchange, with his ironic commentary, in *The Boston Phoenix*.[9] I had already told *The Boston Globe*, when it called, that Sontag's stonewalling was making her seem "crazy."[10]

When I appeared on his show (my third visit) the following March, a chuckling Lydon ran a clip of Sontag's remarks and asked me to respond to what he called her "massive denial." Laughing, I compared Sontag to Anne Bancroft as the prima ballerina in *The Turning Point*: "She is literally being *passed* by a younger rival, and she's not handling it, I'm afraid, very gracefully. . . . *I* am the Sontag of the Nineties, there's no doubt of it." Lydon spoke with amazement of Sontag's contempt for television and popular culture. I replied:

> Oh, she is so out of it! . . . Miss Mandarin did me such a favor by coming out with this novel. Everyone remembers the *old* Sontag, you see. They remember her as being beautiful, as being interesting, and suddenly they really see her, okay, for the first time. And they realize she's *dull*, she's boring, she's solipsistic. She knows nothing about contemporary life. She is not a very good writer any longer. And even this new novel—she's become the toast of the bourgeoisie! She's no longer even avant-garde.

What is the moral of this story? First of all, enormous early success of the Sontag kind can be destructive, not giving one time to develop as a thinker and writer. Celebrity can create an addiction to adulation, which is what I feel happened in Sontag's case, as in Madonna's. Intellectuals must take strong measures to remain outside the establishment and to avoid cronyism. Unchallenged power is absolutely corrupting. Sontag's abandonment of academe removed her from the daily challenges, frustrations, scutwork, and ego-leveling routine of teaching, which keep one honest. As I told Francesca Stanfill, when I rise, cursing, at six A.M. and drive into the city for my 8:30 class, I often remind myself, "Susan Sontag never did this!" Over time, a real job, in limiting and unglamourous circumstances, gives one a sense of reality, of the human norm. Leftists who don't work become bourgeois parasites.

My rivalry with Sontag went international, notably in Brazil and the Netherlands, which pitted us against each other in big, splashy pictorials. Sontag now responds to queries by calling me a "fool" or "repulsive," and saying, "Camille should go join a rock band"—an insult for her, of course, but a vision of nirvana for Sixties people.[11] Sontag's dated aesthetics were vividly demonstrated in the fall of 1993 by her bizarre descent, Beckett in hand, on Yugoslavia. When I heard that Sontag was directing *Waiting for Godot* in Sarajevo, I burst out laughing. "Little Susie Sunshine," I cried, "bringing good cheer to shellshocked Bosnia!" I was already on record as having called *Godot* "a repressive anxiety-formation of defunct modernism."[12] The play is the paradigmatic work of the pre-pop era of passive, nihilistic gloom, of loss of faith in nature, religion, or politics. Perhaps unfairly, I viewed Sontag's Sarajevo adventure as a ghoulish attempt to re-create her glory days, using other people's misery as a backdrop. "Gee," I remarked to a colleague, "I guess she can't find any plays to direct in Harlem."

Because she is divorced from mass media, Sontag may not have realized that her pilgrimage to Sarajevo had already been done six months earlier by several melodramatic American celebrities, including a soap opera star, photographed by *People* magazine as she wandered, looking very worried, through the rubble.[13] Bosnia had become the cult charity of television news shows. I angrily condemned it as a compulsive turning away from the more immediate and pressing subject of race relations in America, following the Los Angeles riots of April 1992. Given the crisis state of our urban neighborhoods, I found the national media's endless sob stories about wounded Bosnian white girls to be gratuitous and offensive. Where were the cameras in Philadelphia or the South Bronx?

Sontag's chic alienation from her country was eloquently expressed in her flight to Sarajevo. When a network news show dubbed her "Person of the Week" for this exploit, her publisher said onscreen, "Susan goes wherever there is suffering"—at which I guffawed so hard, I nearly sprayed my beer across the room. Her own city has plenty of suffering, but for various reasons it seems to be invisible to her. On the same program, Sontag called herself "conscience-driven."

If only Oscar Wilde were alive to do justice to the sanctimonious moralism of the old-guard literary world. Sontag's son and sneering coterie sit around like mournful basset hounds on deep-think talk shows sighing about Bosnia and denouncing the American government for not intervening, a dangerous exercise in which other people's sons would be killed. Our literary leftists have only themselves to blame for their failure to influence public policy.

Surely, intellectual style in the twenty-first century must be radically different. Popular culture cannot be wished away. Global politics will be refracted through telecommunications, the new universal discourse. Pondering Sontag's career, I feel with renewed conviction that progressive values have strayed too far from direct experience and become imprisoned in outmoded verbal categories. An elitist leftism is a contradiction in terms. But it's Sontag's party, and she can cry if she wants to.

1. *Time*, October 24, 1988.

2. For the end of the Parker presidency in a campus revolt, see Nora Ephron's shrewd account, "The Bennington Affair," *Esquire*, May 1976.

3. *The New York Times*, August 22, 1992. *Los Angeles Times*, August 16, 1992.

4. *Vanity Fair*, September (released mid-August) 1992.

5. "Page Six," *The New York Post*, August 14, 1992.

6. "Page Six," *The New York Post*, August 24, 1992.

7. *New York*, August 10, 1992.

8. *Entertainment Weekly*, September 18, 1992.

9. *The Boston Phoenix*, November 27, 1992. The interview was recorded September 23 and aired October 9.

10. *The Boston Globe*, October 24, 1992.

11. Zoë Heller, "The Life of a Head Girl," *The Independent* (London), September 20, 1992. Profile of Sontag.

12. "Junk Bonds and Corporate Raiders," *Sex, Art, and American Culture* (New York, 1992), pp. 210–11.

13. *People*, April 5, 1993.

BOOK REVIEWS

BOOK REVIEWS

THE STAR AS SACRED MONSTER

DAVID SHIPMAN'S

JUDY GARLAND: THE SECRET LIFE OF

AN AMERICAN LEGEND

The glamourous, tawdry lives of Hollywood stars are the hero sagas of modern life. Born in obscurity, driven by a dream, the great stars fight their way to fame and win their date with destiny. But fortune's wheel is ever turning: a combination of hostile external forces and swirling internal pressures transforms triumph and adulation into disaster and despair.

This classic paradigm, half Greek tragedy and half soap opera, is remarkably demonstrated in David Shipman's absorbing new biography, *Judy Garland: The Secret Life of an American Legend*. Mr. Shipman, a British film historian, treats his sensational material with a sober earnestness that at first seems flat and unadventurous but that eventually wins our respect and trust. A fan of Garland's since he "fell in love with her in a record shop in Oxford in 1955," he presents her flamboyant personality with unflinching honesty, neither moralizing nor minimizing her faults. Mr. Shipman's scandal-packed book reads like the war chronicles of a laconic, unflappable battle-front correspondent, with explosions going off and casualties everywhere.

Judy Garland was born Frances Gumm in 1922 in Grand Rap-

[*New York Times Book Review*, June 6, 1993]

ids, Minn. Her father, a singer and manager of a movie theater, had
left Tennessee with visions of show business. He was also, according
to Mr. Shipman, a homosexual. Garland's mother, who knew of and
later bitterly resented her husband's proclivities, had two daughters
by him and then tried to abort Frances, the third. Garland claimed
that her pushy mother took "great delight in telling rooms full of
people" about these attempts to prevent the child from being born.

As "Baby Gumm," Frances made her singing debut at 2½ and
brought down the house with her strangely powerful voice, out of
which came her mature "belting" style. Garland said her talent was
"inherited": "Nobody ever taught me what to do onstage." The
Gumms moved to southern California in 1926 to promote the career
of their tiny song-and-dance trio, the Gumm Sisters. Frances was
already spoiled and given to "sudden, terrible fits of temper." She
rapidly turned into an androgynous tomboy, "as if," says Mr. Shipman, "she were becoming the son" her father had craved.

Before long a boom time began for child actors: Hollywood
studios beat the bushes for the next Shirley Temple, who was America's panacea for the Depression. One night, George Jessel, intro-
ducing the Gumm girls, renamed them the Garland Sisters. Frances
boldly took the name Judy from a Hoagy Carmichael song. Jessel
later said of Judy, who had been billed as "the little girl with the
leather lungs," that even at 12 she sang like "a woman with a heart
that had been hurt."

Now began the period in Garland's life most familiar to us.
Under contract at 13 to Metro-Goldwyn-Mayer, she made several
films, including her first with Mickey Rooney and leading up to *The
Wizard of Oz* (1939). Garland said of these years, when she shuttled
between the set and the studio schoolroom, "My life was a combination of absolute chaos and absolute solitude." She was made to
starve what Mr. Shipman calls her "naturally pudgy" body, and
she secretly squirreled away cookies and candy bars from the studio
spies watching her every move.

Garland, Mr. Shipman reports, was soon taking appetite-
suppressing amphetamines, as well as Seconal prescribed by the
studio doctor. She needed pills to fall asleep and pills to wake up.
By 20, she was seriously addicted, in a vicious lifelong cycle that
would be dramatized in Jacqueline's Susann's wonderful *Valley of*

the Dolls, which was inspired by her. Mr. Shipman says that near the end of her life (she died in 1969) Garland was taking large quantities of alcohol and barbiturates, as well as up to 20 Ritalin tablets a day.

While her public image in the late 1930s was as "America's favorite kid sister," studio insiders knew, as Mr. Shipman puts it, that "the real Judy Garland was intense, headstrong, volatile." She married impetuously and found herself "completely unfitted" to run a house. She had her first two abortions and began to have affairs with both men and women.

Always drawn to gay men, Garland finally married one, the director Vincente Minnelli, who became her second husband and— to the astonishment of Hollywood sophisticates—the unmistakable father of her daughter Liza. Garland's behavior was becoming "increasingly erratic." Mr. Shipman reproduces fascinating M-G-M memos from such troubled productions as *Meet Me in St. Louis,* which tartly record Garland's lateness and surliness. Paralyzed by insecurity, she kept the whole set waiting day after day, much as Marilyn Monroe would do a decade later. After completing *The Pirate* (1947), Garland made her first suicide attempt and was forced to enter a sanitarium.

In 1950, after repeated incidents in which Garland's unreliable behavior added "as much as 20 percent" to the budget of her films, M-G-M fired her. She slashed her throat but lived. When the news of her suicide attempt leaked and made headlines, her career entered a bizarre new phase. Jobless and tormented, she was startled to find herself mobbed by idolatrous fans screaming, "We love you, Judy!" Her humiliation and suffering had made her an international diva, locked into a passionate symbiotic relationship with a cult audience that was heavily gay.

Garland's successive comebacks were engineered by her third husband, Sid Luft, whom Mr. Shipman credits with shrewd business sense and the patience of Job. There were stunning live performances in long sold-out engagements at the London Palladium and the Palace Theater in New York, which are still remembered by those lucky enough to have attended as peak moments in twentieth-century music. Garland's film career, except for *A Star Is Born* (1954), a box-office failure, was essentially over.

Mr. Shipman's book is strongest in documenting Garland's uniqueness and mesmerizing virtuosity as a stage performer in the 1950s and '60s. There are lavish citations from ecstatic British and American reviews, which strain for language to describe Garland's exquisite theatrical instincts, her stamina, vitality, and trembling tension, her operatic emotional depth and dynamic range. Like Puccini's Tosca, she lived for art. She was a creature of extremes, greedy, sensual and demanding, gluttonous for pleasure and pain. Her personal appearances were extravagant and, as one critic put it, "orgiastic," like tumultuous pagan festivals.

Psychology is not Mr. Shipman's forte, and he does little to explain Garland's hostility to her mother or her violently unstable union with Sid Luft and competitiveness with her own daughters. But his book admirably demonstrates the intricate interconnection of commerce and art in Hollywood. We get the grit of management, agents, contracts, bookings and ticket sales. And Mr. Shipman implicitly recognizes the link between genius and criminality. The great stars are sacred monsters, amoral vampires who drain those around them to feed the world. Judy Garland the person was a martyr to Judy Garland the artist, a supernormal being who destroyed as she created. Whew!.

MADONNA IN THE SHALLOWS

MADONNA'S *SEX*

Like a gleaming battleship with its publicity guns blazing, Madonna's long-awaited, aluminum-clad book, *Sex,* was launched on October 21—and promptly ran aground in shallows of its own making.

Jumbled and gimmicky, *Sex* was assembled with all the design skills of the average high-school yearbook. Pictures are drowned in an alphabet soup of cutesy typography. Color is chaotic. Cropping and pasting are banal.

The shocking amateurishness of this production casts doubt on Madonna's ambitions as an art collector. *Sex* should have been a major achievement, documenting and exploring Madonna's important artistic ideas for her core audience and a whole new one, the serious reading public who doesn't listen to pop music and whose view of Madonna is a tabloid caricature.

Apparently, no one among Madonna's advisers ever realized they were producing a *book*. A book is not a record or video. Provocative phrases must be patiently fleshed out on the page, not thrown into the air like confetti. Because of her flippant indifference

[*US,* December 1992]

to literary history and style, Madonna's attempts to be avant-garde self-destruct in a blizzard of clichés.

Is there anything of value in *Sex?* Yes, the battered but loyal Madonna fan, like a melancholy beachcomber sifting through the wreckage, can find glints and glimmers of the book-that-might-have-been.

Madonna boldly attacks establishment feminist ideology head on. She denies that "pornography degrades women." She praises *Playboy* and later poses with a *Playboy* bunny tail. I applaud her. The puritanism of American feminism is proved by the failure of its pro-porn wing to publicly embrace the men's sex magazines.

Even more daringly, Madonna shows a rape scene in a high-school gym as faintly pleasurable to the girl. She poses with legs spread on the rapists' pinball machine from *The Accused*. Many women, she asserts, stay in abusive relationships because they're "digging it"—a psychological truth ignored in our victim-obsessed culture. But Madonna's treatment of sadomasochism wavers: sometimes it's a decadent power trip, sometimes just a fun fashion statement. The book begins: "Sex is not love. Love is not sex." This is brilliant and momentous but isn't sustained.

The pictures are grouped in an ascending pattern, as in Dante: We go from the hellish prison-world of urban s & m sex clubs back to nature, the paradise of sun and surf. The southward movement from New York to Miami has European echoes: from Dietrich-era Berlin, with its jaded cabaret-crawlers, to the exuberant Mediterranean (Madonna flirts with Italian, eats pizza, and mimics Brigitte Bardot and Nancy Sinatra).

Unifying the book is the theme of bisexuality, or sensuality in general, as a liberated view of life. There are dozens of sexual combinations. Tactile sensations—fabric, fleece, leather, hair—are emphasized. Liquids stream or are swum in; there is frank dabbling in urination and sexual secretions. The book has Freud's "polymorphous perversity," the infant's indiscriminate total responsiveness.

Madonna's hypnotic autoeroticism is the most powerful thing in the book. She has the charismatic narcissism of all great stars. But this is what destroys the book as a whole. The pictures are best of Madonna alone, mistily communing with her own divinity. The pictures with others are awkward, sexless and contrived, "high-concept" bright ideas that fall with a thud. The star is a vampire sucking out everyone else's energy, including Naomi Campbell and Isabella Rossellini, who look sheepish and uncomfortable.

That Steven Meisel, a virtuoso of fashion ads, is an inept photographer of sex scenes was obvious a year ago in his waxy, sepulchral spread of Madonna as a Twenties lesbian for *Rolling Stone*. Herb Ritts is the supreme photographer of Madonna's smoldering sensuality. *Sex* struggles for Helmut Newton's elegant sophistication and never comes near it.

There *are* a few great images here. A masked Madonna slouching in a black-leather bikini. Bejeweled Madonna as a slinky Circe tapping along a herd of male slaves with her crop. Acrobatic Madonna as a pagan water sprite arched on a bronze porpoise. *My fave.* Tough-gal Madonna crouching to light a cigarette or, booted, straddling a radiator. Hitchhiking Madonna, hilariously nude except for high heels and a purse.

The list of bad or mediocre pictures is long, but standouts are a ridiculous series with tattooed lesbian skinheads, who look like scrawny plucked chickens and radiate all the sinister sexuality of *Yuk.* *The Brady Bunch*. Among trick pictures playing with androgyny and transvestism: Madonna's trampy kickoffs appear on the macho Vanilla Ice. There are lukewarm experiments in voyeurism, pederasty and bestiality, a very dull porno comic strip, and several steamy word-fantasies. But Madonna's eerie persona as Dita dominatrix finally fizzles. Dietrich Dita ain't.

Sex, wrapped in Warhol silver like an interstellar candy bar, promises a flight of imagination but delivers a very bumpy ride. The important issues it raises—the relation of love to lust, the sluttishness of the fully sexual woman—are never developed. That the book contains a CD signals an inescapable truth: in music and dance, Madonna does her deepest thinking. This is her emotional bond with her audience, a marriage of true minds on a global scale. And no matter how she acts, we will never divorce her.

MADONNA AS GAUGUIN

MARK BEGO'S

MADONNA: BLONDE AMBITION

Since her arrival on the scene ten years ago, Madonna has become so synonymous with sex and publicity that it may be hard to remember that she started as a *musical* phenomenon. As an ambitious young dancer, she dropped out of college in her native Michigan and arrived in New York in 1978 virtually penniless. Homeless and scrounging for food in garbage cans, she clung to her dream of fame and fortune and eventually caught the attention of a series of nightclub disk jockeys and record producers, who were struck by her eccentric fusion of avant-garde dance moves, disco-funk music, and hip urban waif fashion style. The rest, as Muse-mothering Mnemosyne might say, is history.

I write at a moment (February 1993) when Madonna's career is in an unprecedented trough. In the fall of 1992, she released a $50 coffee-table book of pornographic photographs, *Sex* (New York: Warner Books) that became a worldwide bestseller but that lost her crucial support among many people in publishing, media, and the fashion industry—not because the book is shocking but because it is boring, derivative, and sloppily thrown together. Yet *Erotica*, the moody album released simultaneously with the book, was Madon-

[*American Musicological Association Notes*, September 1993]

Limited # 6/37 taboos,

na's most personal and artistically adventurous, breaking the mold of frantic, upbeat dance music that had become her signature. Here she speaks honestly as an artist to her audience, heart to heart, below the level of that increasingly tiresome sexual persona that has run out of taboos to break.

Yup.
No
more
taboos.

Despite its dark beauty, *Erotica* did not have the blockbuster sales Madonna was accustomed to, partly because of its lack of peppy hit singles, and we soon saw pushy advertisements by her record company on MTV, something she never needed at the height of her career. Matters worsened when the first two videos for the album were either dull and murky ("Erotica") or ugly and silly ("Deeper and Deeper"—a brilliant song that deserved better). Madonna, who had pioneered the music-video revolution in the 1980s with dozens of stunningly conceived and photographed videos, most of which are now classics, seemed to be losing her magic touch. Had her real-life romantic problems sent her into a tailspin?

Madonna's longing for screen stardom began with her wonderful performance as a street scamp (based on herself) in the film *Desperately Seeking Susan* (Orion Pictures, 1985) and led to her central casting in two notorious bombs and a series of modestly successful supporting roles. But came the deluge: the debacle in January 1993 of the faux-s&m *Body of Evidence,* which was hilariously shredded by critics and audiences alike and may go down in Hollywood history as one of the worst turkeys ever made by a celebrity.

But Madonna has the ability to surprise you, to remake herself and rise phoenixlike from her own ashes. She has a bedrock support from loyal fans worldwide, who lived through her meteoric early career with her and will not abandon her now, even if her diversion of energy into movies causes some uneasiness among those (including me) who believe her real talents lie in music and dance. It is most unfortunate that Madonna's public-relations overkill and extracurricular escapades (baring her breasts at Jean-Paul Gaultier's fashion show, for instance) have overshadowed her artistic achievements and made it difficult, if not impossible, for cultivated and discriminating people outside the pop realm to see that she *is* an artist, a contention that seems to me indisputable.

Ironically, the temporary fall in Madonna's reputation has come at the very moment of a flash flood of the first serious books about her. The strongest of several biographies is by Mark Bego, *Madonna: Blonde Ambition*. Two essay collections have also appeared, the first academic and absurdly pedantic, the second largely journalistic but a lot more fun: *The Madonna Connection,* edited by Cathy Schwichtenberg (Boulder: Westview Press, 1993), and *Desperately Seeking Madonna,* edited by Adam Sexton and including a newspaper article by me (New York: Delta, 1993).

Current academic writing on Madonna—indeed, on American popular culture in general—is of deplorably low quality. It is marked by inaccuracy, bathos, overinterpretation, overpoliticization, and grotesquely inappropriate jargon borrowed from pseudotechnical semiotics and moribund French theory. Under the misleading rubric "cultural studies," intensely ambitious but not conspicuously talented, learned, or scrupulous humanities professors are scrambling for position by exploiting pop culture and sensitive racial and sexual issues for their own professional purposes.

In my opinion, writing on American popular culture should be simple, lucid, and concrete. If Jacques Lacan is mentioned, you can be sure you're dealing with an incompetent. The Madonna material produced by these desperately trendy academics is shot through with clumsy, pretentious terminology like "intertextual," "diegesis," "significations," "transgressive," "subversive," "self-representation," "subject position," "narrative strata," and "discursive practices." This would be comical, except for its ill effect on students and an increasingly corrupt career system.

Bego is the author of more than twenty celebrity biographies, many of whose subjects have been singers—among them Barry Manilow, Michael Jackson, Whitney Houston, Cher, Bette Midler, and Aretha Franklin. *Madonna: Blonde Ambition* profits from his deep familiarity with the modern music industry, whose commercial dynamic he understands without condemning or excusing it. The weaknesses in the book come from his unwillingness to press or explore legitimate criticisms of Madonna in the detail they deserve, perhaps because as a professional biographer he needs to preserve his access to and guarantee the goodwill of his famous subjects. Nonetheless, I highly recommend Bego's *Madonna* as a generally reliable and entertaining introduction to the career of this superstar. Its chronology of events fills gaps in our knowledge of Madonna and is invaluable to the student of recent popular culture.

Bego's account of Madonna's early years in New York vividly documents the carnival-like downtown dance-club scene, just emerging from the crazed, cocaine-fueled, more upscale Studio 54 era. Madonna's musical tastes from adolescence on had been Motown and soul rather than rock, which Bego notes was more her brothers' style. (Her recent dismissive remarks about a remarkable Guns n' Roses double album, heavily influenced by the Rolling Stones, bear this out.) In New York Madonna was exposed to Latino influences, coming from the clattering metallic percussiveness and complex polyrhythms of salsa, and with the help of an early boyfriend, the producer Jellybean Benitez, she fused them with the melting lyricism and earthy big bassline of black music. Bego is very helpful in his evenhanded reportage of Madonna's early collaborations with Benitez and his rival, Reggie Lucas. This period of Madonna's music, which produced the superb "Burnin' Up," remains my favorite, and I was delighted to see that so much about it was retrievable for the historical record.

Madonna was frequently accused of sleeping her way to the top or of simply being a puppet of Svengalis in the production booth. Bego's book lays such rumors to rest once and for all. As even her early and still bruised manager, Camille Barbone, admits, Madonna may have always used her sexuality to get what she wants, but her master plan for herself, and her grit and tenacity in bringing it to pass, is worthy of Cecil B. DeMille. But while Madonna has had enormous popular success, the respect of the music establishment and many rock critics still eludes her: she has never been nominated for a Grammy and claims to be resigned that she never will. Considering the number of highly individualistic and gorgeously produced hits that she has written or co-written and that became instantly canonical, this would appear a serious injustice.

Bego gives the first detailed descriptions of Madonna's crucial mentoring by a gay male dance teacher in Michigan; her magpie fashion borrowings from the stylist Maripol and the street-smart Debi Mazar; her public flirtation with the comedian Sandra Bernhard; and the sketchy negotiations with Pepsi-Cola that led to the scandal of the "Like a Prayer" video. However, Bego is not so satisfactory on a number of other episodes, for example, Madonna's performance as Marilyn Monroe for the Hollywood power elite at the Oscars, which was, he seems not to realize, a disaster. Similarly, he skims over Madonna's needling of a visibly irritated Arsenio Hall on his talk show, which led to another disaster, her next appearance there with the comedian Rosie O'Donnell, when Hall let the oafish, tittering women hang themselves before a mass audience.

Madonna's cruelty to her childhood friend, Moira McFarland, in the documentary *Truth or Dare,* goes unmentioned. The psycho-biography of Madonna's hot-and-cold relations to her siblings is a bit thin, as is the treatment of the lawsuit against her by three of her dancers. And there is little probing inquiry into Madonna's involvement with AIDS activism, which, while admirable in an eth-ical sense, has also addicted her to a tone of preachy self-righteous-ness that has not always benefited her or her causes.

While he frankly admits her "inability to deliver simple dia-logue" in her movies (p. 235), Bego lets Madonna off the hook about too many artistic matters, such as her failure to research the Phil-adelphia working-class accent required for her role in *Who's That Girl?* (Warner Brothers, 1987), which she arrogantly winged on the inept assumption that it is identical to a Bronx accent. He also records without comment the increasing number of projects she has been simultaneously engaged in, which has led, in my view, to the embarrassing failures of quality control in her recent work. She is seriously overextended.

Like Michael Jackson, Madonna may have become a prisoner of her own celebrity. Natural instincts are stunted and mutilated by the isolating artificiality of wealth and power. The most significant contribution of Bego's book is its establishment of Madonna's story as a Romantic saga of the artist-as-hero. Like the affluent Paul Gauguin, Madonna *made* herself deprived, as if to obliterate her protected middle-class origins in the squalor of a hand-to-mouth reality. Bego proves her suffering and sacrifice. What Madonna has, she earned. But can she survive success? Aging Romantics are in a race with themselves.

TYRANNY OF THE TECHNOCRATS

JOHN RALSTON SAUL'S

VOLTAIRE'S BASTARDS

John Ralston Saul is a Canadian writer whose four novels of international intrigue include *The Birds of Prey* and *The Paradise Eater*, set in Bangkok. His practical experience has been extensive: he managed an investment firm in Paris and served for ten years with the Canadian government oil corporation. Saul also has a doctorate from King's College, London; his thesis was on Charles de Gaulle.

Voltaire's Bastards, Saul's first published work of nonfiction, is an ambitious 600-page meditation on modern culture, tracing the roots of our troubled political, economic and intellectual systems back to the rationalism of the Enlightenment. Despite its frequent overstatements, ponderous format, and excessive bleakness, *Voltaire's Bastards* is a rich, rewarding, highly original book that casts a fresh perspective on all aspects of our public life. There are innumerable brilliant insights. Even when he gets his facts wrong—as sometimes happens in his rushed survey of literary and artistic history—Saul is suggestive and stimulating.

Saul argues that democracy is subverted by the dominance of rational systems of control that are essentially unreformable. The modern science of administration is king. Capitalism has been trans-

[*Washington Post Book World*, September 6, 1992]

formed; it is not the owners, the stockholders, but their amoral, faceless hirelings, the managers, who have unbalanced and bled the marketplace at no risk to themselves. The West is obsessed with a frenzied, sterile quest for ultimate efficiency. "Our obsession with expertise" has produced a master caste, technocrats who are consummate mediocrities. Whether in corporations or government, they are merely "number crunchers," "highly sophisticated grease jockeys" with "a talent for manipulation," who keep the machine humming. Our elites, like sycophantic eighteenth-century courtiers, stand for nothing but "cynicism, ambition, rhetoric, and the worship of power."

Saul's blistering indictment hits a great variety of targets—though not, regrettably, American academe, where self-propagating, overpaid technocrat-administrators are strangling education in a way that exactly proves his points. His account of the origins and influence of the Harvard Business School is fascinating: the founding Harvard deans were admirers of Frederick Winslow Taylor, whose theories of "Scientific Management" for industrial reorganization were also adopted by Lenin, Trotsky, and Stalin, and by Albert Speer in Nazi Germany.

The business schools and schools of public policy in America and Europe enshrine "abstract, logical process" and an "obsession with structures." Their students become "addicts of pure power," without goals or vision. The economic transition from manufacturing to a top-heavy service sector has exacerbated social problems. Nearly three-quarters of business-school graduates go on to cushy non-manufacturing jobs like consulting and banking. They avoid Pittsburgh and Birmingham, where the factories are, and settle in "the great centres of postindustrial self-gratification," like New York and London. Saul thinks this steering of top managerial talent away from nuts-and-bolts experience is a major cause of our industrial decline.

In some of the most startling material of his book, Saul argues that the modern, discreet, ruthless administrative style was created by Ignatius Loyola, founder of the Jesuit order, who was wounded by a cannonball passing between his legs. Though he claims religion is dead and comes perilously close to demonizing Catholicism, Saul is at his best in his comparison of the arbitrary investigative method of the Inquisition to that of today's police-state torturers. He makes clever connections: Descartes, pillar of the Age of Reason, was educated by the Jesuits.

But Saul tries too hard to build a case against the last five centuries, when in fact the trends he identifies are also discernible in antiquity. For example, his cold, cynical company man is the Caesar of Shakespeare's *Antony and Cleopatra* or the Creon of Sophocles' *Antigone*. And the amoral style of interrogation Saul claims was invented by the Inquisitors is already evident in Pontius Pilate's treatment of Jesus.

Voltaire's Bastards would be stronger with some consideration of the evolution of commercial and political bureaucracies in Mesopotamia and Egypt, which would demonstrate that the negative principles Saul isolates are universal and intrinsic to civilization and its discontents. The book also lacks sustained attention to the Greco-Roman origins of Western logic as well as to the complex status of reason in medieval theology. Even the presentation of post-Enlightenment culture suffers from a curious blankness about Romanticism, which Saul rarely mentions but which powerfully critiqued Western institutions and ideology from within.

Saul is superb, however, on military history, which is glaringly absent from the overliterary worldview of poststructuralism. With a novelist's instinct for historical sweep, he presents the staggering development of the arms trade, which has distorted and impoverished the world economy. Secondly, he shows how this "Armada complex" is a direct result of the victory of staff officers over field officers in the past two centuries, a phenomenon that led to the carnage of World War I.

Although he is unfair to Napoleon, whom he blames for inaugurating the pattern of godlike hero that would produce Hitler but that again has ancient precedents, Saul's profiles of military men from Lord Kitchener to General William Westmoreland are models of quick-take psychological astuteness. There are dramatic juxtapositions, such as a wonderful comparison of Cardinal Richelieu to Robert McNamara, against whom Saul levels devastating charges of incompetence.

The last chapters of *Voltaire's Bastards* feel like an awkwardly appended coda. Saul zips through five hundred years of literature and art, flinging out opinions from the fruitful to the bizarre. The current crisis in literary criticism, perfect grist for his mill, is passed over with a few disparaging remarks about deconstruction. Popular culture is treated in a dismissive, harrumphing way all too familiar these days. The discussion of Christian images ignores Protestant iconoclasm. But the book ends with a thrilling celebration of the revolutionary power of clear, simple language against the "professional obscurantism" of the establishment. I was moved and inspired by Saul's vision of the writer as "faithful witness."

Despite huge leaps, frustrating repetitions and organizational uncertainty, *Voltaire's Bastards* is a vigorous, continuously interesting rereading of the principal issues of our time. Its enormous cast of characters includes Machiavelli, Marie Antoinette, Walt Disney, James Baker, and T. Boone Pickens. Massively grounded in hard fact, the book unintentionally exposes the flimsiness and amateurism of New Historicism, a recent fad in literary criticism influenced by Michel Foucault that finds imperialism under every doormat. Saul's intricate analysis of the cold, mechanical operations of Western institutions and policy-making is informed and convincing where that of the careless, culture-bound Foucault was not. *Voltaire's Bastards* should be required reading for graduate students in the humanities. It would break through interdisciplinary barriers without the posturing and clichés of poststructuralism.

After so dire a picture of Western culture, we might expect some concrete proposals for reform. But Saul insists, perhaps to our disappointment, that the writer's mission is "questioning and clarifying," not providing solutions. In this, he has certainly succeeded. Rejecting the exhausted stereotype of left versus right, he opens up new lines of inquiry and creates new constellations of meaning. With his sophisticated international perspective and blunt freedom from cant, Saul offers a promising persona for the future: the intellectual as man of the world.

A WOMAN OF THE CENTURY

GERMAINE GREER'S *THE CHANGE*

Germaine Greer is back. Unfortunately, she's in a very bad mood.

Publication of *The Change* offers young American women an opportunity to get to know one of the great lost figures of feminism. When her wonderful first book, *The Female Eunuch,* was released in 1970, Greer cut a brilliant track across the cultural sky. She was witty, learned, sexy, and stylish. In her uproarious debate with Norman Mailer at New York's Town Hall, she tartly put men in their place and created a sophisticated sexual persona for female intelligence that has never been surpassed.

But Greer and feminism took a wrong turn. Within three years, the thrilling vivacity and humor had turned into dreary ranting. As feminist ideology hardened into political correctness in the Seventies, the dazzlingly gifted Greer tragically cheered it on instead of protesting. Her subsequent books, unevenly researched and shot through with dogma, never won Greer the academic respect that once seemed hers for the asking.

The Change, along with Gail Sheehy's recent best-seller about menopause, *The Silent Passage,* heralds a major shift in thinking about

[*People*, November 30, 1992]

gender. After more than twenty years of "social constructionism" (which attributes all sexual differences to social conditioning), women are ready to think about nature again. Hormones are back in fashion.

In *The Change*, Greer searches the lives of prominent women of the past for references to menopause—and finds frustratingly few. She surveys the history of menopause as a medical category and deftly outlines woman's fantastically complex endocrine system. To relieve menopausal distress, Greer endorses traditional herbal remedies and aromatherapy. She is skeptical about estrogen replacement, which she feels simply postpones the inevitable aging process. She argues that spiritual renewal, not plastic surgery, is menopausal women's best hope for happiness.

In her most fascinating chapter, Greer transforms the stereotype of the cursing, half-cracked crone or witch into a symbol of elderly women's solitude, freedom, and vision. This will surely prove inspirational to lonely widows or dutiful wives callously abandoned for younger women. But Greer backs away from her aggressive, malicious crone. Her last chapter—glorifying the noble, plucky female spirit bravely carrying on against all odds—is cloyingly sentimental, the kind of airy, uplifting effusion that was a staple of genteel ladies' magazines in prefeminist days. She strains for a glowing finale to what is a very dark book.

The robins and crocuses that suddenly pop up cannot conceal the fact that *The Change* seethes with vindictive bitterness toward men, who appear only as smelly, grotesque caricatures. Science and medicine are too often maligned here as a greedy, brutal, monolithic "male-supremacist" establishment. There are scattered slaps at "consumer culture" but no sustained political analysis. And let's face it: for all her professed socialism, Greer lives like a duchess.

Greer's glum sense of isolation may owe less to menopause than to her own misjudgments, as well as to a failure to rethink her rigid antimale feminist ideology. When she left the University of Warwick after the heady success of *The Female Eunuch*, Greer and academe both lost. Outside the discipline of the academic world, Greer's scholarly skills never developed. Her thinking is always stimulating but tends to dissipate itself in flashy spurts. She recently returned to teaching as an unofficial fellow of Cambridge University, but too much time was wasted.

Whatever the defects of her work, Greer is one of the women of the century. Her sharp tongue, vibrant personality, and spiritual odysscy will be just as vivid a hundred years from now as they are today. Indeed, Greer may be an even more powerful figure, freed from the burden of our expectations as her contemporaries and disappointed fans.

SCHOLAR, AESTHETE, ACTIVIST

EDWARD SAID'S

CULTURE AND IMPERIALISM

Edward Said, one of the leading literary critics of his generation, is a rare example of an American academic who is also an intellectual in the European sense. As a professor at Columbia University, he has produced ten books in more than twenty-seven years on subjects ranging from Joseph Conrad and French theory to Orientalism and musicology. As a Christian Palestinian educated in Egypt, he has analyzed and protested against the West's destructive misunderstanding of the Arab world. In short, Said is a brilliant and unique amalgam of scholar, aesthete, and political activist, an inspiring role model for a younger generation of critics searching for their cultural identity.

Said's new book, *Culture and Imperialism,* a collection of revised lectures originally given in the late 1980s in Great Britain and North America, extends his ideas into a rich variety of new as well as familiar areas, from the nineteenth-century realist novel to Italian opera and Irish poetry. Said's learning, like the humanistic perspective he espouses, is global. He is deeply immersed in comparative literature, and his omnivorous interest in and citation of recent groundbreaking interdisciplinary work by scholars of Africa, the

[*Washington Post Book World,* March 7, 1993]

Middle East, India, and the Caribbean are impressive and useful.

Culture and Imperialism has an eloquent, urgent topicality rare in books by literary critics, whose political thinking these days tends to be long on ideology and short on facts and practical experience. Said, unlike his pampered, cloistered brethren on American campuses, is a true man of the world. His most telling charge against such trendy styles as academic Marxism, New Historicism, postmodernism, and jargon-infested deconstruction is that they are "ahistorical." Said's efforts to mesh literary and political analysis into a single broad discourse succeed because of his own precision of mind and complex and unsentimental engagement with current affairs.

The largest theme of Said's book is the crossroads America faces after the disintegration of the Soviet Union: will we become the new British Empire, coercive caretaker of the world? Said notes a "depressing" similarity between the rhetoric of "self-congratulation" and "triumphalism" of pundits and politicians about the 1991 Gulf War and that of British sahibs in imperial India. Has America taken up "the white man's burden" as arrogant "civilizer" of other races and nations with their own traditions and destinies?

Said argues that Western culture of the nineteenth and twentieth centuries was formed in tandem with the political processes of imperialism, resistance, and decolonization. The complete interpretation of a significant number of masterworks from this period depends on acknowledging their implication in the formation and reinforcement of imperialistic assumptions. Said's thinking has been influenced by Michel Foucault and Frantz Fanon, but he uses their ideas sparingly and judiciously, without the coarseness of many less cultivated literary theorists today. For Said, art and politics are intermeshed; neither is subordinate to the other.

Said's view of "the consolidation of authority" in the novel form is strikingly illustrated in his penetrating discussion of Jane Austen's *Mansfield Park,* which he sees structured by a contrast between pastoral England and slave-holding Antigua—an opposition overlooked by mainstream readers. As always, he scrupulously cautions against reductiveness: he thinks of his reading as "completing or complementing others, not discounting or displacing them." In such memorable, finely turned phrases, which fill the book, Said shows his superiority to the dull run of overpoliticized critics with their tin-eared prose.

A short review cannot fairly summarize the important issues touched on in this book. In an ingenious analysis, Said movingly contrasts "the opulence of India's space" in Rudyard Kipling's *Kim* to "the lusterless world of the European bourgeoisie" as portrayed by nineteenth-century French novelists. The chapter on Verdi's "Aïda" was of special interest to me. Perhaps Said, in building this indictment against the imperialist commissioning of the opera by the Khedive of Egypt, unfairly underestimates the impact that the finale's dramatization of political tyranny has on an audience. Nevertheless, Said's rhythmic weaving of art, finance, and history feels natural and unforced. His account of the fate of the Cairo Opera House built for Verdi is tersely ironic: it burned down in 1971 and became a parking lot. As Said presents it, this comic decline seems to epitomize Europe's failure to comprehend or fundamentally alter the cultures it invaded.

The severe chapter on Albert Camus's *The Stranger* is wonderful. For Said, "the blankness and absence of background in the Arab" murdered in the book came from Camus's repressed awareness of the magnitude of French domination in Algeria. Against the norm, Said sees in Camus an "incapacitated colonial sensibility." The treatment of William Butler Yeats similarly stresses Ireland's legacy of imperial servitude to England, though Said might be allowing local references to overshadow the vastness of "Leda and the Swan," which sees Western history as a panorama marked by eruptions of cataclysmic violence.

Said opposes "identity politics" as a splintering new tribalism and criticizes Afrocentrism as much as Eurocentrism. He wants us to read "contrapuntally," with sharpened attention to all competing voices and themes in a work. My reservations about Said's approach are, first, that only a critic with his disciplined, surgical skill can succeed with it. In lesser hands, art gets mutilated by the rush to polemic.

Second, the problem Said is remedying may be confined to university literature departments, which lost contact with the research-based old historicism during the latter days of the New

Criticism, with its increasingly threadbare <u>middlebrow formalism</u>.
Time and again, I was dismayed by Said's caricature of the disciplines of anthropology, Egyptology, and Oriental studies, whose
massive scholarship in the nineteenth century is the foundation of
today's knowledge. As in his uncritical citations of Martin Bernal's
regrettably overideological *Black Athena,* he tends to accept others'
dismissal of a massive body of work of awesome learning and continuing relevance. Perhaps <u>what we need in the movement toward
multiculturalism is not new strategies of reading but a return to a
general education based on hard fact and respect for scholarship.</u>

Third, Said's definition of imperialism may be too limited by
overconcentration on the past two hundred years. <u>A political theory
must take in the full span of history, from the Egyptian, Persian,
and Roman empires to those of the Moors, Inca, and Japanese.</u> The
idea that exploration and empire-building are motivated only by
greed has to be modified by an acknowledgment that <u>economic
development has always been tied to hierarchical organization,</u> expansion, and exploitation of natural resources, <u>from the first state-
sponsored irrigation projects of the Tigris and Euphrates valley in
ancient Mesopotamia.</u>

Fourth, Said, like Foucault, neglects Romanticism in his portrait
of the past two centuries. <u>Romantic literature is itself a critique of
the limitations in imperial, patriarchal society that Foucault and
feminism claim to have discovered.</u> Said's equation of land with
property may be too materialistic: <u>Romanticism sees land as nature,</u>
the great missing term in the Foucauldian equation.

Fifth, Said's description of the international dominance of
corporate-owned mass media overrelies on negative Frankfurt-school
formulas that predate World War II. Media is more than news.
<u>American popular culture has seduced the youth of every nation
and may indeed be the best hope yet for international and communal
life.</u>

My other nagging questions would address why the British imperial system was so powerful in the first place. Military force alone
cannot explain it. <u>Objectivity and efficiency may be Western Apollonian myths, but they have been enormously fruitful as well as
oppressive.</u>

[Handwritten marginalia:]
Real criticism thats valuable

All of H. (not just some)

Camille's look is on all of history, not just part of 4!

Romanticism beat Foucault & feminism to the critical punch of patriarchy! LAND = NATURE ✓ early realist visual artists ✓ naturalists

D-

Said is a writer who challenges and stimulates our thinking in every area. He is a man of profound feeling and ethical imagination. His prose reminds me of that of <u>Walter Pater</u>'s *Marius the Epicurean:* it is sober, stately, lucid, and melancholy. Literary criticism, which is struggling to bridge the gap between art and politics, has everything to learn from listening to Edward Said's dialogue with himself.

Her favorite
mentor.

THE CORPSE OF FASHION

FRED DAVIS'S

FASHION, CULTURE, AND IDENTITY

This slim book has a most appetizing title. A scholarly exploration of fashion, culture, and identity should penetrate to the heart of our time. But Fred Davis, emeritus professor of sociology at the University of California, San Diego, seems ill-prepared to deal with any of these subjects in depth. The University of Chicago Press, following the lamentable lead of Routledge in mistaking trendiness for substance, ought to reexamine its editorial procedures, which have slickly repackaged Davis's earnest, plodding prose without offering him basic help in organization or conceptualization.

Neither the author nor the publisher of *Fashion, Culture, and Identity* seems clear about what audience it is intended for. Davis nervously eyes an invisible chorus of scowling fellow sociologists, to whom he attributes a snorting dismissal of the "frivolous" fashion industry and anyone silly enough to study it. To propitiate this baleful battalion of hanging judges, Davis loads his pages with a slag-heap of mind-dulling jargon and labyrinthine abstraction, so that the reader has the sensation of tunneling through debris to find the corpse of the subject. But then the tone changes, and we get a simple, unpretentious passage on some interesting but familiar mat-

[*Times Literary Supplement*, London, May 28, 1993]

ter, like the history of blue jeans. A few flying references to Barthes, Baudrillard, and Foucault seem added on as hasty afterthoughts to prove the book *au courant*.

Davis's primary thesis is that the rapid cycle of clothing fashion, spurred by capitalism, has been whirling since the court of Burgundy in the late Middle Ages and is somehow unique to Western culture. To prove this, Davis would have to show how changes of fashion in ancient Egypt and Babylonia, Mogul India, or imperial China and Japan were dissimilar. But his research into non-European cultures is nil. Davis's passing assertions that changing styles in clothing are inherently different from changing styles in literature, rock music, cars, or coiffures are unconvincing since, again, he has made no systematic inquiry into those areas.

A troublingly high percentage of Davis's material consists of long quotations from other authors, which unfortunately constitute the best-written passages in the book. In one of the clichés of current academic practice, *Fashion, Culture, and Identity* tries to disguise its failures of research and reasoning by jazzy chapter titles ("Boys will be Boys, Girls will be Boys") and piquant epigraphs. Then we are left on our own to thrash around in the jumbled, repetitive text, with its vague chronology and tortured English.

Davis's introductory chapter hails semiotics as our future salvation, in particular "its seminal notion of *code* as the binding ligament in the shared understandings that comprise a sphere of discourse." Leaving aside the flurry of mixed metaphors here, one notes the provincialism of this widespread belief: self-strangling semiotics did not invent the idea of "code," which was already central to anthropology, comparative religion, and art history, notably in Erwin Panofsky's theory of iconography, which has heavily influenced scholarship and classroom teaching for over fifty years.

Western culture, claims Davis, suffers from ambiguity and ambivalence of identity, which our ever-changing fashions serve to explore and express. This is a promising idea, but Davis's learning is not wide enough to do it justice. He has little familiarity with modern psychology or ancient Western history. Vague generalizations about Western identity that begin with medieval France and can't take in Sophocles, Catullus, or Nero are useless. Davis also makes wild overstatements about the prevalence of androgyny or cross-dressing in Western fashion, which has been only a sporadic phenomenon geared to specific transformations in sex roles. He is right to insist that fashion signifies far more than status, but he never fully nails down what that "more" is.

In a chapter with the promising title "The Dialectic of the Erotic and the Chaste," Davis again shows his limitations. Jean Fouquet's fifteenth-century painting of a stylish enthroned Virgin with a bared breast is simplistically underinterpreted for its "erotic-chaste tension." Here, as throughout the book, Judeo-Christianity is treated as a huge, monolithic, body-denying, sex-hating institution. The differences between Mediterranean Catholicism and Northern European Protestantism, or among different denominations of Protestantism, are not seen. Nor does Davis have the slightest inkling about similar conflations of exhibition and concealment in the pagan tradition: the virginal Archaic *kore* sculptures, the bare-breasted "Dying Amazon," the stately, bosomy, lounging goddesses of the Parthenon pediment, with their plastered, wet-look draperies, and the Hellenistic bathing Aphrodites, leading up to the Roman "Venus Pudica," or modest Venus, revived by Botticelli.

In "Stages of the Fashion Process," Davis tries to analyze the dynamics of the fashion industry from the designer's initiating idea through its material embodiment and display to the manufacturing of scaled-down versions of the garment for distribution to middle-class stores. But he bounces all over the map, with no feeling for period or place. We get newspaper cuttings and bland quotes from anonymous interviewees thrown in at random, and end up with a mushy pudding that will enlighten no one. For heaven's sake, the mechanics of the rag trade are common knowledge to us through dozens of movies and television mini-series. Susan Hayward has it all down in *I Can Get It for You Wholesale* (1951).

The fashion advertisements sprinkled through the book are striking and well-chosen, but Davis's commentary on them is usually inadequate or just plain wrong. For example, he misses all the complexities in the appealing jacket photo of a straw-haired gamine in a baseball cap: Huckleberry Finn, Li'l Abner, Jean Seberg, and 1950s beatniks (fisherman sweater and leotards). He grandly dubs the chic beard stubble of a young dude in a Perry Ellis suit a "disingenuous mistake," when it's an allusion to Jean-Paul Belmondo and 1930s gangster films.

I found this book tedious, uninformed, and unperceptive, first because, as a student twenty-five years ago, I grounded my own thinking about clothing in the excellent, rich, and still reliable fashion histories produced from the late nineteenth century to the second world war by such shrewd analysts as J. C. Flugel and James Laver. Second, I have been heavily influenced by gay men, with their keen sensitivity to and encyclopedic knowledge of the art of fashion and gesture, a connoisseurship of aesthetes descending through Oscar Wilde from Gautier and Baudelaire.

The witty gay style, dramatic and incisive, is our best hope for a sophisticated fashion discourse free from the moralistic anti-beauty ideology of establishment feminism and the incompetence and theory-mad cant of the "cultural studies" movement, from which Davis's work has emerged. Afternoon tea with your average drag queen is likely to be more rewarding and informative about fashion than is this choppy, meandering, confused book.

CRY OF THE INVISIBLE MEN

WARREN FARRELL'S

THE MYTH OF MALE POWER

Warren Farrell, author of *The Liberated Man* and *Why Men Are the Way They Are,* served for three years on the board of directors of the National Organization for Women in New York City. In his latest book, *The Myth of Male Power,* he describes how his career as one of "America's Sensitive New Age Men" skyrocketed when he endorsed the standard feminist view of women as "enlightened" and of men as "Neanderthals." He received standing ovations, lecture invitations, financial rewards.

But, Farrell states, as his position evolved toward one more sympathetic to men, the applause died and the money began to dry up. Reviewing tapes from his workshops and personal appearances, Farrell was troubled by his earlier double standard: "When women criticized men, I called it 'insight,' 'assertiveness,' 'women's liberation,' 'independence,' or 'high self-esteem.' When men criticized women, I called it 'sexism,' 'male chauvinism,' 'defensiveness,' 'rationalizing,' and 'backlash.' . . . Soon the men were no longer expressing their feelings. Then I criticized the men for not expressing their feelings!"

The Myth of Male Power is a quirky book, part confession, part

[*Washington Post Book World,* July 25, 1993]

polemic. Its organization, consisting of short passages with blazing headlines and overabundant boldface type, is somewhat awkward, choppy, and repetitious. Systematic argumentation is scanted, and there is sometimes a questionable selectiveness or credulity about historical sources, both present and past.

But Farrell's vices as a writer are also his virtues. His gruff, blunt manner breaks through the decorous white middle-class conventions and victim-obsessed sentimentality that have paralyzed establishment feminism in recent years. *The Myth of Male Power* is a bombshell. It attacks the unexamined assumptions of feminist discourse with shocking candor and forces us to see our everyday world from a fresh perspective.

Farrell feels that feminism's primary objective as a political movement—equal protection under the law, as guaranteed by the Fourteenth Amendment—has been lost in the "anti-male sexism" of affirmative action programs and other preferential regulations and grievance procedures that guarantee special protections to women and thus ironically perpetuate the pernicious old stereotype of "woman as child." The media, far from opposing and obstructing feminism (as Susan Faludi claims in *Backlash*), has cynically pandered to feminist pressure groups and indulged in "a quarter century of male bashing." As a student of media, I think Farrell is dead right about this.

In brutal, grisly language, Farrell dramatizes the carnage of "male-killing" throughout history—the one million men, for example, slain or maimed at the Battle of the Somme in World War I. Men are not, he insists, the powerful sex but "the silent sex" and "the suicide sex." They are "disposable," dispensable, slaves to higher powers. Men have sacrificed and crippled themselves physically and emotionally to feed, house, and protect women and children. None of their pain or achievement is registered in feminist rhetoric, which portrays men as oppressors and callous exploiters.

Farrell's blistering indictment makes powerful use of contemporary anecdotes. During the 1991 trial of boxer Mike Tyson for rape, the hotel where the jury was sequestered caught fire; two firefighters died. The media, obsessed with the tunnel-vision feminist view of "men-as-rapists," ignored this contrary evidence of "men-as-saviors." According to Farrell, there are a million municipal volunteer firefighters in America who valiantly "risk their lives to save strangers." A startling fact that should disturb and embarrass every feminist: 99 percent of these firefighters are male.

Again and again, Farrell demonstrates that, for all the official talk about desiring equality, the overwhelming majority of contemporary women continue to avoid hazardous, dirty, low-prestige jobs that men take in order to earn a higher income for their families. Miners, loggers, roofers, garbage collectors: Farrell celebrates the invisible men whose backbreaking and sometimes fatal work makes modern life smooth and efficient for pampered, feminism-spouting professionals in their safe, well-lit offices.

The Myth of Male Power is a muckraking exposé for the nineties. It uncovers an unsettling pattern of collusion between government-funded commissions on women and a coterie of feminist leaders and career consultants who claim to speak for all women. It demonstrates how biased surveys and shaky statistics have been used to swell the numbers of reported rapes or prove discrimination against women in employment, medical research, and the justice system. It quotes astonishing pieces of gloomy, anti-male agitprop from such putative reference works as *Encyclopedia of Feminism* and *The Women's History of the World*.

In the largest sense, Farrell sees contemporary gender problems as flowing from our historical transition from an epoch ("Stage I") where survival was the basic issue to one ("Stage II") where communication and cooperation, rather than competition, are required. Here Farrell's theories dovetail with the best in feminist theory: he sees the killer male as a dominant Stage I type unable to adapt to Stage II economic and ethical realities. Now we have a pressing need "not for a women's movement or a men's movement but for a gender transition movement" that would revolutionize both behavior and perception.

The Myth of Male Power is the kind of original, abrasive, heretical text that is desperately needed to restore fairness and balance to the present ideology-sodden curriculum of women's studies courses. Despite its technical flaws and raw inelegance, the book is filled with stunning insights and haunting aphorisms, such as "female beauty is the world's most potent drug."

Warren Farrell is one of many voices urging a critique and

reform of current feminism in order to strengthen it for the twenty-first century. As Farrell says, "discrimination begets discrimination begets discrimination." Equality means not just "equal options" but "equal obligations," a rejection of the passive role of perpetual victim. Government must not become modern woman's "substitute husband." Farrell calls for an end to the blame game and a new stress on personal responsibility, social maturity, and self-enlightenment.

SATIRES AND

SHORT TAKES

ASK CAMILLE PAGLIA:

ADVICE FOR THE LOVELORN,

AMONG OTHERS

When *Spy* asked me to write an advice column, I was delighted. I've loved this snappy American genre since I grew up reading tart-tongued Ann Landers in the Fifties—I even made up both the questions and the answers for satiric advice columns in my high school newspaper. The following letters are authentic, though sometimes condensed.

FEBRUARY

Dear Camille:

I've been with a woman for ten years. Should I propose marriage? My concerns are (1) her loathsome, self-pitying complaints and (2) my suspicion that I could not remain faithful.

Despondent in Oregon

Dear Despondent:

The crystal ball shows a tacky picture of a nag and a philanderer hurling crockery around the kitchen. Misery has enough company already. In fact, they're parking on my lawn.

[*Spy*, 1993. Though locations are real, Paglia supplied all but three of the closing epithets.]

Dear Camille:

What can I do with this PoMo relationship of mine? My boy-friend is a stand-up comic constantly touring the country. I'll be in grad school for the next four years. Can long-distance relationships work?

Down-at-the-Mouth Dan in Northern California

Dear Dan:

I foresee many a moon of quick-fix, laugh-a-minute phone sex. Every relationship is a triumph of imagination. Yours will be tested to the credit limit.

Dear Camille:

I'm an overeducated, underemployed, bored and bisexual, fit and femme woman of the twentynothing generation. I fall for scrumptious young men "raised right" by their mothers. They're intrigued, then intimidated by my ferocity in bed. I'm in love with a sensitive, affectionate boy who is scared to death of me. Should I forget my affinity for boys and find myself a feisty female?

Too Sexy for the Boy in Baton Rouge

Dear Too Sexy:

This is a classic case of the Diana and Endymion myth: a ma-ternal Amazon goddess smacking her lips over androgynous boy-flesh. I'd say keep him as a side dish and supplement the menu with more robust confections. As for feisty females, I hope you have better luck than I do! Ha!.

Dear Camille:

I've been severely disappointed in my lady friends, who come across as intelligent women with common sense but end up making bad choices when it comes to men.

Jolted Joe from Brooklyn

Dear Joe:

You are puzzled by the irrational perversity of sexual attraction. Dionysus is a maelstrom. Love will never be tidy or safe. Jump in the boat and row for your life. Ha!

Dear Camille:

My fiancée and I revere you as a goddess. I once had an un-healthy, mutually manipulative relationship. Two weeks after we stopped speaking, she came into my dorm room to talk. We started to fool around. She seemed to be enjoying it, though when I asked if she wanted to have sex, she said, "I don't care." I went ahead and had sex with her. She later publicly denounced me as a rapist. But she never resisted or even *told* me to stop. Was it rape?

Confused in Kansas City

Dear Confused:

No, it's not rape. It's a scene from an Antonioni movie, all Weltschmerz and ennui. Feminist dogma keeps people from recognizing good old-fashioned decadence. Go for it!

MARCH

Dear Camille:

I'm a sixty-year-old man who has been married five times. I'm currently courting a fifty-three-year-old Catholic medical missionary nun. How do I ask her to give up her vows and marry me?

Amorous in Sarasota

Dear Amorous:

Hot dang! Violate them taboos, baby! You're Perseus rescuing Andromeda from the toils of that old devil Church. You may need a can opener, but it's worth a tumble.

Dear Camille:

I'm a biochemist who must keep up by attending lectures that contain fast-breaking data. The leader in our field shows nude slides of his girlfriends during his lectures and provides copies to men who request them. Women have walked out of his lectures, protested to the hosts, thrown things at the screen, to no avail. What does this man gain from our discomfort? What should we do?

Stumped in Toledo

Dear Stumped:

Unfortunately, I enjoy nude pictures in any context. A biochemical porn show has Broadway possibilities. But the guy sounds like an unprofessional klutz with a microchip wee-wee. Try scorn and satire. They work for me.

————

Dear Camille:

If you were really born in 1947, why do you look as though you were born in 1937 or even 1927? I want to avoid whatever you did to get those deep, saggy lines!

Bilious in Maryland

Dear Bilious:

Listen, pinhead, I'm a short, fast-talking comedienne with dimples who imitates Keith Richards to avoid looking like Sally Field. Get lost! Haggard is hip.

————

Dear Camille:

Women I hardly know come up to me all the time and give me that deep, knowing, womanly look. I feel these women have a terrible power over me. Should I just screw them? Does it matter that they're my students?

Baffled on Long Island

Dear Baffled:

The gals (white and middle-class, right?) are battin' their eyes at Big Daddy. You've discovered the truth: Sexual harassment is a hot-tar, two-way street. Wait till they graduate, then dive right in.

————

Dear Camille:

I used to think Rousseau was the stupidest asshole in the history of philosophy. Now that I'm getting on in years, I wonder if I would have found assholes of greater magnitude if I'd pursued that subject further. Who is *el sphinctero grande* of all time?

Curious in San Francisco

Dear Curious:

Michel Foucault, naturellement!　*Ha!*

Dear Camille:

I know that consumerism is the modern pagan religion and that the media is the altar upon which we offer up flesh sacrifices. I *do* enjoy watching the succession of heroes and heroines devoured by television. But I have lingering feelings of guilt, as if I am worshiping Satan. Yes, sometimes I wake up in the middle of the night shouting, "Consumerism is the Beast 666!" How can I loosen up, become more modern, and enjoy life?

Anguished in Oregon

Dear Anguished:

I prescribe a daily dose of my favorite soap, *The Young and the Restless*. What metaphysical anxiety could survive the soothing presence of plucky Nikki, trampy Jill, and teen queen Christine? Television is our Circe, and she's a date rapist. Just lay back, relax, and spread your sense organs.

Dear Camille:

The first time we met, the electricity was unbelievable. I'm married and white; he's black and ten years younger. He's also my boss. After two years of flirting, we became lovers. We have nothing in common but work and sex. Our Baptist-Cracker conservative company doesn't condone intraoffice or interracial dating. I can't stop thinking about him. I'm a headstrong, independent, take-charge woman. So why can't I handle this relationship? Why am I so irrational?

Reeling in Fort Lauderdale

Dear Reeling:

Sex is the biggest electric company of them all. It shocks, short-circuits, overloads, and generally fries the brains. When the wires go underground, they raise their own voltage. It's like snake-handling: Keep at it till the chills outnumber the thrills.

APRIL

To the many readers who asked me for a date:

I am reviewing applications from all genders. But why hasn't Drew Barrymore written to me yet?

Dear Camille:

I'm in my late twenties and haunt L.A. coffeehouses searching for an intellectually stimulating female partner among the patrons. But I find myself more attracted to the waitresses. In the Male-Confused-Nineties, I fear that making advances on these working women is sexual harassment. Is it wrong to flirt with them?

Anxious Alex

Dear Anxious:

I too get starry-eyed over waitresses. I suspect there is a Cosmic Mammary archetype behind all this. Waitresses have more on the ball, anyhow, than the chi-chi literati you're pursuing. Proceed cautiously, but give it a shot.

Dear Camille:

I'm an attractive twenty-three-year-old gay male. In bars, I notice that attractive men usually have ugly boyfriends. Why is this? How am I supposed to get a boyfriend when all the good ones are dating Ernest Borgnine look-alikes? When I *do* meet someone who doesn't need a bag over his head, he turns out to be a flaky, slutty jerk.

Single in Seattle

Dear Single:

A lesson of eros—only one megastar per household, please. Every god needs a priest in polyester.

Dear Camille:

Two buddies of mine who live thousands of miles from each other were unceremoniously dumped a couple of years ago by their girlfriends. Right after chucking their excess baggage, both girls adopted all the significant traits of their former boyfriends. One went from being a pampered trust-fund baby who read Woolf and subscribed to trendy political causes to being an ardent backpacker in love with Conrad. The other changed her major from environmental science to classical anthropology and philosophy and her music from Depeche Mode to the Lime Spiders. You get the picture. Why would these women become the men they no longer love?

Musing in Kankakee

Dear Musing:

I am stunned by this colorful evidence of the ancient principle of female vampirism, recorded everywhere in world mythology. Having sucked men dry, like marrow from a bone, woman calmly sails on to her next adventure. Sublime! *Ha!*

Dear Camille:

I supplement my unemployment checks by selling phone-sex scripts. I'd rather sell short stories, but nobody's buying. I seem to have a knack for cranking the stuff out. But I don't know whether to think of myself as a cheap media whore or a valuable public servant. Nothing gobs up the creative flow more than the image of a fat, lonely, middle-aged insurance salesman lying on his bed and pulling on his weenie while he listens to my words coming over the line. He and millions of other schmucks may need the help of a prosthetic imagination. Perhaps I am helping to release potentially dangerous sexual energy in a quick, tidy gush at the end of the day.

Pondering in Portland

Dear Pondering:

Though it might seem like a drainage ditch, you too labor in the vineyards of art. Apollo and Aphrodite bless all makers of erotic images.

Dear Camille:

My lesbian girlfriend and I have a running argument about the last scene in Djuna Barnes's *Nightwood*. I guess I'm WASPy and prosaic, but I think it's about having sex with a dog. My lover is French, however, and claims she cannot understand it this way, having read Lacan and Derrida. The argument becomes so heated that I wonder if I can live with a poststructuralist. What can I do?

Stymied in North Carolina

Dear Stymied:

How did your poststructuralist escape deportation? I heard they were reclassified as illegal aliens. Take her to McDonald's and deprogram her. If that doesn't work, box her and return to sender.

MAY

Dear Camille:

I have no trouble getting women in bed, but I just can't hold back. The evening ends before I can undo my belt.

Mortified in Madison

Dear Mortified:

You overeager acolytes of the Goddess have an ancient lineage. At Cnidos, Praxiteles' famous marble statue of Aphrodite was stained by a worshiper's ejaculation. Curtail your excitement by imagining something depressing—like being trapped in an elevator with the leaders of NOW.

Dear Camille:

I'm a thirty-five-year-old married woman. Lately I've been eyeing the kinds of guys I liked when I was fifteen: lean, long-haired, vacant, flannel-shirt-wearing hunks. May I have one?

Lustful in Los Angeles

Dear Lustful:

You mirror my mood exactly. Gather ye flannel while ye may. When lust unbridles, can menopause be far behind?

Dear Camille:

Recently I went camping in the Catskills with three buddies. One night I put out the campfire by urinating on it. I thought my friends would applaud my decisive, manly gesture, but they protested loudly. The whole experience left me feeling hollow.

Dejected in New York

Dear Dejected:

Freud felt urinary fire-extinguishing was early man's first proof of prowess. Today, writing girls' names in the snow is the more favored piss poetry. Expand your repertoire!

Dear Camille:

I'm a female who has rape fantasies featuring ex-convicts, aliens, postapocalyptic mutant gang leaders, etc. While I invent dialogue for both sexes, I feel more "inside" the male character, even after the female has gained the upper hand, which always happens. Am I bisexual, sadomasochistic or just strange?

Is This Hell? No, This Is Iowa

Dear Hell-in-Iowa:

Make movies as soon as possible. Surf's up in your sharkish libido. It's the cyberpunk 1990s, so take us for a ride on the wild side.

Dear Camille:

I'm a big WASP boy who has an ongoing thing with an older, burly Sicilian man. He's on the jealous side and says he would "cut out my heart" if he caught me with another man. But he admits having fantasies about watching me in the act with someone else. Another Sicilian man has come into the picture. Have I bit off more than I can chew?

Italophile in California

Dear Italophile:

Two Sicilians, one knife, and a hunk of white bread. Hmmm.

Better keep your panettone covered and your eye on the nearest fire
escape.

———

Dear Camille:

What's your advice about the ever-popular male pastime of
verbally harassing women on the street? My gut instinct is to snap
back with "Fuck off," but it's interpreted as an invitation to further
dialogue.

Irate in Chicago

Dear Irate:

Nothing made me angrier during my militant-lesbian-feminist
phase twenty years ago. I now feel the street is a combat zone and
modern women should not expect middle-class overprotection.
Men's guttural lunges are primal mating rituals, a crude homage.
Take the mentally superior position of mother or teacher and respond
with quiet withering boredom or comic repartee. I've seen African-
American women dish it right back with humor, not rage, and win
the exchange.

———

Dear Camille:

I'm a twenty-five-year-old full-blooded Italian rock musician. I
had a deep, loving, sexually *hot* relationship for three years with a
woman nine years older. Since we broke up, I've dated and slept
with a lot of girls. But (1) they're total intellectual duds; (2) their
idea of sex is lying in bed like a cadaver; or (3) they complain about
their lives but don't have the balls to do anything about it. I'm so
frustrated that sometimes I wish I were gay!

Glum in L.A.

Dear Glum:

I sympathize. A good gal is hard to find, and don't I know it.
It seems your taste buds are primed for more mature wine. (See
American Gigolo and "Lustful," above.)

———

AUGUST

Dear Camille:

I was making love with a beautiful feminist grad student. As we climaxed I mentioned your name, causing every muscle in her body to tense up immediately. It was the best orgasm in my life. I realize I was exploiting your name, but do you mind?

Wondering in West Hollywood

Dear Wondering:

Your partner's Harpy-like clutching is called vaginismus. Popular myth tells of men trapped and requiring surgical extrication. Use and abuse my name as you please. I love causing friction!

That's hysterical!

Dear Camille:

I'm a bisexual female who passionately loves hard rock and heavy-metal music. The guys I like only want the typical "heavy-metal bimbos." And gay women spout the usual "feminazi" dogma about hard rock being degrading, exploitative, and misogynist.

Lonely in Iowa

Dear Lonely:

Rock 'n' raunch is sexual reality. The new feminism will cut its teeth on heavy-metal power chords. Crank up your own wattage, and don't take no for an answer.

Dear Camille:

As a teenager in the States, I felt extremely abnormal because my foreskin was intact. I felt freakish and unpatriotic and suffered. What's your opinion of America's assembly-line snippage of infantile prepuce?

Feeling Normal in Frankfurt

Dear Normal:

Cut or uncut? Torpedo or lampshade? That is the question. In this deodorant-obsessed land of the bald eagle, gleaming Mr. Clean is our naughty little flesh-puppet.

Dear Camille:

I was involved with a comp lit major for seven years and was haunted by a sense of failure for not understanding the "conference cant" of the Derrida posse. Luckily I escaped the California infestation of these maniacs, but not before this woman had demasculated me to the point of premature ejaculation.

Recuperating in Rancho Mirage

Dear Recuperating:

Polluters of the brain commit crimes against humanity. Dante's Inferno has a special reserved foxhole for the followers of Lacan, Derrida, and Foucault, who will boil for eternity in their own verbal sludge.

———

Dear Camille:

When I'm using the office urinal, one of the dorkiest managers comes in, stands next to me and talks about the stupidest things. Is there a polite way to ignore him, or should I wet his leg? Does this problem happen to women?

Pissed Off in Hackensack

Dear Pissed Off:

Women adore gabbing in the john. It's a freaking hen party! As for your manager, can it be love?

———

Dear Camille:

After her orgasm from oral sex, my girlfriend starts laughing hysterically. What does this mean? Is my hard work being taken seriously?

Concerned in Calgary

Dear Concerned:

Bursts of irrational emotion, like weeping, are reported of orgasmic women. Beware of manic Maenads! The female worshipers of Dionysus tore goats and heifers limb from limb with their bare hands.

Dear Camille:

I'm a twenty-three-year-old gay male who planned to get a sex-change operation to make myself more appealing to a straight co-worker. My current boyfriend is threatening to leave me because of this. Then there's a woman who wants me desperately.

Wavering in Lompoc

Dear Wavering:

I envy your ability to draw a crowd. Your life is a Fellini film lacking only Anita Ekberg with a cat on her head. I would advise putting the operation on hold. Some merchandise is nonreturnable.

Dear Camille:

My girlfriend has started ejaculating and I've stopped. Through Tantra, we trade spontaneous combustion for hours-at-a-time ritual, with astounding results. Can all women ejaculate? We're talking cupfuls—you haven't seen an "arc of transcendence" until a five-foot fountain of amrita erupts from your beloved's yoni

Electro-Shakti'ed in Kansas City

Dear Shakti'ed:

In Coleridge's Xanadu, a geyser blasts up from a chasm, as if the earth is in orgasm. Pagan nature cults release titanic energy. Female ejaculation is the latest thing, demonstrated by Annie Sprinkle in her sacred-orgy video, *Sluts and Goddesses*. Bring an umbrella.

FEMINIST FATALE

From an edition of Man Alive, *with host Peter Downie. Produced by Sam Levene and David Cherniak for the Canadian Broadcast Company. Filmed on September 4, 1991, in Philadelphia. Aired in Canada December 14, 1992, and on public television in the United States in early 1993.*

PETER DOWNIE (*in CBC studio in Toronto*): Tonight on *Man Alive*—

(*Cut to pages of* Sexual Personae, *then* PAGLIA *in violet suit.*)

CAMILLE PAGLIA *(with Downie in Philadelphia)*: In paganism you have a unity between sexuality and spirituality, which is a great ideal. . . . I love the *sleaziest* parts of TV. . . . Madonna and I have a pornographic imagination. It's coming from the repressions of the Catholic Church. . . . I feel very lucky that somehow I wasn't drawn to drugs. I'm not sure why. I think I'm addicted to my own hormones—my adrenalines or whatever they are. I'm the speed-freak Sixties, you know? I never had to *take* anything, because that's just *me*, all right? I feel like I'm coming out of the Bob Dylan electric period, that kind of, like, speed-freak jive, kind of that rap—

(Back to DOWNIE *in Toronto. He freezes* PAGLIA's *onscreen image.)*

DOWNIE *(laughing)*: Hi, I'm Peter Downie, and *her* name is Camille Paglia. And this *(gestures with the remote control)* is about the only way I have to stop her. She's been called "Hurricane Camille" and the "Joan Rivers of Academe." But make no mistake about it: it's her ideas, not her delivery, which have made her the hottest critic around, whether she's writing in *The New York Times* or in *Penthouse* magazine. She has provocative ideas on just about everything—from feminism to rock and roll and from Madonna to political correctness, and those ideas come at you like fire from a machine gun. Her book, *Sexual Personae,* took twenty years to publish, and it's really become a launching pad for her, from where she now sits and takes careful critical aim at life. Trying to neatly package the energy of her mind for a television program is a bit like trying to grasp a bolt of lightning. As soon as you think you've got it, it's off in another direction. You might be angered by what you're going to hear, and you might be pleased. But I don't think you'll be bored—by Camille Paglia.

(With DOWNIE *in Philadelphia)*

PAGLIA: I know that my personality was not *made*. My personality was *born*. I'm an Aries woman like Joan Crawford, Bette Davis, and so we have a lot of problems with people because of this. We're just so *obnoxious*! I'm forty-four years old, and people are *still* having to speak to me like, you know, "*That* was very rude. You shouldn't behave like that, you shouldn't." Even today, people are always lecturing me about my excessive behavior and the way I completely ignore social forms and decorum and so on and so forth. So it's been a *struggle* for me. This is why I see society as civilizing. I don't see society as oppressive, because in my case, my barbaric energy *needs* to be contained. It needs to be contained. Otherwise, I'd be *killing* people and, you know, stealing and God knows what else! I'm just like this *egomaniac*. I'm an Aries—pure egomania, all right? Frankie Frank

DOWNIE: Let's begin by looking at the Sixties. What happened to the realism of the Sixties? What happened to the idealism of the Sixties?

PAGLIA: I think the whole thing just got out of control. I think a part of it was the contempt for the older generation. In the sense that, "We have nothing to do with you, and we have something new, something new to offer, and we don't have to listen to you at all." And part of that came from the fact that our parents— one didn't realize it at the time, but as the years went on, I saw it very clearly—our parents were *resting*, after decade after decade of the Depression, the rise of Fascism and Nazism, World War II, the bomb, the discovery of the concentration camps, the Cold War and so on. And our parents wanted a better life for their children than they had had. They had had *nothing* since they were young but worry, but anxiety, but darkness, all right? So they were determined to create an environment that would protect their children from what they had suffered. As a consequence, they did not tell us about the realities of the world.

And I think that's what I felt like growing up in the Fifties. I thought, *what?* This is so *boring!* This is so sanitized. I can't *stand* this! I felt like I was in prison in the sex roles of the Fifties, in the politics of the Fifties. I mean I'm still claustrophobic from it. We have this TV series down here, you know, *Happy Days,* which has given a very biased picture of what the Fifties were like. This idea that somehow, you know, a black-jacketed guy like Fonzie could be received at the house of the red-haired boy, okay—that's *absurd!* The hoods could *never* be received! There was absolutely a repressive era where the hoods represented the criminality and sexuality and everything that was outlaw, all right? And so I feel *The Twilight Zone* very accurately represents the Fifties' instability, that is, a sense of normality which is then disturbed by eruptions of what has been *repressed,* okay, what has been repressed in the cellar, what has been put up in the attic. And I feel that my work—in *Sexual Personae,* I feel that what I'm doing is going down into the cellar and up into the attic and bringing *into* the eyes of everyone what our parents did not want to think about. Everything. Whether it's pornography or aggression or Nazism, you know, the inner aggression of the human soul, the inner evil of the human soul.

So I think that our parents' reaction was excessive. That that tranquillity was a *false* tranquillity. The sunny Rousseauist optimism of the Fifties, the normality of the Fifties—that was an excessive reaction to something that had *been* excessive. And then *our* reaction was excessive *to* the Fifties, and out of that came another excess, the conservative backlash. But I think we're waking up from everything now. It's the end of the century, it's the end of the millennium, all right? We're reassessing. And *I* feel there is something happening. I have been saying my ideas for twenty years. No one listened. I couldn't get published. I couldn't get hired. And suddenly, people are listening and understanding what I'm saying. And it suggests to me that there is a kind of cyclical pattern at work, and we've gone through a full cycle, and we're coming back.

DOWNIE: Well, so there was excess, but I'd rather have excess with passion than no passion.

PAGLIA: But the point is, it self-destructed, and you had a conservative backlash. It's something much *worse* that happened, okay? Because law and order must go on. We must have law and order. We cannot have a situation where everyone does his own thing. We cannot have rioting in the streets. One has to be realistic about achieving political aims. What I have learned is how slowly institutions change. And in fact, if an institution would change rapidly, that's fascism. I began to realize that *slowness*—which I *hated* when I was young—that the *slow, boring* movement of the law in the courts is what prevents mob hysteria from lynching you, okay? Because I felt it myself. [She is referring to the violation of due process at Bennington College.] I am very obnoxious still, and I'm still—I mean, just yesterday I was, like, carrying on in a meeting and so on.

But the thing is now I'm more realistic. I understand that institutions change *slowly*. So my thing is not now, "We want the world, we want it *now!*" My thing is—all right, *one* year from now, if I keep on, you know, steadily, *two* years from now, it'll change. And I also had to learn how to pick my fights. My thing was, like, *everything!* I had endless energy. Ooh, people think I'm energetic *now!* I am a shadow, a shadow! I had so much energy I could stay up all night. And my thing was *this* issue! *That* issue! *That* issue! Now I've learned how to pick my fights and also how to present in a way that does not alienate the very people I need for a consensus in order to get my aim achieved. And that's maturity. . . .

DOWNIE *(in studio)*: Camille Paglia doesn't look down her academic nose at television or movies or sports or rock and roll. In fact, it's just the opposite. Her seven-hundred-page book was written while she enjoyed them all—sometimes simultaneously! So if you're tempted to yell at your child for having the stereo or the television too loud when homework is being done, consider this.

PAGLIA *(in Philadelphia)*: Technology for me—see, this is one of the ironies of my generation. Our generation was looking to nature and being very disrespectful about society and about capitalism. At the same time *(laughing)*, it was the most *electronic* and *electrified* generation in history. I was the first person that I knew to have a stereo, to go to college with a stereo in 1964. No one had stereos. Now everyone has every kind of music-making equipment. And I had the earphones—I was completely *plugged in*. And this is my attitude toward the world. On the one hand, I see all of nature and I honor it—the moon, the stars, the planets, all of that. As an astrologer, I just see it so clearly. But then, I cannot go anywhere when, you know, I just feel so *happy* at home, when I have the TV on and I have the music, the earphones on. I have the telephone, and I have the radio on, and the wires are crossing the floor, and I'm always tripping over the wires. And I just feel like I'm in this kind of *space capsule*, you know. I'm just totally connected to the universe, and I think that's part of the universality of our vision—the fact that we're connected into the universe through all this electronic machinery.

DOWNIE: But you're only connecting with an electronic universe, not the natural one.

PAGLIA: No, not really, because I think that on cable TV you can flick one channel, and you'll see animals in Africa, you'll see things in nature. That's the way of God himself, checking in on what's happening on every possible station in the entire universe! I think this is definitely the wave of the future. I feel that technology offers the Western version of expanded consciousness, all right? Because my ability to simply *concentrate* with all this going on, with a sensory flood of stimuli—*that* is what's different about my brain, okay, from the brains of the scholars who came before me. Because one part of my brain is totally rigorous and analytic in the traditional way. The other part is this *electrified brain* that people have found no machine to measure yet. It's completely lurid. It's like neon. It's like *this*, all right? *(vibrates hand near head)* My ability to *think* in the face of, incredible noise, for example—people say, "How can you think with that noise?" But I can *only* think when there's noise. I have to *flood my senses* in order to *really* think, all right?

I feel that the brain has many tracks. Everyone in my generation—for *thirty-five years* I've been listening to rock music! All of rock music has gone through this head again and again and again. It's all in there. And so I feel that I have a track in my brain. I wake up in the morning, it's playing. It's constantly playing music, all right? Then I have another one that's a visual track. So I love to write when I have the earphones on, listening to music. It could be classical music, it could be movie music— I love, like, *Ben-Hur* and all those great scores. It could be rock, or it's disco, which I love when I'm writing. *All* kinds of things. And then I have the soap operas on without the sound, okay? So I have the sound going very loud, and I have the images coming into my brain. If I don't have it, I can't concentrate. If I am trying to write without the sound and without the images, my mind wanders. I have to *supply* it. I have to supply the music; I have to supply the images, okay?

So I'm saying that our brains are completely different. It's something new, and I think we're moving outward toward that moment when we leave the earth and go into outer space. *Star Trek* was a great phenomenon of my generation. Let's say we have to take forty years for a person to get from earth to some planet. People will be born and will live and will die in space capsules, okay? And it was my generation which was the first, through this technological machinery, to be able to have a sense of being a *citizen of the universe*. We are citizens of the universe. We have a truly international perspective *through* TV and through technology.

It's very interesting: they use metaphors like this in Buddhism and so on—the idea that the mind should be like a still pond receiving messages from the universe. That's *exactly* how I feel when I'm looking at TV, all right? I go completely *blank (sweeps open hand over face in "cut" gesture), absolutely blank*. And that's why it's so refreshing to me. And I just want to sit there and go completely blank. Like, after I've had dinner, and I've had a glass of wine, you know, I'm just sitting there with *Entertainment Tonight*, and suddenly there's this completely glitzy, sensationalized story—I just *love* that! I have such *pleasure* at it, okay? And I can feel that it's *palpating* a part of my brain that's *not* the other part of the brain. *(goes all daffy/misty, imitating it)* You know, there's Liz Taylor, coming out of the hospital again! And it's like that area of sleazy eroticism and so on. I just *feel* it, right? The TV is literally an *emanation*, in some sense, of the popular mind. I feel that *everything* on TV is of interest to me. I *love* advertisements. I just wrote an essay talking about ads as an art form. I *love (snaps her fingers) the speed* of them—

DOWNIE: But it really is the medium, isn't it? I mean, you're saying that television itself is important.

PAGLIA: Yes, the medium itself. I love the *sleaziest* parts of TV. I mean, some academics like to say, "Oh, yes, I like PBS," or "I

like these documentaries." *(snorts scornfully)* That's not *my* attitude! Or they want to talk ponderously about the problems with
the news programs. Well, that's not what *I* regard as TV, you
know? I regard TV as *this river. (makes flowing motion with hand)*
It's like a river of images, okay? Especially *now* with cable. You
can get like thirty-seven different channels, and you can go . . .
sometimes I just sit there and go *zap! (flips imaginary remote control)*
Zap! Zap! Zap! It's like an *art form,* where you have this weird
collage, you see, of completely discontinuous images.

You'll go from the face of a religious figure, you know, holding
the Bible, then suddenly the next thing, a girl dancing with her
boobs hanging out of her bra, like *that (raises arms and does a
shimmy).* I think, this is *fabulous!* This is *the culture!* The way we
have all these strange things which cannot formally come together—these two figures, the evangelist preacher and the stripper, let's say. Those two people can never meet. But television
brings them together. They are both aspects of reality, and
therefore the mind of the person watching TV is this *universal
mind.* So I feel totally open. I try to have an attitude of total
openness to everything I see. And I have such enjoyment, such
sensuous pleasure of enjoyment, okay, in watching television. And
the colors, the movements, everything about it, everything which
strikes very book-oriented people as tinsely or squalid and so
on. Those very things are exactly why I *love* TV!

DOWNIE *(in studio)*: From television to belly dancing to striptease to
pornography, Camille Paglia writes and teaches about popular
culture and sexuality. Where is there a place for the sacred in
her world?

PAGLIA *(in Philadelphia)*: I'm saying, in *Sexual Personae,* that Western
culture has been formed by this tension between the Judeo-
Christian and the Greco-Roman traditions. And that it is *not
true* that Judeo-Christianity *ever* defeated paganism. In fact, paganism went underground and has erupted at various moments:
at the Renaissance, in Renaissance art; in Romanticism; and
now again in modern popular culture. And that paganism *does*
indeed have a spirituality. In paganism you have a unity be-

tween sexuality and spirituality, which is a great ideal. Christianity was not able to *do* this, because it regards nature as a fallen realm and our bodies as belonging to that fallen realm. The soul is, you know, the thing that was created in God's divine image, so the closer you can come to God, the less sexual you are. And this produced the monasticism, of course, and celibacy of the Middle Ages.

So yes indeed, that's what I'm trying to show in my work. I'm trying to show the actual spiritual vision that's inherent in this highly eroticized point of view that paganism had, all right? And it's so difficult for people to understand this. Like I regard all strip tease or belly dancing today as part of that long line, coming down from when dance was *sacred* in the cult around the Great Mother. This is really true, you know, that belly dancing is the last remnant of this long tradition going back. These movements of the hips, the overtly sensual and provocative pelvic motions of the belly dancer—to provoke *(laughs)* the *fatigued libido* of the various sultans and caliphs—all that goes back to the temple prostitutes around the Great Mother, in the ancient Near East and so on.

It's difficult for people trained in Judeo-Christianity to look at overt sexuality and regard it as in any way having anything to do with God, all right? But it *does*. In Hinduism, there are temples in India which have copulating nude couples, sometimes threes and fours, on the temple. I am entirely pro-pornography. When I look at pornography, for example, I see the *energies of nature*, all right? For Hinduism, those are creative and fertile energies. People who look at pornography and see simply oppression, see male dominance and female submission!—which, by the way, is completely false about pornography. That's simply not true. Often it's exactly the reverse.

DOWNIE (*in gallery of ancient sculpture*): For years, Camille Paglia's colleagues tried to avoid her, despite having impeccable credentials from Yale University. She just didn't seem to fit in. But something has happened. Her ideas are now noticed and debated, and not just by academics. Her book, *Sexual Personae*, is available in paperback now, and it continues to sell amazingly well. But while her *ideas* are reaching more and more people, *she* remains an enigma. And she finds comfort in history.

PAGLIA (*in Philadelphia*): From my earliest years, I feel I was such an alienated being—I think from my rebellion against my sex role in the early Fifties. Right from the start, I felt when as a tiny child I went to the museum, the Metropolitan Museum, and I saw the great artifacts from Egypt and so on, I always felt, from the study of history, that they gave me a kind of perspective upon my own culture. It allowed me to see my own identity in a larger frame of reference. And I think that the study of history has been for me—my early passion was to be an archaeologist, an Egyptologist—the study of history has been for me a liberation from the conventions of my own time.

DOWNIE: For a lot of people, though, I think history is seen as something to be overcome, and your point is that it's something that has to be appreciated and delved into and brought to bear on what's happening now.

PAGLIA: That's why I see history in huge rhythms, enormously long rhythms. That's why I think most people are just *trapped* in the present. If you don't understand the whole path, you can't see where we're going, because you don't see where we've *been*. So I just see these huge rhythms operating, and I see that popular culture has been this enormous transformation that happened, I feel in the 1920s, with the birth of sound pictures. That was the moment when, I think, high art lost its exclusive status, and popular culture took over. And I think we're still in this rhythm, but I believe that we're still in the *Romantic* rhythm.

My mentor Harold Bloom also believes this, that we're still in the Romantic era. That is, the movement initiated by Rousseau's ideas in 1760. So that's what I see—one long huge pattern. Rock and roll is simply, you know, another eruption of that Romanticism. I see us still in that. And I think that the next—to *predict*, all right? *(laughs)*—I think the next rhythm will be inaugurated by someone from outer space. I mean, when— if—we discover another civilization, another planet, if it turns out there's evidence for that, then that's the beginning of a new phase, I think, when the people of the world, presumably, will see that we look more like each other than we do like that creature there which looks like a blob of Jell-O, all right? I think that that may happen, at a certain point, and I think that that may terminate the phase we're in. . . . I often feel when I talk to people who are older than me, a generation older than me, academics and so on, that their brains are very *slow*, okay? Very *slow*. The speed of my mind is part of the stimulation I have received from all these sensory things—from rock and roll and MTV. When MTV came along, I felt it was exactly the way my brain had been operating for the prior twenty years. Flash! Flash! Flash!

BOBBITT VERSUS BOBBITT

CNN & Company, *January 12, 1994. Host: Mary Tillotson. Guests: Susan Estrich, Susan Milano, and Camille Paglia (in London). On the ongoing trial in Virginia of Lorena Bobbitt for severing her husband's penis.*

PAGLIA: I have to say I am not surprised at this new evidence [of Lorena Bobbitt having battered her husband]. I have *always* regarded the Bobbitt relationship as a sadomasochistic one *on both sides*—both physically and psychologically. And my opinion remains that, on the one hand, I feel that Lorena Bobbitt committed a cruel and barbarous act, and a cowardly one, by attacking her husband while he was asleep. I reject *any* prior claim of victimization. On the other hand, I have to say, I think this *will* be having the effect of a revolutionary act by a woman, somewhat equivalent to Charlotte Corday killing Marat in his bath just after the French revolution. . . .

Let me cut in here. I absolutely agree with Susan Estrich about the vigilantism. It *is* that. I have to say, however, that at certain moments of history, when law and order break down, there may be a *need* for self-defense. I do not *excuse* Lorena Bobbitt for what she did. I think it is *criminal* and she *must* go to prison!

However, we're at a time in the history of women when the old controls, the old protections—the fathers and the brothers and so on—are no longer there to protect you against abuse. And I think we have a return here to that great period at the close of the Sixties when you had women like Valerie Solanas—Society for Cutting Up Men—who shot Andy Warhol. I don't want to praise *that* act, but I'm all for personal responsibility and self-reliance again. So on the one hand, I think that Lorena Bobbitt is a neurotic, that she has to go to prison, *but*—what I've always said, you see—she's from a *Latin* country, and she has a sense of *honor*. And when her honor is offended, she *acts* on her *own*. I think there's going to be *more* of this. . . .

I just don't agree that her life was in danger! What I *do* think was going on was a very complex power dynamic. Now the problem of feminist rhetoric of the last twenty years is that it's been totally unable to *deal* with the fact that *women* are as aggressive in sexual relationships and as vengeful as *men*! So what I think we have here is a *wonderful* demonstration of the darkness, irrationality, and turbulence of sex relations and the inadequacy of the normal victimization rhetoric of feminism. . . . I don't want a situation where women go *after the fact* for help to agencies and so on. I want to allow women to diagnose their own *addiction* to a certain kind of s&m relationship—that I believe is going on here. . . . [re: the recent trial in Los Angeles of Erik and Lyle Menendez for the murder of their parents] What I love about that case, the Menendez case, is that it exposes once again the aggressions, the homicidal urges that Freud—who was thrown out of feminism twenty years ago—said were inherent in all of us. I totally agree: the Menendez case is a *fraud*.

We can't keep relying simply on *the system*! I *applaud* the kinds of agencies that are there to give help to desperate women, but in my opinion it's only a minority of battered women that in fact are financially dependent on their husbands, and—*(furiously)* I'm sorry! I *reject* your figures! And I reject *all* those figures of the feminist establishment! It's a bunch of *malarky*! I'm sick and tired—*(shouting)* I'm *sorry*! Until you people begin to understand the *complex psychology* of men and women in relation to each other, *more* such women are going to be killed or are going to cut the penises off their husbands! A woman who stays after she has been battered—*as* in this case—is psychologically addicted to that relationship. *She* was getting something out of it too! Until we look to *great art*—to Bizet's *Carmen* and things like that—we're never going to understand that! There was a love relationship going on here—*a love-hate relationship* of ambivalence. She was *not* a pure victim!

DIARY: SEX, ART, AND SELLING

From The Guardian, *London, January 21, 1994.*

Wednesday. At breakfast en route to London, the steward offers me "bubble and squeak" [a British dish consisting of fried leftovers]. I am dumbfounded and think he is making a sexual proposition. Vaudeville visions of Gypsy Rose Lee dance before my eyes. On landing at Heathrow, I am greeted by Sarah Such, the lively head of publicity at Penguin, who has arranged this tour for the paperback of *Sex, Art, and American Culture.* As we drive into the pitch-dark city, I begin the first of my tutorials in racy British slang. Of the many pungent words Sarah will add to my vocabulary during my visit, my favorite is "prat," which I soon publicly apply to the Prince of Wales.

Caught in traffic near the Basil Street Hotel, we see a strange stir in front of Harrods, as a dogpack of cameras circles an invisible prey. Richard Gere is opening the annual sale. "Penguin always puts me where the action is," I remark. Eighteen months ago, during my visit for *Sexual Personae,* my hotel window looked into topsy-turvy Kensington Palace the week before Andrew Morton's *Diana: Her True Story* broke upon the world.

After a few hours' rest, punctuated by fire alarm bells, I begin my week of interviews, sustained by oceans of Pepsi and Evian and rafts of scones and exquisite tea sandwiches, which I devour with obscene relish.

Thursday. I have an unpleasant encounter with the hotel's European hair dryer, which looks like a vacuum cleaner and blasts me against the wall with hurricanelike force. The interviews continue, back to back. By day's end, I have ejected a belligerent reporter for incoherence and inaccuracy. When informed that this woman is considered an "expert" on feminism, I reply, "I have gazed into her mind, and it is mush."

Highlight of the day is my costume session for the "Dressed to Kill" feature in the *Daily Mail*. When asked, via transatlantic fax, about my favorite contemporary designers, I urged that the stylist find vaguely transvestite Sixties wear, either Diana Rigg *Avengers* outfits or Portobello Road historical regalia of dandy or cavalier. Confronted with a crowded rack, I fall ecstatically on an opulent purple-velvet Moschino jacket with pearl buttons. Two people are needed to zip me into the thigh-high black suede boots. I am in gender-bending heaven.

British news events swirl round us. Every day, some delicious sex scandal shakes the government. I steal an *Evening Standard* poster off the street (LOVE CHILD MINISTER FORCED TO QUIT) to hang in my Philadelphia office next to my lifesize Babylonian icon of Joanne Whalley-Kilmer as Christine Keeler.

Friday. The *Guardian* declares me "a flash in the pan." I eject a photographer for constructing a hellish oven in which I am expected to put my head. *The Late Show* films my predictions for 1994: "Madonna and Diana will be revealed to be one person, a hybrid Hindu goddess named Madiana. They will withdraw to a Tibetan monastery, run by Richard Gere, to which women and hermaphrodites can come for flagellation by Madonna and then nursing and healing by Diana."

We fly to Belfast, where I deliver a lecture at Queen's University. Here, as elsewhere, I complain about my acute television deprivation in Europe and the UK—the few channels, the lack of late-night programming. At a bar afterward, I savour Guinness and marvel at the extraordinary beauty of Irish youth.

Weekend. We are driven to Dublin by a security-cleared driver of James Bond expertise. We pass a ruined Doric temple, a bombed-out courthouse where five policemen were killed. I am fascinated by the ancient stone farmhouses and omnipresent sheep of the Irish countryside.

Arriving at a television studio for the *Kenny Live* show at 10 P.M., we see three handlers struggling with a baby tiger in the street. Sarah, having forgotten her leash, also fails to get me through the door, as I carry on about Blake and *Bringing Up Baby*. I lose a button. In wardrobe, Sarah heroically sews it on, as I wander about exclaiming at boxes labeled "Ladies Bras for Men" and "Ladies Shoes for Men," the latter containing gigantic, battered pink pumps. On the show, a caller says I am a combination of "Groucho Marx and Hitler." The host and I kiss.

Back in London, I film risqué presentations for two Channel 4 programs, on the penis and lesbians, following last year's shows on Diana and Lolita. The artist, Alison Maddex, rightly dubbed my "inamorata" by the press, arrives from Germany. We feast on partridge, steak and kidney pie, and flagons of ale at Rules, where we sense positive spirit presences.

Monday. More interviews, leading up to my lecture at the National Theatre. Alison and I are entranced by a gorgeous Thirties portrait of Olivier as Hamlet in the green room. Andrew Morton comes backstage to say hello. We find him wildly handsome but go off on our own for an Indian cuisine extravaganza.

Tuesday. *Elle* magazine arrives with costumes for a photo shoot. I try on gold mail trousers but reject a black-rubber cat suit and red vinyl dominatrix thigh boots. I select a studded black leather jacket and motorcycle boots and pose with a medieval broadsword. I feel like Mel Gibson in *Mad Max. The South Bank Show* interviews me about the changing image of fat women in cultural history. I am aggravated as reporters claim my "chic" jet black suit was "navy."

Later that week. Alison and I visit Hampton Court, Vivienne Westwood's shop, and a chocolate-wall art exhibit. We see *Oleanna* (tedious but all-too-true) and *Medea* (electrifying), after which I send a thank-you note backstage to Diana Rigg, one of my heroines.

The *Sunday Times* compares me to Dame Edna Everage, which is, as Sarah would say, spot on. I thank the ghost of Coco Chanel that the cover photo definitively documents my maligned black suit. Alison and I fly back to America. The moment I get home, I rush through the house, turning on all three of my television sets at once.

EXTRACTS

"A gentleman is . . . ," *from* Esquire, *Spring–Summer 1993.*
    The idea of the modern "gentleman" is a product of British
culture. It originates in the Italian Renaissance, in Baldassare Cas-
tiglione's *The Courtier,* a handbook of elegant aristocratic manners.
The gentleman is half feminine. Though he may be a warrior or
athlete, he has smoothed and softened his masculine aggression for
indoor politicking. Because of his refinement and attentiveness, the
gentleman is always highly attractive to women and is often a skilled
seducer.
    Film history is full of great gentlemen, from Fred Astaire and
Cary Grant to George Hamilton, whose persona tends toward the
gigolo. Hugh Hefner has never received the credit he deserves for
creating a sophisticated model of the suave American gentleman in
the Marlboro Man years following shoot-'em-up World War II.
Contemporary feminism has tried to ditch male gallantry and chivalry as reactionary and sexist. Eroticism has suffered as a result.
Perhaps it's time to bring the gentleman back. He may be the only
hero who can slay that mythical beast, the date-rape octopus, currently strangling American culture.

* * *

From The Washington Post Book World, *Christmas feature, 1992. Writers were asked what books they would read over the holidays, what books they hoped to write, and what books influenced them in childhood.*

No current books will be read by me for some time, since I am still making my way, with heavy sighs and a magnifying glass, through Madonna's *Sex.* As for planned books of my own, it would be too cruel to spoil the holiday season with dark visions of future Paglia tomes, portable only by wheelbarrow.

However, I eagerly answer the query about the ultimate book of my childhood. It was the boxed set of Lewis Carroll's Alice books, a special edition with tinted Tenniel illustrations, published by Random House in 1946. The contrasting wear of the two tattered volumes clearly shows that it was *Through the Looking-Glass,* rather than *Alice in Wonderland,* that most obsessed me as a child.

The Alice books were my bible, and I studied them religiously. They have a dreamy, hallucinatory quality. Order and chaos oscillate. Time and space melt. Vivid personalities, cantankerous and egotistical, appear as humans, animals, plants, and assorted objects, including a leg of mutton in a paper hat. Everything in the universe is capable of cryptic, bossy speech.

The curt, explosive sound of Carroll's sentences seemed to echo the choppy, vigorous Italian dialects I heard all around me as a child but was unable to understand. I probably identified the rumpled, sweet-tempered White Queen and the forceful, dogmatic Red Queen with, respectively, my paternal and maternal grandmothers, the stately matriarchs to whom I dedicated *Sexual Personae.*

Alice was a model heroine for a small child. Isolated, plucky, and inquisitive, she wanders through gleaming drawing rooms, tangled gardens, and rough forests with a kind of baffled stoicism. At five, I was Alice for Halloween, in a pinafore, apron, and yellow-yarn wig made by my mother. My other admirations were male: Prince Valiant, Robin Hood, and Bizet's Escamillo. The observant and quietly determined Alice would remain my ruling female persona until my adolescent passion for Katharine Hepburn and Amelia Earhart. In college, I rediscovered Carroll's arch, haughty rhetoric in Oscar Wilde and my potent, ultraverbal new allies, gay men and drag queens.

*   *   *

"I, the Jury," from The Washington Post Book World, *December 5, 1993. Writers were asked to make nominations for the Nobel Prize for Literature.*

The Nobel Peace Prize has not been awarded in years where it wasn't deserved. A similar standard should govern the literature prize, in which case there would have been no winners for the past twenty years. The declining importance of the written word in our age of mass media is all too eloquently expressed in the diminishing distinction of winners of the literature prize after the high period of Jean-Paul Sartre (1964), Samuel Beckett (1969), and Pablo Neruda (1971). The literature prize, a relic of a genteel pre-modernist era, should be abolished or redefined as a culture prize. Artists of far greater achievement and world stature than recent Nobel prizewinners are Ingmar Bergman, Federico Fellini, and Bob Dylan. If we must stick to literature, I say give the prize to our brilliant Beat shaman, Allen Ginsberg. I'd love to see Ginsberg disrupt the pompous Nobel ceremony with one of his trademark pieces of performance art—cross-legged, incense-burning, cymbal-clanging, and chanting some mystical ode of juicy gay porn.

* * *

Paglia has publicly condemned "advance blurbs" as a corrupt practice of the publishing industry, and she refuses to write them. However, she occasionally provides comments after a book is published, and these have appeared (along with phrases from her book reviews) on paperback editions.

For the Doubleday/Anchor reissue in 1992 of Leslie Fiedler's *Love and Death in the American Novel* (1960):

Leslie Fiedler, Norman O. Brown, and Allen Ginsberg were the three central literary figures of the American Sixties. In college, I read Fiedler intensely and deeply. *Love and Death in the American Novel* is immediately behind my book *Sexual Personae*. In it, Fiedler made the first important synthesis of practical criticism with psychoanalysis and progressive politics. He created an American intellectual style that was truncated by the invasion of faddish French theory in the Seventies and Eighties. Let's turn back to Fiedler and begin again.

For the New American Library paperback edition of Gordon F. Sander, *Serling: The Rise and Twilight of Television's Last Angry Man* (1992):

Rod Serling was one of the central creators of twentieth-century American imagination. He was a sci-fi visionary, surrealist poet, and political moralist. The impact of *The Twilight Zone* on my Sixties generation was like that of T. S. Eliot's *The Waste Land* and Samuel Beckett's *Waiting for Godot* on the two generations before us. Serling was a primary inspiration to me as a writer. I revere him as the modern heir of Edgar Allan Poe.

* * *

From The Essential Frankenstein, *ed. Leonard Wolf, Penguin, 1993.*

I have always found *Frankenstein,* in its book and movie versions, profoundly and unpleasantly disturbing because of my identification with the split personae of the story. In Dr. Frankenstein I felt my detached scientific consciousness, that cool observing eye that I cast on human behavior from my preschool years. In the monster I sensed my alienated sexuality, which began with the gender dysfunction of my childhood and continued through the ambiguities of sexual orientation that still trouble me today. The monster has my uncouth brute power and psychological isolation, and in its challenge to and flight from authority I saw my own Romantic affronts to the conformist humanitarian values of the "community." But *Frankenstein's* mode is horror, while mine is comedy. I found my way out of Mary Shelley's existential dilemma by rejecting Aristotle's "fear and pity" for Aristophanes' bawdy, vital energy.

* * *

From The New York Observer, *July 5–12, 1993. Dan Cogan asks celebrities about memories of summer camp.*

I went to Spruce Ridge Camp in the Adirondacks and Lourdes Summer Camp, a Catholic camp. For me, these all-women environments were prelesbian heaven. It was just so romantic. I had mad crushes on all the counselors. It was fabulous, a paradise state.

At one camp I had a male name briefly. I had just taken the confirmation name Anastasia, after the movie. You're supposed to name yourself after a saint, so I named myself after Ingrid Bergman. I began calling myself Stacy, already an androgynous name. Someone got it wrong and called me Stanley, and I liked that, so I was called Stanley that summer. It was great.

Outside of my normal school environment, where you would have to wear a skirt or a dress or a gym uniform, I really could be my androgynous, butch self for days on end. It's probably why I felt happy while I was there. The way I've always gotten attention from women is by being funny. Camp was the only place you could get sustained attention from pretty girls. People like to criticize me, saying, "Oh, she's such a showboat," but that's one of the things I developed to get attention from women. I can't get them into bed, but I could still get their attention. And I'm sure camp was pivotal.

But it was still a very innocent age. Today, I think I would have been much more physically aggressive than I was. There were a million opportunities to do things, for heaven's sake. There was some experimentation, sitting in bed and pretending we were boys with each other. It was very hot. Things were never that hot again. I *don't* think counselors would have permitted it if they knew what was going on.

But this is also one of my primary alien experiences. The idea of everyone sitting around the campfire and singing "Que Será Será," Doris Day's greatest hit. It is one of the experiences that formed my temper as the kind of totally obnoxious person that I am now, my total intolerance for sappy sentimentality and handholding. I hate campfire singing. To me, it typifies the Fifties. The false *gemütlichkeit* of these camps is part of what formed my rebellion as a Sixties revolutionary. It's why I love Keith Richards.

And of course I created some incidents. The biggest happened when it was my task to deal with the latrine at Spruce Ridge. The instructions on the five-pound bag of lime that was handed to me said to put half a cup into the latrine. I thought it said half a package. So I dumped in half the bag. Well, I know enough about chemistry now to know what happened. Methane gas is produced by decay. The lime exploded as soon as it hit the gas in the latrine, and I was flung out backwards and clouds and clouds of white-brownish smoke were pouring out of the latrine upwards past the unsullied pine trees into the heavens. And I was so stunned, I thought, God, what's happening, because in those days you didn't know anything. And I jumped onto a fallen tree to warn people, and it was so moss-covered that my legs flew out from under me, and I fell about eight feet down, BOOM!, and I lay there stunned, watching the clouds go and go and go. It was just endless. I knew I would be in trouble.

That was a very archetypal experience. It symbolized everything I would do with my life and work. Excess and extravagance and explosiveness. I would be someone who would look into the latrine of culture, into pornography and crime and psychopathology and so on, and I would drop the bomb into it. I would terrorize everyone, create complete disorder, and then I'd be lying on my back watching the explosion that I made rise helplessly into the sky.

* * *

"Critical Mass Media," *from the* PEN *Newsletter,* October 1993. *Members of PEN were asked what motivated them as writers in today's changing world.*

My primary inspiration remains the rebellion of my Sixties generation against bourgeois convention. So many of my contemporaries lost themselves in drugs or dissipated their energies outside the system, which they refused to enter and therefore never transformed. Television and popular music shaped the imagination of my generation, but the academic and literary establishment is still dominated by dull, moralistic, slow-thinking people who came to consciousness fifty years ago, before the triumph of mass media.

As a writer, I am committed to the enterprise of setting down my generation's inner experience for the historical record. Not since Gutenberg, as Marshall McLuhan observed, had there been such a dizzying communications explosion. Since the Sixties there has been a radical shift from words to images in world culture. The modern writer must be able to negotiate between these realms. Like Alexandrian scribes, we carry the sacred burden of the literary past in a lively, decadent, commercial age increasingly indifferent to books. But I remain convinced that words have both power and permanence.

* * *

From "Symposium—In the Media, A Woman's Place," Columbia Media Studies Journal, *Winter/Spring, 1993.*

In the past two years, feminism exploded into the media and became hot news again. But the serious, legitimate issues of date rape and sexual harassment were done to death and turned into mass hysteria. Feminist books became best-sellers, but they also exposed deep divisions within feminism itself that the media had lazily ignored. For twenty years, dissident feminist voices like mine could not get heard. From the moment Gloria Steinem founded *Ms.* magazine and became a power on the New York social and political scene, the media servilely surrendered to the white, middle-class lady's view of feminism, which many of us from the Sixties found genteel, sanitized, and repressive.

Since my recent notoriety, I have had many opportunities to observe the inner workings of the major media. With few exceptions, the sloth, superficiality and ignorance about long-standing feminist issues are not to be believed. Media people just repeat the simplistic Steinem party line like robots. Catharine MacKinnon, a puritanical anti-porn extremist endorsed by Steinem, is trotted out on program after program as if she were Grandma Moses. I am constantly battling to get the opposing position heard and have pulled out of several network shows when producers began to buckle under hardline pressure. And there are many programs and major print organs that are completely closed to me.

My message to the media is: Wake up! The silencing of authentic debate among feminists just helps the rise of the far right. When the media get locked in their Northeastern ghetto and become slaves of the feminist establishment and fanatical special interests, the American audience ends up looking to conservative voices for common sense. As a libertarian Democrat, I protest against this self-defeating tyranny of political correctness.

*   *   *

From In A Word: A Harper's Magazine Dictionary of Words That Don't Exist But Ought To, *Jack Hitt, ed., 1992. Contributors were asked to invent, define, and illustrate a new word.*

whuffle [*whine + wheeze + snuff + sniffle*]: The annoying, scratchy sound made by weepy feminists as they lament the sufferings of women and, houndlike, sniff out evidence of male oppression in oliterature, art, and the media. Some compare it to the rustle of

Victorian crinoline skirts. Others speak of a badmintonlike spank and whoosh. Still others think of a jumbled feathery flapping, as in the attic torture of Tippi Hedren in *The Birds*. Of a feminist theorist: "She whuffled her way to the top." Of a feminist conference: "The room overflowed with whufflers." Of a feminist lecture: "The whuffling was unbearable."

* * *

Letter to the editor, London Review of Books, *March 11, 1993. Reprinted in* Harper's, *June 1993.*

Elaine Showalter's review of my new book, *Sex, Art, and American Culture,* was generally fair and accurate in its detailed overview of my career. However, her account of my appearance in December at her own institution, Princeton University, is a dismaying collage of distortions, malice, and wishful fantasy.

I have never in fact been invited to lecture at Princeton, partly because of the solipsistic insularity of the feminist establishment that Elaine Showalter represents. I was not giving a lecture at Princeton on the day in question. I had been invited by Alisa Belletini, producer of MTV's "House of Style," to sit on a 40-minute panel with her, supermodel Cindy Crawford, and Linda Wells, founder and editor-in-chief of *Allure* magazine, to help defend them against the insane feminist charge (obsessively pushed by one-note Naomi Wolf) that the fashion industry causes anorexia.

As one of four panelists focused on a single issue, I could hardly jump to my feet, take over the occasion, and regale the audience with my usual Joan-Rivers-meets-Jane-Harrison comic monologue. Had I done so, I expect Professor Showalter would have used that as evidence of my dreadful selfishness and daffy narcissism. Here, as in her books, she shows her inability to read simple cultural symbolism. At Princeton I was dressed in casual butch blue jeans, rather than my usual ultra-femme, high-maquillage, Auntie Mame performance drag, to signal that I was not the central focus: Cindy Crawford was. It was for the gorgeous, willowy Crawford, not me, that the huge crowd paid a $5 entrance fee.

I suggest that Professor Showalter, who was clearly stung by the respectful coverage my attendance at the conference received

before and after the event in *The New York Times* and New Jersey
newspapers on and off campus, should concentrate her energies on
the deplorable condition of Princeton education. We visitors were
shocked at the mediocrity and inarticulateness of most of the student questioners, who seemed to have no command even of syn-
tax, much less thought, aside from their parroting of passé feminist
clichés. Ivy League education in the humanities is obviously in
the pits.

In conclusion, Professor Showalter tries to make a grand point
of my refusal to "debate" other academic feminists—as if I had ever
been invited by anyone anywhere in the country to such a debate
(except for a Madonna panel at this student-organized conference). The unpleasant truth is that the American feminist establishment categorically refused to read my book or to take me or my
ideas seriously until now, three full years after the release of *Sexual
Personae*.

I'm afraid it's too late, ladies. You have abundantly shown your
true character, in all its vicious, Kremlin-walled Stalinism. The
reform movement that I helped launch is at your gates. Your desire
for debate is touching, even pathetic. But the time for negotiations
is long past. History has moved on and left you behind.

* * *

"On Picasso," *from* Art News, *April 1993.*
On the level of creativity, Picasso is equal to Michelangelo.
Therefore it's appalling that feminists have removed him from study
for women artists, who are brainwashed that he was mean to his
girlfriends. Yes, mainstream and radical feminists are anti-Picasso.
You can't treat him seriously, they claim. This is absolute nonsense.
They're blind to a vital fact: you must separate the person in real
life from the artist.

Now, we may be interested in biographical compulsions, but
art—I stress—exists separately from real life. Young women in Ivy
League schools are told art history was written by men, so there's
a heterosexist conspiracy to keep them from knowing about women
artists in history. We've revised the reputation of some minor women
artists I find interesting. Romaine Brooks. I've always liked her.
Frida Kahlo. Fine. But not one major woman artist has ever been

rediscovered. Then Germaine Greer says there are no great women because they have mutilated egos. I say great art *only* comes from mutilated egos.

Western culture is about the solitary, obsessive individualist. Usually artists of non-Western traditions subordinate themselves to collective style and "speak" for the tribe. In Michelangelo and Picasso we see Western art and personality. Everything that is Western about cultural history is encapsulated in Picasso.

* * *

From interview by Edie Magnus with Camille Paglia on premiere of Connie Chung's Eye to Eye, *CBS, June 17, 1993, in regard to sexual harassment lawsuits against schools by parents on behalf of their children.*

PAGLIA: Well, I think it's a very dangerous trend—very dangerous indeed.

MAGNUS *(voiceover)*: Writer and controversial social critic Camille Paglia sees a danger in the surge of laws which might appear fashionable now but which she feels undermine the kids they're designed to protect.

PAGLIA: The idea of the state and the law stepping in to make sure everyone's feelings are not bruised—this is *madness.*

If the girl's feeling's aren't hurt now, they will be hurt some time in the future—again and again and again. If you haven't built up the armor to deal with some reverse in junior high school—what are we *doing* to people? We are crippling them. We are *crippling* our young women!

(Program continues.)

PAGLIA: We cannot have constant legal remedies for every single thing that goes wrong with kids in junior high school.

MAGNUS: What would you say to the eighth grade girl who comes home crying every day, whose grades have fallen, who says she cannot concentrate enough to be able to get a good education because the boys in school are calling her dirty names?

PAGLIA: I have to ask: is it happening in the *classroom?* If it's happening in the classroom, that cannot be tolerated. If it's happening *outside* the classroom, tough cookies, okay? Get a grip. This is called life. L-I-F-E is life. We cannot constantly make a kind of cushion around our white middle-class girls *(makes earmuff gesture and mimics sulky adolescent)*, protecting them from any obscene thing that comes to their ears!

APPENDICES

CARTOON PERSONAE
A MEDIA CHRONICLE

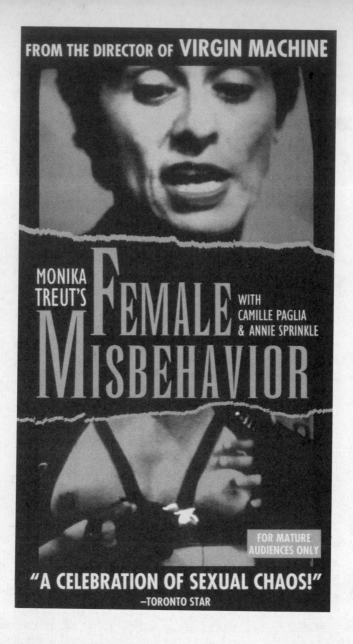

6. Movie poster for *Female Misbehavior* (1992). A. Piccolo Graphics/NYC. From Part 1, "Dr. Paglia" (above); from Part 3, "Bondage" (below). First Run Features.

"You have an air of Camille Paglia about you."

Fig. 7. *Camille Paglia: her operatic tough-girl voice rings out into the cloistered academic air.* Drawing by Victor Juhasz originally appeared in *The New Yorker*. Copyright © 1992 by Victor Juhasz. All rights reserved.

Fig. 8. Drawing by Victoria Roberts originally appeared in *The New Yorker*. Copyright © 1993 by Victoria Roberts.

Fig. 9. Drawing by Gail E. Machlis originally appeared in the *San Francisco Chronicle*. Copyright © 1992 Chronicle Features Syndicate.

Fig. 10. Drawing by Carole Cable originally appeared in the *Chronicle of Higher Education*. Copyright © 1994. Reprinted by permission of University of Texas Press.

"*Lennie's so much more fun since he read Camille Paglia.*"

Camille Paglia Oprah Winfrey Dalai Lama

Fig. 11. Drawing by Doug Sneyd reproduced by special permission of *Playboy* magazine. Copyright © 1993 by *Playboy*.

Fig. 12. Drawing by Demetrios Psillos originally appeared in *Self* magazine. Copyright © 1993 by Demetrios Psillos.

Fig. 13. Copyright © 1993 by Bill Holbrook. Reprinted with special permission of King Features Syndicate.

Fig. 14. Originally appeared in *The New York Native*. Copyright © 1992 by C. Bard Cole.

Fig. 15. Paglia as St. Sebastian. Originally appeared in
The New Republic. Copyright © 1992 by Vint Lawrence.

Fig. 16. Paglia with Madonna and fig leaf. Originally appeared in
The New Republic. Copyright © 1993 by Vint Lawrence.

Fig. 17. Paglia as Diva. Drawing by Charles Hefling originally
appeared in *The Harvard Gay and Lesbian Review*.
Copyright © 1994 by Charles C. Hefling.

Fig. 18. Copyright © 1992 by Tom Roberts and Jim Siergey.
Nationally syndicated in alternative newspapers.

Fig. 19. Copyright © 1993 by Tom Roberts and Jim Siergey.
Nationally syndicated in alternative newspapers.

Fig. 20. Inspired by Paglia's *Modern Review* essay on revivals.
Her books are shown in frame 7. Drawing by Mick Kidd and
Chris Garratt. Copyright © 1994 by BIFF Products.
Originally appeared in *The Guardian*, London.

Figs. 21, 22, & 23. Three strips inspired by *Sexual Personae*. Copyright © 1992 by Bill Griffith. Reprinted with special permission of King Features Syndicate.

Fig. 24. Copyright © 1992 by Bill Griffith. Reprinted with special
permission of King Features Syndicate.

Fig. 25. The box contains copies of Paglia's *Sex, Art, and American
Culture*. Excerpt from the ongoing strip courtesy of
Firebrand Books. Copyright © 1994 by Alison Bechdel.

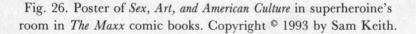

Fig. 26. Poster of *Sex, Art, and American Culture* in superheroine's
room in *The Maxx* comic books. Copyright © 1993 by Sam Keith.

Fig. 27. Copyright © 1993 by Raymond Lowry.
Originally appeared in *The Guardian*, 1993.

Figs. 28 & 29. Copyright © 1993 by John Callahan.
Reprinted by permission. Gift of the artist.

Figs. 30 & 31. Copyright © 1993 by John Callahan.
Reprinted by permission. Gift of the artist.

Fig. 32. Gloria Steinem aboard drifting ship; Paglia as Siren.
Copyright © 1993 by John Callahan. Reprinted by permission.

Fig. 33. Paglia as Samson—the final caricature as published in
the *San Francisco Examiner*. Copyright © 1992 by Zach Trenholm.
Reprinted by permission.

Fig. 34. Paglia as Marlon Brando—the original caricature that was rejected by the *San Francisco Examiner* as "unsuitable for a family newspaper." Copyright © 1992 by Zach Trenholm. Reprinted by permission.

Figs. 35–39. Preliminary sketches for the *San Francisco Examiner* caricature: Paglia as bull in china shop, Byzantine evangelist, Venus de Dietrich, bikini-barbell powerlifter, and La Pasionaria. Copyright © 1992 by Zach Trenholm. Reprinted by permission.

Fig. 40. Gift from the staff of Penthouse Comix. Presented to
Paglia by George Caragonne at Bob Guccione's Manhattan
townhouse. Copyright 1994 by CDI. Drawn by Bill Vallely and
written by George Caragonne, editor in chief of Penthouse Comix.

A MEDIA CHRONICLE

Selected articles regarding Camille Paglia. The bibliography of *Sex, Art, and American Culture* ended with June 1992. The bibliography of *Vamps & Tramps* picks up from that point, with some earlier additions. Annotations by Paglia.

"*My* Name's Camille Paglia," *Philadelphia*, February 1992. Article with photos of the two feminist/astrologer Camille Paglias, unknown to each other until one wrote *Sexual Personae*. When Lesbo A-Go-Go, a troupe of lesbian go-go dancers from Washington, D.C., tried to contact pro-porn professor Paglia to defend them on *Donahue*, they reached the other one by mistake. The latter then appeared on the show (November 1991) and attacked the dancers from the anti-porn feminist position. Author Paglia tells *Philadelphia*, "It's like that episode on *The Twilight Zone* where Vera Miles meets her double in the deserted bus depot."

"Female Problems at Brown," *Heterodoxy*, May 1992. The satirical anti-p.c. newspaper quotes a Stalinist broadside by feminist English department faculty at Brown University denouncing Paglia's appearance there in March 1992, which they boycotted and which drew one of the largest crowds in 30 years.

"Camille Paglia: 'As feministas vulgarizam a grandeza da mulher': Uma das provocações da polêmica professora da Philadelphia's University of the Arts," *Jornal da Tarde* (Brazil), May 12, 1992. Big spread on Paglia.

Joan Juliet Buck, "The Annette Effect," *Vanity Fair*, June 1992. Cover story on Annette Bening: "Now she's reading Camille Paglia, and finds the concept of 'humanist rather than feminist' to be attractive. 'Nature comes first.' "

Kathy Healy, "The New Strippers," *Allure*, June 1992. Paglia defends stripping.

"Speech Codes and Censors," *Wall Street Journal*, June 6, 1992. Editorial about assaults on free speech on American campuses. Condemns the campaign against *Sexual Personae* by feminist faculty at Connecticut College.

"College reading list causes controversy," *Chronicle of Higher Education*, June 17, 1992. On the furor over *Sexual Personae* at Connecticut College.

"The Real Camille," *QW* (New York), June 21, 1992. A gay magazine prints vicious false allegations about Paglia, whose long, angry letter in response appeared July 19.

Emily Harrison Weir, "The Academic Dominatrix: Camille Paglia's Incendiary Cultural Criticism," *NewsSmith* (Smith College), Summer 1992. Account of Paglia's lecture in April at Smith.

Katherine Farrish, "Tempest over a summer selection: Anti-feminist book has college in uproar," *The Hartford Courant*, July 12, 1992. Account of the controversy at Connecticut College over *Sexual Personae*, which some professors called "trash." Janet Gezari, the college's director of women's studies, says about *Sexual Personae*, "Let's not be fooled by packaging into mistaking any hate-speech or sexist or racist doctrine for ideas."

Spy parody issue of *The New York Times*, July 15, 1992. Distributed as a prank at the Democratic National Convention in New York City. Headline: "Perot Set to Pick TV's Oprah Winfrey as Running Mate." On the op-ed page are parodies of articles by Paglia, Anna Quindlen, A.M. Rosenthal, and Michael Dukakis. The Paglia piece, written by Jamie Malanowski, is the lead, "A Hot-Button Candidate: Seeing Clinton as Slick Willie and Liking It." A montage shows Clinton in a jeweled white Elvis suit.

"Women We Love," *Esquire*, August 1992. Listed as "Bad Girls for Good Times": Drew Barrymore and Camille Paglia.

Robert Rockwood, "The Emperor Is Naked: Baring the Truth Behind NAMBLA's Bad Press," *NAMBLA Bulletin,* July /August 1992. Magazine of the controversial North American Man/Boy Love Association. Long excerpt from *Sexual Personae* about what Rockwood correctly summarizes as "an underlying religious impulse" in the ancient cult of the beautiful boy.

"Camille Paglia," *Current Biography*, August 1992. Cover story. Visible in photo of Paglia in her office: poster of Madonna in a black bra; photo of porn king Jeff Stryker, clipped from a gay newspaper.

Camille Paglia, "The Diana Cult: What's *really* behind our obsession with the Princess of Wales?" *New Republic*, August 3, 1992. Cover story. Reprinted in *The Guardian* (London), *The Globe and Mail* (Toronto), and *The San Francisco Chronicle*.

Robert F. Moss, "The 1992 Literary Olympics," *New York*, August 10, 1992. Fantasy athletic contests for literati: "Freestyle Repartee" at the "Dorothy Parker Pavilion" and, "the glamour event," "Literary Feuding" at the "Lillian Hellman/Mary McCarthy Arena." Paglia versus Sontag proposed for the latter. Same issue: Marilyn Webb, "The Right Course." Announces that fall's five-night lecture series on feminism at the 92nd Street Y, with Gloria Steinem the first week and Paglia the second. [It was at this event that Steinem, presiding onstage with Susan Faludi and Naomi Wolf, was caught by the *60 Minutes* cameras declaring to the audience about Paglia, "We don't give a shit what she thinks!"] Paglia says, "My brand of feminism is totally unlike establishment feminism" [a term, along with "feminist establishment," that she coined].

Joseph P. Kahn and Mark Muro, "Woody: The fall of a Hollywood icon," *The Boston Globe*, August 20, 1992. Paglia calls the Woody Allen scandal "a wonderful cold douche for feminist naivete" [apparently the first appearance of that slang term in the *Globe*].

Richard Weizel, "College Reading List Provokes Debate," *The New York Times*, Connecticut supplement, August 23, 1992. Account of the controversy over *Sexual Personae* at Connecticut College. Paglia is described as a "renegade feminist" [a term first applied to her by Diane Sawyer on ABC's *Primetime Live*]. Janet Gezari, director of the college's women's studies program, calls Paglia "a woman hater" and says, "She is a misogynist in the best tradition of Western misogyny. And we should not be recommending that students read books that present those kinds of opinions about women." Weizel states: "[Gezari] said she strongly opposed the book's inclusion on the summer reading list and took part in an organized effort to have it removed because the book 'is racist and sexist and just doesn't belong on a list of books that this college should be recommending.' She said she agreed with some professors who compared it to Hitler's *Mein Kampf*." A male professor says of *Sexual Personae*, "Besides, it's just a bad book from a literary point of view and it shouldn't be read by students. What really strikes me about the book is that both conservatives and liberals have blasted it. That must tell you something." [Gee whiz! A book that thinks for itself!] Lauren H. Klatzkin, the student who originally suggested *Sexual Personae*, "said she was appalled by the efforts to have it removed. 'I was really shocked so many people got so upset about it. The view of feminism expressed in the book may not be fashionable these days, but it is a true form of expression and one as worthy of discussion as any other form.' "

James Wolcott, "Paglia's Power Trip," *Vanity Fair*, September 1992. Profile of Paglia, with schoolday photos of her as Cleopatra, Amelia

Earhart, and Clyde Barrow. Headline: "Since the publication two years ago of her slash-and-burn manifesto, *Sexual Personae*, Camille Paglia has been bullying her way around the intellectual circuit, ambushing the new feminism—and almost single-handedly resurrecting the pop-cult debate. Now the woman who compares herself favorably to Simone de Beauvoir *and* Madonna is busy promoting herself as the female role model of the next century." Photo by James Hamilton (who shot Paglia as bantam-weight super-dyke for *The Village Voice* in 1991) of a vampy, cleavage-baring Paglia and her handsome African-American "Centurions," bodyguards Rennard Snowden and Brian Roach.

Lynn Hirschberg, "Strange Love," *Vanity Fair*, September 1992. Profile of rock diva Courtney Love, who says about her "*Kinderwhore*" style of dress and makeup, "It's a good look. It's sexy, but you can sit down and say, 'I read Camille Paglia.' "

Reed Woodhouse, "Hitting 'em with her best shot: Camille Paglia and *Bay Windows*' Reed Woodhouse have a nice long chat," *Bay Windows* (Boston), September 3, 1992. Part two appeared September 10. Paglia considers Woodhouse one of the most cultivated and knowledgeable interviewers she has encountered. Also in second issue: the lesbian office manager's editorial, "Camille Paglia: A Dangerous Woman," which calls Paglia a "misogynist," groups her with ultra-conservatives like Pat Buchanan, and scolds gay men for liking her.

Chris Culwell, "Camille Unbound: Bitchy academic pushes everyone's buttons," *The Sentinel* (San Francisco), September 10, 1992. Paglia quoted under a photo of Michel Foucault: "Foucault is one of the most misogynist writers of the past 100 years; there isn't a single woman anywhere in his books." Asked what she was "trying to accomplish" with *Sexual Personae*, Paglia replies: "Ultimately, I'm trying to record how the mind works. The book is not about fixed ideas. It's about the epic struggle between the Apollonian—the form-making aspect of mankind—and the Dionysian, between reason and nature, mind and emotion. The book shows the Apollonian dissolving into the Dionysian, back and forth in this kind of rhythmic, oscillating motion. I call the book psychedelic because it's inspired by the kind of thing we were doing in the Sixties. My book is doing what people had to take acid to do; it's exploring parts of the brain we don't ordinarily use in everyday life." [The only reviewer who caught the rhythmic oscillations and critique of polarities in *Sexual Personae* was Pat Lee, "The Eyes Have It," *Yorkshire Post*, April 12, 1990.]

Roger Kimball, "Dragon Lady of Academe," *The Wall Street Journal*, September 17, 1992. Review of *Sex, Art, and American Culture*. Says about Paglia's academic exposé "Junk Bonds and Corporate Raiders": "Don't look for moderation or understatement here. This is criticism as an exercise in saturation bombing."

Elizabeth Tippens, "Mastering Madonna," *Rolling Stone*, September 17, 1992. Courses at various schools around the country that make use of Madonna, including Paglia's "Women and Sex Roles" at the University of the Arts.

Tim Appelo and Meredith Berkman, "Fighting Words," *Entertainment Weekly*, September 18, 1992. The Paglia versus Sontag battle. " 'There's a jealousy factor here,' Paglia snorts. 'I'm saying, "You're the heavyweight who used to be the bully on the block and here comes the new girl!" ' " Describes incident at a Philadelphia Madonna concert where "a young male peed on her seat" and Paglia punched him in the face. [Paglia said to herself, "This is ridiculous! I'm a 40-year-old woman with a purse!"]

Robert L. Pincus, "Paglia's 'Sex, Art' essays infuriate and/or enthrall," *The San Diego Union-Tribune*, September 20, 1992. Review by an art critic: "Her attacks on the American academy's obsession with French theorists like Michel Foucault and Jacques Derrida are brave. As she observes, their influence has given rise to a lot of dry, badly written, and unnecessarily complex commentary on the arts. Paglia offers an alternate method of writing erudite, insightful criticism on literature, art, and pop culture that is both accessible and relevant to a wide range of readers."

Laura Shapiro, "An Intellectual Amazon: Is Paglia a radical thinker or a media marvel?" *Newsweek*, September 21, 1992. Photo of Paglia with bullwhip. Caption (from a classic Ann-Margret movie): "Kitten with a whip: Paglia en garde."

"People in the News," *San Jose Mercury News*, September 22, 1992. "Today's Quote": Paglia comments on what the newspaper calls "Madonna's hotly anticipated photo-fantasy book, titled *Sex*, a work so racy it will be encased in a Mylar bag—penetrable only with the help of a sharp object." Paglia says, "Short of going into a convent, I don't know how she can top herself after this."

Stephanie Zacharek, "Uppity Bitch: Camille 101 is a richer course than critics admit," *Boston Phoenix Literary Supplement*, September 25, 1992. Caption under photo (from 1991 M.I.T. lecture): "Brickbat Tosser: Camille Paglia builds a tough argument with playful prose." Begins: "If you sat down with a group of women's-studies majors and told them the story of a woman academic who, despite her fierce intelligence and encyclopedic knowledge of world culture, is despised in certain academic circles, they'd be the first to chalk her fate up to the oppressive patriarchal system. The reaction of many feminists to Paglia's 1990 opus, *Sexual Personae*, and to the media blitz that followed it, proves that the desire to squelch ideas that don't square with your own isn't a purely white, masculine trait. Curious how, even in the Nineties, a woman runs the risk of getting lynched for being uppity."

Nat Hentoff, "Forbidden Books at Connecticut College," *Washington Post*, September 26, 1992. Criticizes the fight over *Sexual Personae* and says it was the students who "saved the book—and the intellectual credibility" of the college: "Paglia sees literature and the rest of the world as a tournament, and her mission is to unhorse fashionable literary and intellectual figures and theories." See also Hentoff, "When Students Teach Professors," *The Progressive*, February 1993.

"Feminism and Its Discontents: Susan Faludi, Camille Paglia, and Naomi Wolf on Men, Women, Sex, Family Values . . . and each other," *Image* magazine, *San Francisco Examiner*, September 27, 1992.

Entire magazine devoted to full airing of the issues. See also letters, October 25. [Significant that this debate was conceived (by editor David Talbot) and published on the West Coast. The East Coast media were then too dominated by the feminist establishment.]

Don Savage and Christine Wenc, "Camille Paglia: Boy, She Sure Does Talk Fast!" *The Stranger* (Seattle), September 28, 1992. Interview. Part two: October 5.

Melinda Bargreen, "Camille Paglia: thorn in the feminists' side," *The Seattle Times*, September 29, 1992. Inside headline: "A literary pit bull attacks the conventional feminist wisdom." Paglia says: "Let the feminists try to dismiss me. My feminism predates Steinem. Today's feminists are the lackeys and minions of the tyrant, Gloria Steinem. I evolved past the point where they began!"

Diana Walker, "Camille Paglia strikes a pose in lecture on feminism" and "Camille Paglia loosens up," *The Daily of the University of Washington* (Seattle), September 30, 1992. Account of lecture at university. Photo outside the hall of *60 Minutes* cameraman filming socialist protesters, none of whom had read Paglia's work. [In widely rebroadcast footage from this lecture, Paglia declares: "My task as a feminist intellectual is to attack cant, convention, and cliché wherever they appear, in order to save feminism from its worst excesses. I'm not trying to get rid of feminism. I'm trying to reform it from within."]

Joan Smith, "The Original Feminist? Camille Paglia's no shrinking violet, that's for sure," *San Francisco Examiner*, September 30, 1992. Account of Paglia's lecture at the Herbst Theater. Huge photo by Mike Macor of Paglia looking like a wind-blown La Pasionaria, inflaming the crowd.

JoAnn Garflin, "Sex, Art, and American Culture," *East Bay Express* (Los Angeles), October 1992. "It's time to board up the windows, bury the silver, and send the children to stay with relatives in the country. Camille Paglia is back. Reading Paglia is like knocking back three espressos in a row. Your blood races, your eyes bulge, you hyperventilate. Camille Paglia is the person Dorothy Parker would have been if she'd had a Ph.D."

Fenton Bailey, "I, Paglia: Camille Paglia's greatest hits," *Paper* (New York), October 1992. Review. "Whether you agree—or violently disagree—with Camille Paglia's porn of plenty (I love it), there is no doubt that she has performed an invaluable service—reviving the academic establishment from irrelevant extinction. From Oxford to Harvard, academia has failed to make any sense thus far of popular culture. Either it has stuck its nose in the air, tut-tutting over the lowbrow philistines swarming the plain, or it has condescended to perform a cultural ascension on pop, making the comprehensible incomprehensible by trussing it in a criticalese that is mere babble to anyone but the snobs who have constructed the semi-idiotic code for their elitist onanism. 'The Dionysian is no picnic!' Paglia proclaims, a 21st-century Boadicea with chain saws on her chariot wheels, the better to cut down chaff like Susan Sontag, Naomi Wolf and Meryl Streep—and anyone else who gets in her way.'"

Stuart Whitwell, "Nietzsche, Meet Madonna," *Booklist*, October 1, 1992. One of the best analyses yet of Paglia's thought. Whitwell identifies "four overarching themes" in *Sexual Personae* and says that, if readers keep them in mind, "*Sex, Art, and American Culture* will begin to seem less like a fireworks display and more like a concerted effort to shift the intellectual focus of twentieth-century thought." His third category: "While liberals and conservatives were bickering over how to deal with the historical changes brought about by the collapse of religious authority, the rise of democracy, and the furious pace of technological evolution, pop culture has risen up like a tidal wave and changed the world so dramatically that the old quarrels of liberals and conservatives now look facile and outdated."

Pat Califia, "Radical assessment," *The Philadelphia Inquirer*, October 4, 1992. Attack on *Sex, Art, and American Culture*. Those who think the pro-sex wing of feminism is free of rabid political correctness must see this uninformed, maladroit review, with its humorless, grindingly formulaic Seventies-era politics. It calls Paglia "a failed academic," "repetitious, hateful, and in the end dreadfully dull."

"The Cultural Elite: Who They Really Are," *Newsweek*, October 5, 1992. Cover story about Vice-President Dan Quayle's charge that a liberal "cultural elite" wields too much power in America. *Newsweek* lists 100 people, including Paglia, in art, politics, academe, and the media who constitute the "cultural elite." Paglia is identified as "Cultural terrorist, author": "Why is the Ivy League so frightened?" The false statement that Paglia "calls date rape 'sex as usual' " was retracted by *Newsweek* on February 15, 1993.

MTV, interview with Madonna (Milan), October 6, 1992. *Questioner* [British male voice]: "Are you familiar with the work of Camille Paglia?" *Madonna* [correcting pronunciation]: "Paglia, yes." *Q*: "She says female beauty is a potent form of power. Do you agree?" *Madonna*: "Absolutely." *Q*: "In what way are you using your power?" *Madonna*: "You mean I have to tell you? [laughs] How am I using my power? By doing what I do. Well, it depends on what you do. I mean, you could be a beautiful girl who just sits around the house filing your nails all day, or you could be a beautiful girl who's out there saying something, taking risks and trying to change people's way of thinking, which is what I think I am. But I have to preface all of that by saying that beauty is in the eye of the beholder. There are plenty of people who don't think I'm beautiful, so in that case Camille's ideas are out the window [laughs loudly]."

Robert Taylor, "Camille Paglia's fiery essays on sex, art, and education," *The Boston Globe*, October 7, 1992. Review. "The ideas of Camille Paglia go rat-a-tat-tat like the ammo clip of a Chicago piano. As for feminism, Paglia suggests it might evolve if feminists started reading Dante and Shakespeare instead of each other. The tradition of learned eccentric—someone who's smarter than anyone else until you realize he or she is also loopy—thrives in Paglia."

"This Week," *San Francisco Weekly*, October 7, 1992. Photo of Paglia (signing books after lecture at Herbst Theater) rising to bow to and kiss the hands of two majestic drag queens in black. In same issue: Ann Powers, "Both sides now: Camille Paglia's vitriol doesn't make room for an Axl Rose." Feminist attack on Paglia (alleging her incapable of appreciating androgynous Axl Rose) that produced a flood of letters, printed November 4. Sample: "Apparently Powers has not bothered to read *Sexual Personae*, which examines and celebrates androgynous sex appeal from Lord Byron to Elvis Presley." [Paglia's admiration of Guns 'n' Roses had been a matter of public record for over a year.]

Adair Lara, "Dealing with Paglia's Sticks and Stones," *San Francisco Chronicle*, October 8, 1992. Entertaining account of Paglia's lecture at the Herbst Theater. "There's been such a depressing amount of political correctness around lately, and Paglia reminds me of the good old days of journalism, when you said whatever the hell you liked and hoped no one showed up in your office the next day, looking for a duel."

Edna Gunderson, "Lady Madonna: Who is that girl?" *USA Today*, October 9, 1992. A weary Madonna, goaded by a reporter, gloomily insists no one understands her. "Even rebel feminist Camille Paglia, who hails Madonna as the feminist ideal, has miscalculated, she says. 'I've heard her say things, under the guise of being adoring, that make it very clear that she doesn't get me at all. I'm flattered to a certain extent, but sometimes I think she's full of shit." Though this was a minor item in the article, the inside headline blared: "Paglia misses Madonna's point." [Paglia furiously phoned the office of Madonna's publicist to lodge a protest: "Do you know the *crap* I've taken for two years from the rock press because of my endorsement of Madonna?" During an interview that week on a New York radio talk show, Paglia was prodded about Madonna's remark but refused to criticize her, declaring that whatever Madonna-the-person might do or say, nothing would shake Paglia's admiration for Madonna-the-artist, the higher being.]

Jim Windolf, "Off the Record," *New York Observer*, October 12, 1992. Account of incident at feminist panel discussion at the 92nd Street Y on September 30, when CBS associate producer Claudia Weinstein tried to ask moderator Gloria Steinem about Paglia but was repeatedly cut off. "Steve Kroft, the *60 Minutes* correspondent who is reporting the segment on Ms. Paglia, felt that Ms. Weinstein had walked into a trap set by Ms. Steinem. Ms. Steinem, he explained, declined to be interviewed concerning Ms. Paglia until after Election Day [November 3], but suggested herself that *60 Minutes* attend the talk at the Y. 'I think we were set up,' Mr. Kroft said. 'This is not designed to be a glowing profile of Paglia—I don't want to characterize it, actually—but one of Paglia's main points is that Steinem and Faludi and mainstream feminist leaders don't tolerate any dissenting opinions. Without passing judgment on what happened, I think Steinem proved Paglia's point.' "

Kathryn Robinson, "Camille Paglia's Ego: Feminist Camille Paglia is the smartest, sexiest, most provocative intellectual of our time. Just ask her." *Seattle Weekly*, October 14, 1992. On Paglia's lecture at University of Washington: "Part of what's funny, you realize as you sit watching her with your brain whirring and your jaw hanging open, is that she's not, well . . . *ladylike*. In pronouncing herself every superlative in the book, Paglia—who claims to have learned whatever femininity she possesses from drag queens—busts loose from the constraints of modesty and delicacy that have bound women for centuries, the very constraints that piqued the women's movement into being. Most of the power-trippers throughout history have been men. Her intellectual strutting may appear shocking for its novelty—but it is also, for this feminist anyway, a full-on *thrill*. Camille Paglia in high swagger not only promotes the feminist goal of authority—she embodies it. That her self-proclaimed authority sticks in so many critics' craws strikes me as sexism of the most patronizing sort. . . . In every hot, exclamation-pointed pronouncement lies her *passion*—the very element that she believes has been clinically excised from the movement by a crop of feminist prudes who regard men as evil, sex as oppressive, and feminism as indisputable dogma. I, for one, am grateful: feminists need role models this confident. Ironically, she has managed to arouse more rigorous and relevant debate than any other feminist has done in recent memory. Her detractors seem to believe that she's dangerous to the cause of feminism. That's absurd—the only way feminism can hope to stay sharp for the next century will be to hone itself against a whetstone of unusual size and strength. Camille Paglia's ego will do nicely."

Ernest Hardy, "Blah, Blah, Blah: Cultural Critic Camille Paglia Dishes It Out, and Out, and Out," *Village View* (Los Angeles), October 16–22. Cover story on Paglia with superb photographs by Ian Johnson.

John Updike, "She's Got Personality," *The New Yorker*, October 19, 1992. Review. "She is a lusty, feisty bisexual scholar swooping into prominence from an outsider's perch. . . . 'Junk Bonds and Corporate Raiders' takes on a comic-strip vitality as the superheroine, in her Sixties Frye boots and hot pants, clobbers one villain after another; you can almost see the capitalized concussion sounds in their little spiky balloons. POW! . . . BIFF! . . . ZAP! . . . WHAMMO! Take to the hills, evildoers; No-Nonsensewoman is here, with her trusty sidekicks Elvis Presley, Jimi Hendrix, and Keith Richards. . . . Tune in the further adventures of the Amazon quester."

Robin Tyler, Letters, *The Advocate*, October 20, 1992. Responding to Paglia's positive reference to her in *The Advocate*, the lesbian co-median insists "we do not agree on most things." [Paglia thought this contemptible hypocrisy and wrote Tyler to say so. After Paglia's talk at London's Institute of Contemporary Art the prior June, Tyler invited her to a benefit performance, where, backstage, Tyler complained about the paralyzing political correctness in feminism and said most feminist leaders acknowledged it privately. In her letter, Paglia suggested that perhaps Tyler's business interests (she organizes all-women cruises) were preventing her from admitting the truth in public.]

Robert Myers, "Suburban Amazon: Pop-culture critic Camille Paglia discusses sex, suburbia, and family values," *Eastsideweek* (Seattle), October 21, 1992. Interview on postwar American suburban culture. Paglia says: "The worst thing is when people meet me and they say, 'Oh, she's very nice.' I am not very nice! *(bounces on the couch, punching the cushions)* Don't say that! Don't say that! Don't say that! That's the one thing they trained me to be. I try to be Keith Richards as best as I can. But you can't get the suburbia out of the girl, I'm telling you."

B.W. Powe, "Joan of Arc in jackboots," *The Globe and Mail* (Toronto), October 24, 1992. Review of *Sex, Art* beginning, "It's truly an accomplishment to offend everyone." Says of specific passages, the book "spells out what may be among the first intimations of a 21st-century rhetoric."

Bill Marve, "Who is Camille Paglia and *why* is she saying all these *outrageous* things?," *Dallas Morning News*, October 28, 1992. Subheading: "Outspoken scholar deems politically correct feminism wrong, wrong, wrong."

"Beyond the Year 2000: What to Expect in the New Millennium," *Time*, special issue, Fall 1992. "The Century Ahead: Great Goals." Celebrities are asked, "What should humankind aim to accomplish in the coming decades?" Paglia replies: "We should smash the current educational curriculum. I see the multiculturalism being promoted now as a fraud. History is being distorted. It is regarded as nothing but a record of pain, oppression, disaster, and atrocities. My master plan for world understanding is a new kind of education based on comparative religion and archaeology, on an arts-centered curriculum. I am also calling for a Reform feminism instead of the hatred of men now being peddled. Feminism must turn back toward men."

Brooks Peters, "Vintage Vidal," *Out*, Fall 1992. Paglia laments Gore Vidal's long residence abroad: "As a gay figure he certainly could have critiqued the rise of this very pernicious feminist theory which I think is damaging the cause of feminism. We needed someone like Vidal present in the country all the time, attacking it and satirizing it from the point of view of the left. But it has been left to the Jesse Helmses—the far right. And that is not good. Vidal was at his most seditious with *Myra Breckinridge*. It pushed the power base in ways that haven't even been assessed yet. . . . He is a true gay role model, a man of culture and learning and style who represents the best of a worldliness that is conspicuously lacking today. With his courtly manner, Vidal is a patrician throwback. I love his acerbic, waspish style. His fearlessness. The bold attacks."

Robert L. Caserio, "Journalists, Legislators and Ideologues in the Classroom: An Impolitic View," *Western Humanities Review*, Fall 1992. On the politicization of literary studies. Includes a mordant close reading of nasty academic reviews of *Sexual Personae*.

"Meet Camille Paglia," *Motorbooty* (Ann Arbor, Mich.), Fall 1992. Hilarious satire of Paglia in teen-magazine form. ("Favorite Pastime: Smashing the entire structure of feminist ideology.")

James Childs, "In Print," *Yale Alumni Magazine*, November 1992. Snide review of *Sex, Art* that admits, "If size of audience is a yardstick, Camille Paglia's *Sexual Personae* is the most popular literary study of the 1990s."

Stephen O'Shea, "When Elle Met Ollie: Or how Elle Macpherson and Oliver Stone had a heart-to-heart date," *Elle*, November 1992. Director Oliver Stone says: "The man-woman issue oversimplifies and misguides; the economic and legal issues I understand, but culturally I find the issue to be very blinding. I try to avoid labels and definitions. I'm very influenced by Camille Paglia. I don't agree with everything she says, but she's conflated a lot of the tension around modern thinking, and I don't think there's much to modern thinking about women that will last. We go through cycles; most women I meet don't feel the way the intellectuals tell them they must feel."

Jim Powell, "Sensational individualist Camille Paglia strikes the corrupt intellectual establishment like a thunderbolt," *Laissez Faire Books*, November 1992. "Paglia has emerged as a dynamic apostle of individualism." Harvard's Stephen Macedo says, "Camille Paglia is a phenomenon: an intellectual incendiary and a scourge to the feminist and literary criticism establishments."

"Camille Paglia: De gesel der vrouwen." Cover story on Paglia: four articles by critics and journalists. *De Groene Amsterdammer* (The Netherlands), November 1992.

James Servin, "Chic or Cruel? Gianni Versace's styles take a cue from the world of S & M," *New York Times*, November 1, 1992. Asked

about Versace's use of bondage as a "couture esthetic," Paglia replies: "In my publicity shots I've been trying to do Helmut Newton
without Helmut Newton. His Berlin dream of the world is everywhere in the S & M Versace. I also see [in Versace's designs]
historical allusions to Roman gladiators and Minoan snake goddesses. It's also the imagery of the age we're in, the age of AIDS,
in which we are under the whip of the dominatrix Nature."

M.G. Lord, "Politics Is a Hardball Game," *Newsday*, November 1,
1992. Quoted about Geraldine Ferraro et al., Paglia supports Lord's
thesis that "New York female politicians are among the worst sports
in the nation."

"The New Voyeurism: Madonna and the Selling of *Sex*," *Newsweek*,
November 2, 1992. Cover story. Madonna, asked by *Newsweek*
whether she would like to meet Paglia, replies: "First, I'd like to see
her across the room and then I'd like to decide whether I want to
approach her." [Paglia responded, "What is this, a sorority party?"]

Ray Conlogue, "Books: Ray Conlogue regards Camille Paglia as
feminism's rescuer," *The Globe and Mail* (Toronto), November 5,
1992. Excellent analysis of Paglia's views. "For those wondering if
they *dare* go hear Camille Paglia speak Monday night at Toronto's
Winter Garden, I can offer little cheer. She does bite, I'm afraid.
She's fierce. And she may even be the publicity-seeking narcissist
about whom Robert Fulford fretted in this column some weeks ago.
But if it's any consolation, she is innocent of the major charge:
betraying feminism. On the contrary, she's the towtruck that can
haul it out of its current dead-end street. Her greatest service is to
the philosophy of feminism, which is already shipwrecked on the
shoals of Rousseauian absurdity. One doesn't need to look far for
examples. There's the filmmaker who told me last year that 'construction workers whistling at women and men who rape six-month-old
babies are morally indistinguishable.' Or the newspaper columnist
who believes she is oppressed because men look at her breasts when
she is nursing: by an act of Rousseauian amnesia she has forgotten
whether or not, in bikini or ballgown, she ever took pleasure in that
concealing and revealing. In the popular media of North America,

this kind of sophistry has become the norm. Paglia calls it to account, and not a moment too soon."

Susan G. Cole, "Author Camille Paglia the Ayn Rand of the Nineties," *Now* (Toronto), November 5–11, 1992. Subheading: " 'I am the first great woman guitarist. I don't use guitars. I use words.' " On front cover: "Camille Paglia's Poison Pen."

Janice Turner, "Paglia pans 'old feminists' at sellout show," *Toronto Star*, November 10, 1992. Headline in another edition: "Feminist maverick pans old guard."

Val Ross, "Social critic spices lecture with stand-up comic touches. Provocateur: Author Camille Paglia, who calls herself a 'one-woman liberation movement,' wants to redefine feminism," *The Globe and Mail* (Toronto), November 10, 1992.

Marco R della Cava, "The road from babes to babies," *USA Today*, November 16, 1992. Profile of Hugh Hefner. Paglia says about Hefner: "He ushered in a revolution in American sexual consciousness. Some say the women in *Playboy* come across as commodities, like a stereo. But I think *Playboy* is more about an appreciation of pleasure of all kinds."

Victor Dwyer, "Woman warrior: An author makes a frontal assault on feminism," *Maclean's* (Canada), November 16, 1992. "Heather Smith, a lecturer in political science at Acadia University in Wolfville, N.S., has added two chapters from *Sex, Art, and American Culture* to the reading list in her women-in-politics course. 'Feminist courses too often become little more than love-ins where hard questions are never asked,' says Smith. 'Paglia is asking some very hard questions—and has some pretty good points to make. After all, what she's really saying is that women should stop acting as victims and take control.' " Paglia says, "What people find energizing about me is that I question everything, everything. That was Susan Sontag's obligation. But I occupy her throne right now and she can't get back into it. I mean, I'm sorry, I'm sitting in it."

Jim McKeever, "Hurricane Camille," *Syracuse Herald American*, November 22, 1992. Profile.

Rebecca Mead, "A Spy in the house of love," *Sunday Times* (London), November 22, 1992. Announces Paglia, "the bitch-goddess of American feminism," will write advice column for *Spy*. "This is rather like hiring Nikki Lauda to be a chauffeur." Amusing fantasy (using Paglia's published words, with invented questions) about the future column, illustrating what Mead calls "Paglia's brand of 'snap out of it, sucker' succour."

"A ghost? No, just Sandra Bernhard," "Page Six," *New York Post*, November 24, 1992. A vexed Paglia denies rumor she was "channeling Gertrude Stein" backstage at premiere of Sandra Bernhard's one-woman show at the Paramount.

Ingela Lind, "Konst på blodigt allvar: Libertinen och kulturkonservativa Camille Paglia vill dränka de franska filosoferna," *Dagens Nyheter* (Stockholm), November 29, 1992. Article on Paglia, with *Vanity Fair* photograph of Paglia with bodyguards.

Christina Bevilacqua, "Interview: Camille Paglia," *Italian Americana*, Fall/Winter 1992. Account of Paglia's Italian-American family and upbringing. [Paired with much shorter, duller interview with feminist professor Sandra Gilbert, who, despite her haughty ethnic pose versus critic Frank Lentricchia, turns out to be only half-Italian and to have had few formative Italian-American experiences.]

Jamie Malanowski, "Madonna: The Next Fifty Years," *Esquire*, December 1992. Satire. Prediction for November 2003: Madonna "discusses her plans to cooperate with newly appointed *New Republic* magazine editor Camille Paglia on an eighteen-hundred-page biography-cum-diatribe entitled *Madonna as Yahweh: Ontological Post-Post-Feminism and the Era of the Meta-Celebrity*."

Paulo Francis, "Um direto no estômago do feminismo: Verve, tiradas extraordinárias e fúria polêmica são os ingredientes mais apetitosos de *Personas Sexuais*." *O Estado de S. Paulo* (Brazil), December 1, 1992. Splashy spread on Paglia.

Flavia Sekles, "A bruxa está solta: Escritora americana que virou inimiga publica número 1 dos politicamente corretos bota fogo na eterna guerra entre os sexo," *Veja* (Brazil), December 2, 1992. Interview with Paglia. Headline: "The witch is back."

Stu Bykofsky, "Sez who?," *The Philadelphia Daily News*, December 3, 1992. Asked how she could write an advice column for *Spy* when she complains she has "trouble getting dates," Paglia replies, "That's exactly the point. When you're outside the realm of combat, you have a clearer view, like a coach in football."

Charles Allen, "Paglia goes after the 'beauty myth' swinging," *Daily Princetonian* (Princeton University), December 3, 1992. Paglia calls for the "mass destruction" of women's studies programs and defends the cult of beauty, from antiquity on.

Kara Hailey, "Acid Tongue: *Nassau* listens to controversial author Camille Paglia," *Nassau Weekly* (Princeton University), December 3, 1992. On cover: "Iconoclast Camille Paglia trashes feminist academia." Paglia praises Annie Sprinkle and attacks the highly successful "careerism" of academic feminists like Diana Fuss and Judith Butler. [Butler was a student at Bennington when Paglia was in full cry as a militant lesbian feminist faculty member (1972–80) who gave public lectures on controversial gender issues. Butler's close friends were repeat students of Paglia's. Paglia finds Butler's academic writing on sex unpersuasive and jargon-ridden and notes the significance of Butler's transfer from Bennington to Yale at the high point of trendy French theory.]

Sergio Augusto, "Popstar acadêmica lança 'Personas Sexuais': Bissexual, movida a rock e louca por futebol, Camille Paglia é a mais brilhante inimiga dos politicamente corretos." Sucursal do Rio, "Paglia diz ocupar 'trono' que foi de Sontag." Arthur Nestrovski, "Erudição da autora é di tirar o fôlego." Sucursal do Rio, "Livro quase morreu na gaveta." *Folha de Sâo Paolo* (Brazil), December 4, 1992. Four articles on Paglia.

Nadine Brozan, "Beauty and feminism converge at a Princeton University conference," *New York Times*, December 4, 1992. Announces December 5 appearance of model Cindy Crawford, Linda Wells, editor of *Allure*, and Paglia on a panel organized by Alisa Belletini, producer of MTV's *House of Style*. Paglia says she is "prepared to answer any criticism that might arise of Ms. Crawford and the modeling profession. . . . 'To call great fashion models sex objects, that is revolting. They show flair, style, energy, and personality. Ivy League feminists contend that homemakers who buy fashion magazines are pawns, brainwashed pawns. That's not so. Those magazines are works of art for the masses. The lighting, photography, makeup are gorgeous. You can revel in beauty looking at them.' "

Harry Stein, "A firebrand with a showboating style easily steals the show," *TV Guide*, December 5, 1992. Review of *60 Minutes* segment on Paglia, with Malcolm X-like photo of her jabbing finger in air. Stein praises correspondent Steve Kroft for his "gutsy profile" of "maverick feminist" Paglia, which shed light on "the cutthroat world of modern sexual politics." Says Paglia's view of her critics as "thought police" was proved accurate by Gloria Steinem's behavior on camera. "That Paglia seems to have gotten a fair hearing on TV's most popular magazine show is itself amazing. Mainstream feminism finds some of its fiercest adherents in top media circles. Paglia has routinely gotten far less time on the small screen than opponents with far less influence. Indeed, Kroft—who makes clear he by no means endorses all of Paglia's views—notes there was a strong ad hoc effort within the *60 Minutes* shop to derail the piece. Kroft, as well as producer Frank Devine, are to be congratulated for persevering—and for learning a hard lesson. 'A week earlier,' laughs Kroft, 'I did a piece where I drove around Kuwait among undetonated mines. And I thought *that* story was dangerous.' "

Lois Blinkhorn, "Ideas flying, a maverick breaks the feminist mold," *Milwaukee Journal*, December 6, 1992. "Talking with Camille Paglia feels like trying to interview a force of nature." A woman professor says Paglia "makes a career of being outrageous": "The way she does it is to hate women. In our day and age, it is not very cool for men to express their hatred of women. Since not everyone will do it, the price and the rewards for women who do it are very high." Blinkhorn says, "Paglia's response to this charge drips with sarcasm. 'That really makes a lot of sense,' she says. 'I've written about Madonna, Elizabeth Taylor, Cleopatra, Amelia Earhart. Whenever anyone talks like that, you know they're incompetent.' " [A Stalinist big lie of the feminist establishment: criticism of feminists equals hatred of women.]

Howard Gertler, "Panelists clash on feminism," *Daily Princetonian*, December 7, 1992. Account of Princeton feminist conference. On "The Power of Beauty" panel, Paglia says women's studies programs are "run by mediocre careerists who have never seen a painting in their lives."

Buffy Vouglas, "Paglia rips academic feminists, puts down women's studies," *Princeton Packet*, December 8, 1992. Account in town paper of the conference. Paglia says she is "sick and tired of the provincialism of feminist ideology on the question of beauty."

Howard Gertler, "Women's Studies program responds to Paglia," *Daily Princetonian* (Princeton University), December 8, 1992. Paglia says women's studies is "completely corrupt" and teachers in it are "third-rate." "Nor has she shied from naming names. This weekend, she particularly singled out English professor Elaine Showalter, who serves on the Women's Studies program committee. Paglia has also placed university administrations directly in her line of fire. She argues that many of them—especially Princeton's—put Women's Studies programs together to keep up with competitors and installed 'sycophants' in the newly created posts. 'The programs were put together to catch up fast,' she said." A female Princeton professor of history who teaches in women's studies "dismissed Paglia as 'an academic mediocrity who has found a way to make money out of marketing her own resentments.' " [Another feminist big lie: reduce opponents' motives to financial greed; ignore huge profits of Naomi

Wolf, Susan Faludi, and Gloria Steinem, with their $600,000 and million-dollar book advances.]

"Fireworks and Dazzle at Panel Talk on Beauty: An audience at Princeton is partly star-struck and partly hostile," *The New York Times*, December 9, 1992. Report on the conference. "But if Cindy Crawford was the panel's bombshell, Camille Paglia was its Molotov cocktail, filling the room with fiery outbursts. Charles Allen, a Princeton junior, said Ms. Paglia had expressed 'a lot of men's and women's discontents with feminist rhetoric. Men at Ivy League schools are tied to feminist apron strings,' he said. 'They've been de-sexualized, and are terrorized about having any kind of romantic or emotional relations with women.' "

"Cindy: Quiet, Camille," "Page Six," *New York Post*, December 9, 1992. "When Camille Paglia starts talking, it's hard to get a word in edgewise. But supermodel Cindy Crawford managed to insert two beauts over coffee at her sister-in-law Joanne Gere-Rein's house over the weekend. As the gaggle of gals gabbed prior to attending a feminist forum at Princeton University, Paglia admitted that heretofore she'd had three 'major' relationships with women. When Paglia was asked what her partners had been like, Crawford quipped 'deaf mutes' before the fast-talking feminist could reply. Paglia insists it was in good fun, but later, as she shoved a [free-lance professional] photographer, raged: 'I said no flash, asshole. I'm not Cindy Crawford, I'm an academic talking ideas here,' the *Daily Princetonian* reports."

Roee Rozen, "Ha'isha she margiza et kulam" ["The woman who infuriates everyone"], *Yediot America*, supplement of *Yediot Aharonot* (Israel), December 11, 1992.

Julia Phillips and Anne Thompson, "If Women Ran Hollywood," *Entertainment Weekly*, December 18, 1992. 50 ways Hollywood would be different. Number 35: "Author Camille Paglia would get a development deal."

"Best of 1992," *Entertainment Weekly*, December 25, 1992. Asked for the three most memorable moments in entertainment in 1992, Paglia replies: "No. 1: Sharon Stone's fabulous performance in *Basic Instinct*. No. 2: the Deee-Lite album *Infinity Within* with Lady Kier Kirby's brilliant vocals. No. 3: the En Vogue video 'Free Your Mind,' in which the group catches up to Madonna and surpasses her."

Edney Silvestre, "Paglia faz 'terrorismo cultural,' " *O Globo* (Brazil), December 27, 1992. Interview. Inset quote from Paglia: "Susan Sontag é uma intelectual vaidosa, preguiçosa, afetada e muito pretensiosa."

"The 100 Worst People and Events of 1992," *Spy*, January 1993. Number 89 is "Feminist Infighting." "Misdeeds: Paglia vs. Sontag; Faludi and Steinem vs. Quinn; Quinn vs. Graham; Holtzman vs. Ferraro; Greer vs. Sheehy; Madonna vs. Paglia; Madonna vs. Sinéad; Madonna vs. Lauper. Mitigating Factor: Nothing beats a good catfight."

Robert S. Wieder, "Holiday Parties of the Rich and Famous," *Playboy*, January 1993. Satiric invitations. "Susan Faludi requests the honor of your presence. Join Susan, Gloria Steinem, Susan Brownmiller and others for an evening of male-free jubilation." Party game: "Pin the Penis on Camille Paglia."

Stewart Brand, "Paglia: Brash, Self-Promoting and Possibly the Next Marshall McLuhan," *Wired*, Premiere Issue, 1993. Interview with Paglia on mass media and her admiration for Marshall McLuhan. She lauds her favorite soap opera, *The Young and the Restless*. "Like Andy Warhol, I have been in love with ads since my earliest childhood. That is the way I think." Photomontage of Paglia as enthroned Hindu goddess, with psychedelic orange and blue sun rays: "Scream of Consciousness."

Michael Kilian, "Feminism's gadfly likes the limelight," *The Arizona Republic*, January 5, 1993. Reprint from *The Chicago Tribune*. Paglia says, "There are many faces of feminism. You can be against the current feminist establishment and still be a feminist. All revolutions start well but go bad. This one has degenerated into ideology and dogma—groupthink. They're like the Kremlin: there's only one way to see things, especially any form of art. To them, art is the servant of political correctness."

Gail Shister, "Radical feminist Camille Paglia is a Howard Stern fan—but a wary one," *The Philadelphia Inquirer*, January 6, 1993. "Radical culture vulture Camille Paglia loves Howard Stern, but she'd do his show only 'if I could carry a bullwhip and a cattle prod.' She compares him to the old Marx Brothers. 'He is a true '60s spirit. He's completely anarchic, outside the establishment. He's bawdy, lewd, lustful. Constantly attacking sacred cows. He's also genuinely funny. He treats sex in a lustful manner. That's what we need.' " [Excerpts later appeared in Stern's autobiography, *Private Parts* (1993).]

Christina Hoff Sommers, "A genie strikes back: Correctness, subversion, and the risks of freedom," *The Times Literary Supplement*, January 8, 1993. On cover: "Camille Paglia's revenge." Review of *Sex, Art* by the philosopher-author of *Who Stole Feminism?*

"Diary," *The Times* (London), January 9, 1993. Totally inaccurate reproduction of flawed dustjacket of Viking British edition of *Sex, Art*, with factual misstatements about why it was withdrawn and publication delayed. Similar misstatements were repeated in the *Sunday Express* on January 10 and *Times Higher Education Supplement* on January 15.

"Books: Diary," *The Sunday Times* (London), January 10, 1993. Highly inaccurate account of dustjacket controversy. An unauthorized editorial note to Paglia's protest letter (Jan. 24) falsely claimed the article had been "checked with the BBC and [Paglia's] publisher." A letter (Jan. 31) from her publisher, Clare Alexander, refuted the note and article: "We have at all times accepted that the problems with the cover were Viking's responsibility and not of the author's making." [Paglia's British publicity tour, scheduled for the Jan. 1993 release of *Sex, Art*, was postponed when the defective dustjackets were withdrawn. Because the new publication date fell during the spring academic semester, Paglia went to London for the paperback release in Jan. 1994 instead.]

Sue Wilson, "Mouthing off: Sue Wilson talks to maverick American academic Camille Paglia," *The List* (Edinburgh), January 15, 1993. "Rarely has a woman of letters been such a motormouth, so unashamedly upset so many people, been so unafraid to hold unfashionable views. 'Five foot three of New York Italian intellectual Semtex' . . . Her style is up-front, aggressive, funny, and infuriating, her views a bewildering mixture of the profound and the simply provocative."

David Rossie, "Don't give Lucretia Borgia a bad rap," *The Binghamton Press* (Binghamton, New York), January 15, 1993. Attorney Bruno Colapietro, Paglia's uncle, defends the honor of Lucretia Borgia, whom he declares "more interesting than Amy Fisher."

Corinna Honan, "Men, manipulation, and my need to dominate," *Daily Mail* (London), January 16, 1993. Interview with Paglia.

Julie Burchill, "Women are wimps," *The Spectator* (London), January 16, 1993. [The review that began an avalanche of falling dominos. The Burchill-Paglia wars broke out a month later, when editors of the Burchill-founded *Modern Review* invited Paglia to write for them. Paglia declined because of Burchill's review, and Burchill responded with the first of the hostile faxes.]

Zoë Heller, "Shooting from the hip: Camille Paglia sends feminists into a frenzy." *The Independent on Sunday* (London), January 17, 1993. Profile. Paglia says, "Men are never free from women. First it's their mothers and then it's their wives. For years I've seen middle-aged women in shopping malls dragging their husbands around, saying, 'No! You can't have that hot dog!' This is the reality! Men are on the leash!"

Charles A. Radin, "An ivory cower: Some say 'PC cops' making professors cringe," *The Boston Globe*, January 20, 1993. On political correctness in academe. "[Paglia states] 'When people say the media has exaggerated the problem of PC, that's nonsense. The media hasn't begun to report the depth of the problem with PC.' One of the most sought after and most vilified speakers on the campus lecture circuit, Paglia says she sees demoralized faculty everywhere she goes. 'Everyone is exhausted from the left-versus-right battles,' she said. 'People are afraid to speak out because they know they will be abused. They're walking on eggshells.' "

Craig Lambert, "The Radical Conservative: Harvey Mansfield," *Harvard Magazine*, January–February 1993. Profile of the Thomson Professor of Government. Account of Paglia's lecture, "What's Wrong with Harvard?," to a crowd of eight hundred at Harvard in March 1992, with excerpts from Mansfield's introduction: "Every once in a while, God, who is watching over our affairs, sends a messenger. . . . Professor Paglia is an enemy of the namby-pamby, the hoity-toity, and the artsy-fartsy. She fires back when fired upon— and sometimes even sooner. She restores the art of invective to the academy. There are places where angels fear to tread, but there is nowhere that Professor Paglia fears to tread."

Susie Bright, "Camille Anonymous," *The San Francisco Review of Books*, January–February 1993. Susie Bright, trimming facts at will, does a lot of complaining about why Paglia is mad at her. Paglia replied in a letter to the editor (March–April).

Nicholas Lezard, "Masterclass: Camille Paglia," *The Modern Review* (London), February 1993. Review of *Sex, Art, and American Culture* that ends: "But the essays in the book, their wild claims, their rabble-rousing enthusiasms, her talent for making us stomp our feet to her beat, without exactly knowing why, the way she can say 'will-to-power' in one sentence and 'affectionate calico she-cat named Tea-bag' in the next, that's truly Dionysian. We salute her."

"A wish list for Hillary," *Glamour*, February 1993. Celebrities are asked about their wishes for the new First Lady. Paglia says, "I hope that she will speak for women without capitulating to the outmoded feminist establishment." Elsewhere in the magazine, Paglia says (re: *Newsweek*'s "Cultural Elite" list calling Gloria Steinem "the smartest, funniest, most influential feminist"): "Excuse me, okay? *I* am the smart feminist. *She* is the dope."

James Servin, "An Intellectual Pinup: Camille Paglia says exactly what she thinks—and wears whatever she damn well pleases," *Allure*, February 1993. Photo, captioned "two-fisted feminist," of Paglia doing a war dance in a Donna Karan/George Sand black suit.

Ann Magnuson, "Russ Meyer: The king of B-movies on DD cups and XXX ratings," *Details*, February 1993. Interview. Magnuson says Meyer's *Faster, Pussycat! Kill! Kill!* is "the ultimate postfeminist movie. Tura Satana is Camille Paglia's wet dream!" [Paglia, who saw Meyer's films in a grungy, outlying New Haven porn theater while she was in grad school, agrees.]

Joseph A. Mancro, editorial, *The University Review* (Austin), February 1993. Discusses Paglia's lecture to "an overflow crowd of 1,200" at the LBJ Library at the University of Texas.

Elaine Showalter, "The Divine Miss P.," *London Review of Books*, February 11, 1993. Review of *Sex, Art, and American Culture*. [In her response (March 11, printed elsewhere in this volume) Paglia did not address Showalter's silly innuendo about the postponement of Paglia's British p.r. tour, which succinctly illustrates Showalter's propagandistic research methods when she leaves literature for history.]

Letters, *New York Times*, February 12, 1993. Paglia defends Barbra Streisand's slit-skirt inaugural gala suit against Anne Taylor Fleming's op-ed attack.

Bethany Matz, "Paglia slams NOW, political correctness," *The Daily Texan* (Austin), February 15, 1993. Account of Paglia's lecture at the University of Texas, with photo of the mob scene outside the packed auditorium.

"Fernsehen ist wahr," *Der Spiegel* (Germany), February 15, 1993. On Paglia. Unpublished picture from Paglia's prophetically pre-Bobbitt *People* photos (April 1992) with a switchblade knife: here she stands in attack mode by the men's urinals at Swarthmore College.

Geoff Henley, "Venus Envy: Academic celebrity Camille Paglia is lionized by some, demonized by others and ignored by nobody. That's just the way she likes it," *The Daily Texan* (Austin), February 18, 1993. Interview with Paglia after University of Texas lecture. Texan caption to her podium photo: "Stick it to 'em."

Nancy E. Roman, "Paglia's personae: Iconoclast is woman enough," *The Washington Times*, February 25, 1993. Profile. Inside headline: "I Am Woman, Hear Me Roar," over quote from Paglia: "I came in like a Scud. I create total disorder. I just totally undermine authority."

Gareth Grundy, "Sexual Intellectual: Three years ago, Camille Paglia was an unknown academic. Now, just two books later, she's motormouth of the moment," *London Student* (London), February 25, 1993.

"The Paglia Controversy," *Bay Windows*, February 25, 1993. Two reviews in a Boston gay newspaper of *Sex, Art*, one by a man, Reed Woodhouse, the other by a woman, who calls Paglia's book "drivel." [At a symposium on homosexuality at the Harvard Medical School on March 6, Paglia exclaimed on the enormous intellectual gap between these paired reviews.]

Karen Heller, "The 'D' word, as in *Diva*: Barbra! Madonna! Miss Piggy! They're goddesses and don't you dare forget it," *The Philadelphia Inquirer*, February 28, 1993. Inside headline: "The '90s in America: The era of divas, or so the divas think." Paglia pictured with Coco Chanel, Madonna, Barbra Streisand, Diana Ross, Elizabeth Taylor, and Miss Piggy. "Divas are bold broads who don't just command respect, they earn it. They have big voices and dramatic features, large pocketbooks and even larger attitudes. They don't fish for compliments; they inhale them. They don't drown in misery or victimization or co-dependency or all that other maudlin garbage. They say, *yeah, my life's been tough but let's get on with it*. Divas are the overhead smash to the backlash, the better side of bitch. . . . A diva does not make conversation; she makes pronouncements. Consequently, she's a great talker, but not a good listener. She has no fear of what others think of her, and doesn't believe in good press; only in press—and herself."

Sandra Bernhard, *Out*, February/March 1993. "Camille Paglia called me a walking, talking bundle of neuroses in *Vanity Fair* recently [Sept. 1992]. That's great publicity for my new coffeetable book, *Neurotica*. It's filled with shocking pictures of me obsessively rearranging knick-nacks." [Paglia, carrying on about Madonna, had called Bernhard "a walking, talking neurotic." Horrified to see this in print, she spent ninety minutes in a hot summer phone booth tracking down Bernhard's agent to apologize.]

Candida Brady, "Rebirth of Diana: Could this be what the feminist future holds for the Princess of Wales?," *Sunday Express* (London), March 7, 1993. Cover story interview with Paglia.

Corinna Honan, "Diana: A 20th Century Goddess. From the world's most controversial feminist writer, a remarkable tribute to our beleaguered princess," *Daily Mail* (London), March 12, 1993. Interview with Paglia on Diana. Front page teaser for Paglia's article ("Goddess Diana: An extraordinary verdict by the world's most controversial feminist") floats above giant headline about a rural crisis: "The First Victim of Mad Cow Disease?"

Detlev Reinert, "Sex muss extremer werden," *Süddeutsche Zeitung Magazin* (Munich), March 12, 1993. Interview with Paglia. Reproduction of the *Vanity Fair* photo.

"Di Fury at TV Nude," *The Sun* (London), March 12, 1993. Front-page story with screaming headline. "Princess Diana is outraged over a [not-yet-aired] TV show [presented by Paglia] which features cartoons of her naked." Paglia is blamed for the cartoons, about which she knew nothing. Tory Member of Parliament Geoffrey Dickens says, "The producers should get a clip round the ear."

W. Speers, "Paglia's cartoons offend Princess Di," *The Philadelphia Inquirer*, March 13, 1993. The American wire services pick up the *Sun* story. "Princess Diana is said to be livid over a Camille Paglia-produced British TV show to air next Tuesday that features cartoons of her royal self in various states of undress. Two renderings ran yesterday in a tab, *The Sun*, prompting cries of outrage from members of Parliament. One picture depicted Diana in a Union Jack G-string with royal crests on her breasts. The other was from a sequence showing Diana doing a striptease. Explained Channel 4 TV: 'The cartoons are to illustrate the way Ms. Paglia feels that the princess has become a kind of sex icon like Marilyn Monroe and Brigitte Bardot.' Barked Harry Greenway, a member of Parliament: 'This is piling anguish onto an already tortured person and far exceeds the realms of common decency.' His colleague Sir Nicholas Fairburn said Philadelphia's Paglia and her confederates should be 'manacled together naked on the green outside Parliament.' "

Mike Capuzzo, "Paglia gets mad," Newsmakers, *The Philadelphia Inquirer*, March 16, 1993. "Resident Philadelphia celebrity intellectual Camille Paglia is fighting back." Excerpts from Paglia's press release about the Diana cartoons, picked up by the wire services and reprinted nationwide.

"Paglia's Nude 'Toons of Diana Get Zapped," New York *Newsday*, March 16, 1993. "Cartoons depicting a nude Princess Diana have been dropped from a British television documentary after an outcry among royalists who said the drawings were an affront to public decency." [Snappy headline of the London *Sun* article (March 13) from which this came: "Nude Di Spoof Axed."]

David L. Wheeler, "Study of Lesbians Rekindles Debate Over Biological Basis for Homosexuality: At symposium, critics say researchers bring cultural biases to search for 'gay gene,' " *The Chronicle of Higher Education*, March 17, 1993. Report on symposium on homosexuality and biology at Harvard Medical School. "Camille Paglia brought her perspective of looking at the role of sex in culture to the discussion. Ms. Paglia said she was disappointed with the high proportion of gay men and lesbians at the symposium and was concerned that a wide range of views was not represented. 'I don't like the feeling of a clubhouse,' Ms. Paglia said. 'That is not science.' At the same time, Ms. Paglia says, she wants researchers to keep up their search for the origins of homosexuality. 'There is something strange and wonderful about the gay male mind,' she said, 'and I hope scientists can find out what it is.' "

Leslie Forbes, "Camille Paglia: The *bête noire* of feminism talks to Leslie Forbes about her theories on food, sex and culture—and clams," *The Observer Magazine* (London), March 21, 1993. Paglia hails raw clams and her grandmother's snails cooked in tomato sauce and eaten with hat pins: "I miss the decadent, rich smell of my grandfather's wine grapes starting to rot in the late summer sun, and my grandmother's coffee. I identify with all those Homeric warriors who were constantly eating meat. When I was growing up in New York state, my grandfather would slaughter a lamb in the garden on Sundays, then gut and roast it on a brazier he'd made of scrap metal. I remember the superb taste of the lamb fat every time I read descriptions in the *Iliad* of men slaughtering and cooking animals in exactly that way. An early memory is of eating artichokes, a specialty of my mother's region near Rome. Not artichoke hearts but the actual hard, spiny leaves. People often ask where I get my dark view of Mother Nature. Look no further. If you're given spines to eat as a child, as a delicacy, you understand pretty quickly about the dark side of things." [These were not, as Forbes guesses, the "tiny purple-blushed variety" but large Jerusalem artichokes.]

Maralyn Lois Polak, "Jaws: Talking nonstop, the ferocious philosopher attacks—usually Famous Living Feminists and Dead White Males," *The Philadelphia Inquirer Magazine*, March 28, 1993. On cover: "The One-Woman SWAT Team of Academe." Two-part profile of Paglia, concluding April 4.

Nancy Lamar, "Hurricane Camille," *Philadelphia Gay News*, March 26, 1993. [Over three years after the release of *Sexual Personae*, one of two local gay newspapers finally mentions Paglia, after she complained in national magazines about the political correctness and intolerance of the Philadelphia gay scene. A new editor, Al Patrick, inspired this change of direction, which led to representation of a wider range of gay views.]

Stuart Wavell, "Feminist insults fly in battle of the bitches," *The Sunday Times* (London), March 28, 1993. Amusing account of the hostilities-by-fax between Julie Burchill and Paglia. " 'This is a duel,' Paglia said [to the *Times*] last week. 'Boy, did she make a mistake. She is dealing with heavy, heavy artillery. I'm like a battleship. As an Italian, 1 believe in 10 eyes for an eye and 10 teeth for a tooth.' Burchill's [final] riposte on Friday was a blunt, two-lined salute: 'F*** off you crazy old dyke.' Paglia believed yesterday that her opponent had effectively conceded. 'I feel I have my revenge,' she said. 'It's like judo; she came lunging at me, and I used her weight against her. I went over her like a tank, OK? I just drove her into the dust. How different it would have been if she had been more generous.' Germaine Greer, the feminist writer, said, 'You've got two very canny operators using the media and they are all making pay out of it. Female mud-wrestling has always been a spectator sport—we like watching men fight, so I'm told, so I suppose it's just a bit of a change if they've got tits.' "

Anne Eaton, "The *Star* Interview: Shy Di? Hell, She's an Angel of Sex—gushes America's most outrageous woman writer," *Star*, March 30, 1993. Interview with Paglia about Diana. Photos of stars mentioned: Lana Turner, Jane Wyman, Marlene Dietrich, Liz Taylor, Madonna. [As a Sixties pop devotee, Paglia considers this tabloid article a highlight of her career: *The Star*, in simple, uncensored language ("homoerotic," "pagan"), presents Paglia's ideas to a mass audience.]

Richard Johnson column, *New York Daily News*, March 30, 1993. The Burchill-Paglia fax wars hit the American wire services. "If it seems that this feud lacks intellectual underpinnings, it should be noted that almost no one can remember what Norman Mailer and Gore Vidal were fighting about either."

Mimi Freed, "Interview with an Uzi: Camille Paglia Talks at Mimi Freed," *On Our Backs*, March/April 1993.

Paul Elie, "Et in Arcadia Bennington: A professorial fall from grace," *Lingua Franca*, March/April 1993. Controversy over terminated teacher Maura Spiegel. Paglia describes the fisticuffs, administrative misdeeds, and legal negotiations that led to her own departure from Bennington.

Donald P. Eckard, "Camille Paglia: The New Face of Post Modernism?," *Art Matters* (Philadelphia), April 1993. Cover story. "Paglia, like Nietzsche, seeks a vitalism, a liberation of desire, a return of libidinal energy. She supports pornography, prostitution, suicide, life at the edge. She urges a libertarian micro-politics; life is dangerous—get out and feel it!"

Jessica Pegis, "Sex, art and queer culture: Camille Paglia sounds off about the neurotic state of sexual politics," *Xtra!* (Toronto), April 1993. A rare gay-press article accurate about Paglia's radical views. Paglia says: "Once gay men stood for sophistication and insight into sexuality and a kind of breadth of culture. They were the most cultivated people in the world. Once, okay? But not now. Now the neurotics are in charge. There is an increased homosexuality on the college campus which is not of the positive kind. 'Positive' homosexuality is one that is revolutionary, that frees desire to go toward any direction it wants, but this homosexuality comes from people not knowing who they are. The young men are lost—they have no masculine charisma, no confidence, no energy. What is in these boys to want?"

Kevin Sessums, "Stone Goddess," *Vanity Fair*, April 1993. Cover story on actress Sharon Stone. Paglia denounces protests against *Basic Instinct* by gay activists and feminists, who claimed the film portrays woman as "an evil, dangerous bitch." " 'Women *are* bitches!' essayist Camille Paglia shouts at me when I run this argument by her. 'Woman is the bitch goddess of the universe! *Basic Instinct* has to be seen as the return of the femme fatale, which points up woman's dominance of the sexual realm, and Sharon Stone's performance was one of the great performances by a woman in screen history. That interrogation scene in the police station immediately became one of the classic scenes in Hollywood cinema! There you see it: all those men around her, and a fully sexual woman turns them to jelly! The men are enslaved by their own sexuality!' "

Ciao!, April Fool's Day supplement, *The Guardian* (London), April 1, 1993. "Camille Paglia: First exclusive pictures of Camille Paglia's adopted baby son, Adam," with fake photomontage of Paglia and her "son," with his "leatherette diapers." Hilarious spoof.

Letters, *Times Literary Supplement*, April 2, 1993. Paglia responds to columnist's misstatements (March 19) about production of *Diana Unclothed*.

Gillian Glover, "The fine art of an insult: Gillian Glover eavesdrops on a literary slanging match," *The Scotsman* (Edinburgh), April 2, 1993. "Oh what a show: Malice, Abuse, Rage, Racism, Vanity, Sexism, and Ageism, supported by a full array of attendant literary vices—all strutting their vitriol on a transatlantic stage. Mephistopheles couldn't have conjured a more alluring procession. This week's melodrama has been brought to your breakfast table courtesy of a collaboration between Camille Paglia and Julie Burchill. Each in her own style and country defines and decries modern mores with a joint lungpower that is truly awesome, all the more arresting now they are shouting at each other. They may be shouting in print, but this is print that strains the larynx."

Paul Johnson, "The Potter calls the Digger black and the custard pies fly," *The Spectator*, April 3, 1993. "We are cave-man bruisers under the skin. Thus we are all currently enjoying the brawl between Camille Paglia and Julie Burchill, two grotesquely overrated, overpaid and spectacularly aggressive and self-important women—an encounter which has been described by a third, Germaine Greer, as 'mud-wrestling with tits.' What the row is about is as much a mystery as the pie-fight."

Bob Frost, "Camille Paglia," *West* magazine, *San Jose Mercury News*, April 11, 1993. Interview. Frost says, "Some people think you're a flash in the pan." Paglia replies, "Well, I'm not. One reason I know my work is going to last is because the *artists* have heard me. When

[*Sexual Personae*] came out, contemporary artists almost immediately began writing to me—painters and sculptors and musicians and poets. The media has completely missed that—that the artists have heard me. It's very rare that you get an academic critic who is taken seriously by artists. Because most of the writing on art by academics is *stupid*."

John J. O'Connor, "How the Smile of Comedy Has Turned Wolfish," *New York Times*, April 15, 1993. Review of HBO comedy special starring Dennis Miller: "Peeling back an imaginary mask from his face, he announces, 'It's Camille Paglia.' "

"Teenage Plastic Surgery," *People*, April 26, 1993. Cover story. Asked what's wrong with the new fad for adolescent cosmetic surgery, Paglia replies, "Nothing, as long as there is a serious defect which plastic surgery can correct and help a young person feel more confident. But unfortunately the model that has evolved is the Barbie doll."

Tracy Quan, "The Prostitute, the Comedian—and Me," *Puritan*, Number 31, 1993. Interview with Paglia on prostitution and other issues. Quan is an intellectual working prostitute and activist with P.O.N.Y. (Prostitutes of New York). See her letter correcting Francine du Plessix Gray about prostitution in *New York Review of Books*, Nov. 5, 1992.

"One Big Drag," *The Daily News*, May 5, 1993. Announces video collaboration between drag queen Glenn Belverio and "gonzo feminist" Paglia, who says, "I'm awed by drags. They have a deeper insight into feminism, and they understand that women dominate men and that being glamorous doesn't make them passive."

Camille Paglia, "Princess Diana—a goddess for our times," *San Francisco Examiner*, May 9, 1993. Excerpts from Paglia's *Daily Mail* interview on Diana and account of controversy over Channel 4 program. Also David Armstrong, "*Female Misbehavior*: bad girls, good fun." Interview with director Monika Treut about her new film, which includes "bad-girl intellectual Camille Paglia, seen talking faster than any human being alive, male, female or in-between." Treut says, "I wanted to show [Paglia] as she really is. She is very entertaining, like a stand-up comedian. She is almost a female version of Joe Pesci. I've shown *Female Misbehavior* at film festivals in Toronto, Sundance and Berlin. When people see the opening footage of Paglia, they hissed; by the end, they clapped."

Lisa Sewards, "Why women really need supermodels: They are icons of the decade, says top feminist," *Daily Express* (London), May 11, 1993. Paglia says: "I hate the way feminists say supermodels impose an image on women which makes them feel inadequate and suffer a low sense of self-esteem. This is utter b*******, garbage. The ordinary homemaker loves these magazines. She wouldn't go out and spend £3 on one to end up feeling depressed. The Nineties cult of supermodels is a revival of the great system of Hollywood stars. I've never regarded Hollywood glamour as superficial—it's an art form." Of the Hollywood salary gap: "The reason all these female stars who are bitching and complaining are not getting the pay they want is because they've turned their backs on glamour. Who wants to go to the movies to see women who are not interested in glamour? Because of this they can't pull in the same audiences as men. It is the men who have retained their masculine glamour. It is the supermodels who are the heirs of Garbo and Dietrich."

Marion Hume, "Just How Old Can You Get?" *The Independent on Sunday* (London), May 30, 1993. Profile of Lauren Hutton, who says Paglia "has met her match in 'the only broad who is bossier than she is. . . . I'm looking for a man with balls for her. She's ready for a new experience.' "

"Woman of the Year: A Talk with Susan Gubar," *The College* magazine (University of Indiana), Spring 1993. Asked about Paglia, the feminist professor (Sandra Gilbert's collaborator) says: "Paglia is an interesting media phenomenon. This is a woman who has attained amazing renown in a very short time with a really crazy book, the basis of which is biological essentialism. . . . I suspect that Paglia's getting all this publicity because she's a bad girl who flaunts her badness, and because her political incorrectness plays into the backlash against feminism that Susan Faludi has described." [Note how Faludi is now a higher authority for professors of literature.]

Ellen Willis, "Notes on Cam P.," *Dissent*, Spring 1993. Review of *Sex, Art* by a member of the old left that appropriates Paglia's points while ludicrously asserting that Paglia's "Sadeian cosmology" is proof of "conservatism." [For three years, as Paglia and her work were vilified by the alternative press—notably by Willis's career newspaper, *The Village Voice*—Willis did not utter a single word to defend Paglia or acknowledge agreement on any issue with her. Nor did Willis, despite her claim that she is a "sexual libertarian" like Paglia, challenge the feminist establishment by taking a public stand against the date-rape and sexual-harassment hysteria that swept America. By the time Willis's review appeared, Paglia had already had two national best-sellers.]

Kevin Jackson, "Camille the Barbarian: Camille Paglia is a hip academic and high-powered motormouth who thinks that men should be men and women should admit they like it that way. Kevin Jackson loads up and ships out to confront America's self-appointed sex warrior," *Arena* (London), Spring 1993. Cover line calls Paglia "American cleverdick." Photo by Jay Nubile of Paglia in full diva makeup (by Nini Ginsberg) for the Philadelphia filming of Channel 4's programs on Diana and Lolita. Inset quotes from Paglia: "The feminist establishment refuses to credit it, but for God's sake, we're *instinctual beings*! There *is* a hunting thing in male physiology. And it *is* visually based. Men are like *elks*!" "I was driving and I saw this great-looking girl on a bicycle, and I went right into an intersection, and was hit by a taxi. I had this accident because I was gaping *lewdly* at a girl." [This occurred in the mid-Seventies at Bleecker and Macdougal in Greenwich Village.]

"The Price of Fame," *Lingua Franca*, May/June 1993. "Speaking of Camille: If you thought it was hard to get top Hollywood agent Mike Ovitz on the phone, you haven't encountered Professor Paglia's answering machine." Transcript of Paglia's instruction-filled university phone message, "intoned in a crisp, male voice." Same issue: "Road Warriors," the "1992 rankings" of academics in NEXIS, the on-line "spreadsheet of contemporary celebrity." Houston Baker, president of the MLA, "netted a mere two citations" in the media in 1992. Stanley Fish "managed only twenty-four mentions," "compared with the robust 149 citations racked up" by Henry Louis Gates. "The fact is, though, that all these men are eating Camille Paglia's dust. With a stunning total of 297 citations, Paglia pretty much outdistanced all her colleagues, not to mention the MLA itself."

Robin Morgan, "On the Road," *Ms.*, May/June 1993. Editor-in-chief Morgan reveals the kind of "*silly* questions" she was asked by reporters on her trip to Australia. One particularly surprised and annoyed her: "*Q:* What do you think of Camille Paglia? *A*: I don't. Why should we waste energy on a publicity-obsessed, intellectually bereft, rather pathetic person trying to revive the lie that women want to be raped? (This—in the face of the atrocities in Bosnia and Herzegovina.) Ignore the irrelevant; it soon falls out of fashion." [Poor dear, she probably meant "intellectually bankrupt," but it's so hard to use English correctly when you don't read. Is it true there's an intern at *Ms.* permanently assigned to turning the clocks back?]

Christine Hohwieler, "Paglia: Sie is die umstrittenste Sex-Theoretikirin der Gegenwart," *Playboy* (Germany), June 1993. Interview.

George Kalogerakis, "Epistled off: pen pals Camille Paglia and Julie Burchill in epic battle of the (f)axes," *Vanity Fair*, June 1993. On the Paglia-Burchill "transatlantic feud," as well as "a freestanding Paglia-House of Windsor flap over an impious TV show called *Diana Unclothed*." Kalogerakis quotes Paglia's fax to him, after his call for corroboration: "It was the hyper-tabloid *Sun* that concocted Diana's anger over the sexy cartoons. Diana was in *Nepal* and *Bosnia* when all that was happening—it's *ridiculous* to suppose she even *knew* about it. I had to fax Buckingham Palace anyhow (they politely faxed back—with a royal crest on their fax!) to insist that I had *nothing* to do with those damned cartoons." He concludes: "And what have we learned? Maybe just this: that Buckingham Palace has a fax."

Ben Long, "Camillegate: An audience with Camille Paglia, America's self-appointed patron saint of visual culture, is guaranteed to shock." *Black and White* (Australia), June 1993. "Such is the Grand Vision of Camille Paglia, rogue-feminist and self-styled leader of the second American revolution against the (intellectual) decadence of Europe." Paglia says about *Sex*: "Madonna should have contacted me two years ago. I could have saved that damned book in three hours." And: "Susan Faludi and all those feminists are always complaining you never see middle-aged women on the covers of magazines; meanwhile they're attacking me. Well, when I was on the cover of *New York* magazine [March 1991] I looked as Keith Richards-like as I could. That was revolutionary: there was a middle-aged woman looking fierce, unsmiling, and wrinkled." [In *Backlash* Faludi uses Paglia's sudden rise and that cover story specifically as proof of the media's anti-feminism. She ignores the photo, just as she omits the many stridently feminist Fall 1990 major articles and cover stories, to which the *New York* piece was a reaction. The treatment of media history in *Backlash* is disturbingly biased, selective, and distorted.]

Thomas Miessgang, "Viele Frauen hassen mich," *Profil* (Vienna), June 7, 1993. Interview with Paglia.

Hamilton Dos Santos, "Paglia: Comédia é meu modo de vida," *Jornal da Tarde* (São Paulo, Brazil), June 26, 1993. Big splashy spread. [Paglia is asked about Noam Chomsky, who had to admit to the same reporter that he had not attended Paglia's 1991 M.I.T. lecture, which drew thousands of real people, as opposed to trendy academics, to his university from metropolitan Boston and which is now known worldwide because of the transcript in *Sex, Art*. Explaining his absence from that populist extravaganza, Chomsky lamely told the reporter, "Paglia is a supporter of the establishment." A laughing Paglia responds in the article that if anyone is a symbol of the establishment, it is sanctimonious, nebbishy Chomsky, ensconced in a plush position at M.I.T. for thirty-eight years, while she could get no job at a major research institution—including M.I.T. itself, where she was interviewed in the Seventies. Which of the two, Chomsky or Paglia, offered the real threat to the established order?]

"Fax off and die, you bitch: Earlier this year history was made when Julie Burchill and Camille Paglia engaged in the first recorded fax war. This is the complete, unexpurgated transcript of what the press dubbed 'The Battle of the Bitches,' " *The Modern Review* (June–July 1993). The Burchill-Paglia letters (with some errors), interwoven with a narrative of events. Witchy caricatures of the two women glaring at each other with clenched fists and paper-airplane faxes stuck like arrows in their bodies.

Nancy Lamar, "How it all started: Blame it on Camille Paglia," *Philadelphia Gay News*, July 16, 1993. "The media's latest fascination with lesbians began in Philadelphia. 'It probably starts with Camille Paglia,' said Ed Kosner, editor and president of *New York* magazine, whose May cover story 'Lesbian Chic' spawned stories on lesbians in *Vogue*, *Mademoiselle*, *Newsweek*, and *Vanity Fair*. 'She changed the discussion. There began to be a cachet connected to the lesbian scene.' "

George Rush, "Fame Can Be a Drag," *Daily News* (New York), July 17, 1993. Announces first public appearance of "feminist firebrand" Paglia with her "gal pal," Alison Maddex, curator of the In Time Gallery in Washington, D.C., at a party at Club USA celebrating the video collaboration between Paglia and drag queen Glennda Orgasm.

Joe Queenan, "What's New, Pussy-Whipped?," *GQ*, August 1993. Account of real incident, suppressed by major American media, at *The Boston Globe*: a male columnist used the term "pussy-whipped" to a male colleague and was reported by a female staffer to the editor, who fined him $1500 and forced him to apologize publicly. When news of this outrageous infringement of free speech spread outside Boston, the fine was rescinded. Queenan's hilarious fantasy-reconstruction includes grim speechifying by Dworkin and Mac-Kinnon and a loud, furious phone call to the editor from Paglia, defending pussywhipping. Paglia's thank-you letter appeared in December.

"Best of Philly 1993," *Philadelphia*, August 1993. "Local Girl Made Good: Camille Paglia. Yeah, she's a pain in the ass. But she's *our* pain in the ass." [When the surprise award plaque arrived in the mail, Paglia entertained the Italian fantasy of taking it right over and shoving it down the collective editorial throat, since a year earlier, just before release of her second best-seller, the magazine had cynically called for her to leave town.]

Gina Bellafante, "The Brainy and Beautiful," *Time*, August 2, 1993. Announces collaboration between Lauren Hutton and Paglia, "the incendiary academic" and "egghead, antifeminist, and bon vivant," who have made "a short documentary that, according to Paglia, deals with 'sex roles and the condition of humanity.' In the film, Hutton and a Gaultier-clad Camille tackle these lofty issues while seated at a banquet table, a snipe at feminists who, complains Paglia, are obsessed 'with food and anorexia.' "

Maria Miro Johnson, "Why we care about the Lonis and Burts," *The Providence Journal Bulletin* (Rhode Island), August 26, 1993. Interview with Paglia about divorce scandal of Burt Reynolds and Loni Anderson, with whose "kabuki"-like femininity Paglia says the mass audience, unlike the genteel academic and feminist establishment, identifies. Johnson describes her opening greeting to Paglia: "It's good to know she hasn't burned out, I said. Oh, not to worry, she replied. 'I'm Italian. We make other people burn out.' "

"The Perils of Academic Celebrity," *Harper's*, September 1993. Transcript of the long answering-machine message from Paglia's university office. The voice, identified as a staff member, is actually humanities professor Kent Christensen.

Lucia Annunziata, "Tremate femministe, arriva la valanga Camille," *Corriere della Sera*, (Milan) September 8, 1993. ["Tremble, feminists, the avalanche Camille has arrived."] Interview.

David Ritz, "Janet Jackson: The Joy of Sex," *Rolling Stone*, September 16, 1993. Cover story. Ritz says of Jackson: "She then tells me about something Camille Paglia, the sociosexual pop scholar, recently wrote about *janet.*: 'Janet's unique persona combines bold, brash power with quiet sensitivity and womanly mystery. Her latest music is lightning and moonglow.' " [A longtime Janet Jackson fan who thinks "The Pleasure Principle" one of the best music videos ever made, Paglia had provided appreciative remarks when sent the new album by Jackson's manager. A month later, a large box of beautiful gifts arrived from Los Angeles, with an artistically handwritten thank-you note from Jackson herself.]

Robin Bernstein, "Getting a word in edgewise: Author Camille Paglia wants to put women back on their pedestal," *The Washington Blade* (Washington, D.C.), September 17, 1993. Paglia and Alison Maddex, curator of "Walk the Goddess Walk: Power Inside Out," at the District of Columbia Arts Center, are interviewed about their new pro-sex, pro-art, pro-beauty, pro-fashion, pro-food feminism. It is also, Bernstein notes, the first time they had publicly discussed their five-month-old relationship. Photos.

Kim France, "Becoming Juliana Hatfield," *Rolling Stone*, September 30, 1993. "Indie-pop singer/songwriter Juliana Hatfield and rock star wanna-be Camille Paglia have a little something in common. They both believe that women are biologically destined to be inferior guitar players. 'How many girls other than Bonnie Raitt can play a guitar solo?' Hatfield argues. 'I can't, you know? I haven't seen any female guitar players that are really anything special.' She's said this before, and though she knows it makes a lot of people pretty angry, she'll probably say it again." [A lifelong rock fan, Paglia never said "biologically destined" but simply noted that while women have been brilliant vocalists, pianists, violinists, cellists, etc., they have done no major original work in hard-rock lead guitar. In Heart and the Pretenders, for example, superb bands run by highly talented women, the great lead parts have been played by men. Paglia suspects hard-rock solos require youthful male lust and aggression—two commodities currently under cultural attack. Her raising of this issue in *SPIN* (September and October 1991) led to bitter attacks by the politically correct rock press.]

Maximilian Barteau, "Camille Paglia Addresses Milton S. Eisenhower Symposium." Andrew Dunlap, "A Talk with Camille Paglia." *The Johns Hopkins News-Letter*, October 1, 1993. Account of her lecture, "The Question of Sex," at Johns Hopkins University on September 28, which began with her tribute to Hopkins' John J. Money, one of the century's greatest sexologists. In the interview, Paglia scathingly attacks the theory-infested Hopkins literature departments and Judith Butler in particular, whose general learning she questions and whose work on sex she rejects.

Michelle Chihara, "From decadence to date rape: Paglia takes aim," *Yale Herald*, October 1, 1993. Account of Paglia's lecture at the Yale Political Union on September 30. Inset quote from Paglia: "So you had sex with someone and it didn't go well. Big deal." "In her speech, she characterized women's studies departments as 'ghettos of mediocrity.' Laura Wexler, Director of Undergraduate Studies in the Women's Studies program, would not comment on Paglia's writing."

Danielle Neves, "Paglia Criticizes '90s Intellectualism: Self-Described 'Free Speech Militant' Calls 'Yuppies' Phonics," *Yale Daily News*, October 4, 1993. Account of Paglia's lecture at the Yale Political Union. Calls her "infamous for her radically left-wing views." "A murmur of surprise rippled through the crowd" when Paglia attacked Yale's Whitney Humanities Center, taken over by theorists who " 'cast out all of the old-fashioned scholarly values.' " [This was Paglia's first lecture at Yale. She began by sarcastically noting that it was the students who had invited her to speak, not the English Department, even though it was where she had gotten her doctorate and even though *Sexual Personae*, published nearly four years earlier by Yale University Press, had become a worldwide best-seller. But, she said, she loved reproducing the 1970 evening when leftist critic Leslie Fiedler lectured at Yale and was boycotted by the entire English Department.]

"Fabio: Love for Sale," *People*, October 4, 1993. Cover story on the romance-novel king. Paglia says: "Fabio is a skilled seducer who is very attentive to women in the courtly European way. He worships women, and he fulfills their dream of a man who has the physique of a hunk and the emotional sense of an artist or poet."

Julie Hirschfeld, "Paglia Speaks on Feminism and Education," *Yale Daily News*, October 15, 1993. Interview with Paglia. Attacks the "time-servers" and "yuppies" on the Yale literature faculty: "The people of my generation who are in the classroom now, there's not an original mind among them, because the whole system is geared to driving out originality, anything inflammatory, anything exciting, anything flamboyant. The kind of women who are hired now by Yale are women who fit into a certain system, women who are not intellectually challenging to anything, who are not going to challenge the 'patriarchy,' who haven't made a dent in the WASP hegemony at Yale. My self-education occurred in Sterling Library [at Yale]. I feel it is every student's responsibility: self-education."

"Video: Rent Check: Camille Paglia," *Entertainment Weekly*, October 22, 1993. A celebrity is asked what videos he or she has most recently rented. Paglia replies: "*The Women* (1939). It explores the rituals of beauty—the compulsion to exercise, the glamour of fashion. It will raise the temperature of any feminist. *I've Heard the Mermaids Singing* (1987). Here's a smaller product with no budget, and you get this wonderful realism and comedy. This girl's kind of aimless, yet plucky. It's the twentysomething problem with self-definition. Very minimalist."

"Beyond 1993," *U.S. News and World Report*, October 25, 1993. Social theorists are asked to project what the world will be like in the year 2053. Paglia replies: "The men's movement will spread as men are no longer able to just sit around and listen to what feminists want. The more men do, the less the women want them. Men will have to define themselves."

Matt ffytche and John O'Reilly, "The Jacques Pack," *The Modern Review*, October/November 1993. "In a special pull-out-and-keep wallchart, *The Modern Review* profiles the stars of the postmodern catwalk." Satirical sketches and photos of Habermas, Kristeva, Foucault, Rorty, Benjamin, Derrida, Baudrillard, Lacan, Paglia, Barthes, de Beauvoir, Deleuze. Paglia, whose style is "butch femme, dominatrix," is "associated with an Elizabeth Taylor fertility cult." Her "chat-up line": "Wolf-whistle, animal cluck." [On seeing this chart,

Paglia said, "How nice to have swept Hélène Cixous into the dust-bin of history."] Two Paglia letters appear in this issue, with others in following issues.

Kim Masters, "Sex, Lies, and an 8-Inch Carving Knife," *Vanity Fair*, November 1993. Profile of Lorena Bobbitt, who cut off her husband's penis. "However controversial the ubiquitous critic Camille Paglia may otherwise be, she seems to speak for women across the country when she suggests that Lorena Bobbitt committed a rather thrilling act of revolution. 'It's kind of like the Boston Tea Party,' she says gleefully. 'It's a wake-up call. It has to send a chill through every man in the world.' " [Paglia also repeatedly said, as in a November 12 *CNN & Company* debate with Susan Estrich and Annie Gottlieb, that she rejected Lorena Bobbitt's claim of victimization and that Lorena had committed a criminal act and should stand up in court and accept responsibility for it.]

"Women of the Year," *Playgirl*, November 1993. Paglia, declared "Most Daring," is chosen to inaugurate the magazine's "first women of the year salute." Among the others: Sandra Bernhard, Emma Thompson, Maya Angelou, Christie Hefner, Janet Jackson, Ann Richards, and Roseanne Arnold.

Rick Marin, "What's the Problem? He Won't Say," *The New York Times*, November 7, 1993. On the "inaction heroes" of recent films, "the new breed of man, the kind that sexual theorist Camille Paglia says she encounters when she lectures at Ivy League campuses. 'The totally P.C. male is so anxious about whether he's doing the right thing, he's afraid to do anything,' Ms. Paglia says. 'They're like "nowhere men," blank and affectless.' "

Anthony Flint, "Camille Paglia riles them at Wellesley," November 7, 1993. Account of her lecture at Wellesley College on October 28. "The campus is still recovering from her intellectual flame-throwing routine." Gross inaccuracies about Paglia's speaking fee, described as "reportedly $16,000, though she agreed to come for closer to a quarter of that to Wellesley." [Paglia's speaking fee is $2000, which is what Wellesley paid her. The Women's Studies Department refused to make its usual financial contribution to the student Committee for Political and Legislative Action for the visit, which meant that the committee's annual budget was exhausted and the students penalized for wanting to hear ideas different than their teachers'. In his November 21 retraction, Flint made another error, producing an exasperated letter from Paglia printed November 28.]

James Kaplan, "Lauren Hutton: A Model Life," *New York*, November 8, 1993. Cover story. Hutton talks about her early interest in *Sexual Personae* and her subsequent friendship with Paglia. Paglia says, "I had heard for years that she was a lesbian. People speak with absolute confidence about these things. But I said to everyone [after getting to know Hutton], 'That is absolute *nonsense!*' Because—this is my big conceptual breakthrough—the most *dominant* women are heterosexual. And Lauren Hutton really made it clear to me. Because she is *so* butch you can't even *believe* it! She dominates every single social occasion."

Charlotte Hays, "Charlotte's Web," *Daily News* (New York), November 12, 1993. Account of the *60 Minutes* 25th Anniversary party on November 10 at the Metropolitan Museum of Art. Correspondent Steve Kroft "was the mastermind who insisted that Rush Limbaugh and Camille Paglia be seated side by side at dinner—just to see if a food fight might break out between the right-wing commentator and the maverick feminist. Alas, they got along like a house afire." [Congratulating Limbaugh for his courageous anti-establishment stands and defense of free speech, Paglia said, "The number one intellectual problem in America today is liberalism in its present decayed form. You are critiquing it from the right, and I'm critiquing it from the left."]

Jeannie Williams, "Priceless moments at *60 Minutes* gala," *USA Today*, November 12, 1993. "Did Rush Limbaugh give a cigar to a renegade feminist? Limbaugh was seated with fiery feminist Camille Paglia, with Regis Philbin to moderate. Paglia admitted she watches Rush's show, and he gave her a Cuban stogie, which she said she would smoke."

Richard Johnson, "Page Six," *New York Post*, November 18, 1993.
"That was Camille Paglia—in her continuing assault on politically
correct feminism—posing with a dozen strippers the other day at
Stringfellow's Presents Pure Platinum. The photo shoot was for *Penthouse*. Paglia appreciates the female form. She arrived at last week's
60 Minutes 25th anniversary party holding hands with an attractive
brunette [Alison Maddex] she introduced as her 'significant other.'
And she gladly assumed a somewhat 'butch' persona when Rush
Limbaugh presented her with a cigar of Churchillian dimensions."
[After dinner, Limbaugh said, "One cigar smoker always recognizes
another," pulled out an alligator case, and gave Paglia a huge cigar,
which he described as "the best smoke in the world." On his television show the next morning, the cigar incident was described by
Regis Philbin, who had been seated with his wife at the same table
and who quoted Paglia telling Limbaugh, "You have been demonized by the New York media." Limbaugh opened his own television
show that day with a lively account of the exchange and flashed a
60 Minutes shot of Paglia with a cartoon cigar comically superimposed
on her lips.]

Patricia Edmonds, "Sex: News is making life a little sleazier," *USA
Today*, November 18, 1993. The recent flurry of sexual allegations
involving John and Lorena Bobbitt, Heidi Fleiss, Joey Buttafuoco,
Michael Jackson, [falsely accused] Joseph Cardinal Bernardin, and
Sen. Robert Packwood. "While some flog the media for making sex
hot news, Paglia says the media is only—finally—reporting reality.
Before, she says, the [major] media's 'genteel power structure' sanitized sex. Now 'we have bursting out in the media the hard, savage
reality of human sexuality that can never be fully controlled. People
recoil; it's horrifying to them. But it's also fascinating, because on
some level we recognize, 'There but for the grace of God go I.' ' "

Karen Burgess, "American feminist critic defends Yaqzan: Camille
Paglia calls UNB administration's move 'fascist.' " *The Brunswickian*
(University of New Brunswick, Canada), November 19, 1993. Luke
Peterson, interview with Paglia on suspension of male mathematics
professor for writing a controversial article on date-rape. Paglia says:
"In a democracy, free speech must be our paramount principle. It

must supersede all questions of ideology. I believe that the more offensive the speech, the more it's in the best interests of a democracy. We're not going to get anywhere in the sex debate until there is total freedom for everyone to speak their minds. But people don't want the truth. No, no, no. They want sugar-coated pleasantries; they want a return to the Victorian period of propriety and decorum. The history of humanity is nothing but a history of censors trying to squash original ideas. My generation of the 1960s was all about being disrespectful. That's what the free speech movement was about at Berkeley. What is the point of going to university if not to learn how to be disrespectful, to break free of the authority figures who raised you? My God, this is absolutely pablum, pablum! Certainly, [Yaqzan's article] is occasionally coarsely phrased, but one does not punish someone in a democracy for coarse phrasing."

Clare McHugh, "The Prophet of Power Feminism," *New York*, November 29, 1993. On Naomi Wolf's new book. "*Fire with Fire* echoes the work of several prominent feminist thinkers, including, most recently, the ideas advanced by Wendy Kaminer and Camille Paglia. Kaminer won't comment on Wolf's work, but Paglia, who has clashed with Wolf in the past, is typically outspoken on the subject. 'I don't think Naomi has any deep beliefs,' Paglia says. 'She's derivative, picks up on whichever way the wind is blowing, and uses that to advance herself. . . . I can't stand her airhead, totally parent-pleasing way of talking and writing.' " [To McHugh's question about the half-dozen of Paglia's ideas that run through Wolf's latest book, Paglia replied, "As a teacher, I am happy to be completing Naomi's education, which was so deficient at Yale." She also expressed satisfaction at the confirmation of her early portrait of Wolf's "yuppie feminism."]

Richard Nalley, "The Naked and the Nude," *American Photo*, special issue: "What *Is* Erotic?," November/December 1993. Interview with Paglia about eroticism in photography. "Paglia is not your typical teacher. When she met Richard Avedon [at S.I. Newhouse's party celebrating Tina Brown's appointment as editor of *The New Yorker*], Paglia says, 'I screamed. I went down on one knee. I made this huge to-do and kissed his hand and said, "*You* are a great artist!" ' "

Expresses her admiration for Helmut Newton, Gosta Peterson, Robert Mapplethorpe, and Herb Ritts: "Helmut Newton is an enormous hero of mine. I regard him as the living continuity of the Dietrich era of old Berlin. What we get in his work is European sophistication from the prewar era that in turn was part of the heritage of the decaying Austro-Hungarian empire. So Newton is to me this sort of living flame. His influence has just pervaded the culture. Everywhere, in photography and fashion. Helmut Newton photographs are always 'artificial' to the point of decadence. Newton has the most incredible sense of archetype, and of how to manipulate the iconography of both nature and culture, always to decadent effect." [Newton's images directly influenced Paglia's thinking as she was writing *Sexual Personae* in the mid Seventies.]

Woody Hochswender, "Tempest in a B-cup," *Esquire*, December 1993. "Are men ready for women to go topless on the street? An article in *The Village Voice* last summer reported that feminist and lesbian groups had been demonstrating around New York to affirm their right to go shirtless in public." Men are photographed reacting to topless fashion models on Fifth Avenue. "We asked Camille Paglia, the author and Darth Vader of postfeminism, to comment on the topfree phenomenon. 'I applaud confrontations of this kind,' Paglia says. 'I want to see more boobs myself. Unfortunately, the women who tend to do this, in gay parades and such, are big, fat dykes. Also, the ideology behind it is incoherent. These are the same women who would object to men staring at their breasts. I say, flaunt it, but be prepared to handle the sexual response.' "

Richard Johnson, "Page Six," *New York Post*, December 2, 1993. Announces "an art show devoted to the male organ" in Washington, D.C. "Curiously, the curator is Alison Maddex, the artist who is known for her photomontages as well as for her romance with renegade feminist writer Camille Paglia."

Paul Richard, "Beneath the Fig Leaf: At Clark & Co., 'True Phallacy' Takes a Look at a Symbol of Power," *The Washington Post*, December 4, 1993. Review of multimedia art show, "True Phallacy: The Myth of Male Power," curated by Alison A. Maddex at a

Georgetown gallery. 150 images of the phallus from 36 East Coast artists. A project in the Neo-Sexism movement co-founded by Maddex and Paglia.

Bill Zehme, "The Cindy Chronicles," *Rolling Stone*, December 23, 1993. Cover story on supermodel Cindy Crawford. Paglia comments on Crawford's "dusky" multicultural quality, like "an Apache princess."

Lindsey Lane, "Back at the Backlash," *The Austin Chronicle* (Texas), December 3, 1993. Interview with Susan Faludi, who identifies Paglia with Phyllis Schlafly as "women who have discovered they can promote themselves by denigrating the women's movement." Faludi claims that Paglia did not get tenure [false] and that she "blames feminism" for it; that she is motivated by nothing but a "craving" for celebrity and has simply "figured out a line that will get her there"; that she says "the same thing over and over again"; and that she is not a real feminist—the media have simply "packaged" her as one. [These remarks demonstrate that Faludi, a Harvard graduate whose snobbish scorn for everything outside the Ivy League was clear in her negative and characteristically error-filled portrait of Paglia in *Backlash*, has still not read *Sexual Personae*, which may be too hard for her.]

Daniel Radosh, "Beyond the Second Sex," *Planet Magazine* (New Zealand), Summer [December] 1993. Interview with Paglia, "the raging belle of the new sexuality."

Sandy Auriti, "Camille Paglia va alla guerra: sola contro tutte," *Marie Claire* (Milan), December 1993. Subheading: "Eccessiva. Egocentrica. Scandalosa." Interview.

Pythia S. Peay, "Wild Woman Within," *New Woman*, December 1993. Clarissa Pinkola Estés (*Women Who Run with the Wolves*) names five "modern wild women": Georgia O'Keeffe, Maya Angelou, Isabel Allende, Judy Chicago, and Paglia, who is "unfettered" and "says what she thinks."

"Speech Marks: The things they say about Camille Paglia," *The Independent* (London), January 4, 1994. Satiric list of epithets from the media.

Marina Conti, "Tremate, le seduttrici son tornate!" *L'Espresso* (Italy), January 7, 1994. Interview with Paglia on sexy female stars.

Neil Lyndon, "Dear," *The Independent* (London), January 7, 1994. Calls Paglia "the nearest thing to a complete adult that American feminism has produced."

Linda Grant, "The fem fatale." *The Guardian* (London), January 7, 1994. Interview with Paglia. In same issue: editorial about her. "Well heeled feminism," declaring, "There is a new tide in feminism, and it owes much to Paglia."

Pauline Peters, "It's not my fault I'm a lesbian." *Evening Standard* (London), January 7, 1994. Interview with Paglia.

Nicci Gerard, " 'I'm a cartoon figure, an Italian opera,' " *The Observer* (London), January 9, 1994. Interview with Paglia.

"Maria Lexton meets Camille Paglia," *Time Out* (London), January 12, 1994.

Ita O'Kelly Browne, "The passion of Paglia," *The Irish Independent*, January 12, 1994. Paglia says of her childhood, "My father taught me to put up my fists and defend myself like a man."

Ruth Picardie, "Overheated, overhyped, and over here," *The Independent*, January 13, 1994. Attack on "Hot American Feminists" in London: Roiphe, Wolf, Paglia.

Peter Grosvenor, "Camille the firebrand is turning heat on feminism," *Daily Express* (London), January 13, 1994.

Eileen Battersby, "Exasperated voice of common sense," *The Irish Times*, January 13, 1994. Interview with Paglia.

James Barron, "Who Are You?" *The New York Times*, February 13, 1994. Celebrities asked for a one-word self-portrait. Paglia: "Ambition, but that can be easily misunderstood. From the outside, people would probably say her mad egotism. My ambition was always the development of my talent."

The Weasel, "Up & Down the City Road," *The Independent Magazine*, January 15, 1994. Witty account of Paglia's lecture at the National Theatre in London.

Chrissy Iley, "The Mouthtrap: Camille Paglia, the talker of the town," cover story, *The Sunday Times* magazine (London), January 16, 1994. Calls Paglia "the love child of Quentin Crisp and Dame Edna Everage" and describes her as "ludicrous, heroic, and sweet." [In the stylish cover photo, Paglia, enthroned at the Basil Street Hotel, is secretly sitting on the London telephone book, a leg-flattering trick she learned from Mary Matalin and Jane Wallace, then co-hosts of CNBC's *Equal Time*.]

Irvine Hunter, "Rebel without a pause: Camille spreads the feminist message by word of mouth," *Today* (England), January 19, 1994. Paglia says, "I'm a comedian. Sex is a comedy, not a tragedy. The problem with feminists is they want to turn it into this *melodrama*."

Anne Simpson, "Motormouth in overdrive," *The Herald* (Glasgow), January 19, 1994. Interview with Paglia, who says of her teaching at an anti-establishment art school in Philadelphia for the past decade, "In Europe that would be proof of my intellectual authenticity."

Tony Dunn, "Lip Service," *The Tribune* (London), January 21, 1994. Interview with Paglia, about whom Dunn says, "She isn't sexy. She has pared off her eroticism with the knife of her energy and her will. But she is a star."

Denis Scheck, " 'Ich bin eine Kriegerin,' " *Börsenblatt* (Frankfurt), January 21, 1994. Interview with Paglia.

Joel Achenbach and Rich Lieby. "We Find the Defendant," *The Washington Post*, January 22, 1994. Reactions to Lorena Bobbitt's acquittal for sexually mutilating her husband. An Indiana waitress says, "Actually, I think they should have taken the penis off him and sewed it onto Camille Paglia."

Simon Price, "Making Camille of It," *Melody Maker* (London), January 22, 1994. After seeing her National Theatre lecture, Price calls Paglia "the Nineties' first intellectual-as-rock-star" and "the most exciting rock 'n' roll icon of the year."

N.B., *Times Literary Supplement,* January 28, 1994. "Camille Paglia has once more overcome her natural shyness," having achieved "near ubiquity" in London.

James Servin, "Can Lipstick Change Your Life?" *Harper's Bazaar,* February 1994. "Paglia rattles off her Lipstick Personae. . . . 'For my really grand appearances, for my theatrical persona, for La Paglia, as they call me in Italy, I put on Lancôme's Rouge Decor Creme. That's the perfect lipstick for her. Or should I say it.' "

"You Go Away, Girl!" *GQ,* February 1994. "Gals we've had enough of": RuPaul, Shannen Doherty, Susan Powter, Marianne Williamson, Demi Moore, Barbra Streisand, and Paglia.

Mark Abernethy, "Feminist Fatale," Australian *Penthouse,* February 1994. Quotes Robin Morgan on Australian TV saying about Paglia, "You have to understand that every year for the past 25 years, someone like this has sort of burped to the surface. If they didn't exist, the boys, the patriarchs, would have had to invent them. They make a bit of money. They say women really want to be raped." Paglia tells Abernethy that Morgan is a "dinosaur" and "philistine," with "no feeling for art" or culture. "She's withered up, she's cynical, she's bitter. . . . She's responsible for the fact that 85 percent of young women in this country don't identify with the word 'feminist.' "

Marcus R. Wohlsen, "Paglia Criticizes Women's Studies: Calls for Elimination of These Programs in Favor of 'Sex Studies,' " *The Harvard Crimson,* February 4, 1994. Account of Paglia's speech on education reform at Harvard's Kennedy School of Government.

Florence Graves, "There is no female Mozart because there is no female Jack the Ripper. They are monsters at the extremes of personality," *The Boston Globe*, February 6, 1994. Interview with Paglia in Cambridge, the morning after her Harvard speech. Huge photo of her at lunch with the *Globe* editors, as she protested the newspaper's recent political correctness. Paglia tells Graves: "I was a feminist long before Gloria Steinem. She had to be dragged into the movement by Betty Friedan. I am one of the leaders of the reform movement in feminism, which is trying to bring it back to its old principles of personal responsibility and concern for equal rights." Of her proposed "sex studies": "What is going to be the credential for someone to work in gay studies? That they are gay? That's a wonderful credential. That is absurd. For every assertion of gay pride, there should be the other counter-argument that the Bible condemns homosexuality. You've got to have the opposition. If you don't, that's not truth. You've got propaganda. And the elite colleges have totally given themselves over to propaganda."

"Hurricane Camille Howls at Wolf," Intelligencer, *New York*, February 7, 1994. Tipped off by a media mole that Naomi Wolf's publisher was falsely claiming Paglia's support of Wolf's latest book in an ad in *The New York Times Book Review*, Paglia raises the roof and gets her name pulled at press deadline. [The ad foolishly trumpeted: "From Gloria to Camille—the word is *yes!*"]

Marcus R. Wohlsen, "Paglia Attacks Faculty," *The Harvard Crimson*, February 7, 1994. Interview with Paglia, who "blasted" three members of Harvard's Committee on Women Studies for gaining power by "playing the career game." Of the chair, Susan R. Suleiman, a professor of comparative literature, she asks, "Why is that woman in charge of women's studies? Has she ever studied science? Does she know anything about history? Does she know anything about anthropology? Does she know anything about the history of psychology?" "Paglia's thinking is rather incoherent," Suleiman tells the *Crimson*. "It's very difficult to be a serious thinker when you're giving TV interviews all the time." [Gosh, whatever happened to the chi-chi theorists' infatuation with the media as "text"?]

Daniel H. Chol, "The Odd Couple?" *The Harvard Crimson*, February 9, 1994. Sophisticated analysis of the political positions of Harvard's Harvey Mansfield, "a tenured, Fifties conservative," and Paglia, "a radical Sixties libertarian." Issues addressed: liberalism, idealism, human nature, tolerance, justice.

Thomas C. Palmer, "Paglia offers prescription for higher ed," *The Boston Globe*, February 13, 1994. On Paglia's proposals for education reform.

Douglas Davis, "The Genders Are Ready to Kiss and Make Up," *Newsday*, February 13, 1994. "For the first time, almost anyone can detect a counterrevolution within feminist ranks. The intrepid, isolated Camille Paglia, whose books scorch feminist puritanism, is now joined by a stream of reformers."

Camille Paglia, "The Blank Page," *The Observer Magazine* (London), February 13, 1994. Feature asking guests to fill two pages as they wish. Paglia chose 24 celebrity photos from *Observer* files and gave them fake *Mad* magazine captions. Cindy Crawford amid Israeli soldiers: "Today's well-dressed lady has a no-dust bust, a tote-a-tot marsupial pouch, and a knee for the groin." Zsa Zsa Gabor beating conga drums: "In an emergency landing, smart blows to the rump of the lady next to you will automatically inflate her approved flotation devices." Olivia De Havilland exclaiming in *Gone with the Wind:* "Oh, God, it's Madonna flashing those tired old tits again."

Lance Morrow, "Are Men Really that Bad?" Cover story, *Time*, February 14, 1994. Calls Paglia "an intellectual gunslinger."

Jean Marbella, "Catfight Fever," *The Baltimore Sun*, February 19, 1994. Tonya Harding versus Nancy Kerrigan. Paglia, "currently involved in any number of what she freely calls catfights," says, "People love it when one woman goes after another. It's primitive and primeval. There's something tigress-like about women. The clawing. It's carnivorous."

Ruth Picardie, "Why I adore the penis, by a radical lesbian feminist," *The Independent* (London), February 28, 1994. Subheading:

"Professor Camille Paglia, famous for her attacks on the politically correct school of feminism, has now made a film in praise of the male organ."

"Camille Paglia Unleashed," *Playguy*, March 1994. Splashy photo spread on *Glennda and Camille* in a deliciously hardcore gay-male porn magazine.

Claudia Steinberg, "Porträt: 'Ich bin ein Monster': Camille Paglias Loblied auf den Krieg der Geschlechter fasziniert Amerika und schockiert die Feministinnen," *Vogue* (Germany), March 1994. Profile of Paglia.

Melissa Benn, "Sex, power, and rock 'n' roll," *Everywoman* (England), March 1994. Profile of Paglia. Of Paglia's lecture at the National Theatre, Benn says: "She is terribly funny in a high camp way. Her famous insults have a quite different resonance in performance than in the cold light of print. In this, she returns to a premodern standard of public life where rudeness, even abuse, is part of the acceptable cut and thrust of public debate and polemic."

"The Two-Faced Phenomenon: Camille Paglia at the Kennedy School of Government," *Peninsula* (Harvard University), March 1994. "In a written statement to this publication" about Paglia, Susan R. Suleiman, Harvard's Chair of Women's Studies, says, "*Sexual Personae* is shoddy scholarship, I'm afraid. It would not earn its author tenure at Harvard."

Camille Paglia, "Where Gay Boys Come From," *The Harvard Gay and Lesbian Review*, Spring 1994. Excerpted transcript of Paglia's talk at a March 1993 symposium on homosexuality and biology at the Harvard Medical School.

Jeremy J. Beadle, "Camille Paglia: Hot?" *Gay Times* (London), March 1994. Lively profile. Calling Foucault a "fraud," Paglia says of poststructuralists, "What these people are doing has already been done in English. James Joyce's *Ulysses* does what Foucault claims to be doing but never gets around to. The points Foucault makes about insanity and normality, my God, all these points have been raised from Blake on—it's part of Romanticism. The claims for Foucault that he's 'challenging the whole idea of the Enlightenment'—surprise, surprise, guess what, that's what Romanticism *is*! Nothing Foucault did was original. Even when he shaved his head, he was just imitating Genet."

Frank DiGiacomo, "Who's Redhanded?" *The New York Observer*, March 14, 1994. On the banning of *Glennda and Camille Do Downtown* by the New York Lesbian and Gay Film Festival, whose director tells Glenn Belverio that Paglia's "backlash politics were too problematic." Paglia says about the festival's entry committee, "These are very dangerous people because they think they have the truth. They think that my politics do not come up to theirs. They're grand inquisitors, they're not true leftists. I love it when we catch totalitarians redhanded."

Marina Conti, "Nuovo Erotismo," *L'Espresso* (Italy), March 18, 1994. Illustrated article on Paglia's *The Penis Unsheathed* and Alison Maddex's *True Phallacy* show. [Article on the latter: "The Penis as Art," *Penthouse*, April 1994.]

Anne Dempsey, " 'I expected fame!' Writer Camille Paglia seems to attract controversy wherever she goes," *Woman's Way* (Ireland), March 18, 1994. "While she is famous, she is still shunned by the highest echelons of American academia, who feel she doesn't conform."

Tim Campbell, "Docu-farce with Camille Paglia Causes Minor Riot," *Gaze* magazine, March 18, 1994. *Glennda and Camille* sparks a riot but wins "thunderous" applause at the Minneapolis/St. Paul Lesbian and Gay Film Festival.

Robin Bernstein, "Women in Love: How Camille Paglia found love and pancakes in Baltimore," *10 Percent*, March/April 1994. On Paglia's year-old relationship with Alison Maddex.

Yvonne Roberts, "Is this the face of feminism?" British *Elle*, April 1994. Attack on Paglia. Photo: Paglia in a motorcycle jacket.

Lisa Levenson, "Paglia stimulates discussion," *The Daily Pennsyl-vanian* (University of Pennsylvania), April 15, 1994. Paglia delivers the Philomathean Society's annual oration. "Paglia began by ex-plaining that University students, not faculty members, had invited her. 'That speaks volumes for American intellectual life' she said. 'Your faculty would not invite me—they are not interested in ideas, debate, and dissent.' Paglia attacked American faculty members in general as 'inert, passive, and completely out of touch with reality—twerps whose knowledge would fill a thimble. I want the students to have a greater critical sense about the faculty. Students are in a malaise because what they get in the classroom bears no resemblance to the culture they see outside of it.' "

Guy Walters, "A Childhood: Camille Paglia," *The Times Magazine* (London), April 16, 1994. Scenes from Paglia's tomboyish Italian-American childhood. She says, "I got into constant fights. There's an endless series of people I've struck physically—I'm the only leading feminist right now who's done so."

Letters, *The Modern Review*, April–May 1994. In response to Paglia's article on revivals, a reader sends in a satirical graph, "Differences between Camille Paglia and G.W. Hegel."

Boze Hadleigh, "Hollywoodland: The Stars Diss Each Other," *Los Angeles* magazine, May 1994. Germaine Greer says, "Jodie Foster is the type of so-called feminist only Camille Paglia could love," [Wrong: Foster is pure Yale political correctness.]

Colin Richardson, "Camille Paglia in 'censorship' storm," *Gay Times* (London), May 1994. On the banning of *Glennda and Camille* by the New York Gay and Lesbian Film Festival. "Paglia despises 'the dreary, Stalinist, white middle-class gay establishment' for 'turning against the drag queens' after Stonewall. 'I've modelled half my personality on drag queens, God knows. One of the truest things said about me was by a critic [Reed Woodhouse] who said. 'The voice of *Sexual Personae* is the voice of Myra Breckinridge.' "

Ricky Spears, "Cable Ready," *Paper*, May 1994. On Manhattan public access television programs. Photo of Glennda Orgasm and Paglia from *Glennda and Camille Do Downtown*, "now a classic."

Al Patrick, "Camille claims her film was rejected for political reasons," *Philadelphia Gay News*, May 6–12, 1994. On the banning of *Glennda and Camille*.

Michael Logan, "Feminism's gadfly lauds *The Young and the Restless*," *TV Guide*, May 7, 1994. Paglia talks about her favorite soap, which she has watched since its debut in 1973. In part two (May 14), she attacks the other soaps for their "high and mighty" preachiness and their abandonment of the great female "trash-and-sleaze" style of old Hollywood.

Richard Johnson, "Paglia not good enough for gay film fest," "Page Six," *New York Post*, May 9, 1994. "All lesbians are *not* created equal in the politically correct eyes of the New York Lesbian and Gay Film Festival."

Perry McMahon, "Cowgirls and Paglia Face the Gay Fascists," *New York Press*, May 25, 1994. The lesbian *Even Cowgirls Get the Blues*, by "avant-queer director" Gus Van Sant, is also rejected by the New York Lesbian and Gay Film Festival, which has "set many a downtown tongue wagging over the perceived political overtones behind their selection process." [This issue of blatant censorship was suppressed by the American gay and alternative as well as straight mainstream press, which now passively follows gay-establishment propaganda, despite long evidence, leading up to fractious Stonewall 25 (NYC, June 1994), of serious dissent in the gay movement.]

Steve Sailer, "Why Lesbians Aren't Gay," *National Review*, May 30, 1994. Hilarious graph contrasting gay men and lesbians, with Paglia the "exception proving these rules."

Russell Davies, "Man of the People," *The Telegraph Magazine* (London), June 4, 1994. Profile of artist R. B. Kitaj, who says: "I love it when Camille Paglia gets on the box and starts yelling at the feminists, saying she loves pornography. It's great stuff. She uses funny words, like 'You're neglecting a part of your *sensorium*' (he laughs uproariously). She's terrific! I love her!' "

Kristine McKenna, "Keanu's Eccentric Adventure," *Los Angeles Times*, June 5, 1994. Profile of actor Keanu Reeves, "Asked in parting if movies create false expectations of life, Reeves laughs and says, 'Shouldn't you be asking Michel Foucault or Camille Paglia that question?' "

Camille Paglia, "A Horse, a Flame, a Rose," *The Guardian* (London), June 9, 1994. Reprint of Paglia's *New Republic* article on Jacqueline Kennedy Onassis. Another reprint appeared in *The Australian* on June 1.

Nancy E. Roman, "Scales of justice weigh tiers of sexual assault," *The Washington Times*, June 16, 1994. Paglia attacks feminist reasoning about a controversial rape case at Pennsylvania's East Stroudsburg University.

Rachel Fisher, "Femme TV," *The Hollywood Reporter*, June 17–19, 1994. Paglia rejects recent women-ogling-men commercials as a phony "nudge-in-the-ribs" male style.

Matthew Flamm, "Page Turners," *New York*, June 27, 1994. Celebrities' summer reading. Paglia says of A. J. Langguth's *A Noise of War: Caesar, Pompey, Octavian and the Struggle for Rome*: "People who talk about 'negative politics' and 'negative ads' today, well, how ignorant. If you study Greek and Roman politics—human nature doesn't change. Women want to get into politics, then they complain, 'It isn't nice.' Politics is a hardball game. Cicero got his head sawed off."

Thomas J. Ferraro, "An Interview with Camille Paglia," *South Atlantic Quarterly* (Duke University), Summer 1994. Special issue on contemporary American Catholicism. Paglia talks about her Italian-American roots and her theories of religion.

Lois Commondenominator, "High Noon, High Heels: Doing Downtown with Glennda and Camille," *Dragazine* (West Hollywood), Summer 1994.

Colin Richardson, "Famous names join pro-NAMBLA protest," *Gay Times* (London), July 1994. Photos of Paglia, Allen Ginsberg, and others forming Spirit of Stonewall to protest the expulsion of NAMBLA from the International Lesbian and Gay Association. In same issue: letter from Glenn Belverio, with photo of Paglia and him (as Glennda Orgasm) at the Stonewall Inn.

Letters, *The New York Times Book Review*, July 3, 1994. Paglia writes: "Nina Auerbach's inept and shamefully biased review of Christina Hoff Sommers's amusing, invigorating, and superbly researched exposé, *Who Stole Feminism?* [June 12], beautifully demonstrates the moral and intellectual bankruptcy of the academic feminist establishment."

Articles by or about Paglia published too late for inclusion in this volume:

Paglia, "The rise of theory: a symposium, *TLS*, July 15, 1994.

Paglia, a negative review of John Boswell, *Same-Sex Unions in Premodern Europe*, *The Washington Post Book World*, July 17, 1994.

Paglia, "My night with Streisand," *The New Republic*, July 18, 1994.

Paglia, "Questionnaire," *The Guardian* (London), August 20, 1994.

Interview with Suzanne Ramljak, *Sculpture*, Sept.–Oct. 1994.

Interview with Martha Frankel, *Movieline*, October 1994.

Melanie Wells, "Woman as Goddess," *Penthouse*, October 1994. Interview with Paglia on a tour of New York strip clubs.

John Gallagher, cover story on Paglia, *The Advocate*, November 1, 1994.

Paglia, interview with Raquel Welch, *Tatler* (London), November 1994.

Paglia, cover story on the Rolling Stones, *The Boston Phoenix*, August 26, 1994.

INDEX

ACKNOWLEDGMENTS

"The Penis Unsheathed" and "Lolita Unclothed" originally aired on Channel 4, London. Copyright © Channel 4. Reprinted by permission of Channel 4 and Rapido TV.

"The Nursery-School Campus" originally appeared in the *Times Literary Supplement*. Reprinted by permission.

"Gay Stalinism" (which originally appeared in Vox Populi as "Camille Paglia defends her rotten record") is reprinted by permission of *The Advocate*, the national gay and lesbian newsmagazine.

"The New Sexism" (Which originally appeared in the Outlook section of the *Washington Post* as "My Case for the 'New Sexism' ") Copyright © 1993 by The Washington Post. Reprinted by permission.

"Our Tabloid Princess" (which originally appeared as "The Female Heart of Darkness"), "The Female Lenny Bruce: Sandra Bernhard," and "Television and the Clintons" originally appeared in the *San Francisco Examiner*. Reprinted by permission.

"Kind of a Bitch: Hillary Clinton" originally appeared in *The London Sunday Times Style and Travel Magazine*. Reprinted by permission.

"Hillary in the Crossfire," "Laying the Ghost of Anita Hill," and "Bobbitt Versus Bobbitt" Copyright © 1994 by Cable News Network, Inc. All rights reserved. Reprinted by permission.

"Diana Regina" (which originally appeared as "The Diana Cult") and "Mona Lisa in Motion" are reprinted by permission of *The New Republic*.

"Female Misbehavior" is reprinted by permission of Monika Treut.

"Sex War" is reprinted by permission of Luca Babini.

"Glennda and Camille Do Downtown" is reprinted by permission of Glenn Belverio.

"Gypsy Tigress: Carmen" (August, 1992) is reprinted by permission of *Stagebill*.

"Love Poetry" originally appeared in the *Princeton Encyclopedia of Poetry and Poetics* (1993). Reprinted by permission of Princeton University Press.

"Breviary of the Nude: Kenneth Clark's *The Nude*" originally appeared in the London *Times Higher Education Supplement*. Reprinted by permission.

"The Artistic Dynamics of Revival" originally appeared in *The Modern Review* (London, vol. 1, iss. 13, February–March 1994). Reprinted by permission.

"The Star as Sacred Monster: Judy Garland" originally appeared in *The New York Times Book Review* (June 6, 1993) as a review of David Shipman's *Judy Garland: The Secret Life of an American Legend*. Copyright © 1993 by The New York Times Company. Reprinted by permission.

"Madonna in the Shallows" originally appeared in *US* magazine as a review of Madonna's *Sex*. Reprinted by permission of US Magazine Company, L.P. All rights reserved.

"Madonna as Gauguin" is reprinted from *Notes: Quarterly Journal of the Music Library Association*, September 1993, by permission of the Music Library Association.

"Tyranny of the Technocrats" originally appeared in the *Washington Post Book World*. Copyright © 1992 by The Washington Post Writers Group. Reprinted by permission.

"Scholar, Aesthete, Activist: Edward Said," "Cry of the Invisible Men," and "I, the Jury" originally appeared in the *Washington Post Book World*. Copyright © 1993 by The Washington Post Writers Group. Reprinted by permission.

"A Woman of the Century: Germaine Greer" is reprinted from the November 30, 1992, issue of PEOPLE Weekly Magazine by special permission; copyright © 1992, Time, Inc.

"The Corpse of Fashion" originally appeared in the London *Times Literary Supplement*. Reprinted by permission.

The headnote on *Frankenstein* originally appeared in *The Essential Frankenstein*, edited by Leonard Wolf, copyright © 1977, 1993 by Leonard Wolf. Artwork copyright © 1993 by Christopher Bing. Reprinted by permission of Dutton Signet, a division of Penguin Books USA Inc.

"Critical Mass Media" originally appeared in the PEN American Center Newsletter.

Excerpts from transcript of "Feminist Fatale" produced by David Cerniak and Sam Levene. Copyright © 1992 MAN ALIVE—"Feminist Fatale," Canadian Broadcast Corporation. Reprinted by permission.

"Notes on Summer Camp" is reprinted from *The New York Observer*.

The interview with Edie Magnus and Camille Paglia originally appeared on Connie Chung's *Eye to Eye*. Reprinted by permission.

Paglia's contribution to "Symposium—In the Media, A Woman's Place" originally appeared in the *Media Studies Journal* (Winter/Spring 1993), published by The Freedom Forum Media Studies Center. Copyright © 1993.

"Whuffle" originally appeared in *In a Word: A Harper's Magazine Dictionary of Words That Don't Exist But Ought To*, Jack Hilt, ed., 1992.

The "Ask Camille Paglia" column originally appeared in *Spy* magazine.

"Diary of Sex, Art, and Selling" originally appeared in *The Guardian* (London, January 21, 1994).

"On Censorship" originally appeared as "Insanity and Desire" in the *Observer* (London), April 10, 1994.

"The Return of Carry Nation" originally appeared in *Playboy* magazine.

"A Gentleman Is . . ." originally appeared in *Esquire* (Spring–Summer 1993), a division of The Hearst Organization.

Drawing by Carole Cable is reprinted from *Cable on Academe* by Carole Cable, Copyright © 1994, University of Texas Press.

ABOUT THE AUTHOR

Camille Paglia is Professor of Humanities at the University of the Arts in Philadelphia. She is the author of *Sexual Personae: Art and Decadence from Nefertiti to Emily Dickinson* and *Sex, Art, and American Culture: Essays*.